HELPING ADOLESCENTS
WITH
LEARNING AND
BEHAVIOR PROBLEMS

MARY MARGARET KERR

C. MICHAEL NELSON

DEBORAH L. LAMBERT

HELPING ADOLESCENTS WITH LEARNING AND BEHAVIOR PROBLEMS

Merrill Publishing Company
A Bell & Howell Information Company
Columbus London Toronto Melbourne

Cover Photo: Merrill Publishing/
          Bruce Johnson

Published by Merrill Publishing Company
A Bell & Howell Information Company
Columbus, Ohio 43216

This book was set in Garamond.

Administrative Editor: Vicki Knight
Production Coordinator: Linda Hillis Bayma
Cover Designer: Cathy Watterson
Text Designer: Cynthia Brunk

Photo credits: All photos copyrighted by individuals or
companies listed. Merrill Publishing/photographs by Celia
Drake, pp. 3, 281; Jean Greenwald, pp. 51, 83, 149, 205;
Mary Hagler, pp. 207, 255; Larry Hamill, p. 85; and Tom
Hutchinson, pp. 9, 115, 181; Strix Pix, p. 225; University of
Maryland, Division of Photographic Services, p. 1.

Library of Congress Catalog Card Number: 86-63610
International Standard Book Number: 0-675-20511-5
Printed in the United States of America
3 4 5 6 7 8 9 — 91 90

Preface

We're not interested in theory and rhetoric—we're interested in practical strategies that can be implemented in a classroom on a daily basis.

Sarah H., a graduate student

So often I go to workshops hoping I'll learn some new strategies, but as soon as the presentation begins, I know I'm wasting my time. Why is it that every workshop is really designed for elementary school teachers? As a veteran secondary teacher working with socially and emotionally disturbed students, I feel I deserve information geared for adolescents, not younger kids.

Regina G., sixth-grade science teacher

I must see over a hundred kids a year. Every one has different problems, different issues, and different needs. My biggest concern is assessing the situation. The presenting problem is only the tip of the iceberg.

Dean S., secondary school consultant

It would be nice to open a secondary text and find current issues like the problems of drugs in the high school, teenage pregnancy, and vocational training being discussed.

Rose C., liaison counselor

These comments reflect only a few of the many conversations that helped us plan and write this book. Through our work in public middle schools and high schools, our consultation to correctional programs, and our teaching in undergraduate and graduate training programs, we have tried to stay attuned to the audience for whom this book was written. Our goal is to present current practices

and research findings, while maintaining a practical and readable writing style.

Some of you still are preparing for important roles in secondary education, while others have been working in this field for a long time. No matter what your role is, we think you will find new, helpful information in this textbook. To help you understand what lies ahead, here is a brief overview of each chapter and an explanation of how the book is organized.

Chapter One introduces the topics of the book. Chapter Two begins with the important process of assessment and planning. Academic assessment is presented, with plenty of examples to help you understand the model we have selected. Chapter Three continues the assessment and planning process with a focus on nonacademic areas, including social and interpersonal skills, career awareness and vocational skills, and study skills.

Chapters Four through Seven are "strategies chapters," telling you how to intervene on special problems and how to teach important skills. Chapter Four presents a discussion of "school survival skills," or prerequisite skills that enable students to benefit more fully from their classes. These school survival skills include getting to classes on time, being prepared, organizing study time, participating in class activities, and self-monitoring for good classroom deportment. The information in this chapter is new; research on school survival skills has been conducted only recently.

Academic skills dominate the discussion in Chapter Five, where we introduce you to innovative strategies such as self-monitoring and strategy training. As in all of our strategy chapters, you will find a case study to help you understand how to apply some of the interventions in your classroom.

Discipline and behavior management are addressed in Chapter Six, which opens with a section on school-wide interventions (e.g., detention, in-school suspension) and continues to discuss individual strategies suitable for classroom use. These strategies include peer-mediated as well as self-mediated approaches and cover both special and regular education environments.

In Chapter Seven we direct your attention to interpersonal and psychological problems, many of which have their highest prevalence in the adolescent years. For example, we discuss ways to identify and refer depressed, anorectic, and suicidal students. We also offer tips on how to work with school truants and refusers and socially withdrawn students.

Chapters Eight and Nine offer informative presentations on sexual maturation and related problems and on drug use and abuse, respectively. All of us who work in middle and high schools know how important these topics have become.

Chapter Ten helps you to understand the juvenile justice system and its interactions with regular and special education programs. Chapter Eleven takes you past the high school experience for a look at post-secondary transitions. This chapter explores career awareness and vocational options for teenagers.

To summarize, we begin with coverage of the assessment and planning process (Part One), move to specific strategies (Part Two), and conclude with chapters on special topics (Part Three).

To aid your understanding, we have included several instructional aids. Most chapters contain recommended readings to extend your study of a particular topic. In addition, most chapters conclude with a case study to illustrate planning or instructional approaches. In other chapters, illustrations from cases are included within the text. Numerous figures illustrating forms, graphs, charts, or checklists supplement and clarify the narrative. Tables enable you to review and summarize your reading. A glossary at the end of the book will help you to understand unfamiliar words and phrases. Glossary terms are boldfaced in the text.

We hope you will enjoy this textbook and learn from it as much as we have learned in putting it together for you. Feel free to write us with your suggestions and questions, so that we can improve our next edition.

M. M. K.

C. M. N.

D. L. L.

Acknowledgments

These colleagues and friends supported us with their insights, expertise, and encouragement. To each one we extend our heartfelt thanks.

Arsenal Middle School Staff
Wayne Ayres
Deirdre Battle
Debora Bell-Dolan
Donna Bickel
Gwen Brown
Mary Buchanan
Vikki Daniels
Gene Edgar
Kathleen Edwards
Robert Gedekoh
Karleen Goubeaud
Melissa Harrison
Kathryn Hoel
Tamara Hoier
Mary Horvath
Cynthia Langford
Peter Larson
Peter Leone
Laura Lee McCullough
Dona Meddaugh
Steve Miksic

Mary Ann Pace
Bruce Perrone
Elizabeth Ragland
Caryanne Ruffin
Spencer Saland
Deborah Santora
Jim Saski
Vaughan Stagg
Kenneth Stanko
Gail Staresinic
Joseph M. Strayhorn
George Sugai
Sandra Sunday
David Test
Dean Tomko
Bruce Wolford

Our special thanks go to Jamey Covaleski, who cheerfully and competently spent two years editing and typing our manuscript; to Vicki Knight, who kept us on schedule and on target; and to our friends and families, who allowed us to monopolize dinner conversations, to isolate ourselves on weekends, and to take time away from them for this project.

ix

Contents

HELPING ADOLESCENTS
WITH
LEARNING AND
BEHAVIOR PROBLEMS

PART
ONE

Assessment
and Planning
for Adolescents

CHAPTER
ONE

An Introduction

This chapter describes three adolescents with the kinds of learning and behavior problems covered in this textbook. These vignettes lend a perspective on the topics of the coming chapters. Moreover, we hope that you will begin the process of bringing your own situation to bear on the information you will find here, translating our suggestions into direct applications in your workplace.

For those who have yet to begin their professional careers, these vignettes may bring a new perspective on the teenagers you will encounter in your work in secondary education. We have tried to select fairly typical cases from our own work in middle, junior high, and senior high schools. Let us begin with a learning disabled student.

Andrea

Andrea, a 17-year-old senior in high school, was brought to our clinic for assessment by her father, who had noticed that she was unable to read aloud from the newspaper without getting nervous. Her father also reported that she seemed unsure of herself when driving and trying to read road signs and street names. All necessary vision screening had proved that Andrea's present corrective lenses were adequate.

At first Andrea remained very quiet when asked questions about her reading and her school history in general. Gradually she relaxed, explaining that she had been in "pull-out" remedial reading programs throughout her school career. She expressed serious concern about her reading difficulties, stating, " I just can't let my father know how bad it is. . . . He wants me to go on to college and be an engineer like he is. I'll never make it."

After gathering Andrea's school records for review, we decided to conduct a comprehensive assessment of her reading skills. A reading specialist was called in for an assessment of both comprehension and oral reading. After the first appointment, the specialist, Mrs. Donovan, called the assessment team together to discuss a significant

problem: Andrea had become so anxious when confronted with an oral reading task that she was unable to continue the examination. She had left the session in tears, despite Mrs. Donovan's attempts to console her.

The team agreed to consultation from a specialist in child and adolescent psychiatry, who suggested that Andrea might have developed a secondary anxiety reaction to oral reading, because of her continued inadequacy in this skill area. Furthermore, he hypothesized that Andrea might have become fearful about the information her parents would receive regarding her poor performance. The team invited Andrea's parents to meet with them to discuss Andrea's reactions. A series of meetings between the psychiatrist, the parents, and Andrea were arranged. The purpose of these meetings was to determine whether Andrea's anxiety could be alleviated, allowing Mrs. Donovan to proceed with testing.

Andrea did continue with the assessment, which revealed an untreated reading disability and related anxiety. Andrea needed intensive intervention in reading, in the context of a warm and caring environment that could boost her confidence and highlight her strengths in other areas. The solution was found when a work-study student in the clinic offices left for the summer. Andrea replaced the work-study student, thereby taking a low-pressure job among the team whom she had grown to trust. In return, the team members volunteered to assist Andrea with her reading skills.

Four years later, Andrea completed a two-year college degree and took a year off to travel in Europe. Her enthusiastic letters attested to her mastery not only of reading, but of a new foreign language. On a visit back to her friends at the clinic, she agreed to an assessment of her reading skills. To everyone's delight, she had moved from a fourth grade reading level on a standardized test to the twelfth grade level and reported no further difficulties in oral reading.

Not every story has such a happy ending. Unfortunately, too many adolescents never receive the kind of specialized, age- and grade-appropriate assessment and intervention they need. We develop instructional plans for a unique group of students—not quite adults yet, but not really children either. Our students' needs differ from those of elementary-aged students. Instructional planning, then, should be treated very differently from elementary special education. As Gearhart (1980) has stated:

Much of our knowledge in providing programs for handicapped students is based on successful experience with elementary-age children. When we attempt to plan for handicapped adolescents, we find that both the structure and goals of the school and the characteristics and drives of the students are different. (p. 419)

When designing instructional programs in secondary special education, we must resist the temptation of merely replicating elementary school efforts. Instead, middle and high school programming should be linked to vocational and career preparation, as discussed throughout this text.

To help Andrea handle college, our team spent some time helping her learn "school survival skills." Chapter Four is devoted entirely to these skills. Although this is a fairly new area of research and program development, we have pulled together as much information as possible.

For a long time people naively assumed that teenagers would naturally pick up on the cues to become good students. We now realize that a segment of every teenager's curriculum should address such important skills as time management, being prepared for classes, punctuality, and classroom interaction skills. Some of these seem so obvious, yet they have never been dealt with before.

Recent research has made an attempt to figure out what makes the difference between successful and unsuccessful students. In the studies in Chapter Four, large-scale surveys of high school students, their teachers, and their building administrators revealed some of these critical differences (Kerr & Zigmond, 1986). Regular and special educators tended to cite the same problems and skills as critical to an adolescent's failure or success in secondary education, for example, meeting due dates, following teacher instructions, getting to class on time, handling anger appropriately. Yet students, on the other hand, did not entirely agree with the adults' assessments, a finding that reminds us of the importance of clarifying our expectations for teenagers (Kerr & Zigmond, 1986).

Andrea's case also underscores the importance of a multidisciplinary approach to assessment. Not all teenagers will experience such psychological discomfort when faced with difficult academic tasks, but many will. Chapter Seven helps in understanding some of these "internalizing difficulties" and in reaching out to a teenager experiencing them.

Next, let us explore a case in which psychological and behavior problems play the predominant role.

Kevin

Kevin had been enrolled in a public middle school for three months when the seventh grade team decided to refer him for special testing. On his referral form, the team wrote, "Kevin is barely passing his courses, although we all believe he could do the work if he would settle down. He needs close supervision in order to get anything done. It should also be noted that he does not seem to be making friends." Shortly after Kevin's first meeting with the school psychologist, his behavior worsened. He fired a cap gun in the middle of a quiet English test; he was found loitering during lunch and free times in an off-limits area; he brought an old pair of bifocals to school, wearing them to all his classes; and he had repeated trips to the bathroom for reasons that were not entirely appropriate.

The school found Kevin's behavior unbearable and referred him to a behavior management consultant, who visited the school a few days later.

After observing and interviewing Kevin, his teacher, and a "successful" peer, the consultant decided to review the school's disciplinary policies. After all, Kevin had hinted that the school could not make him behave no matter what the staff tried to do. In fact, he seemed to like all the attention (time alone with the psychologist, interviews with the consultant) that his behavior had warranted.

The consultant sat in the **In-School Suspension** room, observed the after-school **detention** program, and followed Kevin to a couple of his classes. She surmised that Kevin was "beating the system." Her recommendation was threefold:

1. A Discipline Committee should be formed to review and improve the school-wide discipline policies.
2. Kevin's parents should meet with the school officials to share information and to develop a home-based contingency contract.
3. The seventh grade team should review their classroom-level disciplinary and social skills teaching practices for all students.

Perhaps you have already encountered a student like Kevin. Other illustrations of problem behavior are found in Chapter Six, in which a wealth of behavior management ideas await, including school-wide, teacher-directed, peer-mediated, and **self-mediated strategies**. School-wide interventions include suspension, detention, rules, and alternative classrooms. In a **teacher-mediated** intervention, the adult takes on primary responsibility for delivery of specified contingencies. **Contingency contracts** and **token economies** may be familiar examples of these strategies. The natural resource of peers is harnessed in **peer-mediated interventions** such as **peer tutoring, group goalsetting** and **feedback**, and **group contingencies**. These strategies, when applied correctly, can be very powerful. Finally, we consider self-mediated strategies such as **self-monitoring, self-reinforcement**, and self-evaluation. This "new wave" in special education is very promising.

What about the other side of teaching behavioral skills—the social skills? Kevin's team helped him to develop friendships by using some of the interpersonal skills ideas encountered in Chapter Seven.

Finally, the following case gives a glimpse of the kind of problems addressed in Chapters Eight to Eleven, our "special topics" chapters.

Martina

Martina's school record at Johnson High School was two volumes thick, reflecting her many scrapes with legal authorities, her early pattern of truancy, and her disordered family life. She was well known in her school district, where she had repeated two grades and seemed doomed to fail a third. One morning, her truancy officer phoned her home, only to discover that Martina had been charged with drug possession and was being detained in a juvenile correctional facility. Shortly thereafter, the school social worker was asked to testify in court. As she reviewed Martina's voluminous record, she was reminded of the various "special problems" this child-turned-young-adult had presented to the school personnel who had tried to help her over the years:

- Martina failed the first grade and was transferred to four different schools during the remainder of her elementary school career. She missed an average of 20 days (4 weeks) of school each year. Her mother had seemed concerned when Martina was in first grade but had failed to keep several appointments thereafter. The family's telephone was often disconnected.
- In junior high school, the school nurse referred Martina to a free women's clinic for an examination when Martina confided in her that she thought she might be pregnant. She was 14 at the time.
- Martina's entry to ninth grade was delayed because she was in a juvenile detention facility for repeated shoplifting. Despite repeated attempts, the junior high school dean was unable to get any information about Martina's educational program while she was in the juvenile facility. By the time she returned to her regular

school, she was hopelessly behind in the curriculum and failed three courses.

- The most recent note in Martina's file expressed the concern of Ms. McClean, the physical education teacher, who had overheard Martina talking with other girls in the locker room about suicide. When Ms. McClean tried to talk with Martina, she "clammed up."

We wish we could predict that you will never meet a Martina. Unfortunately, you will. To help prepare for adolescents whose complicated lives bring so many problems into the school setting, we have included chapters on drugs, sexual development, the juvenile justice system, and after-school transitions.

One of the issues raised by Martina's case, and by the chapters to come, is suicidality. Suicide is the third leading cause of death among adolescents. This tragic problem is one of several that are the focus of Chapter Seven. Others include depression, anorexia nervosa, school refusal, truancy, and social skills deficits. For the most part, educators play a collaborative role in the assessment and treatment of these problems. Collaboration between educators and mental health professionals has expanded greatly during the past few years.

Chapter Eight addresses another problem area, sexuality, raised by adolescents like Martina. All adolescents deserve reliable, honest information regarding human sexuality so that they can cope with life as a sexual beings. Mildly handicapped teenage adolescents often require even more help in dealing with the perplexing aspects of physical and psychological maturation.

Unfortunately, our society makes this task difficult. Sex education remains an exceptionally volatile issue throughout most of the country. Some school systems offer practically no sex education at all, while others insist upon a curriculum so diluted as to be useless. The challenge is to develop effective educational programs that are acceptable to all.

Martina also had drug-related problems, as will many of your students. The information in Chapter Nine helps you make an appropriate referral to an outside agency.

According to a 1985 study by the National Institute on Drug Abuse, our nation's adolescents have the highest levels of illicit drug use in any of the developed countries of the world. Fully 62% of young people try an illicit drug before finishing high school. There is a steadily increasing focus on the school as an instrument to identify and intervene in developing **drug abuse** problems.

More emphasis is being placed on defining the role of the teacher in identifying, and educating, students with drug use or abuse problems. Educators also are being asked to take a more active role in helping their school administrators define drug-use policies and programs.

The school staff working with Martina was faced with still another problem: Martina's involvement in the juvenile justice system. Professional concern regarding the educational rights and needs of handicapped youthful offenders has increased dramatically in the past decade. As documented in Chapter Ten, it is becoming widely recognized that mildly handicapped youth are overrepresented throughout the juvenile justice system.

In juvenile correctional programs, where educational treatment tends to be mandatory, efforts to provide free and appropriate individualized special education programs to handicapped youth have lagged behind similar efforts in the public schools. Nevertheless, correctional education programs are under the same mandate as public school programs to comply with **Public Law 94–142**. Increased recognition of the prevalence and needs of handicapped incarcerated youth, as well as the pressures of litigation and potential loss of state and federal funding, have resulted in increased attempts to develop special education programs in correctional settings. However, these attempts are hampered by the dissimilarities between correctional and public school education programs, by the shortage of trained special education personnel in corrections, and by the negative attitudes toward education programs held by many corrections staff. Moreover, many existing correctional special education programs tend to emphasize a watered-down regular secondary curriculum, or they attempt the remediation of basic academic skill deficits, instead of focusing on functional skills handicapped offenders need to succeed in their communities and in the work force. Chapter Ten presents information about the juvenile justice system, because many special educators working with handicapped adolescents must become involved with the agencies and professionals encompassed within this system.

In our final chapter, we face teenagers' life after school. We have included a chapter on post-secondary transitions to explain some of the options being exercised to help handicapped learners once they leave secondary schools. The current trend is toward a better balance between teaching functional living and occupational skills, providing content instruction in traditional secondary academic areas, and teaching handicapped adolescents effective learning strategies.

SUMMARY

We hope this chapter has given you some new insights about the special needs of teenagers in secondary schools today, as well as an understanding of what this book offers. Chapter Two will begin with assessing the academic areas; Chapter Three helps in assessing social skills. The "how-to" chapters (Chapters Four to Seven) follow, offering interventions in academic and behavior management and in managing and referring special psychological and interpersonal problems. Finally, Chapters Eight to Eleven deal with four "special topics": sexual development and problems, drugs, the juvenile justice system, and facilitating transitions. As you proceed through the text, we hope you remember students you know and think of new ways to reach out to them.

RECOMMENDED READINGS

D'Alonzo, B. J. (1983). *Educating adolescents with learning and behavior problems*. Rockville, MD: Aspen Systems Corporation.

Kauffman, J. M., & Hallahan, D. P. (Eds.). (1981). *Handbook of special education*. Englewood Cliffs, NJ: Prentice-Hall.

CHAPTER
TWO

Academic
Assessment

As a school psychologist I feel there is one thing that most of us will agree on: teenagers with special needs must receive individualized assessments and program planning, designed to give them the best available program.

While I may tire of sitting through inservice workshops that focus on assessment and planning, I still say we need to take the time to be thorough, clear and systematic when designing assessment and programming procedures. (Dr. G., a school psychologist)

We agree! Assessment and program planning receive frequent attention today because it is now realized that these two components set the stage for effective teaching.

Educational assessment is a "systematic process of asking educationally relevant questions about a student's learning behavior for the purposes of placement and instruction" (Wallace & McLoughlin, 1979, p.79). Moreover, special educators at the secondary level (grades 6 through 12) must consider learning in a broad context that includes reading, mathematics, cognition and written language, study skills, social skills, and motor and vocational skills. To integrate these diverse domains of evaluation, we have organized Chapters Two and Three according to the Hawkins (1979) model displayed in Figure 2–1. Note that the figure begins with its broadest side, reflecting "broad-band assessment," or an assessment of all possible deficits and skills. During the assessment process, the focus of the diagnostic efforts narrows until only a few, well-articulated target behaviors remain. For each phase of the assessment process we explain strategies and instruments suitable for secondary school students, while referring to the mandated assessment procedures of Public Law 94-142.

The first section addresses the screening and general disposition phase. In Figure 2–1 this is the first phase of the model. Described in this phase are four activities:

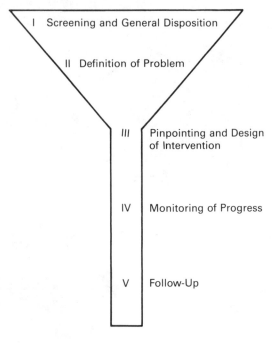

FIGURE 2–1

Five-phase assessment model (Source: Adapted from "The Functions of Assessment: Implications for Selection and Development of Devices for Assessing Repertoires in Clinical, Educational, and Other Settings" by R. P. Hawkins, 1979, *Journal of Applied Behavior Analysis, 12*, p. 502. Copyright 1979 by the Society for the Experimental Analysis of Behavior. Adapted by permission.)

1. referral;
2. screening, through a review of the student's educational history;
3. screening for achievement problems; and
4. screening for intellectual deficits.

In most cases you or a member of your school's staff will complete all of these activities, although the instruments and the sequence of screening steps may vary from school to school. Most of the information gathered at this stage is for the purposes of an eligibility decision, the decision to place a student into a particular **special education** program.

SCREENING AND GENERAL DISPOSITION

The initial phase of educational assessment, *screening,* answers the question, "Does a problem exist?" When screening is completed, we are able to address the next question, "Should further evaluation take place?" *General disposition* refers to the "next-step" decision, or generally the way in which to proceed with the case.

Referral

The first step in screening and general disposition is, of course, a referral. To illustrate the referral process, we have selected a form that reflects **pre-referral intervention**. Pre-referral intervention refers to a process in which a student's problem is diagnosed briefly, several interventions are tried, and results are reviewed, *before* a formal referral for eligibility for special education. This model has several advantages:

1. Pre-referral intervention reduces the number of referrals to special education, many of which may be inappropriate.
2. This model provides assessment information without labeling the student.
3. It reduces the delay between referral and intervention (by shortening the diagnostic process).
4. This approach takes advantage of existing (and often overlooked) data on the student's progress.
5. It relies on the expertise of classroom teachers who know the student best.

To illustrate the connection between pre-referral intervention and referral for eligibility, refer to Figure 2–2. This form, developed by the Maryland Learning Disabilities Project (1983), reflects several important features of pre-referral intervention. First, the teacher is urged to include actual samples of work. Question 3 regarding strengths helps in getting a balanced picture of performance. Also included is documentation that pre-referral interventions have been tried. This is now becoming a requirement in many schools.

Part II of the referral form is completed by *each of the student's teachers.* This *multiple informant approach* is crucial for an adolescent's assessment, because teenagers often receive instruction from, and interact with, six or more adults every day.

If possible, address eligibility issues only *after* you have pursued the pre-referral "screening" steps outlined in this and the next section, which deals with ratings, interviews, and history gathering. Remember that parental permission may be required for these steps, under P.L. 94–142. When in doubt about the requirement for parental permission, check the school district's guidelines for due process.

History Gathering

Often interviews raise important questions about the student's school and developmental histories. This information is critical to understanding the context of the student's present difficulties, including factors that may be contributing to the problem. The history also gives a perspective on how long the problems have existed. *An extensive history, accompanied by student, teacher, and parent ratings and interviews always should precede more formal testing.* A comprehensive history includes background information on health, psychosocial development, present living arrangements, number of school transfers, attendance patterns, achievement data, previous **Individualized Education Programs (IEPs)**, grades, involvement of outside agencies, and such unusual family circumstances as deceased parent, reports of child abuse, or disabled family member. Much of this

Maryland Learning Disabilities Project
Secondary School Student ARD Referral, Part I

Date _____ School _____ Referring Person _____

Student _____ Birthdate _____ Age _____ Grade _____

1. Reason for referral. [Describe the presenting problem(s) and attach work samples.]

2. What would you like the student to be able to do that he/she does not do now?

3. What do you see as this student's strengths?

4. What interventions have been attempted?

☐ Student conference   ☐ Modifying materials and presentations
☐ Alternative methods and techniques   ☐ Change of text
☐ Adjusted workload   ☐ Change in schedule
☐ Referral to guidance   ☐ Parent conference
☐ Behavior management techniques   ☐ Consultation with specialists
☐ Note/call to parent   ☐ Consultation with colleagues
☐ Detention/suspension

5. Complete Part II of the referral form and submit to_____

FIGURE 2–2

Teacher referral form (Source: From *Learning Disabilities: A Diagnostic Handbook* by the Maryland Learning Disabilities Project, 1983, Baltimore, MD: State Department of Education. Reprinted by permission.)

Please return to _____ by _____. Attach Work Samples
(Date)

Maryland Learning Disabilities Project
Secondary School Student ARD Referral, Part II

Student _____ Teacher _____ Subject _____

1. Based on your observations, evaluate the student in comparison to other classmates by checking problems frequently observed.

LISTENING COMPREHENSION
☐ Difficulty understanding spoken language
☐ Difficulty following verbal directions

ORAL EXPRESSION
☐ Difficulty expressing thoughts and ideas
☐ Limited speaking vocabulary

READING
☐ Difficulty with basic skills
☐ Difficulty with comprehension
☐ Difficulty reading assigned text(s) or material presented

WRITTEN EXPRESSION
☐ Difficulty with spelling
☐ Difficulty with mechanics of writing
☐ Difficulty organizing sentences and ideas into paragraphs

MATHEMATICS (if appropriate)
☐ Difficulty with basic operations
  ☐ Addition   ☐ Multiplication
  ☐ Subtraction   ☐ Division
☐ Difficulty solving word problems

MEMORY
☐ Difficulty retaining information over time

ATTENTION/ORGANIZATION/ACTIVITY LEVEL
☐ Difficulty maintaining attention
☐ Easily distracted
☐ Loses or forgets work and/or materials
☐ Late for class

☐ Underactive
☐ Overactive
☐ Difficulty with organization

DAILY WORK
☐ Does not attend class regularly
☐ Incomplete homework assignments
☐ Poor test grades
☐ Does not complete class assignments
☐ Does not participate in class

SOCIAL/EMOTIONAL
☐ Lacks motivation
☐ Sudden changes in mood throughout day
☐ Lacks self-control
☐ Inconsistency in performance
☐ Needs constant approval
☐ Unusually aggressive toward others
☐ Unusually shy or withdrawn
☐ Difficulty interpreting social cues
☐ Difficulty making and keeping friends
☐ Doesn't accept responsibility for own behavior
☐ Easily influenced by others

SPEECH
☐ Stutters
☐ Difficulty articulating speech sounds
☐ Unusual voice quality

2. Rate the student's level of functioning as compared to other classmates:

	Above Average	Average	Below Average
Reading	☐	☐	☐
Mathematics (if applicable)	☐	☐	☐
Written Expression	☐	☐	☐
Oral Expression	☐	☐	☐
Listening Comprehension	☐	☐	☐

3. At what grade level is the student functioning in your subject area?
Circle: 1 2 3 4 5 6 7 8 9 10 11 12

4. Has the student received any deficiencies, interim reports, advisory notices, etc., in your class?
Yes _____ No _____ When _____

5. Report card grades for your subject: 1st qtr. _____ 2nd qtr. _____ 3rd qtr. _____ 4th qtr. _____

6. Student's attendance (days absent) in your class: 1st qtr. _____ 2nd qtr. _____ 3rd qtr. _____ 4th qtr. _____

7. Comments: Please note any additional comments on the back of this form.

13

information is carried in the school's records, which warrant *careful* reading and notetaking.

Parents should be included in the history-gathering process. One vehicle for this is a parent questionnaire such as the one displayed in Figure 2–3.

Thus far, the measures described have been somewhat *informal*. More formal tests supplement (but do not replace) the information gathered through interviews, ratings, and record reviews. First, we illustrate the academic screening measures.

Screening for General Achievement Problems

Annual achievement testing provides teachers and others with current academic information. When administering an achievement test, review the student's own worksheet to examine errors and problem-solving strategies. Even at the screening phase, we encourage gathering as much information *beyond the derived scores* as possible and analyzing systematically the student's strengths and weaknesses. The student may be weak in one particular area of the curriculum. A glance at that student's history may indicate reasons for this isolated deficit (e.g., the family moved and changed schools, resulting in a three-week absence from classes).

Ten of the most frequently used achievement batteries are The California Achievement Tests (CAT), the Metropolitan Achievement Test (MAT), the Metropolitan Achievement Test Survey Test (MATST), the Stanford Achievement Test (SAT), the SRA Achievement Series, the Iowa Tests of Basic Skills (ITBS), the Tests of Achievement and Proficiency (TAP), the Peabody Individual Achievement Test (PIAT), the Wide Range Achievement Test (WRAT), and the Basic Achievement Skills Individual Screener (BASIS) (see Table 2–1). These tests are age-appropriate for high school students and are designed to measure general skill development

in several areas, such as reading, spelling, language, mathematics, and information.

Group Achievement Tests. As a screening device, *a group achievement test* provides a global estimate of a student's present level of functioning compared with others of the same age or grade. Screening achievement primarily helps to identify pupils with low-level, average, or high-level skills in comparison to others. After screening, the teacher will have a general idea where to begin with diagnostic testing, if deemed necessary. The working time for each test ranges from 30 minutes to 2½ hours.

Every test in Table 2–1 is norm-referenced, meaning that it compares a pupil's performance to that of the pupils in the selected norm group. After transforming the raw scores from the norm-referenced achievement tests, the teacher has age- or grade-equivalent scores. Percentile ranks within grades and standard scores and/ or stanines are given also. However, merely learning that an eighth grade student has a grade-equivalent score of 6.9 on the mathematics subtest of the CAT does not tell us which skills the student possesses or lacks. Nevertheless, these test data are usually part of the normal school routine, are readily available, and provide a good starting place for assessment you might want to conduct in your classroom.

Minimum Competency Testing. The basic skills are particularly relevant in high school; 36 states have now implemented minimum competency tests for graduation and grade-to-grade promotion. This movement toward **minimum competency testing** has had substantial impact on general education policies, which in turn influence the goals of special education. McClung and Pullin (1978) claim that insufficient attention has been paid to the special problems of exceptional students in mandated minimum competency testing programs. According to a Children's Defense Fund Report (1985), prior experience and research lend

Parent/Guardian Questionnaire

All information on this form will be strictly confidential and will be used only to help us in determining an appropriate educational program for your child. This form will be kept in your child's confidential folder and will be shared only with your knowledge and consent.

If you have any questions please call _____

                                       Name   Title   Telephone

Today's Date _____ School _____

Student _____ Teacher _____

Birthdate _____ Grade _____

Family Data

Age	Household Members: Relationship	Education (Highest Grade Completed)	Occupation (If Appropriate)

Describe any serious concerns you have about your child.

_____

_____

_____

Describe any school related problems other family members have experienced.

_____

_____

_____

Is English the usual language spoken at home? Yes ☐ No ☐ Other Language _____

Pregnancy and Birth

Describe any serious health problems the mother experienced during this or other pregnancies.

_____

_____

_____

FIGURE 2–3

continued

Parent questionnaire form (Source: From *Learning Disabilities: A Diagnostic Handbook* by the Maryland Learning Disabilities Project, 1983, Baltimore, MD: State Department of Education. Reprinted by permission.)

During what month(s) of the pregnancy did these problems occur? _____

_____

Birthweight _____ Apgar Scores _____ _____

Did any of the following occur during the birth process?

☐ Premature   ☐ Transfusion   ☐ Caesarian section
☐ Breech birth   ☐ Prolonged labor   ☐ Oxygen problem
☐ Blood incompatability (Rh Factor)   ☐ Fetal distress

Other birth problems and/or concerns:

_____

_____

_____

Describe any difficulties your child had in learning to eat, sleep, sit, walk, or talk.

_____

_____

_____

Briefly describe any traumatic events which the child has experienced, for example: death of close relative, divorce, family crisis.

_____

_____

_____

Medical History

Please check below any illnesses or problems the child has had:

☐ Physical defect   ☐ Frequent colds   ☐ Allergies ☐ Speech problems
☐ Eye problems   ☐ Frequent sore throats   ☐ Asthma   ☐ Dietary problems
☐ Ear problems   ☐ Headaches   ☐ Epilepsy   ☐ Serious accidents or injuries
☐ Operations   ☐ Heart disease   ☐ Diabetes
☐ Temperatures above 104°   ☐ Other: _____

Describe any of the problems checked above: _____

_____

_____

Has the child ever been hospitalized? ☐ No ☐ Yes   Reason: _____

Age at time of hospitalization: _____ How long in hospital? _____

Is the child under treatment or medication at present? (If yes, please explain) _____

_____

How would you rate the child's general health? (check)   ☐ excellent ☐ good ☐ fair ☐ poor

FIGURE 2–3

(continued)

16

Social/Behavioral Characteristics

Please check any of the following behaviors which describe your child:

- ☐ Flexible
- ☐ Outgoing
- ☐ Consistently short attention span
- ☐ Daydreams
- ☐ Cooperative
- ☐ Nightmares
- ☐ Temper tantrums
- ☐ Unreasonable fears
- ☐ Gets idea quickly
- ☐ Fantasies
- ☐ Artistic
- ☐ Frequently tells lies
- ☐ Avoids homework
- ☐ Uncooperative
- ☐ Frequently talks to self
- ☐ Sleepwalking
- ☐ Lacks motivation

- ☐ Creative
- ☐ Bedwetting
- ☐ Thumb Sucking
- ☐ Nailbiting
- ☐ Mechanical
- ☐ Overactive
- ☐ Athletic
- ☐ Musical
- ☐ Rocking
- ☐ Underactive
- ☐ Self-confident
- ☐ Enjoys reading
- ☐ Frequently late
- ☐ Doesn't seem to understand questions or directions
- ☐ Difficulty making and keeping friends
- ☐ Easily influenced by others
- ☐ Difficulty using numbers

- ☐ Lacks self-control
- ☐ Frequent sudden changes in mood
- ☐ Excessive inconsistency in behavior
- ☐ Needs constant approval or reassurance
- ☐ Unusually aggressive towards others
- ☐ Unusually shy or withdrawn
- ☐ Difficulty completing jobs and activities
- ☐ Difficulty with changes in routine
- ☐ Difficulty with organization
- ☐ Avoids reading
- ☐ Difficulty telling time

Comment on any behaviors that particularly concern you: _____
_____
_____

Has your child had any evaluations that the school may be unaware of:

☐ educational   ☐ psychological   ☐ medical   ☐ other

Explain (what, when, by whom): _____
_____

What are your child's interests? _____
_____

What does your child do well? _____
_____

What do you like best about your child? _____
_____
_____

How do you think the school can help your child? _____
_____

Is there any additional information which you feel will help us to understand your child better? __
_____
_____

I understand that this information will be used to help find out if my child has a learning handicap and will be used by school professionals only. This material will be kept in my child's confidential folder.

_____   _____
Interviewer's Signature   Parent's Signature

TABLE 2-1
Summary of achievement tests for screening

Test and Publisher	Grade Ranges	Content Areas Evaluated	Norm- or Criterion-Referenced	Scores Obtained	Comments
Basic Achievement Skills Individual Screener (BASIS) New York: Harcourt Brace Jovanovich; The Psychological Corporation	1–12 Post High School	Reading Math Spelling	Norm-referenced Criterion-referenced	Grade equivalents Percentiles Standard scores	Limited behavior sampling
California Achievement Tests (CAT) Monterey, CA: McGraw	1.5–12	Reading Spelling Language Mathematics Use of reference materials	Norm-referenced Criterion-referenced	Grade equivalents Percentiles Stanines Scaled scores NCE	Useful at screening level; multiple choice format; group test; good reliability and validity; evidence of adequate standards
Iowa Test of Basic Skills (ITBS) Boston, MA: Houghton Mifflin	1–9	Reading Language Workstudy Mathematics	Norm-referenced Criterion-referenced	Grade/Age equivalents Percentiles Stanines Standard scores	Useful at screening; standardization is adequate; multiple choice format
Metropolitan Achievement Tests (MAT) New York: Harcourt Brace Jovanovich	K–9	Reading Mathematics Language	Norm-referenced	Percentiles Stanines Grade level Standard scores	Adequate normative sample; reliable valid; adequate multiple choice screening
Metropolitan Achievement Test Survey Test (MATST) New York: Harcourt Brace Jovanovich	K–12	Reading Mathematics Language Social studies Science	Norm-referenced Criterion-referenced	Percentiles Stanines Grade equivalents Standard scores	Standardization, reliability and validity technically adequate

Test	Grade	Content Areas	Type	Scores	Comments
Peabody Individual Achievement Test (PIAT) Circle Pines, MN: American Guidance Service	K–12	Mathematics Reading recognition Reading comprehension Spelling General information	Norm-referenced	Grade/Age equivalents Percentile ranks Standard scores	Superior standardization; adequate reliability (for screening purposes); validity rests on its content validity
SRA Achievement Series Palo Alto, CA: American Institute for Research in the Behavioral Sciences	K–12	Reading Mathematics Language Social studies Science Use of reference materials	Norm-referenced Criterion-referenced	Grade equivalents Stanines National and local percentiles	Standardization; reliability and validity exceptionally good
Stanford Achievement Test (SAT) New York: Harcourt Brace Jovanovich	1.5–9.5	Reading English Mathematics	Norm-referenced Criterion-referenced	Grade/Age equivalents Percentiles Standard scores	Lower and upper extension available; group testing format; standardized; excellent reliability and validity also good
Tests of Achievement and Proficiency (TAP) Boston, MA: Houghton Mifflin	9–12	Reading Written expression Mathematics Use of information sources Science Social studies	Norm-referenced Criterion-referenced	Grade/Age percentiles Stanines Standard scores	Designed to assess broad functional skills; standardization adequate
Wide Range Achievement Test (WRAT) (Revised) Wilmington, DE: Jastak Associates	K–12	Reading Spelling Arithmetic	Norm-referenced	Grade level Percentiles Standard scores	Limited behavior sampling; inadequate standardization; absence of reliability and validity data

doubt to the validity of the test results and even suggest that the testing process interferes with learning. Problems identified include a test design that evaluates a limited range of skills, the prevalence of cultural bias, and scoring processes that cannot yield an objective measure. The trend toward basic skill competency may affect assessment and program planning for the secondary adolescent in special education.

A few of the achievement tests are also criterion-referenced. They compare the pupil's performance to the curriculum rather than to the performance of other students. The CAT (Tiegs & Clark, 1970), the MAT (Balow, Farr, Hogan, & Prescott, 1978), and the SAT (Madden, Gardner, Rudman, Karlsen, & Merwin, 1973) are three of the most frequently used global measures of academic achievement given in public schools today. (The SAT offers a unique special edition designed for visually handicapped and hearing-impaired students.) Because they are group administered, CAT, MAT, and SAT only *screen* the achievement of special education students.

Next we highlight the *individual* achievement tests available for screening.

Individual Achievement Measures. One of the most popular, wide-range screening measures of academic achievement is the PIAT (Dunn & Markwardt, 1970). Like the WRAT and BASIS, the PIAT is an individually administered test, which prevents its widespread use in regular classrooms. However, the PIAT is often used by special educators as a screening and diagnostic tool. A distinct feature of the PIAT is its easel format, which permits examiner/student interaction. For the teacher, this feature may be desirable if, for example, a teenager with attention deficit disorder responds more favorably to an interactive format than to a more independent testing approach. The PIAT assesses five academic areas, providing the teacher with an overview of the secondary student's present academic achievement. The subtests—mathematics, reading rec-

ognition, reading comprehension, spelling, and general information—provide more behavior samples than other individual screening measures.

The PIAT, like the other achievement tests, does not offer the specificity necessary to pinpoint individual instructional targets, but PIAT results can identify academic subjects in which the teenager may be performing below average.

The WRAT (Jastak & Jastak, 1978) is another commonly used norm-referenced achievement test that taps three major curriculum areas—spelling, arithmetic, and reading.

The Woodcock-Johnson Psychoeducational Battery (Woodcock, 1978) is very different from the previous tests inasmuch as cognitive ability, scholastic aptitude, academic achievement, and student interest can be assessed and compared by the education team within one assessment system. Consisting of three parts and 27 subtests, it is a system that provides cluster scores used to diagnose strengths and weaknesses. The key drawback of the Woodcock-Johnson is that the examiner invests a lot of time administering, scoring, and interpreting the results.

Problems with Achievement Tests

Although achievement tests are useful in the initial screening stage, they do have pitfalls in common. First, the results of these tests are absolutely meaningless if the content areas reflected in the test items are not well matched to the curriculum taught. For example, although the technical aspects of the PIAT are very good, certain items on this test do not represent typical classroom performance tasks: in the area of reading comprehension, the secondary student is asked to match a sentence with a picture. How often does an adolescent perform such a task in school? Unlike the WRAT, where the student actually writes the correct word in the spelling subtest, the adolescent is asked on the PIAT to select the correct spelling word from four choices—using recognition rather than recall skills. Again, how often are adolescents given these opportunities in middle or high school?

Secondly, in the secondary schools the achievement tests are usually administered to groups, preventing teachers from observing individual student performance. When a student is referred for academic or behavior problems, systematic testing is performed preferably on an individual basis, providing the examiner with added information.

To understand the limitations of an achievement test better, review the manual that accompanies the test. The O.K. Buros' *Mental Measurements Yearbooks* provide critical reviews of achievement and other tests. Most professional libraries carry these yearbooks in the reference department. The *Mental Measurement Yearbook,* like the testing manual, provides valuable information on testing norms and on measures of reliability and validity. When selecting a test, try to study factors aside from the technical aspects of the instrument. The purpose of the test and the behaviors it samples are key features in the selection process. Ask yourself whether the sampled items match the objectives of the adolescent's curriculum.

Screening for Intellectual Deficits

Perhaps the most controversial aspect of screening is intellectual assessment. Eligibility decisions for special education placements often

include a measure of intelligence. Parental permission is required for intellectual testing. Table 2–2 displays the intellectual measures that might be used by a certified professional for testing students.

Although state standards specify that the testing of intellectual performance must be included in this decision making process, this requirement is being disputed in some states because of suspected discriminatory abuse with minority students. As mentioned earlier, test selection must include issues of acculturation and the comparison to a normative group. Placement should be based on a multiple-measure battery, not the intelligence test alone.

Four instruments assess intellectual functioning by sampling performance on several different types of tasks. They include the Wechsler Intelligence Scale for Children—Revised (WISC–R), the Wechsler Adult Intelligence Scale (WAIS), the Stanford-Binet Intelligence Scale, and the Kaufman Assessment Battery for Children (K–ABC).

Table 2–3 summarizes the basic features of the four major measures of individual intelligence.

The WISC–R, according to its standardized sample population, is best suited for elementary and secondary students between the ages of 6 years, 0 months and 16 years, 11 months. The manual implies that this test is most appropriate for white, English-speaking persons not living in institutional settings for the men-

TABLE 2–2

Classification system for intelligence

	WISC–R/WAIS IQ Range	WISC–R/WAIS Scaled Score Range	Stanford-Binet IQ Range	Performance Classification
I.	IQ 69 and below	SS.3 and below	IQ 67 and below	Below average
II.	IQ 70 to IQ 84	SS.4 to SS.6	IQ 68 to IQ 83	Low average
III.	IQ 85 to IQ 115	SS.7 to SS.13	IQ 84 to IQ 116	Average
IV.	IQ 116 to IQ 130	SS.14 to SS.16	IQ 117 to IQ 132	High average
V.	IQ 131 and above	SS.17 and above	IQ 132 and above	Above average

tally retarded and without severe emotional problems. The test includes verbal and performance scales. Table 2–3 lists each subtest of the scales of intellectual performance measure. The WISC-R, like the WAIS and the Stanford-Binet, requires minimal academic skills since students answer test questions orally.

The WAIS, designed for individuals over 16 years of age, almost identically parallels the WISC–R.

The Stanford-Binet Intelligence Scale, the oldest intelligence test, is one of the most widely used assessment devices and gives two scores: mental age and IQ. Because it has fewer subtests, the Stanford-Binet yields fewer scores than the Wechsler scales and is more appropriate for the assessment of verbal abilities.

A newer intelligence test, useful for students under age 3, is the K–ABC. According to Keith (1985) more research is needed to discover *what* the test measures, but it appears to quantify verbal and verbal-mediated memory, verbal reasoning, and nonverbal (figural) reasoning skills, in addition to giving two measures of reading and one of mathematics achievement. This test has limited uses for secondary school students as the age range is lower than it is for the WISC–R, the WAIS, and the Stanford-Binet. The K–ABC yields a multitude of scores: standard scores, scaled scores, age equivalents, and percentile ranks. Refer to Table 2–3 for a listing of its three scales and a brief description of its subtests.

Problems with Intelligence Measures

The WISC–R, the WAIS, the Stanford–Binet, and the K–ABC tests are used widely outside of the classroom when information regarding intelligence is needed. Measurements of intelligence, like other assessment devices, must be used judiciously in conjunction with other information in order to be useful to the teacher and the adolescent. Regardless of which test the examiner selects, remember that inadequacies exist in every norm-referenced test. As mentioned, many of these standardized tools are culturally biased against minorities. Also, testing conditions are critical, as scores derived from intelligence tests can change over time. The IQ score should never be viewed as a fixed number because there is always a possibility of testing error and inappropriate choice of sample selections.

At the secondary level, according to Wallace and McLoughlin (1979), there are few age-appropriate and subject-appropriate assessment instruments that are valid and reliable. When interpreting results, recall that these tests merely sample behaviors, such as discrimination, generalization, motor behavior, general information, vocabulary, induction, comprehension, sequencing, detail recognition, analogies, abstract reasoning, memory, and pattern completion. The examiner must go beyond the full scale scores and look at the individual performance of the separate subtests. Used judiciously, these intelligence measures may provide valuable information in the problem definition phase of assessment. They are only one component, however, of a comprehensive assessment.

In summary, this screening sequence has examined two domains: general academic achievement and intellectual functioning. Once this point in the screening phase has been reached, you should be able to respond to the general disposition question, "Is there a problem?" Although the use of formal tests such as those described is quite common, remember to look beyond this phase in your instructional assessment. To determine the exact nature of the problem (reading comprehension, math computation) is the challenge of the next phase.

DEFINITION OF THE PROBLEM

Once a problem has been verified through screening, the next phase is *defining the problem*. This phase has two goals:

1. to confirm the results of screening and
2. to identify specific individual strengths and weaknesses (Hops & Greenwood, 1981).

TABLE 2–3
Summary of intellectual performance measures

Test and Publisher	Age Range	Testing Subtests	Working Time (Approximate)	Scores Yielded
Kaufman Assessment Battery for Children (K-ABC) Circle Pines, MN: American Guidance Service	2½ to 12½	*Sequential* Hand movements Number recall Word order · *Simultaneous* Triangles Gestalt closure Matrix analogies Spatial memory Photo series · *Achievement* Faces and places Arithmetic Riddles/Decoding Reading/ Understanding	35 to 80 minutes (depending on number of subtests)	Scaled scores Age equivalent Percentile ranks
Stanford-Binet Intelligence Scale Chicago, IL: Riverside Publishing Co.	2 to adult	General comprehension Visual motor ability Arithmetic reasoning Memory and concentration Vocabulary and verbal fluency Judgment and reasoning	60 minutes (no limit)	Mental age (MA) Intelligent quotient (IQ)
Wechsler Adult Intelligence Scale (WAIS) New York: Harcourt Brace Jovanovich; The Psychological Corporation	16–75	*Verbal* Information Comprehension Similarities Arithmetic Vocabulary Digit span · *Performance* (Picture completion) Picture arrangement Block design Object assembly Coding	60 minutes	Verbal performance Full scale
Wechsler Intelligence Scale for Children-Revised (WISC-R) New York: Harcourt Brace Jovanovich; The Psychological Corporation	6–0 to 16–11	*Verbal* Information Comprehension Similarities Vocabulary (Digit span) · *Performance* Picture completion Picture arrangement Block design Object assembly (Mazes)	50–75 minutes	Verbal performance Full scale

This phase begins with a look at the general measures for following up your screening efforts.

Defining a General Problem in Achievement

The PIAT, the Woodcock-Johnson Psychoeducational Battery, and other individually administered achievement tests screen overlapping areas of academic achievement. If these are concerns regarding additional academic skill areas, supplement these tests with a criterion-referenced or teacher-made curriculum unit test. Criterion-referenced tests represent a means of connecting assessment to current programming.

The BRIGANCE®* Diagnostic Inventory of Essential Skills (Brigance, 1980) which focuses upon the taught curriculum, provides a comprehensive assessment of important skills, behaviors, and concepts taught in the secondary classroom. Another advantage of this multiple-skill battery is that it requires no special training to administer and score. One of the products is a list of mastered and unmastered skills that translates into strengths, weaknesses, and ready-made potential objectives. Figure 2–4 displays a sample from Travel and Transportation that assesses computation of gas mileage and cost.

Other advantages of the BRIGANCE® test include ease of adaptation and results that are expressed as grade equivalents. Because of the large number of behaviors sampled, it is not practical for a classroom teacher or examiner to give the test in its entirety; therefore, its use may be postponed until specific skill areas that need attention have been selected. The flexibility of selecting subtests out of the 165 skill sequences for specific assessment needs is one of the BRIGANCE® test's unique and most practical features.

---

*BRIAGANCE® is a registered trademark of Curriculum Associates, Inc.

In the following sections we review criterion-referenced assessments for specific content areas, beginning with reading.

Defining a Specific Reading Problem

Word recognition, reading comprehension, and application are the reading skills assessed most often. The ability to look at a word and say its name is referred to as *word recognition*. Words that we come upon quite frequently are often learned by sight, earning the name "sight words." Other words may be identified using a phonics approach: the student decodes the words and blends the sounds to form the correct pronunciation. A similar method, structural analysis, requires the person to analyze the root word and any prefixes or suffixes. Finally, the reader can use context clues to help her identify words by their meaning in the given situation. Characteristically, reading measures target at least two of these skills.

Comprehension refers to understanding what is read. This complex skill can be assessed by using either oral or silent reading samples. Questions generally follow a reading passage that may require the secondary student simply to recall information, sequence the events, state the main idea, or identify detailed information. Inferential comprehension requires the middle or high school student to make inferences, draw conclusions, predict outcomes, or make judgments.

Measures of application skills are especially crucial at the secondary level. This final aspect of reading combines the skills of word recognition and comprehension with everyday situations. Each day adolescents and adults are exposed to reading in the form of newspapers, magazines, menus, applications, signs, bus schedules, television logs, and other learning situations.

Table 2–4 describes reading diagnostic tests that enable you to define a reading problem. This table also includes descriptive remarks

DIRECTIONS: Read each problem carefully. Work each problem and write your answer in the blank.

NAME: _____

1. a. Frank's car used 15 gallons of gasoline on a trip of 255 miles. How many miles per gallon does his car get?

   _____ miles per gallon

   b. Marie's car used 22 gallons of gasoline on a trip of 396 miles. How many miles per gallon does her car get?

   _____ miles per gallon

2. a. When she filled the gasoline tank with 12 gallons of gasoline, the mileage on Betty's car was as shown below on the left. She drove the car until the tank was almost empty, and the mileage was as shown below on the right. Then it took 15 gallons to fill the tank. How many miles per gallon of gas does her car get?

   Mileage when tank   Mileage when tank
   was first filled   was refilled

   | 1 | 5 | 8 | 7 | 7 | 8 | | 1 | 6 | 1 | 4 | 7 | 8 |

   _____ miles per gallon

   b. When he filled the gasoline tank with 9 gallons of gasoline, the mileage on Tom's car was as shown below on the left. He drove the car until the tank was almost empty, and the mileage was as shown below on the right. Then it took 14 gallons to fill the tank. How many miles per gallon of gas does his car get?

   Mileage when tank   Mileage when tank
   was first filled   was refilled

   | 2 | 1 | 5 | 7 | 3 | 5 | | 2 | 1 | 8 | 6 | 7 | 5 |

   _____ miles per gallon

3. a. Annetta's car travels 17 miles per gallon of gasoline. How many gallons will she need to go on a trip of 255 miles?

   _____ gallons

   b. Bill's car travels 18 miles per gallon of gasoline. How many gallons will he need to go on a trip of 396 miles?

   _____ gallons

4. a. If gasoline costs $0.89 per gallon, and Fran's car travels 17 miles per gallon, how much will the gasoline cost for a trip of 238 miles?

   $ _____

   b. If Carlo's car uses "No Lead" gasoline that costs $0.92 per gallon and travels 18 miles per gallon of gasoline, how much will the gasoline cost for a trip of 396 miles?

   $ _____

FIGURE 2-4

Excerpt from BRIGANCE® Diagnostic Inventory of Essential Skills (Source: From BRIG-ANCE® *Diagnostic Inventory of Essential Skills*, Copyright © 1981 Curriculum Associates, Inc. Reprinted by permission.)

25

TABLE 2-4

Norm-referenced screening and diagnostic measures—Reading

Test and Publisher	Grade	Working Time (Approximate)	Administration	Content Areas	Features
Durrell Analysis of Reading Difficulty New York: Harcourt Brace Jovanovich	K-6	30–60 minutes	Individual	Oral reading Silent reading Listening comprehension Word recognition and word analysis	Inadequate information on technical aspects
Diagnostic Reading Scales (rev. ed.) Monterey. CA: California Testing Bureau/McGraw-Hill	1–8.5	60 minutes	Individual	Word recognition lists Reading passages Phonics test	Reliability and validity; inadequate information on standardization
Gates-McKillop Reading Diagnostic Tests New York: Teachers College Press	2–6	30–60 minutes	Individual	Speed and accuracy Vocabulary Comprehension	Insufficient data on technical aspects
Gilmore Oral Reading Test New York: Harcourt Brace Jovanovich	1–8	15–20 minutes	Individual	Oral reading Comprehension Reading rate	Insufficient information on reliability and validity; adequate standardization

Test	Grade Level	Time	Administration	Areas Assessed	Reliability/Validity
Gray Oral Reading Test Indianapolis: Bobbs-Merrill	1–12	30–90 minutes	Individual	Oral reading Comprehension (literal)	Limited reliability and adequate validity; inadequate information on norming samples Tape recorder can be used
Stanford Diagnostic Reading Test Cleveland: The Psychological Corporation	4.6–9.5 (Brown level) · · · · · · · · 9.0–12.+ (Blue level)	3 sessions	Group	*Decoding* Phonetic analysis Structured analysis (Brown level) · · · · · · · · Phonetic analysis Structured analysis (Blue level) *Comprehension* Reading (literal & inferential) (Brown level) · · · · · · · · Reading (literal & inferential) (Blue level) *Vocabulary* Auditory vocabulary · · · · · · · · Word meaning Word parts *Rate* Reading rate · · · · · · · · Fast reading Scanning and skimming	Well standardized, adequate reliability and validity (relative to content of local curriculum)
Woodcock Reading Mastery Tests Circle Pines, MN: American Guidance Service	1–12+	30–40 minutes	Individual	Letter identification Word identification Word attack Word comprehension Passage comprehension	Good reliability, insufficient information for validity

27

about the technical aspects, the amount of time needed, and other features.

Because the Stanford Diagnostic Reading Test (SDRT) possesses a number of items, it is to be administered in three sessions, each lasting no longer than 40 minutes. The SDRT is both criterion-referenced and norm-referenced. This test is a useful tool because it is designed to compare an adolescent's skill development with the skill development of her peers. The subtests, many specific to reading behaviors, provide the secondary teacher with a systematic analysis of reading strengths and weaknesses.

The Woodcock Reading Mastery Tests assess these areas of skill development: letter identification, word identification, word attack, word comprehension, and passage comprehension. Generally, the letter identification section is not given to teenagers reading above grade 6; however, if the teenager is a nonreader, this subtest should be given. The Woodcock's unique scoring system permits the examiner to convert the raw scores into special grade scores—Reading Grade Score, Easy Reading Level, and Failure Reading Level. The Reading Grade Score denotes the grade level in which instruction should take place, and the other two levels represent material presumed to be too easy or too difficult. The easel format, like that found in the PIAT and Peabody Picture Vocabulary Test (PPVT), provides continuous one-to-one interaction with the examiner. This feature is advantageous to the special educator who intends to assess individually for multiple reading skills; however, it is a drawback to the instructor requiring a group-administered measure. See Table 2–4 for information regarding the test's technical aspects.

The Diagnostic Reading Scales (Spache, 1972), like the Woodcock, assess several different areas of reading performance—a valuable component. Diagnosing strengths and weaknesses is an integral part of planning instruction, and the Spache checklist is helpful because it targets sight vocabulary, word analysis tech-

niques, oral reading, and silent reading. This collection of norm-referenced standardized measurements is appropriate for students whose reading is between grades 1 and 8.5. More information on this individually administered test can be found in Table 2–4.

The Durrell Analysis of Reading Difficulty (Durrell, 1955), a test designed to cover a range from pre-reading to sixth grade, is popular, though it can be used only for secondary students reading below grade level. This individually administered test taps four measures: oral and silent reading, listening comprehension, word recognition, and word analysis. A special educator or examiner might choose this test to delineate specific strengths and weaknesses, for it yields a checklist that identifies reading skill developments, which is useful to a classroom teacher. A drawback to the test is that the technical aspects are insufficiently documented in the testing manual. Still, with that in mind, the test can be used to collect meaningful qualitative information about an adolescent's reading deficits.

The Gates-McKillop Reading Diagnostic Tests (Gates & McKillop, 1975) are widely used despite the fact that they do not assess comprehension. These tests also have limited use at the high school level because they are designed for students in grades 2 through 7. Still, they can be used to assess middle, junior, or senior high school students who are reading at or below their grade level. The 8 content areas and 17 subtests are listed in Table 2–4. The high number of subtests and multiple scores leaves room for misinterpretation. The manual for this battery of tests, like Durrell's, presents insufficient information about test construction and quality. Again, like the Durrell test, one of the Gates-McKillop's strongest features is the checklist of difficulties and error analysis that is provided for many of the subtests.

The Gray Oral Reading Test (Gray & Robinson, 1985) and the Gilmore Oral Reading Test (Gilmore & Gilmore, 1968) are designed to measure oral reading objectively. One of the differences between these two tests is the targeted age range; the Gray is designed to assess students through grade 12, while the Gilmore reaches grade 8. The Gray and the Gilmore, like the Gates-McKillop, present a series of graded reading passages. Comprehension questions follow the presentation of each passage in the Gray and the Gilmore, but not in the Gates-McKillop. Generally, this individually administered test is given by the regular or special education teacher, a reading specialist, or an outside consultant. Requiring aid, giving partial or gross mispronunciations, omitting, inserting, inverting, substituting, and repeating words—all are recorded as errors. A list of reading characteristics is also available to assist the examiner in identifying observable reading behaviors. The most useful feature, error analysis, provides the secondary teacher with a list of errors and patterns of errors for specific instruction. At the secondary level, the skill-oral reading is far less functional than silent reading, as far less opportunity for reading aloud arises at the secondary level than at the elementary one. Another reason these tests are not frequently used is that oral reading tests are virtually being replaced by informal reading inventories (IRI) because they share many of the same characteristics. Although the IRIs are neither norm-referenced nor standardized, they can be individually designed by the teacher, or commercially prepared IRIs like the *Sucher-Allred Reading Placement* (Sucher & Allred, 1973), the *Classroom Reading Inventory* (Silvaroli, 1982), and the *Analytical Reading Inventory* (Woods & Moe, 1985) can be purchased.

We have tried to describe tests that any school district may use, or that may have been studied in other coursework. Keep in mind that these tests will offer only a general picture of a student's reading performance and that some tests sample only a small number of reading behaviors. Although some districts place students in reading programs based on their scores on these general tests, a more specific, curriculum-based assessment should follow (or replace) this kind of testing.

In the next section we examine some assessments for defining a problem in language.

Defining a Specific Written or Oral Language Problem

Multiple opportunities in the classroom provide the secondary teacher with useful information about writing. The PIAT, WRAT, BRIGANCE®, and the Woodcock-Johnson Psychoeducational Battery provide the teacher with more global information on a teenager's academic performance. Nevertheless, one of these tests requires the student to write sentences with capitalization, punctuation, and spelling. The Test of Written Language (TOWL) by Hammill and Larsen (1978), which measures vocabulary, thematic maturity, thought units (complete ideas), word usage, spelling, handwriting, and such writing mechanics as capitalization and punctuation, can provide additional information. The TOWL is one of the only testing instruments that assesses writing skills. Here, the teenager is asked to compose an original science fiction theme based on three sequenced pictures. The test is easy to administer, but scoring is more difficult because the examiner must make multiple decisions based on the spontaneous writing sample of the adolescent. The subtests, vocabulary, thematic maturity, thought units, and handwriting, are scored herein. The TOWL has been normed with students between the ages of 8 years, 6 months and 14 years, 5 months. The test is norm-referenced; working time is between 1 and 3 hours; and it can be administered individually or in a group. The reliability and validity of the test appear adequate, although the information on standardization is insufficient. This unique instrument offers the regular or special educator standardized results on key areas of written language.

The Picture Story Language Test (PSLT) by Myklebust (1965) is a norm-referenced standardized test that measures several areas of written language. The test is normed for students ages 7 to 17 and may be given individually or to groups. A spontaneous writing sample is obtained after the student is shown a test picture and asked to write a story about it. Typically, the PSLT takes 20 minutes; the areas tapped include productivity, correctness (syntax), and meaning (sentences). Unfortunately, scoring this test is not as easy as administering it.

Another instrument, the Zaner-Bloser Evaluation Scales (1979), provides a way to collect and rate multiple handwriting samples. Students with poor motor skills are often referred by teachers and parents for special education assessment. A special education team usually collects permanent products from informal classroom activities and obtains information from such standardized measurements as the TOWL and the Zaner-Bloser, which assesses letter formation, slant in cursive, spacing, alignment and proportion, and line quality. The scale helps determine the teenager's present level of handwriting in relation to other students 'the same age and specifies areas of strength and weakness.

A relatively new instrument that assesses spoken and written language, reception and expression, and grammar and vocation is the Test of Adolescent Language (TOAL) by Hammill, Brown, Larsen, and Wiederholt (1980). For the most part, the classroom teacher can administer this test in a group, since only two of the eight subtests must be given individually. The test is viewed as comprehensive because both oral and written language are assessed. The results identify weak areas, and further testing can then be recommended before further educational planning occurs. The test, relatively easy to administer but difficult to score, lasts between 1 and 3 hours. The technical aspects include good reliability, fair validity, and standardization.

The *Clinical Evaluation of Language Functions* (Semel & Wiig, 1980) is another language test with two main components for screening and diagnostic purposes. Typically, this individually administered test would be given by a speech pathologist or a resource-room teacher. Remember that the PPVT also tests language reception.

Oral and written language comprise the basic skills in communication. If a teacher suspects severe deficits in the area of oral language, generally he refers the student to the special education team, and the youth is most likely considered for speech and language intervention. At the secondary level, these skills become critical as composition, discussions, and writing become more sophisticated and expectations in the overlapping academic areas more demanding. Adolescents are constantly being assessed informally on their oral skills and their written language, in areas such as science, social studies, English, journalism, and history.

Defining a Specific Problem in Mathematics

Basic math skills are needed in everyday life. There are always students who think they *cannot* do math, and teenagers who have never acquired basic calculation and other math skills easily fall behind in the curriculum. Teachers and parents may refer students for mathematics assessment in special education because of specific problems, including the inability to:

- Read and interpret tables and graphs.
- Make change, when given the cost of a purchase and money available.
- Work problems involving percentages.

The Key Math Diagnostic Arithmetic Test by Connolly, Nachtman, and Pritchett (1976) and the Stanford Diagnostic Mathematics Test (SDMT) by Beatty, Madden, Gardner and Karlsen (1978) are two commonly used tests measuring levels of math achievement and strengths and weaknesses.

Two features that make these individually administered tests popular are that teachers can give them without formal training and that each has specific listings of behavioral objectives for every item. These criterion-referenced measures make the identification of specific strengths and weaknesses easy for the secondary instructor. Table 2–5 displays Key Math's three domains (content, operations, and applications) and their subtests.

The table also illustrates the SDMT's three domains (number system and numeration, computation, and applications), its subtests, and technical aspects. Two of the SDMT's levels (Brown and Blue), representing the appropriate level for adolescents, are included in the table. Both tests reflect sequenced skill development to evaluate a variety of math skills. The tests are relatively easy to administer and score, and the interpretation of deficit skill areas is clear-cut.

One of the major differences between the two tests is the format. The Key Math's test notebook easel format, like the PIAT, allows the adolescent to interact directly with the examiner. The SDMT permits the teenager to work independently using a multiple choice format. The SDMT is designed to identify the instructional math needs of students through the twelfth grade, whereas the Key Math is designed to accommodate only teenagers functioning below the eighth grade. More testing items are found on the SDMT; the test typically takes 1½ hours, whereas the Key Math takes approximately 30 minutes to administer.

If there are concerns about an adolescent's basic computation skills, we strongly recommend the Computational Arithmetic Program (CAP) (Deutsch, Smith, & Lovitt, 1982) designed to assess computational skills and to remedy skill deficits.

So far our discussion has focused on popular, commercially available tests; however, teacher-made tests and other criterion-refer-

enced assessments may fit into any phase of the assessment model. We discuss these more informal measures in the following section. Under no circumstances should an adolescent's assessment stop with the defining of the problem, where only a limited number of academic behaviors can be measured. Eligibility decisions often include only the first two phases of the assessment model, screening and definition of the problem. This is a result of time constraints placed on school psychologists and others who are charged with these initial assessments. Classroom teachers recognize that problem definition, no matter how thorough, does not replace specific pinpointing of academic targets. The next section takes a more precise look at the academic problems addressed in classroom instruction.

PINPOINTING ACADEMIC TARGETS

Pinpointing refers to the specification of behaviors or skills to be modified or taught. In previous sections, we focused on standardized assessment instruments (formal tests) that are commonly used in public secondary schools. Another critical process, informal testing, provides specific information about adolescent skill development.

Table 2–6 offers a 12-step strategy to help in understanding the substeps of pinpointing. Developed by Zigmond, Vallecorsa, and Silverman (1983), this pinpointing model focuses on error analysis, an important feature of criterion-referenced assessments. This approach to pinpointing strategy can be adapted to assess the basic skill areas—mathematics, written and oral language, and reading.

Begin with pinpointing basic skills and then move to other areas of a student's functioning: reading, math, and written language. For the academic areas (reading, math, and written language), we follow 10 steps of Zigmond's 12-step strategy. Our case study explores all 12 steps in the area of mathematics.

TABLE 2–5
Screening and diagnostic measures—Mathematics

Test and Publisher	Grade Range	Subtests	Time (Approximate)	Norm- or Criterion-Referenced	Comments
Computational Arithmetic Program (CAP) Austin, TX: Pro-Ed	5–12	Addition Subtraction Multiplication Division	1 minute timings (by teacher)	Criterion-referenced	Research support; field validation
Key Math Diagnostic Arithmetic Test Circle Pines, MN: American Guidance Service	K–8	*Content* Numeration Fractions Geometry and symbols / *Operations* Addition Subtraction Multiplication Division Mental computation Numerical reasoning / *Application* Word problems Missing elements Money Measurement Time	30 minutes	Norm- or Criterion-referenced	Inadequate data for demonstration of content validity, adequate reliability; incomplete information on sample
Stanford Diagnostic Mathematics Test (SDMT) New York: Harcourt Brace Jovanovich	5.5–8.5 (Brown level) 7.5–HS (Blue level)	*Number System and Numeration* Whole numbers Decimal place value Rational number and numeration Operations and properties / *Computation* Addition of whole numbers Addition facts Addition, no renaming Subtraction of whole numbers Subtraction facts Subtraction, no renaming Multiplication of whole numbers Division of whole numbers Fractions Decimals Percent (Blue only) Number sentences / *Applications* Problem solving Reading and interpreting tables and graphs Geometry and measurement	1½–1¾ hours	Norm- or Criterion-referenced	Well standardized, adequate reliability and validity measures

TABLE 2–6
12-step strategy for assessment for instructional planning

1. Decide what to assess
2. Select or develop a skill hierarchy
3. Decide where to begin
4. Select or develop a survey instrument
5. Get ready to test
6. Administer the survey
7. Note errors and performance style
8. Analyze findings and summarize outcomes
9. Hypothesize reasons for errors and determine areas to probe
10. Probe
11. Complete record keeping forms and generate teaching objectives
12. Start teaching/update assessment information

Source: From Naomi Zigmond/Ada Vallecorsa/Rita Silverman, ASSESSMENT FOR INSTRUC-TIONAL PLANNING IN SPECIAL EDUCATION, © 1983, p. 32, Adapted by permission of Prentice-Hall, Inc., Englewood Cliffs, New Jersey.

PINPOINTING BASIC SKILLS

The basic skills are particularly relevant in the high school; many states have already implemented minimum competency tests for graduation and grade-to-grade promotion. This movement towards minimum competency testing has had substantial impact on special education policies that determine the goals of special education. Although P.L. 94–142 makes no mention of mandated minimum competency testing, the extent to which a secondary student receives special services still must be considered. While educators of exceptional students are being held accountable for the continuous evaluation of learning, there is mixed opinion as to whether competency tests actually measure competency. McClung and Pullin (1978) claim that insufficient attention has been paid to the special problems of exceptional students in mandated minimum competency testing programs. According to a Children's Defense Fund Report (1985), prior experience and research lend doubt to the validity of the test results and even suggest that the testing process interferes with learning. Problems identified are that the design of the test evaluates a limited range of skills, there is a prevalence of cultural bias, and

that the scoring process cannot yield an objective measure. The trend toward basic skill competency clearly will affect assessment and program planning for the adolescent in special education at the secondary level.

Pinpointing Reading Targets

Decide What to Assess. Because reading is a complex process involving multiple skills, we must narrow our scope by pinpointing reading targets. Word recognition, word attack skills, comprehension, and application of reading are areas commonly measured. When deciding what to assess, the administrator must rely on his own judgment. By the time the instructor has reached this pinpointing phase we assume that he has defined the problem area. For example, he may have discovered that many of his students are reading below their grade level expectancy. This information was gathered after a standardized test such as the SDRT was administered. He is concerned with establishing reading levels for one particular student who he suspects is having problems comprehending written material as a result of insufficient decoding skills. He should have the student orally read passages from standardized surveys (e.g.,

SAT, MAT, PIAT, CAT, or WRAT) to determine an appropriate instructional level. This method enables the instructor to identify students needing immediate attention.

Select or Develop a Skill Hierarchy. After deciding what to test, develop a comprehensive skill hierarchy that arranges samples of the student's reading behavior in a systematic fashion. Once the student has read orally, her word attack skills used for unfamiliar words will become clear. Use expertise in establishing a skill hierarchy. For example, if the student is having difficulty with structural analysis, refer to Table 2–7. Secondary level students who are experiencing difficulty with decoding or phonetic or structural analysis will have to be given material geared toward the elementary or middle school level. Table 2–7 provides a scope-and-sequence chart based on a basal series for fifth grade students. A scope-and-sequence chart offers systematic grouping of academic material in a recommended order for testing and teaching. The materials provided in basal series can always be adapted, as the exercises for testing students are closely related to the exercises for teaching students.

Decide Where to Begin. Select a beginning reading level and refer to the skill hierarchy for an appropriate beginning. For example, if structural analysis is a problem area, begin with gathering materials designed to tap knowledge of prefixes, suffixes, and syllabication.

Select or Develop a Survey Instrument. Select a commercially available survey instrument or create one. The instrument should contain enough items or samples to provide sufficient information regarding student mastery of each skill level. Although word recognition or decoding skills can be measured objectively using

oral reading measures such as the Gray Oral Reading Test (Gray & Robinson, 1985) and the Gilmore Oral Reading Test (Gilmore & Gilmore, 1968), we encourage the exploration of such informal reading inventories as the *Sucher-Allred Reading Placement* (1973), the *Classroom Reading Inventory* by Silvaroli (1982), and the *Analytical Reading Inventory* by Woods and Moe (1985). These inventories can provide invaluable, precise information about a student's reading problem. When selecting an instrument or creating one, be sure to mark and analyze errors.

Get Ready to Test and Administer the Survey. Gather the pertinent testing materials. When acquiring any oral information, it might be helpful to use a tape recorder. This will make the next step easier. At this level of assessment, students typically will be tested one at a time. Thus, the instructor needs to schedule her time and the students' time accordingly.

Note Errors and Performance Style. A tape recorder can collect meaningful information for decoding and structural analysis. For example, the following behavior was recorded from a student reading a portion of a teacher-made reading list.

Stimulus	Response	Error Analysis
endlessly	endless	omission of suffix
picture	pitcher	faulty consonant
tangle	triangle	word substitution
employer	employee	careless/faulty consonant
circuit	circus	word substitution
recollection	collection	omission of prefix
additional	addition	omission of sound
wander	wonder	word substitution
corporal	corporate	word substitution
monarch	monar<u>ch</u>	faulty consonant

With the use of IRIs or standard or informal reading measures, you can usually record er-

TABLE 2–7

A scope and sequence of elementary skills that can be adapted
for secondary students

Word Study Skills	Comprehension and Study Skills
1. Antonyms—review and give practice in using context clues	Continue development in the following areas:
2. Expand vocabulary	A. Main idea
3. Review figures of speech and introduce new ones to enrich vocabulary	B. Sequence
4. Homonyms—review and introduce new ones	C. Reading for details
5. Synonyms—review and introduce new ones to expand vocabulary	D. Appreciating literary style
6. Use of dictionary and glossary	E. Drawing conclusions
a. guide words	F. Enriching information
b. accent marks	G. Evaluating information
c. diacritical marks	H. Forming opinions and generalizing
1. review a, ä, u, å, oo, oo, ėė	I. Interpreting ideas
2. review long and short vowels	J. Using alphabetical arrangement
3. introduce, schwa, half- long o	K. Using dictionary or glossary skills
4. introduce italic, u, i, a, e	L. Interpreting maps and pictures
5. introduce an omitted vowel	M. Skimming for purposes
6. respellings	N. Classifying ideas
7. Phonetic analysis	O. Following directions
a. review consonant sounds	P. Outlining
b. review pronunciation of vowel sounds	Q. Summarizing
c. review phonograms	R. Reading for accuracy
8. Structural analysis	S. Skimming
a. compound words	Introduce and teach:
b. words of similar configuration	A. Discrimination between fact and fiction
c. prefixes	B. Perceiving related ideas
1. review un-, im-, dis-, re-	C. Strengthening power of recall
2. introduce in-, anti-, inter-, mis-	D. Using encyclopedias, atlases, almanacs, and other references
d. suffixes	E. Using charts and graphs
1. review -en, -ment, -less, -ish, -ly, -ful, -y, -ed	F. Using index and pronunciation keys
2. introduce -sp, -or, -ours, -ness, -ward, -hood, -action, -al	G. Reading to answer questions and for enjoyment of literary style
e. principles of syllabication	
1. review rules already taught	
2. consonant blends and digraphs treated as singular sounds and usually not divided (ma-chine)	
f. application of word analysis, attacking words outside the basic vocabulary	

Source: From *Reading and Learning Disabilities*, 2nd ed. (pp. 147–150) by G. Kaluger and C. J. Kolson, 1978. Columbus, OH: Merrill Publishing Company. Adapted by permission of the author.

rors that include partial mispronunciations, gross mispronunciations, omissions, insertions, inversions, substitutions, and repetitions.

As a result of her decoding problem, the above student also had difficulty with comprehension. According to Hammill and Bartel (1986), the three broad areas of comprehension include:

- literal—understanding the primary meaning,
- inferential—understanding a deeper meaning that is not directly stated in the passage, and
- critical—passing judgment on quality, worth, accuracy, and truth.

To assess these areas, one must collect information on the student's recognition and recall of details, main ideas, sequencing, cause-and-effect relationships, as well as the student's ability to infer supporting details, main ideas, and causal relationships. The same instruments used to determine decoding difficulties can be employed for this.

Analyze Findings and Summarize Outcomes. After translating all of the accumulated assessment material, you can begin to target very specifically the individual's strengths and weaknesses.

Hypothesize Reasons for Errors and Determine Areas to Probe. The student may be strong in vocabulary but weak in areas of comprehension, or problems in comprehension may be a result of his poor decoding skills.

Probe. Probing consists of creating a specialized test to determine deficit areas. These probes need not take much of the teacher's time to administer. For each area of reading there are multiple tests and inventories available to offer ideas and word lists for probing. Material from such standardized reading tests as the SDRT or the BRIGANCE® can be adapted. Reading pro-

grams such as DISTAR also provide worksheets that can be used for probing.

If the analysis of a student's work leads to the conclusion that there is no mastery of word endings or that the student has problems with vowels or syllabication, a simple probe sheet can be given, which might look like Figure 2–5.

Pinpointing Written or Oral Language Targets

Decide What to Assess. Consider the case of a tenth grader who has a specific problem in written composition. Composition refers to a student's ability to capitalize, punctuate, use vocabulary, and construct sentences. After taking the TOWL, the student shows a very poor vocabulary. This area is thus pinpointed for further analysis.

Select or Develop a Skill Hierarchy. Refer to Table 2–8, which provides a scope-and-sequence chart. In this chart, the scope spans the areas of capitalization, vocabulary, word usage, grammar, sentence construction, and paragraph construction. These behaviors tap the major aspects of written and oral language. The individual skills appear in a developmental sequence for testing and teaching. Naturally, the instructor is encouraged to use her own judgment as to the ordering of these skills. Concentrate on the sequencing of items under the vocabulary category. Focus on exercises that provide information on exactness in choice of words, antonyms, homonyms, contractions, vocabulary, and use of a dictionary.

Decide Where to Begin. Select a beginning, after referring to the skill hierarchy. Let us assume that we begin at the top of the list under vocabulary–antonyms.

Select or Develop a Survey Instrument. Gathering materials for vocabulary assessment is fairly easy. Consider the student's speaking and writ-

Name _____	Correct _____	Errors _____
Date _____	Teacher Comments: _____	

_____

_____

stimulus	*response*	*stimulus*	*response*
special	_____	helpless	_____
healthy	_____	careful	_____
tired	_____	before	_____
poor	_____	after	_____
weary	_____	today	_____
confused	_____	tomorrow	_____
helpful	_____	school	_____
silly	_____	morning	_____
together	_____	evening	_____
anger	_____	clearly	_____
angry	_____	sentence	_____
simple	_____	paragraph	_____
sample	_____	composition	_____
sorting	_____	write	_____
able	_____	writer	_____
fighting	_____	writing	_____

FIGURE 2–5
A probe sheet used to test word recognition

TABLE 2-8

Scope and sequence of skills in written composition for elementary skills that can be applied to students at the secondary level

Grade 5	Grades 6, 7, and 8

Capitalization

Names of streets	Names of the Deity and the Bible
Names of all places and persons, countries, oceans, etc.	First word of a quoted sentence
Capitalization used in outlining	Proper adjectives, showing race, nationality, etc.
Titles when used with names, such as President Lincoln	Abbreviations of proper nouns and titles
Commercial trade names	

Punctuation

Colon in writing time	Comma to set off nouns in direct address
Quotation marks around the title of a booklet, pamphlet, the chapter of a book, and the title of a poem or story	Hyphen in compound numbers
Underlining the title of a book	Colon to set off a list
	Comma in sentences to aid in making meaning clear

Vocabulary

Using antonyms	Extending meanings, writing with care in choice of words and phrases
Prefixes and suffixes; compound words	In writing and speaking, selecting words for accuracy
Exactness in choice of words	Selecting words for effectiveness and appropriateness
Dictionary work; definitions; syllables; pronunciation; macron; breve	Selecting words for courtesy
Contractions	Editing a paragraph to improve a choice of words
Rhyme and rhythm; words with sensory images	
Classification of words related to them	
Adjectives, nouns, verbs—contrasting general and specific vocabulary	

Word Usage

Avoiding unnecessary pronouns (the boy he . . .)	Homonyms: its, it's; their, there, they're; there's, theirs; whose, who's
Linking verbs and predicate nominatives	Use of parallel structure for parallel ideas, as in outlines
Conjugation of verbs, to note changes in tense, person, number	Verb forms in sentences: beat, beat, beaten
Transitive and intransitive verbs	learn, learned, learned
Verb forms in sentences: am, was, been	leave, left, left
say, said, said	light, lit, lit
fall, fell, fallen	forget, forgot, forgotten
dive, dived, dived	swing, swung, swung
burst, burst, burst	spring, sprang, sprung
buy, bought, bought	shrink, shrank, shrunk
Additional verb forms: climb, like, play, read, sail, vote, work	slide, slid, slid

TABLE 2–8
continued

Grade 5	Grades 6, 7, and 8
Grammar	

Noun: possessive; object of preposition; predicate noun
Verb: tense; agreement with subject; verbs of action and state of being
Adjective: comparison; predicate adjective; proper adjective
Adverb: comparison; words telling how, when, where, how much, modifying verbs, adjective, adverbs
Pronouns: possessive, objective after prepositions
Prepositions: recognition; prepositional phrases
Conjunction: recognition
Interjection: recognition

Noun: antecedent of pronouns; collective nouns; compound subject; direct object; indirect object, object of preposition
Verb: active and passive voice; emphatic forms, transitive and intransitive, tenses; linking verbs
Adverbs: as modifiers; clauses; comparing adverbs; adverbial phrases, use of well and good
Adjectives: as modifiers; clauses; compound adjectives
Pronouns: agreement with antecedents; personal pronoun chart; indirect object; object of preposition; objective case, person and number; possessive form
Preposition: in phrase
Conjunction: coordinate; subordinate; use in compound subjects; compound predicates; complex and compound sentences

Sentences

Using a variety of interesting sentences: declarative; interrogative; exclamatory; and imperative (you as the subject)
Agreement of subject and verb; changes in pronoun forms
Compound subjects and compound predicates
Composing paragraphs with clearly stated ideas

Development of concise statements (avoiding wordiness or unnecessary repetition)
Indirect object and predicate nominative
Complex sentences
Clear thinking and expression (avoiding vagueness and omissions)

Paragraphs

Improvement in writing a paragraph of several sentences
Selecting subheads as well as main topic for outline
Courtesy and appropriateness in all communications
Recognizing topic sentences
Keeping to the topic as expressed in title and topic sentence
Use of more than one paragraph
Developing a four-point outline
Writing paragraphs from outline
New paragraphs for new speakers in written conversation
Keeping list of books (authors and titles) used for reference

Analyzing a paragraph to note method of development
Developing a paragraph in different ways: e.g., with details, reasons, examples, or comparisons
Checking for accurate statements
Use of a fresh or original approach in expressing ideas
Use of transition words to connect ideas
Use of topic sentences in developing paragraphs
Improvement in complete composition—introduction, development, conclusion
Checking for good reasoning
Use of bibliography in report based on several sources

Source: Adapted from *Corrective and Remedial Teaching* by W. Otto and R. McMenemy, 1980, Boston: Houghton Mifflin; *Developing Language Skills in the Elementary School* by H. Greene and W. Petty, 1967, Boston: Allyn & Bacon; *Teaching Students with Learning and Behavior Problems* (4th ed.) by D. D. Hammill and N. R. Bartel, 1986, Boston: Allyn & Bacon.

ing vocabulary when selecting word lists. Do not expect students' written vocabulary to be very different from their spoken vocabulary. These word lists can come from standardized assessment instruments like the BRIGANCE®, the PIAT, the SDRT, the TOWL, or any commercially available materials.

Get Ready to Test and Administer the Survey. Gather the pertinent materials or word lists that tap different areas of vocabulary; for example the BRIGANCE® can tap functional vocabulary, food vocabulary, food preparation vocabulary, car parts vocabulary, or others. Perhaps the tenth grade student is interested in working part-time after school; you might select a section of the BRIGANCE® that deals with employment vocabulary. The test provides 25 words matched to definitions. Here is a sample of 10 words.

1. appearance
2. application
3. deduction
4. employee
5. employer
6. equal opportunity employer
7. salary
8. references
9. union
10. pay period

Note Errors and Performance Style. The instrument may offer discriminating items, from which the student must select the appropriate word. Or perhaps a student must define a list of words, with or without context clues. Observe whether or not the student uses prefixes, suffixes, or root words to make meaningful guesses.

Analyze Findings, Summarize Outcomes, and Hypothesize Reasons for Errors and Determine Areas to Probe. Target very specifically the student's strengths and vocabulary after reviewing all of the assessment results. There may be no pattern in the student's problem area—

vocabulary. Perhaps the student never learned how to use root words, prefixes, or suffixes to aid in vocabulary. Perhaps the student has a selective vocabulary in areas that are particularly interesting (i.e., a student may have a strong car mechanics vocabulary and a limited business vocabulary).

Probe. Continue to create specialized tests to determine deficit areas. A sample vocabulary probe sheet might look like Figure 2–6.

Pinpointing Mathematics Targets

Pinpointing areas of strengths and weaknesses in mathematics is very similar to the assessment techniques used in pinpointing behaviors in reading and in oral and written language. We realize that to obtain a clear picture of each individual's areas, testing with standardized instruments is only a beginning. The case study at the end of this chapter deals in detail with the 12-step assessment strategy of Zigmond et al.

In summary, at the completion of the pinpointing phase, specific teaching targets for each of the academic areas have been determined. By following the 12-step pinpointing procedure, no important process of error analysis will be overlooked. Moreover, this process allows the instructor to make assessments using materials taken from the student's regular curriculum. We have illustrated the process in two major academic areas here; the third—mathematics—is exemplified in our case study.

Next we turn to the use of the assessment information for planning.

ACADEMIC PLANNING

Developing Short-Term Objectives

Phase III of the model pinpointed target behaviors. These targets give valuable information about all of the student's deficit areas. The next

FIGURE 2–6
A probe sheet designed to test vocabulary (knowledge of prefixes, suffixes, and root words)

Stimulus	Response	Comment
Prefixes		
repeated		
dislike		
unafraid		
preheated		
biweekly		
semiannual		
Suffixes		
falsely		
friendly		
careless		
neighborhood		
Root words		
neighbor		
invent		
love		
poison		
reason		

Take the five root words and add a prefix or a suffix to create a new word.

neighbor _____

invent _____

love _____

poison _____

reason _____

task is to write these targets into short-term objectives suitable for instructional programming, that is, to add criteria, conditions, and target dates to the previously defined pinpoints, or target behaviors.

Recall the essential components of a sound behavioral objective (Mager, 1975, p. 23):

1. condition
2. specific behavior(s) to be performed
3. criterion

In the next section, we continue the development of the instructional or intervention plan.

Setting Priorities for Short-Term Objectives

Ask yourself these questions when evaluating any short-term objective:

1. Is this really an important skill for the student now and in the immediate future?

2. Is this skill or behavior in keeping with the student's development as an adolescent?
3. Is this objective appropriate for a school setting, or can its instruction be arranged elsewhere?
4. Does this objective unnecessarily repeat past instructional efforts? Is it time for a change of program?

Writing the Short-Term Objectives

It may be helpful to review some guidelines in writing objectives for adolescents.

1. Skills should be relevant to the student.
2. Criteria should be realistic as well as *meaningful*. Saying "90 percent of the time" really says little, when one asks, "What *time*?" Here are examples of this problem: "The student will complete work 100 percent of the time." A better statement would be "The student will turn in all classwork and homework assignments on or before the due date, and will earn a passing grade on at least 90 percent of them."
3. Objectives must be linked to the assessment information.
4. Objectives that cannot be measured are not useful in most special education settings.
5. Objectives ought to specify student, not teacher behavior. For example, "To encourage participation in class discussions" may be better stated, "The student will participate in class discussions."

TABLE 2–9

Relationship among annual goals, short-term instructional objectives, and the instructional plan

Annual Goals	Short-term Instructional Objectives	Instructional Plan
Broad, general statements of anticipated outcomes	Measurable intermediate steps between child's present level of educational performance and the annual goals established	More detailed than IEP; contains specific implementation objectives (daily or weekly objectives)
Serve as basis for the development of short-term instructional objectives	Developed based on a logical breakdown of annual goals	May include listing of materials, strategies, techniques to be used in accomplished objectives
Required as part of IEP	Serve as milestones for indicating progress toward goals	Not required from a federal compliance standpoint
	Used to describe what student is expected to accomplish in a given period of time	
	Used as a "benchmark" to determine the extent to which the student is progressing	
	Projected on a quarterly basis	
	Serves as the basis for developing a detailed instructional plan	
	Required as part of IEP	

Source: From *A Primer on Individualized Education Programs for Exceptional Children* (p. 25) by D. Morgan, 1981. (2nd ed.) Reston, VA: The Foundation for Exceptional Children. Copyright 1981 by The Foundation for Exceptional Children. Reprinted by permission.

6. Objectives written in IEPs do not replace instructional plans or lessons.

Morgan (1981) differentiated between IEP goals, short-term objectives, and instructional plans through the outline in Table 2–9.

Preparing the IEP or Other Document

In special education settings, the short-term objectives and long-term goals are included in an IEP. Adolescents in nonschool settings have their social, academic, or vocational goals on a "Treatment Plan" or "**Rehabilitation Plan.**" These alternative forms often resemble an IEP.

IEPs, Treatment Plans, and Rehabilitation Plans offer an unparalleled opportunity for creative communication—and contracting—among students, teachers, parents, and other professionals. However, the planning document is only as good as the goal statements within it.

The formulation of a workable and comprehensive plan is linked directly to the formulation of short-term objectives drawn from the behavioral targets delineated in the assessment process. Traditionally, long-term goals precede the development of short-term objectives; however, reversing this process may prove more helpful: if the short-term objectives have been carefully worked out, then it will be clear which precise behaviors and skills need to be developed. By setting priorities for meeting as many of the short-term objectives as possible within the school calendar (or time available), the instructor will create *Realistic* long-term goals for himself and his students. Too often, long-term goals do not reflect short-term objectives. Reversing the process corrects for that oversight.

Figure 2–7 illustrates the two IEP sections summarizing assessment results and setting forth annual goals.

SUMMARY

Chapter Two introduced an assessment model and described the way this model applied to academic and intellectual assessment.

Screening is only the first phase in the lengthy process of assessment. Screening procedures, by design, are broad measures that can be misinterpreted if they do not reflect the content of the curriculum being taught. Once screening is completed, a student's academic deficits in specific content areas become clear. After

---

Child's Name _____   Summary of Present Levels of Performance

School _____   _____

Date of Program Entry _____   _____

Prioritized Long-Term Goals: _____

1. _____   _____

2. _____   _____

3. _____   _____

FIGURE 2–7
Excerpt from an Individual Education Program (IEP)

screening, a "general disposition" decision is made whether or not more evaluation is necessary. For example, we might make a decision to evaluate a student further for eligibility in a special education program. In the next phase, the problem is defined more specifically.

Defining the problem is fairly straightforward if screening was comprehensive. During this definition phase, we ascertain the strengths and weaknesses of the individual and determine whether the screening results were accurate. The chapter outlined various tests and informal measures of achievement.

Pinpointing exact target behaviors is the last phase. This phase often results in an Individualized Education Plan (IEP), if the student is identified for a special education program. Finally, the following case study illustrates the assessment process for a specific academic behavior—mathematics.

RECOMMENDED READINGS

For more extensive discussion or technical reviews of the various assessment instruments, we recommend one of the following texts:

McLoughlin, J. A., & Lewis, R. B. (1986). *Assessing special students: Strategies and procedures* (2nd ed.). Columbus, OH: Charles E. Merrill Publishing Company.

Salvia, J., & Ysseldyke, J. E. (1981). *Assessment in special and remedial education.* Boston: Houghton Mifflin.

Models for informal assessment, or how to select and design criterion-referenced tests, have been addressed in:

Howell, K. W., & Kaplan, J. S. (1980). *Diagnosing basic skills: A handbook for deciding what to teach.* Columbus, OH: Charles E. Merrill Publishing Company.

Zigmond, N., Vallecorsa, A., & Silverman, R. (1983). *Assessment for instructional planning in special education.* Englewood Cliffs, NJ: Prentice-Hall.

CASE STUDY

An Assessment of a Tenth Grade Student Having Difficulties in Mathematics

SCREENING AND GENERAL DISPOSITION

Tashina Young was referred to me, a math specialist, after her teacher had administered the CAT to the entire class. Tashina had recently transferred to the school this year, so I waited a few weeks to retrieve past school records to review her educational history. She was in the tenth grade, after repeating the ninth grade. She had a history of poor grades and achievement problems. Although she had never received special education services, she had been assigned to remedial classrooms and after-school math programs. Her current teacher was concerned that perhaps Tashina would do better receiving support from a learning disabilities resource room.

According to her history, Tashina had missed an inordinate amount of school due to a variety of illnesses. Last year she had been absent more than

45 days. Presently, she was living at home with her mother and an older sister, who had a history of school failure. Tashina had been in three different schools over the past three years, with no reason for transferring mentioned.

I screened for general achievement problems using the PIAT and discovered that Tashina's mathematics scores were not commensurate with her mental age. She scored at the 5.2 grade level. According to her scores on the Stanford Binet, given two years earlier, she had an IQ of 92. According to the PIAT, she was functioning on the fifth grade level in mathematics. Tashina was, however, on grade level in the other areas.

Clearly, Tashina would qualify for a math enrichment program, if not for a learning disabilities resource room. I followed the PIAT up with an SDMT, which confirmed my suspicions that Tashina lacked so many of the basic skills as to make any high school mathematics course difficult. Her knowledge of math facts seemed best described as sporadic. At times she would multiply two numbers together and come up with the correct product. At other times she would be given the same numbers and incorrectly complete the task.

In her interview, Tashina disclosed that she felt she had a "math disability," partly due, she thought, to her many past absences, but she was also concerned about her attitude toward the subject. She claimed that the thought of working with numbers made her anxious and that she had never learned the basic skills. She recalled that her math grades began dropping in the fourth grade, and that she more or less lost a lot of footing. She remarked that for periods of time she would try very hard but would become discouraged very easily. Tashina also expressed a lot of embarrassment resulting from her mathematics deficit. She explained that the last remedial classroom was for students with behavioral and academic problems. Often the students were very disruptive, distracting her from the work at hand. Although her teacher appeared very enthusiastic, Tashina revealed that she was constantly confused, even though she normally received one-to-one instruction in the classroom. She shared with me a variety of worksheets that yielded a little bit of insight.

Clearly, a problem existed in the area of mathematics, and further evaluation was necessary. Although I would be responsible for the testing in mathematics, Tashina was referred to the school psychologist to decide whether she was eligible for special education services.

DEFINING A SPECIFIC PROBLEM IN MATHEMATICS

In general, Tashina's overall performance on the PIAT indicated an average grade-level function, although one of her scores (mathematics) placed her significantly below her age-level expectancy. Because Tashina had repeated a grade, age as well as grade equivalents were used to interpret her scores. Her overall general achievement as

measured by this test was at the 8.2 grade equivalent and the 13.6 age-level equivalent. Most notable about Tashina's performance on the mathematics subtest was her difficulty in quickly remembering basic facts (e.g., multiplication tables) and working problems involving fractions. Because Tashina evidenced difficulty on the mathematics subtest (grade equivalent = 5.2, age equivalent = 10.6), she was subsequently administered a more comprehensive math test, the Key Math. It should be noted that the format of the PIAT mathematics subtest permits no written notation or responses on the part of the student. Tashina claimed that she could do better if she could write down her work. This suggested that Tashina had difficulty in remembering math facts quickly.

Tashina was administered some subtests of the Key Math. Her overall performance was typical of a student in the sixth month of the fifth grade. Specific examples are given below.

Multiplication. Tashina correctly answered items involving one-digit numbers. She experienced difficulty multiplying one-digit and two-digit numbers that required regrouping. Examples of her mistakes included:

$$
\begin{array}{llll}
15 & 75 & 25 & 75 \\
\underline{\times6} & \underline{\times8} & \underline{\times14} & \underline{\times75} \\
130 & 740 & 28{,}520 & 4{,}925
\end{array}
\qquad 5\tfrac{1}{2} \times 4 = 20\tfrac{1}{2}
$$

Division. Tashina, when given a one- or two-digit number, was able to divide correctly by a one-digit divisor to obtain a one-digit quotient; however, she was unable to work any problems that required more skill. For example, Tashina was unable to solve a problem that obtained a two-digit quotient (e.g., $4 \div 75$).

Summary of the Key Math. In the area of operations, Tashina was able to perform problems of simple addition, subtraction, multiplication, and division requiring no regrouping. Tashina missed problems requiring more advanced computational processes such as addition of fractions, multiplication involving a two-digit multiplier, multiplication of fractions, division of fractions, division with two or more digit dividends, and word problems that required application of basic math facts.

PINPOINTING MATHEMATICS SKILLS

Decide What to Assess. I had received much beneficial information from the formal instruments. It was clear that there was a need to begin with basic mathematics facts.

Select or Develop a Skill Hierarchy. I developed my own skill hierarchy, after reviewing a scope-and-sequence chart of a mathematics program that was in the school textbook. See Table 1, a portion of a scope-and-sequence chart that targets the specific areas she was concerned about. The content was organized in such a way that the specialist could assess quickly the capabilities and skills Tashina should possess. The plan was to supplement Table 1 (which was based on commonly used commercial texts and curriculum guides) with other items of varying degrees of difficulty.

Decide Where to Begin. From the test information, it was clear that Tashina had basic knowledge of addition and subtraction skills, except with fractions. Therefore, three basic areas became targets: multiplication, division, and fractions. The skill hierarchy indicated beginning with multiplication.

Select or Develop a Survey Instrument. The BRIGANCE® Diagnostic Inventory of Essential Skills was selected for its ease of administration and scoring and because one of the products obtained is a list of mastered and unmastered skills that translate into strengths, weaknesses, and ready-made potential objectives. The areas targeted using the BRIGANCE® were number facts (multiplication and division) and fractions.

Get Ready to Test and Administer the Survey. Tashina's teacher agreed to release her from the classroom for 1 hour to take the survey. Because Tashina expressed discomfort in giving oral responses, paper was provided and no time limits were placed on the exercises.

Note Errors and Performance Style. She was more comfortable providing written responses. See Tables 2 and 3 for samples of the type of checklist that can be used to aid in noting errors in multiplication and division.

Analyze Findings and Summarize Outcomes. Tables 2 and 3 illustrate the types of mathematics errors observed when Tashina was working multiplication and division problems. In the area of fractions, her problems were based on such computational errors as her inability to add and subtract simple fractions with mixed denominators and her inability to add and subtract mixed fractions with common or mixed denominators. She successfully added and subtracted simple fractions with common denominators. She was unable to multiply or divide any fractions successfully.

Hypothesize Reasons for Errors and Determine Areas to Probe. After looking at all of her testing scores and information gathered from Tashina and her teacher, it seemed clear that Tashina needed an intensive remedial program that stressed basic math facts. The probes would be very similar to the survey administration, except with more sample problems that targeted areas of weakness.

Complete Record Keeping Forms and Generate Teaching Objectives. I made a mathematics profile chart that targeted multiplication, division, and fractions. I used the skill hierarchy chart to create and organize a profile chart, with which I could probe and provide mastery checks on a daily or weekly basis. Examples of headings on the profile chart would be addition of simple fractions, subtraction of simple fractions, and multiplication with regrouping.

Start Teaching/Update Assessment Information. Because my assessment process was extensive, those areas that needed to be taught were obvious. I thus used the scope-and-sequence steps to influence the order of my teaching. Probing will continue on a regular basis to update the assessment information on Tashina.

For *pinpointing*, the Zigmond's 12-step strategy for assessment for instructional planning was used. Here assessment is directly linked to instructional planning, which makes my job as a mathematics specialist easier.

TABLE 1
An example of a math skills hierarchy for assessment

Whole Numbers: Multiplication and Division

Demonstrates understanding of math properties:

____ Cummutative $(a \cdot b) = (b \cdot a)$

____ Associative $(a \cdot b) \cdot c = a \cdot (b \cdot c)$

____ Distributive $a(b + c) = ab + ac$

Demonstrates knowledge of how multiplication and division are inversely related to each other. Understanding of:

____ The union of sets and the distribution of these sets into other sets

____ Continual addition and subtraction

____ The number line

____ Horizontal multiplication and division methods

____ Vertical multiplication and division methods

____ Rules involving zero in multiplication and division

____ Rules involving "one" in multiplication and division

____ Multiplication and division by 10 and powers of 10

Solving problems without regrouping

____ One-digit factor or divisor with one-digit sums and dividends

____ One-digit factor or divisor with two-digit sums or dividends

Solving problems with regrouping:

____ One-digit factor or divisor with two- or three-digit sums or dividends

____ Two-digit factors or divisors with any number of sums or dividends

____ Three- or four-digit factors or divisors

TABLE 1
continued

Fractions

_____ Definitions of fractions

Methods of understanding:

_____ Number lines

_____ Subsets

_____ Geometric figures

Demonstrate knowledge of:

_____ Adding and subtracting simple fractions with the same denominator

_____ Adding and subtracting simple fractions with different denominators

_____ Adding and subtracting mixed fractions with the same denominator

_____ Adding and subtracting mixed fractions with different denominators

_____ Muliplication and division of fractions

_____ Rules involving decimal fractions

TABLE 2
Types of mathematics errors (multiplication)

_____ Errors in combinations	__✓__ Confused products when multiplier had two or more digits
_____ Error in adding the carried number	
__✓__ Wrote rows of zeros	_____ Repeated part of table
__✓__ Carried a wrong number	_____ Multiplied by adding
__✓__ Errors in addition	_____ Did not multiply a digit in multiplicand
__✓__ Forgot to carry	_____ Based unknown combination on another
__✓__ Used multiplicand as multiplier	_____ Errors in reading
_____ Error in single zero combinations, zero as multiplier	_____ Omitted digit in writing product
	__✓__ Errors in carrying into zero
__✓__ Used wrong process—added	__✓__ Counted to carry
_____ Error in single zero combinations, zero as multiplicand	_____ Omitted digit in multiplier
	_____ Split multiplier
	_____ Wrote wrong digit of product

Source: From *Diagnostic Studies in Arithmetic* (p. 196) by G. T. Buswell and Lenore John, 1926, Chicago: University of Chicago Press. Copyright 1926 by University of Chicago Press. Adapted by permission.

TABLE 3
Types of mathematics errors (division)

_√_ Errors in division combinations	_____ Derived unknown combinations from known one
_____ Errors in subtraction	_____ Had right answer, used wrong one
_√_ Errors in multiplication	_√_ Grouped too many digits in dividend
_√_ Used remainder larger than divisor	_____ Error in reading
_____ Found quotient by trial multiplication	_____ Used dividend or divisor as quotient
_____ Neglected to use remainder within problem	_____ Found quotient by adding
_____ Omitted zero resulting from another digit	_√_ Reversed dividend and divisor
_____ Counted to get quotient	_____ Used digits of divisor separately
_____ Repeated part of multiplication table	_____ Wrote all remainders at end of problem
_√_ Used short division form for long division	_____ Misinterpreted table
_√_ Wrote remainders within problem	_____ Used digit in dividend twice
_____ Omitted zero resulting from zero in dividend	_____ Used second digit or divisor to find quotient
_√_ Omitted final remainder	_____ Began dividing at units digit of dividend
_√_ Used long division form for short division	_____ Split dividend
_____ Said example backwards	_____ Counted in subtracting
_____ Used remainder without new dividend figure	_____ Used too large a product
	_____ Used endings to find quotient

Source: From *Diagnostic Studies in Arithmetic* (p. 197) by G. T. Buswell and Lenore John, 1926, Chicago: University of Chicago Press. Copyright 1926 by University of Chicago Press. Adapted by permission.

CHAPTER
THREE

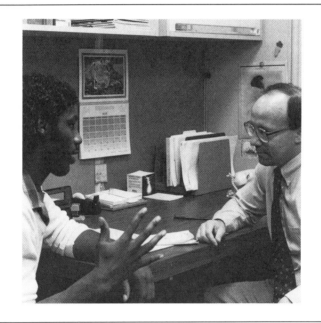

Nonacademic
Assessment

This chapter follows the Hawkins assessment model, changing its focus to social, vocational, and study skills. Again, we go through each phase, from screening to pinpointing, indicating the appropriate tests, checklists, and activities. We begin with a discussion of the issues in assessing social and interpersonal problems.

GENERAL CONSIDERATIONS

Social and interpersonal problems often arise during the referral process. Yet, their assessment is rarely straightforward. Social behavior, after all, is subject to the varying perceptions of all who perceive it. What is upsetting, disturbing, depressing, or even heartening to one person may not be so for another. This naturally leads to team disagreements about the nature of a child's behavior problems. Therefore, a detailed assessment is vital to a team decision, whereby a group of professionals can agree to an intervention; but the process is often hampered by differences in perception.

It is best not to fight against the differing opinions of colleagues; instead, study and learn from these differences in perception. Remember that social behavior is not always the same across all settings; accordingly, it is unrealistic to expect adults to witness or describe the same behavior problems.

A team's discussions may include both behaviors to be *decreased* (refusal to complete assignments, tantrums, self-injurious behavior) or *increased* (completion of assignments, making appropriate requests of peers, keeping hands in lap). Both classes of problems are called target behaviors if they are observable, measurable, and defined so that two persons can agree on their occurrence or nonoccurrence. A criterion can then be set for a desired level of performance. It is important to define the behaviors to be *increased*, rather than decreased, whenever possible. The tendency to cite behaviors to be decreased leads to an emphasis on the negatives (e.g., punishment procedures, focusing on getting the pupil to stop doing something). Greater emphasis on teaching appropriate and useful skills should be the aim of intervention strategies. A positive focus also is much more palatable to students and their parents and is a good model for other teachers.

If each student presented only one behavior to be changed, the task would be simple. However, it is usually necessary for the persons responsible for a student's education and welfare to agree on a *set* of priorities for changes in that student's behavior. In public school settings, a forum for this decision-making activity is provided in the evaluation and individual education program conferences required under P.L. 94-142. If one is working in a hospital or other residential agency, habilitation planning conferences or case conferences serve the same purpose. Group decision making is never easy, and the process may be made even more difficult by the day-to-day pressures exerted on staff members who must work with extremely difficult students. To assist in setting priorities for students, consider the following issues:

1. Is the student dangerous to self or others?
2. What does the pupil need to know? What skills does the pupil lack? What competencies would improve the pupil's interactions with others?
3. Does the student lack important self-help skills (e.g., dressing, feeding, toileting, identifying environmental dangers)?
4. Can you identify behaviors that are preventing the student's access to less restrictive environments (e.g., lack of language or self-help skills, aggressive or disruptive behaviors, defiant or noncompliant behaviors)?

The authors would like to acknowledge the contribution of Cynthia Langford, a vocational specialist at Louisiana State University.

5. What "survival" skills or information does the pupil lack (e.g., following teacher directions, staying with a group, remaining on task, discriminating between a felony and a misdemeanor)?

Finally, ask persons in affected microcommunities which behaviors bother them the most, or which skills the student must have to function successfully in that setting. Figure 3–1, taken from the data-based program modification model by

---

Directions: May be attached to referral form. Ask each person concerned with student to complete a form. Items may be listed by the SERT or each person may generate his/her own list.

Referree: _____ Age/Grade: _____ Date: _____

Name of person completing this form:_____

Specify those goal (terminal) behaviors which you would most like to see attained through program modification.

Academic
Rank   Acceptable Level of Performance

_____   _____

_____   _____

_____   _____

_____   _____

_____   _____

_____   _____

_____   _____

_____   _____

Social

_____   _____

_____   _____

_____   _____

_____   _____

_____   _____

_____   _____

_____   _____

After you complete your list, rank order the list in terms of those most requiring immediate attention.

FIGURE 3–1

Priority-ranking form (Source: From *Data-Based Program Modification: A Manual* by S. L. Deno and P. K. Mirkin, 1978. Reston, VA: Council for Exceptional Children. Copyright 1978 by Council for Exceptional Children. Reprinted by permission.)

Deno and Mirkin (1978), shows the procedure developed by a planning team to establish priorities for a student receiving consultative services.

This discussion of decision making will give some perspective on the outcomes to be achieved after assessing academic and nonacademic problems. Now let us turn to the specific activities to undertake in screening and assessing behavior problems and for interpersonal skills deficits.

SCREENING FOR NONACADEMIC NEEDS

Several tools are available for assessing nonacademic needs; few of them are "tests." For example, teacher interviews and sociometric measures are discussed in this section.

Teacher Interviews

In a referral for problem behaviors, a teacher might be asked several specific questions. These questions may compose an interview such as the one presented in Figure 3–2. This interview helps consultants or those without direct daily contact with the student to understand the context in which problem behavior occurs.

Student Interviews

We almost always recommend talking with a student to find out what the problems are. For example, a student may be able to explain quite clearly why he is late to his first period class, why he teases another student, or why he makes noises in the back of a certain teacher's classes while attending well to the lessons of other instructors.

Moreover, there are certain adolescent problems that simply do not lend themselves to an outsider's evaluation. For example, we do not know to what extent a teacher can report on symptoms of adolescent depression, one of the

"internalizing disorders." (In Chapter Seven, some of these internalizing disorders are defined and guidelines for interviewing students about whom a teacher is concerned are given.)

The Youth Self-Report (Achenbach & Edelbrock, 1983) is one example of a student checklist that might expand an assessment beyond the interview. This measure is similar to the Teacher Form of the Child Behavior Checklist mentioned below.

Teacher Ratings and Checklists

Often checklists or rating forms are sent to teachers and counselors from outside agencies that are planning a treatment program. The Teacher's Report Form of the Child Behavior Checklist (Achenbach & Edelbrock, 1980) is a popular example. The following are sample items.

Compared to typical pupils of the same age:

1. How hard is he/she working?
2. How appropriately is he/she behaving?
3. How much is he/she learning?
4. How happy is he/she?

Sociometric Measures

Because social behavior problems often involve peer interactions, direct information from peers may be desirable. This can be accomplished through a *sociometric measure*. Sociometric procedures may not be considered a traditional part of a school's assessment; however, research has shown that sociometric measures play an important role in identifying students at risk for social behavior problems (Hops & Greenwood, 1981). These measures are valuable predictors of such later social behavior problems as dropping out of school (Ullmann, 1952) and delinquency (Roff, Sells, & Golden, 1972). Before using a sociometric procedure in the classroom, check with the supervisor to de-

Teacher's Name: _____ Interviewer's Name: _____

Date: _____ School: _____

Directions: This interview is designed to gather information about the way a teacher runs her classroom, with an emphasis on behavior management. Try to get answers for all of the questions, but feel free to ask them in any order or with words of your own.

1. What have you said to your student about the upcoming evaluation?

_____
_____
_____
_____
_____
_____

2. In turn, what has your student said to you about the evaluation?

_____
_____
_____
_____
_____
_____
_____
_____
_____
_____
_____
_____

3. Let's talk about your class rosters for a while. Where do you keep your class lists? _____

_____
Would you say these are up-to-date? _____
Are you expecting any new students?_____

Notes: _____
_____
_____
_____

(Document any anticipated student schedule changes here.)

_____
_____
_____
_____

FIGURE 3–2   *continued*
Structured teacher interview

4. Could we spend some time discussing your views on classroom management? First, do you have a set of classroom rules? _____ Where are they posted or listed? _____
_____

How did you develop these rules? _____
Did the students participate in the development of rules? _____

What are the general school rules here? _____
_____
_____
_____
_____

Do your students know the school rules? _____

5. What kind of behavior management system do you prefer? _____
_____

(Ask to see any documents that are used in the teacher's management system; be sure to find out how the system works.)

6. Does your management system involve adults outside your classroom (such as the principal, counselor, mainstream teachers)? _____
_____
_____

7. What is your approach to discipline? _____
_____
_____

8. How do you reinforce/reward/recognize students who have performed admirably?
_____
_____
_____

Notes:

FIGURE 3–2
(continued)

9. These next few questions focus on student interactions. Let's begin with a review of each period and the students in it—How do these students interact with each other? For example, are they assigned to work together? Alone? Do they have assigned seats? Would you say they are cohesive as a group? How would you characterize each group?

   Period   *Notes*

   1   _____

   2   _____

   3   _____

   4   _____

   5   _____

   6   _____

   7   _____

10. Now let's look at student-teacher interactions. Would you say that you encourage students to (a) work alone and independently; (b) with you; or, (c) some of both. If this changes with each group you teach, let's review the groups period by period again. _____

   _____

   _____

   _____

   _____

   _____

   _____

   _____

11. How do students know what to work on each day? _____

   _____

   Do students tell you what they are studying in their mainstream classrooms?

   _____

   _____

FIGURE 3–2
(continued)

12. How do your students let you know that they need help on academic tasks? _____
_____

13. What do your students call you (first name, last name, title)? _____
_____

14. How would you describe your classroom atmosphere? _____
_____

15. What do you like best about the way you run your classroom? _____
_____
_____

16. When do you have your planning period? _____Do you suggest that we meet then?
_____

17. For my information (this may be subject to change), do you interact with your students after
school very often? (Emphasize that you are trying to get a picture of students' expectations of
the teacher's time and that you are *not* asking about the teacher's personal life!)_____
_____
Do students have your phone number at home? _____

18. Do you have regular classroom visitors or observers? _____ _____
_____
Can you tell me something about these visits? _____
_____
_____
_____
_____
_____

19. Where is emergency information on your students kept? _____
(DO NOT SKIP THIS QUESTION!!)

20. Where is other information on your students kept? _____ Do you have records
that you would like me to update while I am here? _____
_____
_____

FIGURE 3–2
(continued)

21. Could we talk a little about your grading policies? (At this point, review the grading policies in force for each period, each student.)

    Notes:

FIGURE 3–2

termine whether parental permission is required for students participating in this assessment procedure.

Sociometric measures can be of two types: nomination measures and rating-scale measures. With nomination measures, students are asked to nominate a certain number of classmates according to some interpersonal criterion (e.g., best friend, social preference). Positive selection criteria are used most often (e.g., "Name three people with whom you especially like to spend time"), but negative selection criteria are also sometimes used (e.g., "Name three people with whom you do not like to spend time").

Because peer acceptance and rejection appear to be independent dimensions (Hops & Greenwood, 1981), a combination of positive and negative choices yields more detailed information than positive choices alone. In particular, adolescents identified as unpopular using only a positive nomination sociometric procedure can be classified with a positive plus negative nomination procedure, as actively disliked or as simply isolated or neglected. A drawback of peer nomination sociometric procedures, though, is that many parents, teachers, and researchers feel that asking students to negatively nominate peers may negatively affect them (e.g., make them feel bad or act more negatively toward negatively nominated peers). Available evidence, however, suggests that this is not the case (Bell-Dolan, Foster, & Sikora, 1985; Hayvren & Hymel, 1984).

In using a sociometric rating procedure, a student is asked to rate each of his classroom peers according to a Likert-type scale. Each person in the classroom thus earns a score, the average of his rating from his peers.

While they present valuable information, sociometric techniques unfortunately are limited by their relatively high cost in teacher time. Also, secondary school scheduling means that pupils move from class to class more often, making it difficult to establish a stable reference group for nominations or ratings (Hops & Greenwood, 1981). Nevertheless, if a sociometric measure is possible, it can yield very helpful information.

Screening for Vocational Needs

The first phase of the assessment model, "Screening and General Disposition," is a starting point for teachers who want to analyze the career and vocational needs of their students. The purpose of screening is to determine students' familiarity with the world of work and their interests and abilities. Frequently, standardized tests are used in formal evaluation settings. Such tests may include interest inventories (e.g., the Kuder, the Strom-Campbell, and the Wide Range Interest Inventory) and performance tests such as the McCarron-Dial. Sometimes work samples are presented and evaluated by the instructor.

It is also important to include career-awareness and vocational screening in the programs, as these are important skills areas for adolescents.

To summarize, at this point in assessment, one should be able to establish whether the student's problems warrant further evaluation and whether the student might qualify for a special placement or service. To establish the latter, one must proceed with the assessment, narrowing the number of considered behaviors until the team finally comes to a consensus on the nature of the problem. Accordingly, we now move to the second phase of the Hawkins (1979) assessment model, "Defining the Problem." Our discussion begins with social behavior.

DEFINING A SOCIAL BEHAVIOR PROBLEM

Defining social behavior problems is not easy. The subtlety of adolescents' social interactions and the often low rate/high intensity of their problem behaviors create elusive targets for measurement. Fortunately, the capacity to observe and record social behaviors has expanded dramatically in recent years, and this direct observational technology has been field-tested in numerous secondary school classrooms.

As mentioned earlier, the focus of this chapter is on *observable* problem behaviors. To help in assessing the behaviors that *can* be detected in the school setting, we present several observation formats, beginning with an analysis of events. This analysis often helps define the behavior problem, its causes, and what seems to be maintaining it.

Antecedent-Response-Consequence Analysis (ARC)

Although its name is quite technical, the **Antecedent-Response-Consequence Analysis** is relatively simple and requires no special materials. The purpose of an ARC analysis (sometimes called ABC, for **Antecedent-Behavior Consequence**) is to determine the context, or causes and effects of a specific problem behavior. This technique involves keeping a brief record of student behaviors, their immediate antecedents, and their consequences. The resulting information will help in analyzing the relationship between a behavior and what happens when it occurs. The ARC is a *preliminary* observation technique to be used to understand an aggressive or **disruptive behavior** in its natural setting (e.g., the classroom). The disadvantage of an ARC analysis is that teachers cannot perform the analysis and instruct a class simultaneously. Therefore, it must be used during a break, in a consultant capacity, or while observing behavior outside the classroom.

Figures 3–3 and 3–4 illustrate the ARC procedure. The examples display two ARC records. Note that one student was targeted for each observation. This technique is too unwieldy for several pupils at the same time.

To try an ARC analysis, first divide a sheet of paper into three columns, as shown in Figure 3–3. Then decide on one or two problem behaviors. Next, set aside at least 10 minutes for observing. When the first problem behavior occurs, note it in the middle column, then quickly record (using abbreviations if necessary) what took place before and after it. Try to avoid subjective descriptions, writing only those actions *actually seen*. With practice, skill at ARC analysis will develop, especially when target behaviors are limited to unequivocal, simple acts (leaving class, cursing, volunteering a question or comment, smoking a cigarette, crying, verbally refusing to work).

At this point in the social behavior assessment, the nature of the student's social behavior problem will be relatively clear. Perhaps other members of the team would assess the student's other nonacademic needs at the same time.

Defining a Specific Vocational Need

The initial screening of the students' vocational needs will probably indicate that they, like most adolescents, have very broad and somewhat unrealistic expectations of work. Typically, mildly handicapped adolescents will have no clear idea of the kinds of jobs available, the skills required to perform those jobs, or the benefits, salaries, and working conditions of particular jobs/careers. Second, most mildly handicapped adolescents tend to have a here-and-now focus, targeting specific jobs that they know are available in the community and are typically open to entry level workers. Because many students must seek employment immediately after high school, defining vocational needs should begin at least as soon as the student enters high school.

To define vocational training needs, begin with **career awareness** presentations. This helps students target occupations or occupational clusters that interest them. Only then can the teacher develop specific, individualized pinpoints, secure **vocational education** training

| Child: Raymond | Date: 10-16-84 | Time: 1:00 to 1:10 |

Behavior: Aggression

Observer: Sheryl Fleck   Class: Language

Antecedent	Response	Consequence
Teacher writes assignment on the board.	Raymond whispers to student behind him.	Teacher says, "There should be no talking now."
Teacher says, "You will need to get your language notebook and a pencil."	Raymond pokes student in front of him with a pencil.	Student screams.
Teacher says to Ray, "If you continue to be disruptive, I will have to ask you to sit in the back of the room."	Raymond yells, "I didn't do anything."	Student behind Raymond says, "You liar!"
Teacher says, "Who remembers what the difference is between an action and a linking verb?"	Students raising hands. Raymond tapping pencil.	Student next to Raymond reaches over and pushes pencil out of Raymond's hand saying, "I'm sick of telling you to quit this, you jerk!"
Teacher says, "Raymond, are you aware that bothers people when you tap pencils?"	"I wasn't tapping my pencil," Raymond yelled pushing his books on the floor.	One student yelled out, "That kid is wierd."

FIGURE 3–3
ARC record

| Child: Randy Fisher | Date: Sept. 12, 83 | Time: 10:15 to 10:30 |

Behavior: verbal & physical aggression; swearing, name calling, touching others or seat, fighting

Observer: N. Deaner   Class: Reading

Antecedent	Response	Consequence
Teacher gives written assignment and class begins individual seat work.	Randy pokes pencil into back of boy in front of him.	Boy yells, "Cut it out!"
Teacher asked Randy if he poked the boy.	Randy says, "no".	Other boy says, "You're a liar!"
Teacher tells both boys to behave and get busy.	Randy threatens to beat up boy at recess, kicks boy's chair.	Teacher reprimands Randy.
Boy turns and knocks Randy's book to floor.	Randy jumps out of seat, grabs boy by the hair, tells boy to pick up his books or he'll kill him. Randy shouts obscenities at boy.	Teacher runs over. Class watching.
Teacher breaks up fight.	Randy gives finger to boy.	Teacher takes Randy to office.

FIGURE 3–4
ARC record

and/or develop specific **work-study** positions for students.

The world of work is a fascinating topic for most high school students. One good way to help students define their vocational training needs is to arrange talks by employers who can speak to the class. The more explicit the invitation to the speaker, the better advice the students will receive. A request like "Would you speak to my class about the qualities McDonald's is looking for in an entry-level employee, the duties entry-level workers usually perform, the good things and the difficult things about the job, and the kind of advancement opportunities available?" gives the employer a sense of what is wanted. Encourage the class to ask questions. Choose speakers based upon student interests and abilities. At the end of each presentation, conduct a brief survey of individuals' vocational training needs in the employment area presented. These activities should give a good picture of the students' needs, while providing them with valuable information that goes beyond pencil-and-paper interest inventories.

Social and vocational screening and problem definition will yield a fairly comprehensive understanding of the adolescent's nonacademic needs. There are a few other areas, however, that one might find relevant in the assessment.

Chapter Four offers an extensive discussion of study skills (or school survival skills). We encourage the inclusion of a school survival skills assessment in all educational evaluations of adolescents. While formal instruments are not yet generally available in this rapidly advancing field, the Estes School Attitude Scale (Estes, Estes, Richards, & Roettinger, 1980) and the School Survival Skills Scale (Zigmond, Kerr, Schaeffer, Brown, & Farra, 1986) cited in Chapter Four might be considered.

The assessment of **adaptive behaviors** is required under P.L. 94-142 for those students being considered for classes for the mentally retarded.

The American Association on Mental Deficiency (AAMD) defines adaptive behavior as "the effectiveness of degree to which an individual meets standards of personal independence and social responsibility expected for age and cultural group" (Grossman, 1977, p. 11). Adaptive behavior, then, may be measured with many of the methods already cited for the screening and evaluation of social skills and behavior problems. In addition to these domains, however, adaptive behavior usually refers to skills such as dressing, grooming, communicating, socializing, managing transportation, and using judgment. More than 136 adaptive behavior instruments were identified by Walls, Werner, and Bacon (1977). The most commonly used adaptive behavior measures include the Vineland Social Maturity Scale-Revised (Doll, 1985) and the AAMD Adaptive Behavior Scale-School Edition (Lambert, Windmiller, Thoringer, & Cole, 1981). Some controversy exists as to the appropriateness of the standardization samples used to norm these scales. Accordingly, the reader might want to explore this topic further by going through Wallander et al. (1983).

Once the team members have a general idea of the problems a student is having, it is time to define them specifically enough for lesson plans, **role-playing** or counselling group sessions, IEPs, or Habilitation Plans. Only through this level of specificity can interventions be accomplished with ease and with the confidence that the exact nature of the problem to be reduced or eliminated has been determined and agreed upon.

PINPOINTING SOCIAL BEHAVIOR TARGETS

An ARC analysis helps describe problem behaviors but does not actually measure those behaviors. The observational methods discussed below rely on more precise measurement, either of **frequency** (how often a behavior occurs), duration (how long a behavior lasts), or a combination of these, such as rate.

Selecting a Comparison Peer

Before beginning any direct observational procedure, try to note the behavior of a peer or two in order to measure any discrepancy between their behavior and that of the "problem" student. This measure of peer behavior can then serve as the student's goal or criterion. A good idea is to select a nonhandicapped student in the mainstream class where your student is to be placed. Consider this example: A student may "goof off" too much of the class period. Direct observational data on that student alone will indicate the time the student spends on-task and off-task but will not provide information on how deviant this student's behavior is from others in the classroom or school. For example, the teacher could simply be noticing this child more than others. Perhaps the student sits near other students who frequently disrupt class. In order to obtain a clearer picture of the extent to which a student's behavior is deviant, then, it is important to collect direct observational data on a random group of *peers in the same class* or on another student who is a "good" student. Figure 3–5 displays data collected on a target student and a selected peer. Note that some of the target student's behaviors were much like his behaviorally acceptable peer.

Using Existing Records to Pinpoint Social Targets

Once target behaviors have been defined specifically and objectively, it is relatively easy to record how often they occur. Event recording is the best method for most behaviors that are brief and discrete (i.e., have a definite beginning and end, and are best characterized in terms of their frequency rather than their duration). In some cases, a simple numerical count will be sufficient (e.g., keeping track of the number of times a pupil is tardy).

Often these records are a part of a school's normal routine: attendance records, critical incident reports, tardy slips, detention rolls, suspension lists. Use these existing records to save time. In some instances, they alone provide an adequate frequency count. For example, in a middle school there may be a special detention held for tardy students. The roster of students sent to this detention would help to measure whether a school-wide intervention is reducing tardiness.

Using an Event Record to Pinpoint Social Behaviors

An event record is a simple tally. Its purpose is to count how many times the target behavior occurs during a specified interval of time. The time interval is chosen by the observer, who must consider the type of behavior being observed and the time available for observation.

Event records have distinct advantages. They are easy to use, require no special equipment, and are often a part of a teacher's everyday routine. Also, event records allow the monitoring of more than one student at a time.

Use an event record with brief and discrete behaviors. (Discrete behaviors are those having a very definite beginning and end such as shouting out a curse word in a classroom. An example of a *nondiscrete* behavior is daydreaming. It would be very difficult to determine when a student begins and ends this behavior.)

When using an event record to pinpoint a social behavior problem or target, be sure to measure a behavior that is uniform in length and is not an extremely high-rate behavior. For example, do not use an event record to record the number of times a teenager converses with his classmates. A dialogue could range from grunts and single-word replies to a 20-minute report on the television program he watched

Behavior Observation Record

Recorder B. Haggerty Student Frank

Date 2/16/82 Circumstance Study Period

+= Behavior observed at least once during interval. Length of time observed 15 min.

−= Behavior not observed during interval.

Target Student

Noise	−	+	+	−	−	−	+	+	−	+	−	+	−	+	+	8
Out of place	−	−	+	+	−	−	+	+	−	+	−	−	−	−	−	5
Off-task	−	+	+	+	+	−	+	+	+	−	+	+	+	+	+	12
Physical contact	−	−	+	−	−	−	−	−	−	+	−	−	−	−	−	2
Other	−	−	−	+	−	−	+	−	−	−	+	−	−	−	+	4

Peers

Noise	+	−	+	−	−	+	+	−	+	−	+	+	−	+	+	9
Out of place	−	−	−	−	−	−	−	−	−	−	−	−	−	−	−	0
Off-task	−	−	+	−	−	+	−	−	+	−	−	−	−	+	+	5
Physical contact	−	−	−	−	−	−	−	−	−	−	−	−	−	−	−	0
Other	−	−	−	−	−	−	−	−	−	−	−	−	−	−	−	0

Note: Each square represents one minute of observation.

FIGURE 3–5

A form for recording observations of behavior in a classroom (Source: From *Data-Based Program Modification: A Manual* (p. 103) by S. Deno and P. Mirkin, 1978, Reston, VA.: Council for Exceptional Children. Copyright 1978 by Council for Exceptional Children. Reprinted by permission.)

last night! To score one mark for every time the student began to speak would not reflect a true picture of the verbal interaction, for some tallies would record a long conversation while others would indicate only brief comments.

High-rate behaviors are not suitable for an event record because the behavior may occur so rapidly that it would be impossible to count accurately the number of times that behavior took place. An example of a high-rate behavior would be thumb twiddling, for which it would be nearly impossible to count the actual revolutions of thumb over thumb for even two minutes.

Here are the steps for using an event record. (T. Avny, personal communication, 1984)

1. Get the necessary materials:
   a. A watch or clock to measure the time of your observation.
   b. Tally instrument:
      —Pencil and checklist
      —Wrist counter or wrist tally (some counting device); or
      —Pennies for penny transfer (move a penny from one pocket to another every time the behavior occurs)
2. Select a brief and discrete behavior.
3. Situate yourself so you can actually observe the behavior.
4. Record the number of times you see (or hear) the behavior.

Using a Duration Record to Pinpoint Social Behaviors

If the *length* of a behavior is of interest, **duration recording** may be the best method. For example, a student may rarely exhibit out-of-seat behavior, but each episode may last several minutes. A duration measure records the amount of time between the initiation of a behavior and its conclusion.

Here are some situations that lend themselves to a duration record:

■ When you want to know the length of time a student spends performing a specified behavior
■ When the behavior being observed is discrete (e.g., out of seat, writing, crying)
■ When the behavior is a high-rate noncontinuous behavior
■ When the behavior has an extended time duration

It is not appropriate to use a duration measurement under these circumstances:

■ When the target behavior has a short duration and the occurrence is more important than duration (i.e., making noises during a class discussion)
■ When the target behavior is not discrete
■ When you want to know how frequently a behavior occurs (e.g., how often a student swears or raises his hand)

Here are the steps for a duration recording (N. Moore, personal communication, 1984):

1. Get a stopwatch or a clock.
2. Get an appropriate recording form and something with which to write.
3. Complete the form as indicated in Figure 3–6.
4. Calculate the duration of the first occurrence and record the time under the Duration column.

Using an Interval Record to Pinpoint

Even with a stopwatch, duration recording may be unreliable and awkward. Interval recording is a versatile technique for recording both discrete and continuous responses. Interval records require the recorder to devote full attention to observing and recording, but one can observe several behaviors or pupils simultaneously. When using this technique, break the observation period into small intervals of equal length (10, 15, or 30 seconds). Gelfand and Hartmann (1975) recommended that the interval be at least as long as the average duration of a single response, but not so long that two complete responses occur in the same interval. Next, observe whether or not the behavior occurs in any given interval. Count a behavior as occurring if the behavior occurred at all during the interval (Gelfand & Hartmann, 1975).

Figure 3–7 shows interval data collected in a middle school alternative program. This in-

Form A

Observer: **Miss Moore**

Student: **Kim**

Target Behavior: **Out of Seat**

Movement from chair when not permitted or requested by the teacher. No part of the child's body is touching the chair.

Session or Day	Duration
10-1-84	51 min. (← Total Duration for 10-1-84)
10-2-84	85 min.

Form A
Stopwatch
Total Duration

Form B

Observer: **Miss Moore**

Student: **Kim**

Target Behavior: **Out of Seat**

Movement from chair when not permitted or requested by the teacher. No part of the child's body is touching the chair.

Date	Response Initiation	Response Terminated	Duration
10-1-84	9:00	9:15	15 min.
	10:45	10:50	5 min.
	10:53	10:57	4 min.
	11:03	11:05	2 min.
	12:00	12:25	25 min.
			51 min. (← Total Duration)
10-2-84	9:05	9:20	15 min.
	10:25	10:35	10 min.
	12:00	1:00	60 min. (← Total Duration)
			85 min. (← Total Duration)

The middle two columns fall under a **Time** heading.

Form B
Watch or Clock
Total Duration

FIGURE 3-6
Duration record (Source: N. Moore, personal communication, 1984.)

terval record and its accompanying codes were used by a paraprofessional. The student behavior codes used to complete the interval record shown in Figure 3–7 are listed in Table 3–1.

These behavioral codes illustrate the specificity of pinpointing behaviors. The examples will be of help in using an interval record in your classroom. The most commonly observed behaviors—off-task, on-task, and disruptive behaviors—are listed. To complete this interval record, the instructional aide simply circled any behavior that took place during a 10-second interval. A tape recording announced the change of interval through an earphone.

Interval recording is very versatile, yet does not require sophisticated equipment. A clipboard and a stopwatch or watch with a second hand are all that are needed. The process is made even easier by using a cassette recording of the intervals to listen to while noting the behaviors. Using this method eliminates the need to check the time.

Interval recording does not provide a measure of absolute frequency, so it is not appropriate to report the total number of target behaviors occurring in a given observation period. Instead, one reports the percentage of intervals in which the behavior was observed to occur. This is calculated by the formula:

$$\frac{\text{Number of intervals in which behavior occurred}}{\text{Total number of intervals}} \times 100$$

Assessing Reliability

For observational measures to be reliable, the behaviors must be defined specifically and objectively (Cooper, 1981). That is, observations must be confined to what the student *actually* does rather than to generalizations or impressions. Human behaviors are objectively defined if two or more persons agree on whether they occurred. Consider the ambiguity of measuring

"hostile remarks" or "irritating noises," for example. High interobserver agreement might not be obtained for either of the behaviors mentioned, because what is "hostile" or "irritating" to one person may not be so to another. To make these behavioral definitions specific and objective, one must ask, "What makes us interpret remarks as hostile or noises as irritating?" To answer this question, prepare a list of specific behaviors, the occurrence or nonoccurrence upon which two independent persons could agree. For example, a student might say to others, "Go to hell," "I don't like you," "Your momma,"; or, the student might tap a pencil against the desk, squeak a chair, or belch.

The primary criterion for evaluating the adequacy of a behavioral definition is the extent to which observers agree that they have observed the same levels of behavior during the same observational period (Hall, 1973). Several methods are used to assess the agreement between observers.

To measure the reliability of event records, divide the smaller obtained frequency by the larger and multiply by 100.

For interval recording, two observers may agree or disagree as to an occurrence. Thus, reliability is calculated by the following formula.

$$\frac{\text{Number of "agreed" intervals}}{\text{Number of "agreed"} + \text{"disagreed" intervals}} \times 100$$

There are no hard and fast rules for determining how much agreement is enough. Generally, 80% agreement is considered satisfactory, but 90% or better is preferred (Gast & Gast, 1981). To rule out gradual changes in the observers' interpretation of behavioral definitions, periodic reliability checks are recommended.

In summary, the measurement of social behaviors is not as straightforward as the measurement of academic skills. Nevertheless, there are now several direct observational strategies

Student _____ Date _____

Class _____ Period _____ Teacher _____

CODE:

Column 1—Mark 1	Column 2—Mark 1	Column 3—Mark 1
O = On-Task	TC = Teacher Command/Request	C = Compliance
F = Off-Task	TT = Teacher Talk	NA = Noncompliance—Active
D = Disruptive	N = No Command or Talk	NP = Noncompliance—Passive
W = Waiting		NO = No Opportunity

Minute	1	2	3	4	5	6
1	O TC C F TT NA D N NP W NO	O TC C F TT NA D N NP W NO	O TC C F TT NA D N NP W NO	O TC C F TT NA D N NP W NO	O TC C F TT NA D N NP W NO	O TC C F TT NA D N NP W NO
2	O TC C F TT NA D N NP W NO	O TC C F TT NA D N NP W NO	O TC C F TT NA D N NP W NO	O TC C F TT NA D N NP W NO	O TC C F TT NA D N NP W NO	O TC C F TT NA D N NP W NO
3	O TC C F TT NA D N NP W NO	O TC C F TT NA D N NP W NO	O TC C F TT NA D N NP W NO	O TC C F TT NA D N NP W NO	O TC C F TT NA D N NP W NO	O TC C F TT NA D N NP W NO

FIGURE 3–7

Student behavior observation form

TABLE 3–1

Student behavior codes

On-Task (O):   The student is on-task if he is paying attention to and participating in a class activity or if he is working on a class assignment or project. The specific behaviors considered on-task depend upon the class period and current activity. The directions that the teacher gives to the class or the target student can help you decide specifically what on-task is for that class period.

Examples of On-Task Behaviors:

1. Student looks at teacher during teacher-directed activity.
2. Student looks at assignment or other class information on chalkboard.
3. Student writes or takes notes.
4. Student works at the chalkboard.
5. Student looks at a class book or worksheet.
6. Student raises hand.
7. Student asks questions related to classwork or student's grade or performance on a test or paper.
8. Student works with or tutors peers (if allowed in that class).
9. Student plays on a basketball team during P.E. class.
10. Student answers a teacher's question.
11. Student engages in a teacher-initiated conversation.

Off-Task (F):   The student is off-task if she is not paying attention to or participating in a class activity or if she is not working on a class assignment or project.

Examples of Off-Task Behaviors:

1. Student looks at fingernails.
2. Student reads a note from a friend.
3. Student puts head down on desk during math.
4. Student folds her paper into a small triangle.
5. Student stares at teacher during individual reading time.
6. Student stares at blank chalkboard.
7. Student draws faces on paper during math class.
8. Student reads a comic book during language arts.
9. Student wanders around room.
10. Student writes a letter (Note: you must be able to see this to know that it is off-task).

Disruptive (D): Students are "disruptive" if their behavior does (or is likely to) interrupt the class and/or makes it difficult for teachers or peers to continue the task at hand or ongoing classroom activity.

Examples of Disruptive Behavior:

1. Student talks out of turn about something unrelated to class.
2. Student "talks back" to the teacher.
3. Student throws something.
4. Student hits, pokes, touches another student.
5. Student fights with a peer (physically or verbally).
6. Student talks or whispers to a peer.
7. Student walks into class late.
8. Student leaves class before the designated time.
9. Student talks loudly during quiet work time.
10. Student laughs out loud when not determined by teacher's cue.

available, including event records, duration measures, and interval records. These procedures allow us to pinpoint specific, observable social skills or problem behaviors and to establish estimates of their rate. Although one may not always be able to collect these kinds of data, we encourage precise measurement whenever possible. Furthermore, we encourage students to collect their own data, using one of the methods outlined in Chapters Four through Seven.

PINPOINTING VOCATIONAL TARGETS

Figure 3–8 shows an IEP for career selection.

To describe all of the possible targets to be pinpointed under career awareness or vocational training is not possible, but the process for pinpointing in this crucial instructional area can be illustrated. As mentioned earlier, each student's values, life-style preferences, interests, and abilities will shape her career choices. As information about occupations is presented, students learn to measure those occupations against their personal requirements. They also learn to modify their expectations, set priorities, and develop more realistic attitudes about careers. For example, a student who wishes to become a "movie star" may also target hotel maid work as a "day job" that will pay the bills and allow her to pursue an acting career. Given the volatility of the labor market, the youth, and the vocational naïveté of many students, a back-up occupation is, for most students, a good idea.

During the information-gathering stage, students may be able to report the kinds of things that they like to do, the types of volunteer jobs they have liked (and why), and the kinds of chores they do around the house that they find interesting (or odious). Leisure activities also provide information about the student's interests and abilities that can be used to target occupations. For example, some students choose very active, group-oriented, outdoor leisure ac-

tivities. These students may prefer to avoid a first job that is indoor, relatively isolated, and sedentary. It is important to remember that people work for a variety of reasons, including socialization opportunities (or lack of them), money, status, and acceptance. Once these kinds of motivators and needs have been identified, it will be easier to target a specific first job to allow the student to discover more about her target occupation.

The initial assessment ends with the pinpointing phase. Next learn to incorporate this important assessment information into plans for instruction, counselling sessions, vocational field-work experiences, and other interventions. Place the results into the context of short-term goals, our first topic.

Setting Long-Term Social Behavior Goals

Most secondary school teachers report difficulty in writing good social behavior goals and objectives. Despite obstacles, the social behavior findings must be incorporated into the IEP and into daily plans for many of the adolescents being taught or advised. The best beginning for this process is an excellent behavioral assessment, resulting in specific target behaviors and short-term goals. Deal first with **social skills** deficits and problems that meet any of these criteria:

- the behavior deficit prevents the student from entering and/or succeeding in a less restrictive environment
- the behavior or skill deficit interferes with the student's own learning or the instructional activities in his classes
- the problem prevents the student from enjoying good health (e.g., eating disorder, anxiety problem, phobia, substance abuse, sexual problem)
- the difficulty significantly inhibits the student's capacity to make and/or maintain friendships

- the problem results in the possibility of danger to the adolescent herself (e.g., suicide) or to others (e.g., property destruction, aggression)
- the behavior may result in an illegal action.

A good second step in using assessment results is to look for relatively recent skills deficits or behavior problems. Often these can be resolved readily, especially if they reflect adjustment reactions to controllable or transitory situations (e.g., a bad match between a student and a teacher with whom he cannot get along).

Carefully consider, with the advice of the adolescent, his family, and other team members, the student's one-year and five-year educational, personal, and vocational goals. These will put the IEP into proper perspective and should help the entire team set priorities. For example, if a teenager intends to finish high school and go on to a trade school, he might need different skills than would a teenager heading for a university engineering major.

Teachers of middle school students may stay abreast of the social demands of the senior high school in their feeder pattern, preparing accordingly a student's social and school survival skills objectives.

Finally, recall the priority ranking form suggested at the beginning of this chapter. If the multidisciplinary team (and parents and students) have taken this activity seriously, social skills and behavior management priorities for IEP inclusion will be more evident.

Designing Noneducational Interventions

As a rule, the results of health, psychiatric, vision, or hearing assessments of outside agencies will become part of the *related services* statement of the IEP rather than become specific short-term objectives. Ironically, these non-educational data may play a crucial or even more important role in an adolescent's life, when compared with more traditional educational results. Yet, some of the issues raised by these sources may not be suitable content for an IEP. The task for professionals is to highlight important information in the IEP *conference*, ensuring that these data are communicated to all concerned. An alternative to incorporation of these findings in the IEP is to record them in letters of understanding, contingency contracts, home-based monitoring forms, pupil personnel or social workers' records, or the student's cumulative record (not usually recommended because of confidentiality issues). Examples of these kinds of information are:

- the dosage and schedule for a prescribed psychopharmacological treatment that physician and teachers deem essential for a student's academic success
- personal information suggesting that a student's home situation includes drug abuse and child abuse, which interfere with the student's welfare (of course, most states require that educators file a formal report on suspected child abuse, but the adolescent may not be the involved child)
- information regarding the teenager's interactions with juvenile court
- knowledge that a teenager is a parent (see Chapter Eight)
- reports of a depressed parent, which places the adolescent at risk for depression
- information about an existing health problem (see Chapter Seven)

In some instances, assessments of behaviorally disordered students highlight the need for psychiatric help for the family and/or the adolescent. This recommendation often creates frustration for multidisciplinary teams that recognize their inability to act on the recommendation in the school environment. (Psychiatric help, counselling, and other mental health services generally are *not* considered related services under P.L. 94-142 and cannot be mandated

FIGURE 3–8
Vocational IEP

Instructional Area: Vocational

Annual Goal: Student will investigate his/her personal preferences that have impact upon career selection.

		Evaluation of Instructional Objectives	
Short-term Objective	Instructional Methods Media/ Material Title(s) (optional)	Tests, Materials, Evaluation Procedures to Be Used	Criteria of Successful Performance
1. Students will list work tasks that they prefer and those that they dislike.	1.1.a Students will list leisure activities that they enjoy and what they like and dislike about those activities. 1.1.b Students will list leisure activities that they have tried but did not enjoy and what they liked and disliked about those activities.	1.1a/b Students will use lists from 1.1a and b to produce a personal preference list.	1.1a/b Students must list at least three activities in each assignment. Lists must include specific tasks that were liked and specific tasks that were disliked. Value judgments will be accepted, but the reasons must be clear (e.g., "Sports are yucky" is unacceptable, but "Sports are yucky because they make you sweat," is acceptable).
2. Students will list life-style variables that are important to their career choice.	2.1 Students will complete a teacher-made life-styles questionnaire. Preferences regarding area of the country, working hours (e.g. 40-hour or extended work weeks), expected level of income, expected status, expected time commitment to job (lifetime, intermittent), expected time commitments to family, etc., will be surveyed. Teacher will ask students to operationalize and clarify their answers but will not influence value base.	2.1 Students will produce a list of life-style preferences.	2.1 All areas must be addressed, and preferences must be clear. Apparently conflicting values will be accepted if the statements are clear (e.g., I want to make $1000.00 a day and work 4 hours per day).
3. Students will compare their likes, dislikes, and life-style variables to possible career choices and list 10 possible occupations that incorporate likes, diminish dislikes, and promote acquisition of life-style variables important to them.	3.1 Kuder Vocational Interest Inventory will be administered. Students will be given feedback on their interests and how those interests are linked to particular careers.	3.1 Kuder Vocational Interest Inventory will be administered.	3.1 Standardization criteria from the Kuder Vocational Interest Inventory will be used to identify possible career interests.

Objectives/Activities	Evaluation	Criteria
3.2 Students will review their personal preference lists and complete a final personal preference list (incorporating activity preference and life-style preference lists) that reconciles and prioritizes conflicting values.	3.2 Combined activity and life-style preference list will be evaluated.	3.2 Preferences and dislikes from activity and life-style list must be included in final list. Preferences and dislikes must be prioritized. Logical improbabilities and conflicting values must be reconciled.
3.3 Students will compare preference list variables, formal preference information (Kuder Vocational Interest Inventory) to the Dictionary of Occupational Titles (DOT) and list at least 10 possible occupations that meet their personal preference criteria.		
4. Students will interview workers from each of the 10 target occupations to acquire direct information about the occupation.		
4.1 Teacher will review standard interview form with student and assist student in contacting persons to be interviewed.	4.1 Results of interview will be evaluated.	4.1 All questions from the standard interview form must be answered. Students will report the results of the interview to class members.
5. Students will list 5 possible volunteer activities that would give them first-hand information about the occupation.		
5.1 From information gained (preference, interest inventories, DOT classifications, and direct interview), students will identify and list volunteer jobs that incorporate their interests, and list activities of 5 occupations of interest to the students.	5.1 Student-made list of possible volunteer jobs will be evaluated.	5.1 Volunteer jobs must (a) exist, (b) be related to the identified occupational preference and interest groups, according to the DOT classification of the occupation's relationship to people, information, and things. Volunteer jobs listed must have at least two items in each category (people, information, and things) that match the DOT listing of the target occupation's relationship to people, information, and things.

by the schools.) In such situations it is important to help the family in taking even small steps toward getting the help they need. Often families complain that professionals direct, request, and complain but never listen. In the case of an impaired family, an educator may feel overwhelmed with the practical obstacles to mental health (or other) assistance. Yet, listening empathically may, over time, boost the confidence of a parent who is otherwise reluctant to seek help.

In other situations involving outside agencies, parents may seek help and then refuse to release the records describing that help to school personnel. Often, the parents' concern is justified (e.g., psychiatric help for parents' marital or substance abuse problems). If, however, a student reports receiving outside help from someone deemed to be an educationally helpful source of information, try calling the parents to see if they would mind non-written information sharing (e.g., telephone conference). Sometimes parents still will refuse to release information, but they might allow a one-way communication from you to the outside professional; *any* communication is better than none.

In summary, important information for an IEP may be available but not suitable for inclusion or not available at all because of parental concerns. We have suggested some alternative strategies for securing and incorporating this non-school information, including alternative documentation and thoughtful communications that respect the rights of parents and show empathy for their difficulties.

SUMMARY

This chapter has delineated the phases of assessing a nonacademic problem: screening and disposition, defining the problem, pinpointing, and summarizing these results in an intervention or instructional plan. Throughout the discussion, we have tried to highlight the special issues that arise in assessing and monitoring social and other nonacademic behaviors: getting the team to agree on the problem; defining the problem so that measures are reliable; setting aside the necessary time for the often tedious but important direct observational assessments, including interview materials from both professionals as well as parents and the target student; and finally, respecting the inevitable differences of opinion that arise in the elusive domain of social behaviors. (This chapter focused upon *observable* problems; "internalizing" problems are discussed in Chapter Seven.)

In conclusion, we offer a case study that illustrates the complete Hawkins assessment model as it applies to a disruptive adolescent's behaviors.

RECOMMENDED READINGS

For readers who are unfamiliar with *applied behavior* analysis and its observational measures, we recommend further reading, as our presentation is merely an overview. Recommended texts are:

Alberto, P., & Troutman, A. (1986). *Applied behavior analysis for teachers* (2nd ed.). Columbus, OH: Charles E. Merrill Publishing Company.

Kerr, M. M., & Nelson, C. M. (1983). *Strategies for managing behavior problems in the classroom.* Columbus, OH: Charles E. Merrill Publishing Company.

We have chosen a noncategorical approach for our presentation of assessment issues, recognizing the ongoing conflicts in special education, psychology, and psychiatry regarding the definitions and prescribed assessment practices for emotional disturbance (or **behavior disorders**), **mental retardation**, and learning disabilities. We urge you to stay abreast of developments in these important areas of assessment. The following readings may provide a helpful orientation to the current controversy.

Bower, E. (1982). Defining emotional disturbance. Public policy and research. *Psychology in the Schools, 19,* 55–60.

Huntz, S. L. (1985). A position paper of the council for children with behavioral disorders. *Behavioral Disorders, 10,* 167–174.

Matson, J. L., & Breuning, S. E. (1983). *Assessing the mentally retarded.* New York: Grune & Stratton.

Federal guidelines for determining eligibility in these categories are set forth in the *Federal Register,* Education of handicapped children: Implementation of Part B of the Education of the Handicapped Act. August 23, 1977, Part II: 42474–42518.

CASE STUDY

Assessment of Social Behavior

CASE BACKGROUND

Tim is a 12-year-old white male sixth grade student. He has recently been referred by his school district for evaluation to determine the appropriateness of a special education placement. After a psychiatric and psychoeducational evaluation, placement into a classroom for socially and emotionally disturbed children was recommended. Armed with a copy of the evaluation report, my job as a school consultant was to help Tim and his teacher deal with Tim's adjustment to the classroom and academic and behavior problems.

PROBLEM DEFINITION

Because the screening phase of assessment had taken place prior to my receiving Tim's case, I immediately began by defining the problem. My first step was to meet with Tim's teacher, Mr. Wilson, which involved a semi-structured interview that addressed academic functioning, social interactions, behavior problems, classroom rules and management techniques, psychological functioning, IEP objectives, and the role of liaison (school, home, and other agencies) involved with Tim's case. I also asked

Mr. Wilson to list problem areas and rank them in terms of importance. Mr. Wilson reported that Tim was doing quite well with his academic work, working at his grade level and turning in high-quality work. He also reported that there were no apparent psychological difficulties. Mr. Wilson was concerned, however, with Tim's interactions. Talking back to teachers and fighting with peers were identified as problems, with fighting identified as the most problematic.

Mr. Wilson also described a point system that he used in his classroom. Each student had a point account, in which deposits could be made for good behavior in the classroom and during lunch, for working hard in class, and for reports of good behavior in other classes. Points could be taken away for misbehavior or not doing assignments. A child could earn daily treats if he did not lose any points during the day. In addition, he could exchange the points earned each week or month for small toys, privileges, etc.

Next, I observed Tim in the classroom and during lunch/free time and made narrative records of Tim's behavior. During classroom observation, Tim participated appropriately in small group instruction and worked steadily during seat-work periods. During lunch/free time, Tim interacted with a few different male peers, but it was difficult to tell which peer interactions were appropriate and which were inappropriate, due to the high rate of rough, fighting-type interac-

---

This case study was written by Debora Bell-Dolan, a school consultant at the Western Psychiatric Institute and Clinic, University of Pittsburgh.

tions. It seemed that Tim was not fighting much more than his peers, but the level of intensity may have been higher.

The third step in the problem definition phase was to interview Tim. During the interview, he was friendly and cooperative. He reported working hard in class and enjoying Mr. Wilson's room. He claimed to have several friends, but admitted he had enemies who started fights with him. He said he rarely started fights, but was usually provoked.

From the interviews and observations, I developed a functional case formulation (see Figure 1). This is similar to an ARC analysis, but its data are derived from multiple sources rather than just direct observation and are considered hypotheses concerning maintaining contingencies to be tested.

PINPOINTING

At this point, I hypothesized that fighting with peers occurred most often during out-of-class time and was often preceded by rough-and-tumble play with peers. Tim probably did not know exactly when the play ended and fights began. For the most part, consequences were neither immediate nor consistent. Talking back to a teacher seemed to occur only in math class and often after trouble with a specific peer. The first step in the pinpointing phase of assessment was to collect data that specifically addressed these hypotheses. To address the hypotheses regarding both fighting and talking back, Mr. Wilson agreed to keep track, in the form of a simple ARC analysis, of the occurrence of fighting with peers and talking back to teachers (see Figure 2). Fighting with peers was defined as any of the following types of contact with another child: hitting, kicking, pinching, pushing, pulling, grabbing, or poking. Talking back to teachers was defined as expressing verbal disagreement or dissatisfaction with a teacher instruction or comment. If Mr. Wilson saw the behavior, he recorded the setting and antecedents, the specific behavior, and the con-

Antecedents	Problem Behaviors	Consequences	
		Benefits	Costs
1. a. unstructured time b. out of SED room c. peers teasing d. roughhousing with peers	1. fighting with peers—kicking, hitting, pushing, pulling, pinching, grabbing, poking	1. a. gets peers "off his back" b. often gets attention from teacher without losing points	1. a. possible reprimand by another teacher b. "bad" note to mother—not usually followed by any consistent consequence c. maintains poor peer relations
2. a. trouble with peers b. Tim's request/demand ignored or denied	2. talking back to math teacher	2. teacher more likely to listen to/grant Tim's request	2. a. "bad" note to mother b. reprimanded by math teacher c. loses points

FIGURE 1
Functional case formulation

sequences. If the behavior was reported by someone else, Mr. Wilson recorded the position of the person reporting the behavior (e.g., student, math teacher, school-yard supervisor), the reported setting and antecedents, behavior, and consequence, and any consequences that Mr. Wilson applied upon receiving the report.

After two weeks of ARC recording, Mr. Wilson, Tim, and I were able to see that fighting occurred an average of 5 to 6 times per week; that it never occurred in Mr. Wilson's classroom but always in the halls, in line before and after lunch, or during free time in the school yard; and rarely occurred in Mr. Wilson's presence. Also, when Mr. Wilson did not see the fighting, he did not subtract points from Tim's point account; the consequence provided by others usually consisted of reprimands. During the two-week period, talking back to a teacher occurred

only once, in math class. The report indicated that the incident involved Tim and another boy and the consequence consisted of moving their desks. These pieces of information were added to the functional case formulation.

The second step in pinpointing the target behavior involved ranking behaviors for intervention and establishing intervention goals. Because talking back occurred so infrequently, Mr. Wilson, Tim, and I decided to focus on fighting. The general intervention goal was to decrease the number of fights that Mr. Wilson saw or heard about. Within that general goal were two subgoals: (a) to decrease fighting in lines between classes and in the lunchroom and (b) to decrease reports of fighting in the school yard (Mr. Wilson was never in the school yard to witness fights). Even though intervention should address increasing appropriate alternatives to

Day	Antecedent	Response	Consequence	
Monday	before school, safety patrol told Tim to walk	Tim grabbed patrol's coat and pulled	patrol reported incident to me; I told Tim that I expected better behavior from him	R*
Monday	kids coming in from recess and jostling each other in line	Tim pushed a boy	boy told me; I made Tim go to end of line	R
Tuesday	group of kids rough-housing in school yard	Tim yelled and kicked a peer	playground supervisor gave Tim a warning	R
Wednesday	kids in line at water fountain	Tim pinched peer in front of him	I sent Tim to end of line and didn't give him points for hall behavior	S*
Thursday	group of kids rough-housing in school yard	Tim tackled a peer	playground supervisor made Tim sit down for five minutes	R
Friday	————————	————————	————————	—

FIGURE 2

Antecedent Response Consequence analysis of fighting with peers and talking back to teachers.

*R = reported by others; S = saw.

fighting, for the purposes of data collection, the negative behavior to be decreased was considered the best dependent measure.

The third step in pinpointing was to design an intervention based on the data collected to this point. The functional case formulation showed that possible maintaining contingencies for fighting in lines (subgoal a) included (1) the antecedent condition of standing by specific children and (2) a relatively long delay between behavior in line and the consequence of the daily class privilege. Thus, intervention focused on assigning line positions so that Tim did not stand by children with whom he usually fought and providing the daily class privilege immediately following lunch/free time. The functional case formulation suggested that the contingencies involved in maintaining fights in the school yard may have included Tim's inability to discriminate between rough play and fights, and the lack of point loss if Mr. Wilson did not actually see the fight. Thus, intervention focused on Tim's learning the definition of fighting that Mr. Wilson (and other school personnel) was using and Mr. Wilson's taking points away for fights reported to him by the school-yard supervisor, respectively. Additionally, Tim earned a special bonus for each week in which he met requirements of a behavior contract specifying a maximum number of "allowed" fights.

PROGRESS MONITORING

After intervention, assessment continued in the form of progress monitoring. Mr. Wilson continued to collect data on the frequency of fights in line and in the school yard, and these data were graphed weekly (see Figure 3). The behavior contract was reviewed and renegotiated weekly, with the maximum number of allowed fights decreasing each week. Additionally, Mr. Wilson, Tim, and I reviewed Tim's point account each week to evaluate his general academic and behavioral performance.

FOLLOW-UP

After several weeks, it was clear that Tim's fighting had decreased substantially in all school settings, talking back to teachers occurred very infrequently, and other areas of academic and behavior functioning continued to be satisfactory. Thus, the final phase of assessment, follow-up, began. This involved fading of the behavior contract (i.e., replacing the written contract with a verbal one, gradually replacing the privilege earned with praise) and only periodically meeting with Mr. Wilson and Tim, while Mr. Wilson continued to keep data on the target behaviors. The antecedent change of line positions and the consequence of providing the class privilege immediately after lunch remained in effect, since they fit easily into the normal classroom routine. Finally, when it was clear that Tim's appropriate behavior was being maintained I stopped visiting and contacted Mr. Wilson by phone at the end of the month.

Although the assessment phase took a fair amount of time and effort, Mr. Wilson and Tim reported that it really helped to see exactly what the problem areas were and to notice when Tim's behavior improved. The time and effort were very well spent.*

---

*In order to examine the effects of each intervention strategy, they would have to be implemented separately. However, in this case, in the interests of time and the teacher's wishes, all intervention strategies were implemented simultaneously.

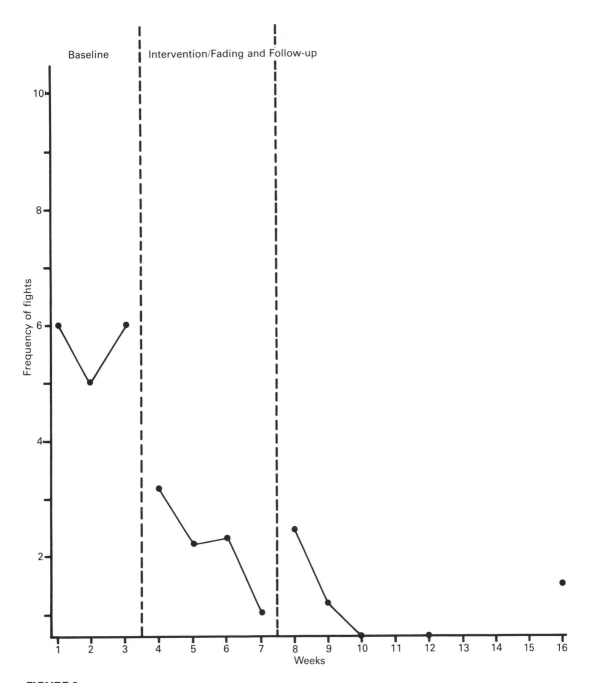

FIGURE 3
Number of fights with peers per week

81

PART
TWO

Strategies for Solving
School Problems

CHAPTER
FOUR

Improving School
Survival Skills

For all adolescents, school is occasionally stressful. Handicapped adolescents, moreover, may encounter *daily* stresses as they attempt integration into regular classes, the "mainstream." The mainstream classroom is the focal setting for this chapter, as we describe strategies for improving school survival skills, or those skills that enable students to meet the demands of the regular curriculum, of regular educators, and of large-group instruction. School survival skills include:

- class attendance and punctuality,
- class preparedness,
- time management,
- assessing teacher demands,
- remaining on task,
- handling transitions,
- and getting others' help.

ORGANIZATION OF THE CHAPTER

Before proceeding with the discussion of interventions, let us review the organization of this chapter (and the three chapters that follow). Chapters Four through Seven are arranged by target behaviors. For example, this chapter covers the skills just named. Strategies for promoting the skill follow each target behavior. These intervention types include:

- school-wide (involving changes in the student's settings),
- adult-directed (in which an adult plays the primary intervention role),
- peer-mediated (in which classmates assist), and
- self-mediated (e.g., self-monitoring or self-instruction).

Each chapter contains a case study illustrating the interventions. These case studies, most often based on real students, serve as source material for the many forms contained within the chapter. Pay close attention to all figures

and tables; they offer important information supplemental to the text.

SCHOOL SURVIVAL SKILLS: WHAT ARE THEY?

We have introduced the general topic of school survival skills. Let us turn now to some more specific questions:

1. Do the students need to learn school survival skills?
2. Do they understand the importance of school survival skills?
3. Which skills ought to be taught?
4. How should the skills be taught?
5. What links school survival skills to real-life survival?
6. How can families help teach these skills?
7. How can one be sure that skills will transfer from special education to regular education classes?

Because these important questions have been addressed only recently in research studies, it would be helpful to review some of the findings about school survival skills. To begin, let us answer the first three questions. These questions all relate to the *assessment process*.

ASSESSING SCHOOL SURVIVAL SKILLS

Recent research has addressed the often-overlooked question of which school survival skills to teach. As Freedman et al. (1978) stated:

Nearly all skill-training studies to date have been treatment oriented, that is, they have been concerned either with evaluating the general therapeutic utility of skill-training programs or with assessing the specific contributions of various training components, such as instructions, modeling, rehearsal, or feedback. Meanwhile, many fundamental questions concerning the underlying assumptions, concepts, and methods of the skill-training approach have been ignored. Some investigators, for example, have developed the content of their skill-training programs without first conducting a thorough and systematic analysis of the performance problems supposedly addressed by the programs. As a result, they have had no way of knowing whether their programs actually focused on the most relevant problem situations for their clients or whether the behaviors taught in the programs represented genuine solutions to these target problems. Furthermore, some investigators have offered skill training without first establishing that their clients actually were deficient in the particular skills being taught. (pp. 1448-1449)

The particular skills being taught have been addressed by our own research group (Kerr, Zigmond, Schaeffer, & Brown, 1986) and by others (see Walker and Rankin, 1983). Figure 4–1 shows a School Survival Skills Questionnaire.

Scanning the skills and problem statements gives an opportunity to think about one's *own* views. Which skills are critical? Which problems cannot be tolerated? We believe it is important for high school personnel to *become aware of their own values* before attempting to teach school survival skills or to insist upon specific classroom behaviors. Compare your responses with other special and regular educators. This activity will help you understand the demands placed on your students in other school settings.

Personnel in the research studies responded to the School Survival Skills Questionnaire. Here are the skills and problems ranked most important by a large group of urban high school special and regular educators, administrators, and counselors:

Important Skills

1. Meets due dates
2. Arrives at school on time
3. Attends class every day
4. Exhibits interest in academic work
5. Accepts consequences of behavior

Problem Behaviors

1. Seldom completes assignments
2. Cannot follow written directions
3. Gives "back talk" to teacher
4. Falls asleep in class
5. Is quick to give up

As a starting point in the assessment of which school survival skills to teach, ask others in the school to rate the skills and problems listed in Figure 4–1. This activity would be useful in planning curricular priorities and IEPs and in assisting students going into mainstream classes.

Student opinions are important, too. Research has shown that students do not always comprehend the demands or expectations of secondary school environments. For example, examine the items rated highly by students taking classes from the teacher represented above:

Skills

1. Goes to class every day
2. Shows interest in grades
3. Turns in work on time
4. Arrives at school on time
5. Plans steps to reach a goal

Problems

1. Cannot read directions
2. Makes poor grades
3. Does not bring necessary pencils, paper, or books to class
4. Gives "back talk" to teacher
5. Fails to finish work

To determine how your students view school survival skills (a set of competencies that many students fail to consider carefully) try the Student's School Survival Skills Questionnaire in Figure 4–1. Engage students in a discussion of the school survival skills—preferably at the beginning of the year or term.

Pinpointing target behaviors (Phase III of the Hawkins (1979) assessment model) can be fa-

Directions: This is a list of things that might be important for a student to be successful in high school. We would like to know what you think. Please mark each item according to how important you think it really is. If you think it is Very Important, circle number 3. If you think it is Helpful, circle number 2. If you think it is Not Important, circle number 1.

Very Important means this is necessary for doing well in high school.
Helpful means this is helpful, but not necessary for doing well in high school.
Not Important means this is not necessary for doing well in high school.

Statement	Very Important	Helpful	Not Important
1. Turns in work on time.	3	2	1
2. Listens to a lecture and remembers what was heard.	3	2	1
3. Is pleased about other people's achievements.	3	2	1
4. Raises hand to get teacher's attention.	3	2	1
5. Can calm down someone who is upset or angry.	3	2	1
6. Handles criticism.	3	2	1
7. Shows interest in grades.	3	2	1
8. Gives opinions in class even if no one else agrees.	3	2	1
9. Accepts consequences of behavior.	3	2	1
10. Takes good care of other people's things.	3	2	1
11. Knows when to leave someone alone.	3	2	1
12. Sticks up for a friend.	3	2	1
13. Can guess the questions a teacher might ask on a test.	3	2	1
14. Has both male and female friends.	3	2	1
15. Keeps busy while waiting for the teacher's help.	3	2	1
16. Goes to class every day.	3	2	1
17. Pays attention to appearance.	3	2	1
18. Volunteers to answer teacher's questions.	3	2	1
19. Has a sense of humor.	3	2	1
20. Asks to be included in activities with friends.	3	2	1
21. Does what an adult says to do.	3	2	1
22. Turns in neat papers.	3	2	1
23. Behaves differently with some teachers than with others.	3	2	1
24. Is a good sport about winning and losing.	3	2	1
25. Is good at taking tests.	3	2	1
26. Handles getting angry or upset in a way that others think is okay.	3	2	1
27. Writes so people can read it.	3	2	1
28. Has an adult in the school who is interested in her or him.	3	2	1
29. Offers help when a person has a problem.	3	2	1
30. Has some ideas about what to do after leaving high school.	3	2	1
31. Stays cool in a tough situation.	3	2	1
32. Figures out how people will react to her or him.	3	2	1
33. Looks at a person when talking.	3	2	1
34. Arrives at school on time.	3	2	1
35. Knows how someone feels and says the right thing.	3	2	1

FIGURE 4–1

School survival skills questionnaire (Source: From *The School Survival Skills Project: 1983–84 Annual Report* by M. M. Kerr and N. Zigmond, 1984 [unpublished grant report]. Reprinted by permission.)

	Serious Problem	Somewhat a Problem	Not a Problem
36. Goes up and talks to teachers and other adults in the building.	3	2	1
37. Keeps track of work in an assignment book.	3	2	1
38. Answers when someone speaks.	3	2	1
39. Figures out people's moods.	3	2	1
40. Has some close friends.	3	2	1
41. Organizes time and papers for studying.	3	2	1
42. Knows how well she or he is doing in school.	3	2	1
43. Is polite.	3	2	1
44. Talks calmly to an adult when she or he feels unfairly treated.	3	2	1
45. Does a favor for a friend even when it's a hassle.	3	2	1
46. Knows what things she or he does well.	3	2	1
47. Plans steps to reach a goal.	3	2	1
48. Waits for teacher's permission before speaking out.	3	2	1

Directions: This is a list of things that might make it hard for students to do well in high school. We would like to know what you think. If you think this is a Serious Problem, circle number 3. If you think it is Somewhat of a Problem, circle number 2. If you think it is Not a Problem, circle number 1.

Serious Problem means this would make it impossible to do well in high school.

Somewhat of a Problem means this would make it hard to do well in high school.

Not a Problem means this would not affect how a student does in high school.

Statement	Serious Problem	Somewhat a Problem	Not a Problem
1. Falls asleep in class.	3	2	1
2. Gets out of seat without asking.	3	2	1
3. Is late to class.	3	2	1
4. Gives "back talk" to teacher.	3	2	1
5. Makes mistakes through quick decisions.	3	2	1
6. Cannot take notes.	3	2	1
7. Says things not related to the topic.	3	2	1
8. Cannot work alone.	3	2	1
9. Laughs when things aren't funny.	3	2	1
10. Does not bring pencils, paper, or books for class.	3	2	1
11. Does not ask for teacher's help even when it is needed.	3	2	1
12. Cannot make decisions.	3	2	1
13. Lets others bother her or him while working.	3	2	1
14. Makes poor grades.	3	2	1
15. Does not belong to a group, club, or team.	3	2	1
16. Cannot read directions.	3	2	1
17. Gives up quickly if faced with a problem.	3	2	1
18. Does not accept people who are different.	3	2	1
19. Fails to finish work.	3	2	1
20. Does not know how to use the library.	3	2	1
21. Irritates others.	3	2	1

FIGURE 4–1

(continued)

cilitated by these attitude surveys. By learning what is expected of students and the discrepancy between student and adult opinions, one can pinpoint the initial objective for School Survival Skills Training: to raise students' awareness of teachers' standards and expectations. For example, an adolescent's long-term objective might read:

To state the requirements of each class according to these categories of school survival skills:
a. What I need for class
b. When I must get to class
c. What kind of assignments and deadlines I will have
d. Of what behaviors the teacher approves and disapproves
e. What outside resources I will need for the class assignments.

Students will find their task—assessing and setting demands—easier if the participating teachers have made their expectations explicit. A very useful tool for teachers as well as consultants and supervisors is the SBS Inventory of Teacher Social Behavior Standards and Expectations (Secondary Version) (Walker & Rankin, 1983). The SBS inventory is especially helpful in assigning adolescents to mainstream classes. The inventory assesses the social behavior expectations, tolerances, and related inservice/consultation needs of a teacher, *with respect to a student considered for placement in her class*.

Once the most important school survival skills have been decided upon, determine *which of the students will need to learn these skills*. You may have identified some students already: the one who is perennially late to class, those who never seem to have a pencil, the youth who never can turn in work on the due date.

Unfortunately, research has shown that special educators cannot always identify accurately students who need school survival skills training for mainstream classes. Too often, special and regular educators lack planning time to-

gether to discuss their students' specific skill deficits. To remedy this situation, try a rating scale such as the School Survival Skills Scale (Zigmond et al., 1986). This simple form allows teachers to rate the skills shown by their students and to communicate their evaluations to others. Figure 4–2 illustrates the School Survival Skills Scale.

In summary, we have shared the research findings that answer three assessment questions:

1. Which skills ought to be taught?
2. Do the students understand the importance of school survival skills?
3. Which students need to learn school survival skills?

Selecting which skills to teach is an important task that is accomplished through attitudinal surveys, discussions, and direct observations. These activities facilitate an understanding of how students view school survival skills, too. To identify candidates for training, try direct observations and teacher ratings. Throughout all phases of the assessment process, communication between professionals and students is vital.

TEACHING SCHOOL SURVIVAL SKILLS

The remainder of the chapter will address questions about teaching school survival skills. This section is organized by skill areas.

Class Attendance and Punctuality

Perhaps the most basic school survival skill is getting to classes. Interventions for the problem of truancy have increased in recent years, as the rate of high school dropouts reaches alarming levels. System-wide interventions for truancy and strategies for the related problem, school refusal, appear in Chapter Seven. Here we discuss strategies for other important problems: cutting classes and late arrivals.

Environmental Strategies. No doubt your school has adopted some of these environmental strategies to promote class attendance.

- hall monitors
- written passes
- random checks on attendance, by periods
- hall sweeps
- late bells
- assigned seats

Hall monitors refers to nonprofessional individuals hired by the school to check non-classroom areas for students who may be unauthorized "trespassers." In some buildings, security guards serve this function, while in others parent volunteers may monitor the corridors. In any event, these individuals are not usually trained in the special needs of handicapped youth. Like bus drivers, cafeteria workers, and custodians, they do not attend inservice sessions tailored to their interactions with handicapped students. Subsequently, they may "excuse" a behaviorally disordered student who needs "regular" treatment with respect to the enforcement of rules, or unfairly penalize a mentally retarded student who has not understood school policies. We recommend that special educators review the operations of hall monitors with a goal of helping these ancillary personnel to individualize (when appropriate) their approaches to certain students. In turn, handicapped youth should receive (and review as often as necessary) a clear explication of class attendance and hall monitoring policies. In this explanation, teachers should make the real-world link to individuals with whom adolescents may have similar interactions:

- ticket takers at athletic events, concerts, and movies
- traffic police officers
- airport security personnel
- department store security agents and dressing room monitors

Drawing such "real-world" analogies can reduce adolescents' feelings that only teenagers are scrutinized in moving about an environment. Taking the illustrations one step further, you can talk about managing interactions (especially confrontations) with persons in these authority positions.

Naturally, it is important to discuss school hall monitoring early in a teenager's career in a building—before the student develops a problem (or a poor reputation) with security people.

Hall passes, if they are to be effective, must be produced in a manner that prevents counterfeit. They, like tokens in a token economy program, should be

- durable (if they are to be reused),
- unique (to avoid counterfeit),
- convenient to produce, and
- age-appropriate.

Random attendance checks may curb absenteeism and tardiness. Each day (or check), a class period is chosen for monitoring. The period is, of course, not announced in advance. Once attendance has been taken, the names of late or absent students are announced for penalties. Alternatively, the students who arrived on time for class might be recognized and/or reinforced. Although it has never applied specifically to secondary school absenteeism, Van Houten's research on **public posting** offers principles that warrant our consideration. His work on public posting involves publicly listing the names of persons who have (or have not) engaged in a target behavior. In one middle school, these principles are being applied to the problem of class cutting and tardiness as follows: Whenever a student arrives late to class, a detention slip for the next afternoon's detention is assigned. The names of all students earning detention for tardiness or cuts are posted throughout the school in highly visible areas such as the cafeteria. (Detention is discussed in Chapter Six.)

DATE: _____

STUDENT'S NAME: _____   TEACHER'S NAME: _____
(please print)   (please print)
Circle the appropriate response.
STUDENT'S GRADE: 9 10 11 12   THIS STUDENT IS IN YOUR CLASS FOR:
STUDENT'S SEX: M F   Homeroom   Social Studies
STUDENT'S SPECIAL ED CLASSIFICATION: English   Science
SED LD EMR VH HI PH   Math   Other _____

DIRECTIONS: *Please read each statement and circle the corresponding letter that best describes this student's typical behavior. Be sure that you mark every item.*

THIS STUDENT:	NEVER	SOMETIMES	USUALLY	ALWAYS	NOT OBSERVED
1. . . . stays awake in class.	N	S	U	A	X
2. . . . gets to class on time.	N	S	U	A	A
3. . . . complies with requests of adults in authority.	N	S	U	A	X
4. . . . stays calm and in control of emotions.	N	S	U	A	X
5. . . . brings necessary materials to class.	N	S	U	A	X
6. . . . is persistent even when faced with a difficult task.	N	S	U	A	X
7. . . . asks for help with schoolwork when necessary.	N	S	U	A	X
8. . . . responds to others when they speak.	N	S	U	A	X
9. . . . arrives at school on time.	N	S	U	A	X
10. . . . completes assigned work.	N	S	U	A	X
11. . . . behaves appropriately in a variety of settings.	N	S	U	A	X

FIGURE 4–2

School survival skills scale (Source: From *The School Survival Skills Curriculum* by N. Zigmond, M. M. Kerr, A. Schaeffer, G. Brown, and H. Farra, 1986. Pittsburgh: University of Pittsburgh. Reprinted by permission.)

THIS STUDENT:	NEVER	SOMETIMES	USUALLY	ALWAYS	NOT OBSERVED
12. . . . manages conflict though nonaggressive means.	N	S	U	A	X
13. . . . organizes study time efficiently.	N	S	U	A	X
14. . . . can concentrate on work without being distracted by peers.	N	S	U	A	X
15. . . . works well independently.	N	S	U	A	X
16. . . . accepts the punishment if caught doing something wrong.	N	S	U	A	X
17. . . . turns in assignments when they are due.	N	S	U	A	X
18. . . . speaks appropriately to teachers.	N	S	U	A	X
19. . . . follows written directions.	N	S	U	A	X
20. . . . talks calmly to an adult when perceived to be unjustly accused.	N	S	U	A	X
21. . . . uses time productively while waiting for teacher.	N	S	U	A	X
22. . . . attends class.	N	S	U	A	X
23. . . . exhibits interest in improving academic performance.	N	S	U	A	X
24. . . . is good at taking tests.	N	S	U	A	X
25. . . . appropriately handles corrections on classwork.	N	S	U	A	X
26. . . . identifies the central theme of a lecture (demonstrates by stating or writing the main ideas and supporting facts).	N	S	U	A	X

PLEASE CHECK TO MAKE SURE ALL ITEMS ARE MARKED.

FIGURE 4–2
(continued)

Adult-Directed Strategies. Explicitly stating the expectation that adolescents will attend class and arrive on time is itself a powerful—and often overlooked—intervention. Conversations with teenagers suggest that they differentiate between "strict" and "easy" teachers, and they tend to rise (or sink) to the level of expectation. One way to underscore your expectation for prompt arrival at class is to have a daily "warm-up activity" written on the board. Students are to take their seats and begin this activity with no help from the teacher. Another idea is to have a firmly established routine for the beginning minutes of class, thus eliminating the complaint, "There's nothing to do!"

Because class attendance and punctuality tend to be issues of motivation, an adult-directed strategy of rewards and punishments is appropriate. In Chapter Six we offer guidelines for contracting and token economies. These two contingency management systems are helpful in reducing class absences.

Another adult-directed approach is to teach the skills directly. Discussions of the importance of getting to classes on time are needed. Consider this interview between a researcher and an adolescent:

> **Researcher:** People thought it was important for students to *arrive at school on time*. Do you think it's important?
>
> **Student:** Yes and no.
>
> **Researcher:** Why do you think it's important to get to school on time?
>
> **Student:** If you have an important first class, then it is important.
>
> **Researcher:** What happens if you don't?
>
> **Student:** *If late to homeroom nothing; if after homeroom, write it in the book in office.*

Teaching a lesson (or lessons) on the importance of arriving at class on time is a short-term, but important, intervention. The School Survival Skills Curriculum (available from Dr. Naomi Zigmond, Department of Special Educa-

tion, University of Pittsburgh, Pittsburgh, PA) is a series of lessons, one of which addresses getting to class on time. Figure 4–3 illustrates this lesson.

Peer-Mediated Strategies. Peers play such an important role in adolescence that we consider them major resources in training. In a peer-mediated strategy, classmates and/or friends serve as behavior-change facilitators.

Peer monitoring is a straightforward approach to the problem of class attendance (and other school survival skill deficits). During a peer monitoring intervention, a classmate checks on the behavior of another student. Students also may monitor one another reciprocally. Peers may monitor class attendance and being on time, too. However, we advise that students begin with only one or two recorded activities. Note also that peer monitoring may extend to times outside of the school day. Families can participate (if desired) in this strategy by letting teenagers use home telephones.

Another peer-mediated intervention for class attendance is a group contingency. Contingencies related to group characteristics take advantage of social reinforcers controlled by the peer group and are adaptable to a variety of situations. Group-oriented contingencies also reduce the number of individual consequences the teacher must deliver.

The basic characteristic of group-oriented contingencies is group reinforcement. Whether the target is an individual student or the entire class, the group shares in the consequences of the target's behavior. In many cases, group-oriented contingencies are devised to deal with specific problem behaviors. Nevertheless, they can be used to establish appropriate behaviors and to prevent problems from occurring. A full description of group contingencies and the way to set them up is contained in Chapter Six.

Group contingencies may be combined with other peer-mediated strategies. For example, a

SCRIPT:

Today I want to talk about *Attending Class Every Day* and *Getting to Class on Time*.

1. Q: Why do you think it's important to attend class every day?
   A: 1) so you don't miss assignments
      2) so you can learn what the teacher is teaching
      3) so you can have an easier time passing tests and getting good grades
      4) the teacher will view you as an interested student, as someone who tried to do well

   Q: Why do students miss classes?
   A: 1) they are sick
      2) they're not good in that subject, so they skip that class
      3) they think it's not important to learn that subject
      4) they don't like the teacher

   Q: What can you do about these things?
   A: 1) If you are sick and miss a class, call a classmate to find out what you missed. Or next day, ask your teacher what you missed.
      2) If you're not good in a subject, GET HELP! Ask your teacher for help; work after school with a friend; ask your counselor to set up a tutor for you. Not coming to class won't change the fact that you need help in that class.
      3) Even if you think that the subject matter in a class isn't important, you know that it's *much* better to pass a class than to fail it. You can't pass if you don't attend.
      4) Nobody likes every single teacher. But if you don't go to class, and you fail, you are only hurting yourself.

2. Q: Why is it important to get to class on time?
   A: 1) so you won't miss things (announcements, assignments)
      2) so you start off class "on the right foot"
      3) so you won't disturb the class by coming in late
      4) so the teacher won't have to repeat things
      5) so you don't make the teacher angry
      6) so you develop good habits
      7) so your teacher will think you care about how you are doing in school

   Q: Why are students late to class?
   A: 1) they are talking to friends
      2) they have to get things from their lockers
      3) their next class is far away from the class they are leaving

   Q: What can *you* do to make sure you get to your class on time?
   A: 1) Don't have long conversations with friends between classes.
      2) Plan to take all materials you need for your classes with you so you don't have to stop at your locker. If you have a lot to carry, try to get a knapsack or canvas bag to carry them in.
      3) If your classes are far apart, walk quickly. Don't make any stops.

   Q: How much time do you have between classes?
   A: 1) 5 minutes

      That seems like very little time, but actually, it's a lot of time. Let me show you how long it is. (GET OUT STOPWATCH. GIVE TO 1 STUDENT. TELL OTHER STUDENTS TO SEE IF THEY CAN KEEP THEIR EYES CLOSED, AND STAY PERFECTLY STILL FOR 1 MINUTE.)

FIGURE 4–3

Class attendance lesson (Source: From *The School Survival Skills Project: 1983–84 Annual Report* by M. M. Kerr and N. Zigmond, 1984 [unpublished grant report]. Reprinted by permission.)

class may skip assignments once a week if every dyad has arrived at 27 or 30 classes on time during the previous week. Group contingencies also may supplement self-monitoring, a strategy described in the next section.

Self-Mediated Strategies. Among the self-mediated strategies applicable to adolescents are self-monitoring, self-instruction, and self-reinforcement. Self monitoring refers to a student's observing, counting, and recording his own behaviors. **Self-instruction** means that an individual gives herself spoken directions about a task or social encounter. Self-reinforcement occurs when a person rewards himself for a designated act. In this section we will concentrate on self-monitoring activities for class attendance.

First, review the general guidelines for self-monitoring displayed in Table 4–1. Here are some examples of target behaviors that can be used in self-monitoring class attendance:

- to arrive at class before the late bell
- to be seated by second bell
- to be at third period class all this week
- to punch the time clock in Industrial Arts class before the instructor checks attendance
- to earn "attendance list" (public posting) for three weeks
- to stay at school through the last period for two consecutive weeks

Note that some of these goals fall short of many of our aims for high school students. These objectives are included as examples of initial goals for students with severe attendance problems. Remember the importance of **shaping** in modifying behavior problems. Shaping refers to the gradual reinforcement of behaviors leading to a desired, more difficult behavior.

Figure 4–4 depicts a self-monitoring form completed by an adolescent monitoring class attendance for the first time. Only two days were monitored at first. Note the reliability checks (indicated by teacher initials) on Jon's **self-re-**

cording. A student's goal written directly on the form serves to remind him of the progress he is making. Most teenagers prefer also that the self-monitoring form be as unobtrusive as possible. For this reason, use plain white paper with the form photocopied and reduced to make it less obvious to others.

Family-Involved Interventions. Because arriving at school on time usually begins at home, we offer a few ideas for including families in the intervention. Families may assist through a home-based contingency management program. In such a program, families give recognition and/or rewards for school performance. This arrangement may be formalized through a home-based contract. (See Chapter Six for a step-by-step contracting procedure.)

Families can be instrumental, of course, in early morning monitoring to see that adolescents wake up, leave home, and go to school. There is a current program whereby parents are called every morning for a report on whether their child got to school on time or not. Parents have come to appreciate this regular contact, especially because they receive both "good news" and "bad news." One mother even called her son at school when he missed his bus! The inclusion of positive phone calls seems crucial to the close communication between the school and home—a communication vital to the remediation of truancy and tardiness.

In summary, we have described several strategies for promoting class attendance. Students may monitor their own and others' behavior, in combination with environmental and adult-directed strategies, the most common of which are contingency management programs. Families can help, especially in recognizing and prompting these important school survival skills.

Class Preparedness

Bringing Materials and Equipment. Having all the materials and equipment for class tasks

TABLE 4-1
Guidelines for training students to use self-monitoring

1. Identify target behaviors. Include behaviors to be increased as well as those to be decreased (e.g., on-task, off-task).
2. Discuss target behaviors with the student. Redefine target behaviors, using the student's own words. For example, one teenager defined study behaviors as follows.
   On-task:
   —writing, or
   —reading, or
   —thinking about the content area.
   —conference with teacher, or other adult, work.
   —charting data
   Off-task
   —anything else!
3. Select a practical way to measure the target behaviors.
4. Train the student to use the measurement system (e.g., to mark a 3 × 5 card with (/) marks for off-task behaviors) in the classroom. You may find it helpful to provide external monitoring (the teacher scores the student's performance and provides feedback) prior to moving to self-monitoring.
5. Once the student is self-recording behaviors, conduct an occasional reliability check to ensure that the evaluation was done accurately.
6. Provide reinforcement to students who reduce their disruptive behaviors. Consider using a response cost if disruptive behaviors continue above designated level.
7. Display an optimistic attitude when explaining the program to students. You may benefit from the placebo effect!
8. Encourage students to develop a visual image of the behaviors they are performing. This is called imaginal training.
9. Use shaping of successive approximations when training students. In other words, teach and reinforce even small attempts to use the procedures.
10. Don't forget to use fading to reduce the number of teacher prompts and reinforcers to students after the program has been well underway and progress has been seen.
11. Remember that self-instruction that includes statements of positive affect will be more productive than rote instructions.
12. Don't forget that you can use self-management with individuals or with a classroom group. Do remember each student evaluates himself, not others.
13. See that students receive thorough training so they understand the procedures. The program is not a success unless it's used!

Source: The material for this table was taken from *Self-Management Strategies: A Review and Guide for Use* by F. Albion, 1979, Nashville, Tenn.: Peabody College, unpublished manuscript.

is another school survival skill. *materials* include textbooks, assignment book, handouts, paper, and notebooks. *Equipment* includes locker keys, pens, pencils, calculators, and other tools used to complete classwork.

Adult-Directed Strategies

Too many handicapped teenagers either lack or cannot locate (in their disorganized backpack rubble) the items they need to succeed in

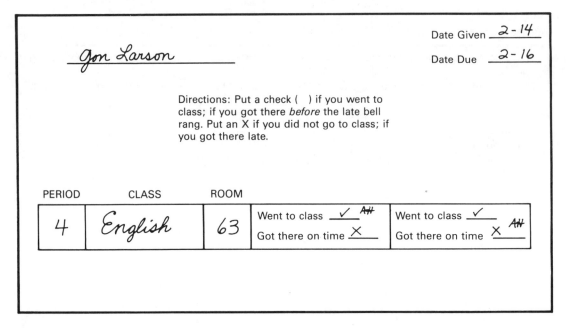

FIGURE 4–4
Self-monitoring form (Source: From *The School Survival Skills Curriculum* by N. Zigmond, M. M. Kerr, A. Schaeffer, G. Brown, and H. Farra, 1986, Pittsburgh: University of Pittsburgh. Adapted by permission.)

classes (Brown, Kerr, Zigmond, & Harris, 1984). On the other hand, secondary school teachers may inadvertently reinforce their students' poor habits by providing them with paper, pencils, and books in the classroom (Kerr & Zigmond, 1984). Clearly, the first step in solving the problem of ill-equipped students is to set the *expectation* that students take responsibility for their own preparedness. Use the ideas in the opening section of this chapter to reconsider the expectations you and other staff have for class preparedness. Assess *your* contribution to the problem, too, by asking these questions:

1. Have I explicitly asked students to bring their own materials and equipment to class?
2. Have I posted a list of items that students must bring to class?
3. How do I respond to students who chronically come to class unprepared? Is this re-

sponse reinforcing the problem behavior?
4. Do I recognize and reinforce well-prepared students?
5. What are my school's policies on class preparedness? Am I enforcing (reviewing, developing, revising) them? (A senior high school teacher once commented, "It's not enough to list 'pencils.' Say, 'sharpened pencils!' ")
6. Do I encourage students (a characteristic of successful students) to call on one another, instead of on me, for items?
7. Are my expectations the same or different from less restrictive settings? How much different?
8. Have I informed parents of my expectations?

Some teachers "rent" (for a quarter or so) materials and equipment for limited periods, or demand "collateral"–an ID card, driver's license, locker key, or bus pass–in return for loaned materials. These simple measures avoid reinforcement of inappropriate behavior, while allowing students to complete classwork. Teachers may collect a "security deposit" at the beginning of the school year: students contribute materials (e.g., two pencils, some notebook paper) to a classroom pool of items that may be borrowed later.

Figure 4–5 shows an excerpt from a lesson on class preparedness.

Peer-Mediated Strategies

The peer-mediated strategies mentioned in previous sections apply to class preparedness as well. Specifically, students can learn to monitor one another's class preparedness by simply asking each other about necessary materials prior to class. A recent study of successful high school students (Brown et al., 1984) demonstrated that they frequently borrow materials from their classmates. This straightforward peer-

---

Hi. On Monday, we talked about why it's important to go to your classes every day, and why it's important to be on time. We also talked about SELF-MONITORING, and I gave each of you your own MONITORING SHEET. I will ask you to take out your monitoring forms in a few minutes. First, I want to talk about *bringing necessary materials to class*.

Q: What materials are necessary for you to bring to class everyday?
A: 1) something to write *with* (pen or pencil)
   2) something to write *on* (paper, notebook)
   3) books for that class

Q: Why do you need to have these things?
A: 1) If you have nothing to write with, you can't do the classwork that day.
   2) If you don't have paper, you can't take notes or do assignments.
   3) If you don't have books, you can't keep up with your own work or with what the class is doing.
   4) If you often don't bring materials, your teacher will think you don't care about your class or your grades.

Q: What happens if you don't bring them to class with you?

Q: What can *you* do to make sure you have everything you need for class?
A: 1) Put all your materials together in one place the night before—don't try to find things in the morning when you're in a hurry.
   2) If you lose a book, tell the teacher. Find out what you have to do to get a new one.
   3) Keep extra pens or pencils with you; ask a friend if you can borrow a pen or pencil.
   4) Keep an assignment book with you. Write down your assignments and what materials you need to bring with you to class.

And just to make sure there are *no* excuses for not having a pencil and paper, I'll give each of you a brand new pencil and some paper. Now, just remember to bring them with you!

FIGURE 4–5

Class preparedness lesson (Source: From the *School Survival Skills Curriculum* by N. Zigmond, M. M. Kerr, A. Schaeffer, G. Brown, and H. Farra, 1986. Pittsburgh: University of Pittsburgh. Reprinted by permission.)

mediated strategy may not appeal to all high school teachers but clearly has merit. After all, in post-secondary environments, students often borrow from one another. Taking this example one step further, adult officemates swap materials frequently.

Teacher intervention may be required if some students develop a pattern of borrowing but never lending. As part of the initial orientation offered to students, teachers might suggest appropriate and inappropriate ways of being prepared for class. Needless to say, adults should be very clear about the issue of borrowing answers to tests or copying other students' work. Borrowing should always be clearly differentiated from stealing.

Self-Mediated Strategies

Most students manage their own class preparation without help from adults. Nevertheless, handicapped adolescents, especially those entering mainstream classes, may need help in monitoring their own behaviors. Self-monitoring, described in an earlier section, is a good tool for helping adolescents monitor their class preparation. Students who are overly dependent on adult supervision and assistance may "wean" themselves from teachers by using a self-monitoring strategy. Figure 4–6 and 4–7 show self-monitoring forms completed by a student who was overly dependent on teacher help. Notice that this self-monitoring program involved a contingency contract between the student and her teacher. Also notice that Jerry was asked to try several alternate sources of help, including asking her assigned study partner. The assignment of a study partner may help students to develop autonomy in an age-appropriate manner. Teachers who can organize homework and classwork projects for pairs or small groups of students will help students learn the important skill of cooperative work.

Be sure to review with students the materials necessary for each class, before expecting stu-

dents to respond successfully to *any* of the strategies named in this section. Until students understand what is expected of them, they will not change their behavior effectively.

Adults, classmates, and target students themselves can work in collaboration to improve class preparedness skills. Adult intervention is almost always required, to set up expectations and review them with students. Classmates may assist target students through reciprocal peer monitoring and through the straightforward strategy of sharing necessary materials and equipment. Finally, students eventually must learn to monitor their own class preparedness.

Time Management

In this section, we review time management, a relatively new area of training and research. Unfortunately, little has been done in the area of teaching time-management skills to adolescents. Therefore, adult time-management literature must supply our lessons and strategies. Teachers interested in building time-management skills in their students should consult one of the following books to gain an introduction to this important field: *Doing It Now* by E.C. Bliss (New York: Bantam Books, 1984), or *Getting Things Done*, also by Bliss (New York: Scribner's, 1983).

Time management for teenagers includes organizing one's environment for studying, allocating time effectively for major class projects, balancing extracurricular and studying schedules, and completing assignments on time.

Adult-Directed Strategies. The best thing adults can do for teenagers who need to learn time-management skills is to *teach* time management. However, adults must first learn something about time management themselves, by reading the available literature and practicing what they read. *Doing It Now* (Bliss, 1984) is an especially helpful volume for those who procrastinate—a behavior common to many un-

Contract

This contract is between ___*Jerry*___ and ___*Mrs. Rothchild*___
                         (Student)   (Teacher)

and is effective on ___*4-8*___.
                            (Date)

I, ___*Jerry*___ agree to try these behaviors.

(1) to stop and think, "Do I really need help?", before calling on the teacher.

(2) to use at least one other source of help before calling on ___*Mrs. Rothchild*___

These other sources are:

___*textbook*___
___*study partner*___
___*the blackboard*___

(3) to check off on my "help" sheet which kind of help I tried to use.

My goal is to have at least three (v) per English period, showing that I tried to use other kinds of help.

If ___*Jerry*___ meets her goal, I, ___*Mrs. Rothchild*___, will provide her with an extra 5 points on the assignment for that period. If there was no graded assignment, she will be issued a 5 point credit to be used when she chooses.

Signed: ___*Jerry Kudo*___   Date: ___*4/8*___
       (Student)

Signed: ___*Mrs. E. Rothchild*___   Date: ___*4/8*___
       (Teacher)

Signed: ___*H. Morton.*___   Date: ___*4/9*___
       (Principal)

We will review this contract on ___*4/15*___.
                             (Date)

FIGURE 4–6
Contract to promote independent classwork (Source: From *Strategies for Managing Behavior Problems in the Classroom* (p. 162) by M. M. Kerr and and C. M. Nelson, 1983, Columbus, OH: Charles E. Merrill Publishing Company. Copyright 1983 by Charles E. Merrill Publishing Company. Reprinted by permission.)

Alternate Source of Help	Date: 4/9	Date: 4/10	Date: 4/11	Date: 4/12	Date: 4/13
1. Reread the assignment on the board.	✓	✓	✓	✓	✓
2. Consult the index of the textbook for other information.	✓		✓	✓	✓
3. Reread the chapter material that's relevant.	✓	✓	✓	✓	✓
4. Use a reference book (thesaurus, dictionary, etc.)					
5. Ask my assigned study partner		✓			
6. Asked the librarian later (Other)					✓
Total:	3	3	3	3	3̶ 4

Name: Jerry

Week of: 4/9

Rev'd by: E. Rothschild.

FIGURE 4–7

Checklist for using classroom resources (Source: From *Strategies for Managing Behavior Problems in the Classroom* (p. 163) by M. M. Kerr and C. M. Nelson, 1983, Columbus, OH: Charles E. Merrill Publishing Company. Copyright 1983 by Charles E. Merrill Publishing Company. Reprinted by permission.)

successful teenage students. For example, one of Bliss's chapters recommends visible reminders, shown in Table 4–2. Consider these for classroom posters.

We often take time-management skills for granted. Unfortunately, many adolescents do not develop time-management skills on their own. Every teacher should spend at least one or two class periods discussing the assignments for the course and assisting students in estimating the time required to complete these assignments. Ideally, this time-management orientation would take place in the early grades, but it is essential in secondary school programs where assignments tend to be lengthy. Help students by giving them an opportunity to practice estimating and allocating their time for assignments. When students turn in work after the deadline, talk with them about how they planned their time, checking to see that they have learned time-management skills. Too often, teachers accept late work without discussing with a student the reasons for the delay.

Expecting students to maintain an assignment book not only gives them a way to practice time-management skills, but also provides the teacher with a permanent product for monitoring time management and planning. Keep in mind, moreover, that if your own time-management skills are weak (e.g., if you never quite complete the lesson you set out to teach), students may come to question the value of your time-management instruction. Be a good role model by managing classroom time and planning lessons carefully.

Peer-Mediated Strategies. Students may help one another plan time for homework as illustrated in the example in Figure 4–8. This activity, entitled "peer monitoring," is designed to have students help each other with homework. Pairs of students remind each other about homework completion three days a week for several weeks. A **homework completion checklist** structures this activity for the students, who spend about 5 to 10 minutes three days a week checking each other's homework completion. Each student initials his partner's checklist if homework assignments have been completed and turned in on time. The student who gets

TABLE 4–2
Time management
slogans
	MAKE TODAY.
	DOING BEATS STEWING.
	DO IT ANYWAY!
	PEOPLE DON'T FAIL BECAUSE THEY INTEND TO FAIL; THEY FAIL
	   BECAUSE THEY FAIL TO DO WHAT THEY INTEND TO DO.
	BE A DOER NOT A DAWDLER.
	HAVE A HAPPY TOMORROW: DO TODAY'S WORK TODAY.
	YOU DON'T FIND TIME—YOU MAKE IT!
	TODAY: USE IT OR LOSE IT.
	LEAD TIME: THE GIFT THAT ONLY I CAN GIVE MYSELF.
	DUE TOMORROW: DO TODAY!
	WELL BEGUN IS HALF DONE.
	WINNERS DON'T WAIT.
	DO THE WORST FIRST.
	THERE'S A TIME TO WORK AND A TIME TO PLAY . . . IT'S TIME TO
	   WORK.

Source: Edwin C. Bliss, excerpted from *DOING IT NOW.* Copyright © 1983 Edwin C. Bliss. Reprinted with permission of Charles Scribner's.

Here are a few examples of questions to ask your partner. Check each question that you asked.

1. Did you complete your assignment? ___
2. Did you put your name on the paper, the class and teacher's name? ___
3. Did you check your spelling? ___
4. Did you read the assignment? ___
5. Did you take notes? ___
6. Did you bring your assignment, your assignment book, your notebook, and textbook? ___
7. Did you write down the assignment book? ___
8. Do you understand the assignment for tonight? ___
9. Do you understand the directions? ___
10. Do you have your book and notebook for tonight's homework? ___
11. When are you doing your work tonight? ___

This homework assignment is:

	YES!	NO
1. turned in on time.	☐	☐
2. complete.	☐	☐
3. neat and easy to read.	☐	☐
4. done according to directions.	☐	☐

Student: _____
Date: _____
Class: _____
Checker: _____
　　　　　　(initial)

Did you call to remind your partner?	☐	☐

FIGURE 4–8

Homework helper checklist (Source: From *The School Survival Skills Project: 1983–84 Annual Report* by M. M. Kerr and N. Zigmond, 1984 [unpublished grant report]. Reprinted by permission.)

her homework in on time and completed and who helps her partner receives special privileges made available through the school survival skills project. Students are encouraged to remind each other of due dates, to check in with each other about what to do (for example, which chapters to study for a test), and to help each other understand written or verbal directions. **Task analysis** is a primary strategy involved in this peer-mediated program. In the time-management literature, dividing a large (and overwhelming) responsibility into smaller, more manageable steps is called the **Salami Technique** (Bliss, 1984). Bliss's explanation may be used to introduce this peer-mediated strategy:

Whenever a task seems overwhelming, pause for a moment and do a little thinking on paper. List chronologically every step that must be taken to complete the job. The smaller the steps, the better—even little mini-tasks that will take only a minute or two should be listed separately. I call this the Salami Technique because it seems to me that contemplation of an overwhelming task is like looking at a large uncut salami: it's a huge, crusty, greasy, unappetizing chunk; you don't feel you can get your teeth into it. But when you cut it into thin slices you transform it into something quite different. Those thin slices are inviting; they make your mouth water, and after you've sampled one slice you tend to reach for another. Cutting up your overwhelming task into tiny segments can have the same effect. Now, instead of looking at a gargantuan project, you're looking at a series of tiny tasks, each of which, considered separately, is manageable. And you begin to realize that they will indeed be considered separately. (Bliss, 1984; p.20)

Having given an introduction to this peer-mediated Salami Technique, allow about 15 minutes for each pair of students to talk about the homework planning forms.

Self-Mediated Strategies. Throughout all of the strategies discussed for time management is created a theme of students taking responsibility for their own assignments. Eventually, students must allocate their time by analyzing their schedules and setting aside pleasurable activities for those less pleasurable tasks. The first step in teaching students this self-discipline is to have students schedule their own time. Typically, schools issue schedules that begin at 7:00 A.M. and end at about 3:00 P.M. In our experience, students need to plan their time from waking to sleeping, seven days a week. Figure 4–9 displays a time-management schedule designed by a high school junior. Note that his schedule begins with wake-up, ends at night, and covers an entire week.

In Figure 4–10, you will see the same student's daily planning form, which he designed for himself. Students may be encouraged to design their own assignment books, planning sheets, or modifications of commercially available "to do" lists. In the example given in Figure 4–10, the student also put an estimation of his grades for the period (a concession to his parents).

We have discussed several strategies for time management, including direct instruction, peer monitoring and task analysis, and self-scheduling. These strategies may be used in combination or singly, although teacher instruction must not be overlooked. Too often we assume that students have developed time-management skills, although school curricula ignore this important school survival skill altogether.

Appropriate Classroom Behavior

One can hardly overemphasize the importance of behaving appropriately in regular and special education classes. In fact, classroom behavior may have more to do with an adolescent's successful mainstream experience than his academic skills (Walker & Rankin, 1983). In this section we discuss the way in which students exhibit an interest in their work, respond appropriately to adults, manage "down time" in class, and remain on-task.

Before describing strategies specifically designed to improve class behavior, we remind you that Chapter Six is devoted to more serious behavior *problems*, while this chapter section relates to the development of appropriate skills.

We cannot overstate the importance of straightforward expectations combined with clear contingencies. When students understand the format and rules for a class and know that there are consequences for acting outside of these expectations, they will be more likely to manage their own behavior during class time. Several contingency management strategies may be used in combination with the specific interventions named in this section. These general contingency management strategies include:

1. group contingencies,
2. token economy,
3. contingency contracting,
4. grades,
5. suspension, and
6. time out.

These contingency management systems are described in detail in Chapter Six.

Teacher-Directed Strategies. The format of instruction offered will influence students' on-task behavior. Review the curricular suggestions in Chapter Six to see how you might improve your teaching.

Part of your instruction—especially if you are preparing handicapped students for **mainstreaming**—should be devoted to the school survival skill of showing an interest in class. Figure 4–11 shows a handout to promote discussion of this essential skill. Talk with students about their in-class behavior. You may be surprised to discover that the students are not even aware of their off-task behaviors. The next two strategies—peer-mediated and self-mediated—

Planning form for study time, high school level (Source: From *Strategies for Managing Behavior Problems in the Classroom* (p. 157) by M. M. Kerr and C. M. Nelson, 1983, Columbus, OH: Charles E. Merrill Publishing Company. Copyright 1983 by Charles E. Merrill Publishing Company. Reprinted by permission.)

Time	Monday	Tuesday	Wednesday	Thursday	Friday	Saturday	Sunday
7:00	breakfast	snooze	breakfast	breakfast	breakfast	snooze	snooze
8:00	3 classes	breakfast	breakfast	3 classes	3 classes	breakfast	snooze
9:00	3 classes	2 classes	2 classes	3 classes	3 classes	free	breakfast
10:00	3 classes	2 classes	chapel break	3 classes	3 classes	free	breakfast
11:00	break / 1 class	break / 1 class	4 classes	break / 1 class	break / 1 class	free	free
12:00	lunch	lunch	4 classes	lunch	lunch	lunch	lunch
1:00	school meeting	3 classes	lunch	break	school meeting	free	free
2:00	2 classes	3 classes	free	2 classes	2 classes	free	free
3:00	2 classes	3 classes	free	2 classes	2 classes	free	free
4:00	free	free	free	free	free	free	free
5:00	free	free	free	free	free	free	free
6:00	free	free	free	free	free	dinner	dinner
7:00	dinner / free	dinner / free	dinner / free	dinner / free	dinner	free	free
8:00	mandatory study period	mandatory study period	mandatory study period	mandatory study period	free	free	mandatory study period
9:00	mandatory study period	mandatory study period	mandatory study period	mandatory study period	free	free	mandatory study period
10:00	free	free	free	free			free
11:00							

As of Friday, Sept. 11

Course	Grade

French level three .... |70|

comments _____ I was well prepared for the two small quizzes we had, one

on grammar and the other on vocabulary _____

American Literature Advanced .... |—|

comments _____ no grades thus far: working on a short paper due Monday—

will be our first grade _____

History .... |85|

comments _____ This is the same as last week. I expect a test next week. ____

Elementary Physics .... |41|

comments _____ I was barely able to grasp a simple principle and did poorly

on a quiz. Afterwards I went in for HELP. I understand it now. _____

Algebra and Trigonometry Advanced .... |90|

comments _____ I am keeping up so it is not so bad as I might have expected. ___

FIGURE 4–10

High school student's grade and progress monitoring form (Source: From *Strategies for Managing Behavior Problems in the Classroom* (p. 168) by M. M. Kerr and C. M. Nelson, 1983, Columbus, OH: Charles E. Merrill Publishing Company. Copyright 1983 by Charles E. Merrill Publishing Company. Reprinted by permission.)

The following statements describe *BEING RESPONSIVE* to the teacher:

1. raising your hand when the teacher asks a question	Y	N
2. getting out your book and turning to the chapter the teacher mentioned	Y	N
3. saying and doing nothing when the teacher asks a question	Y	N
4. trying to figure out a math problem the teacher wrote on the board	Y	N
5. taking out your homework when the teacher is standing at your desk, instead of when she told you to get it out at the beginning of the class	Y	N
6. saying the answer to yourself when the teacher asks the class a question	Y	N
7. raising your hand to ask a question	Y	N
8. volunteering to help the teacher	Y	N
9. volunteering to skip class	Y	N
10. sharpening your pencil	Y	N
11. listening to what your teacher is saying	Y	N
12. asking a friend for a piece of paper	Y	N
13. taking a test	Y	N
14. passing in your homework	Y	N
15. singing during class	Y	N
16. cleaning your glasses	Y	N
17. putting on nail polish	Y	N
18. answering the teacher when she speaks to you	Y	N

FIGURE 4–11
Student handout (Source: From *The School Survival Skills Curriculum* by N. Zigmond, M. M. Kerr, A. Schaeffer, G. Brown, and H. Farra, 1986, Pittsburgh: University of Pittsburgh. Adapted by permission.)

will enhance adolescents' awareness of how they conduct themselves during class times.

Peer-Mediated Strategies. Students are often aware of one another's in-class performance. Yet, until recently, we overlooked this valuable teaching resource. Reconsider peer interactions as a positive aspect of your classroom's environment rather than a force to be overcome. Naturally, one cannot teach while teenagers converse constantly, but one may be able to channel their interactions to produce better in-class behavior. Group goalsetting and feedback, described in Chapter Six, offer a structure in which adolescents share their feedback on each other's behavioral goals.

A group contingency for appropriate classroom behavior provides group reinforcers contingent upon the performance of the group members. To introduce the concept of on-task to students who will participate in a group contingency, ask these questions:

Which of these behaviors is on-task?

1. looking at the teacher while he is talking
2. taking out your books when the teacher tells you to
3. catching a quick snooze during a film
4. jotting down some notes during a film
5. writing a letter during a film
6. looking out the window
7. looking through your text while the teacher is busy
8. talking to your friends
9. reading your English book in math class

Figure 4–12 displays a group contingency worksheet used in our research on school survival skills. Notice that this group contingency has been combined with another effective strategy, self-monitoring. You may notice also that students were self-monitoring *several* school survival skills including on-task behavior.

Privileges or reinforcers awarded to adolescents could include:

- notebooks and other school supplies
- tickets to school functions
- bus or lunch tickets
- gasoline vouchers
- fast-food coupons

- the right to drop a low grade, select a guest speaker, or skip classwork or homework

Many businesses will donate the coupons or gift certificates used in school survival skills training.

Self-Mediated Strategies. We have described how self-monitoring can help adolescents develop new school survival skills. Figure 4–13 shows a self-monitoring form used in conjunction with the group contingency strategy. This form covers a week of monitoring for one selected class. In our experience, students succeed when their self-monitoring is limited in

---

WHAT YOU EARN FOR SELF-RECORDING

A. There are 12 different ways students may earn privileges for self-recording:

1. Bring back a *completed* self-record form.   _____

2. Go to class.   _____

3. Be on time.   _____

4. Bring a pen, pencil.   _____

5. Bring a notebook, paper.   _____

6. Bring a text.   _____

7. Record whether you used your assignment book.   _____

8.–12. Use your assignment book. (5 points)   _____

13. Record whether you were being on-task.   _____

14. Be on-task.   _____

15. Have your record match closely with the observer's record.   _____

B. After each student checks the list, we will add the numbers for the entire class.

For this week, this class must earn ____points (or __% of the total points possible) in order to receive privileges.

Week: _____ to _____

Student: _____

Adult Signature:_____

FIGURE 4–12

Group contingency form (Source: From *The School Survival Skills Curriculum* by N. Zigmond, M. M. Kerr, A. Schaeffer, G. Brown, and H. Farra, 1986, Pittsburgh: University of Pittsburgh. Adapted by permission.)

Name _____

Directions: Put a check (✓) if you did each step.
Put an X if you did not.

Date Given _____
Date Due _____

PERIOD	CLASS	ROOM		Monday Date:	Tuesday Date:	Wednesday Date:	Thursday Date:	Friday Date:
				Went to class ___ Got there on time ___	Went to class ___ Got there on time ___	Went to class ___ Got there on time ___	Went to class ___ Got there on time ___	Went to class ___ Got there on time ___
				Brought to class pen, pencil ___ notebook, ___ paper ___ text ___	Brought to class pen, pencil ___ notebook, ___ paper ___ text ___	Brought to class pen, pencil ___ notebook, ___ paper ___ text ___	Brought to class pen, pencil ___ notebook, ___ paper ___ text ___	Brought to class pen, pencil ___ notebook, ___ paper ___ text ___
				assignment book ___	assignment book ___	assignment book ___	assignment book ___	assignment book ___
				being on-task ___	being on-task ___	being on-task ___	being on-task ___	being on-task ___

FIGURE 4–13

Self-monitoring form (Source: From *The School Survival Skills Curriculum* by N. Zigmond, M. M. Kerr, A. Schaeffer, G. Brown, and H. Farra, 1986, Pittsburgh: University of Pittsburgh. Adapted by permission.)

one of two ways: (a) to one or two behaviors across classes, or (b) to several behaviors in only one class.

In summary, paying attention to classwork and to one's teacher is a crucial school survival skill. Yet many teenagers are unaware of their classroom behavior. Once the rules and expectations have been stated clearly, teachers may choose from several strategies, including direct teaching, group contingencies, and self-monitoring. Combining these interventions is an excellent approach to improving on-task behavior.

The case study for Chapter Four describes a strategy for getting students to come to class prepared. Class preparedness is an important prerequisite for the behaviors discussed in Chapter Five, "Improving Academic Performance."

SUMMARY

This chapter has addressed a relatively new but important aspect of educational programming for mildly handicapped adolescents: promoting school survival skills. We began with an introduction to the research, highlighting strategies to help students become more aware of school survival skills, including getting to classes on time, being prepared, participating in class, and getting along with teachers.

After this introduction, school-wide strategies that foster class attendance were reviewed. These interventions play an important role by supporting an individual classroom's rules and ensuring consistent expectations across a building. Teacher-mediated strategies often consist of skills lessons, such as those from the School Survival Skills Curriculum (Zigmond et al., 1986). Accompanying such didactic activities are strategies to improve generalization, or transfer of learning: self-monitoring and peer monitoring. These interventions greatly improve the chances that a student will practice school survival skills outside the special education classroom.

In conclusion, school survival skills interventions provide teenagers with important prerequisites to successful academic and interpersonal skills for less restrictive environments. Take a little extra time to include one or more of these strategies in your educational program.

RECOMMENDED READINGS

Lovitt, T. (1984). *Tactics for teaching.* Columbus, OH: Charles E. Merrill Publishing Company.

Zigmond, N., Kerr, M. M., Schaeffer, A. L., Brown, G. M., & Farra, H.E. (1986, September). *School Survival Skills Curriculum.* (Available from Department of Special Education, 5M30 Forbes Quadrangle, 230 Bouquet Street, University of Pittsburgh, Pittsburgh, Pennsylvania, 15260).

CASE STUDY

Employing Access to the Computer as a Reinforcer for Secondary Students

Recently, there has been an increase in the development and use of computer technology in special education (Bennett, 1982; Hofmeister,

Source: From "Employing access to the computer as a reinforcer for secondary students" by F. J. Salend and D. Santora, 1985, *Behavioral Disorders, 11,* 30–34. Copyright 1985 by *Behavioral Disorders.* Adapted by permission.

1982). Computers have been employed in a variety of ways by special education teachers and administrators (Chaffin, Maxwell & Thompson, 1982; Ragghianti & Miller, 1982). These uses include: (a) assessment of educational needs (Hasselbring & Crossland, 1981), (b) educational planning and management (Brown, 1982; Wilson, 1981), (c) direct and supplemental instruction (Thorkildsen, Bickel & Williams, 1979), (d) administration of special education programs (Ragghianti & Miller, 1982), (e) inservice and preservice training of special educators (Hofmeister & Thorkildsen, 1981) and (f) as prosthetic devices for physically handicapped and sensory-impaired students (Foulds, 1982; James, 1980).

One novel and practical use of the computer may be as a positive reinforcer to increase and maintain appropriate behavior. In such a system, access to the computer is contingent upon students demonstrating appropriate behavior. This use of computers in the classroom is based on the motivational aspects of computers (Frederiksen, Warren, Gillote & Weaver, 1982; Malone, 1981). While the motivational aspects of computers have been used to develop educational skills (Chaffin et al., 1982), there has been limited research to validate empirically the use of access to computers as a vehicle for promoting appropriate social behaviors. An extensive review of the literature revealed that no studies have examined the motivational value of computers for teaching appropriate social behaviors (Santora, 1983). The present study was developed to illustrate the use of access to computers as a positive reinforcer to increase appropriate social behaviors. In the study, the target behavior was to increase the number of times the students came to class prepared. Coming to class prepared was defined as attending class with the necessary work materials including textbooks, notebooks, writing utensils, and assignments.

METHOD

Subjects. A group of five high school students attending a mixed category resource room served as subjects in this study. Their ages ranged from 15 years, 0 months to 19 years, 2 months ($\bar{X} = 7 - 2$). Their IQ's as tested by the WISC-R ranged from 72 to 94 with a mean of 83. Three of the subjects were males and two were females. The group consisted of two twelfth-graders, two tenth-graders, and one ninth-grader.

Three of the students were labeled learning disabled and two were labeled mentally retarded by placement teams in accordance with New York State guidelines. They received their academic instruction (e.g., math, English, science, social studies) in a departmental regular education program with their nonhandicapped peers. In addition to their regular education placements, students in the group were attending the resource room program for remedial assistance in reading and math. All of the subjects were identified by their resource room teacher as "frequently coming to class unprepared" and "forgetting their materials."

Setting. This study was conducted during the group's daily resource room instructional period, which lasted from 11:15 A.M. to 12:40 P.M. and included a 30-minute lunch period from 11:40 to 12:10. The classroom was typical of many resource rooms in size, design, and availability of instructional materials.

The group's daily resource room was divided into two activities: assistance with their regular education assignments and individualized instruction in reading and math. Once every two weeks, the class was taken to the school's computer room to use the computer.

Experimental Design. The study employed a reversal design (Baer, Wolf & Risley, 1968). The procedures for evaluating the group's increase in coming to class prepared are described below.

Baseline 1. Prior to instituting the intervention, a frequency count was taken to measure the number of necessary work materials the students failed to bring to the daily resource room instructional period. The teacher reacted to each group member's being unprepared in her usual manner (reprimands, reminders) and made no unusual attempts to influence behavior. The baseline 1 period lasted six days.

Intervention 1. The intervention was an interdependent group positive reinforcement system whereby access to the computer was made contingent upon the entire group coming to class prepared. At the beginning of each session, the teacher noted if the students had come to class prepared (bringing the necessary textbooks, notebooks, writing utensils and assignments to class). If all the group members were prepared, the group earned access to the computer for 25 minutes. During this time, students worked on academic skill and drill programs and played academically oriented computer games. However, if a group member came to class unprepared, the entire group was denied access to the computer. Intervention 1 conditions were maintained for six days.

Following the baseline period, the teacher explained the intervention conditions to the group, including a description of the target behavior, the treatment conditions and the reinforcer (Salend & Ehrlich, 1983). When the teacher completed the review of the intervention, the subjects were quizzed on their knowledge of the intervention conditions by answering questions related to the teacher's explanation (Salend, 1985).

Baseline 2. This period replicated the conditions described in Baseline 1. Baseline 2 conditions lasted for nine days.

Intervention 2. This phase marked a return to the conditions described in Intervention 1. Intervention 2 conditions were maintained for seven days.

Reliability. Interobserver reliability measures were obtained by having two trained observers independently record the target behavior. Reliability was calculated by dividing the smaller number by the larger number for each observation and multiplying by 100 (Alberto & Troutman, 1982).

Interobserver reliability measures were taken on 29% of the sessions and across all the experimental phases. All reliability measures were 100%.

RESULTS

The results are presented in Figure 1. The findings revealed that access to the computers resulted in a substantial increase in the group's preparedness for class. The number of materials forgotten during Baseline 1 ranged from 6 to 7,

with a mean of 6.3. During the Intervention 1 phase, the group members were prepared for each session. The mean number of materials not brought to class during Baseline 2 was 2.8, with a range of 1 to 4. Data collected during Intervention 2 showed that the entire group was prepared for each session.

DISCUSSION

The results of this study suggest that access to computers can be an effective reinforcer for promoting appropriate behavior in special education classrooms. When access to the computer was made contingent upon coming to class prepared, all students came to class prepared. This finding is consistent with the research on positive reinforcement (Alberto & Troutman, 1982; Kazdin, 1975) and adds to the potential uses of computers in special education (Bennett, 1982; Hofmeister, 1982).

The motivational value of access to computers adds to the availability of reinforcers that teachers can employ in their classrooms to increase appropriate behavior. In fact, access to computers may be superior to other reinforcers used in schools because of the educational value of the computer. Thus, while appropriate social behaviors are being taught by earning access to the computer, educational skills are simultaneously being enhanced through direct exposure to the computer. For example, in this study while working on the computer, students were developing and practicing academic skills such as capitalization and decimals as well as keypunching skills. Furthermore, the teacher noted that the motivational value of the computer led to a decrease in other inappropriate behavior in the classroom as well as a 40%; increase in completed assignments.

The motivational aspects of the computer may have particular implications for teachers working with secondary level handicapped students. Frequently, secondary level teachers have difficulty identifying appropriate reinforcers for their students since traditional reinforcers available in the schools are generally appropriate for elementary rather than secondary students.

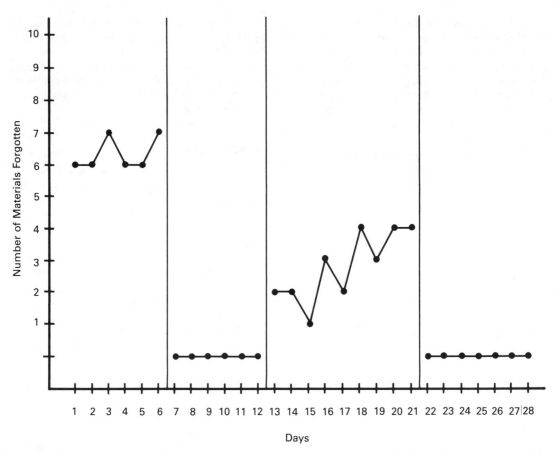

FIGURE 1
Coming to class unprepared

However, the computer provides secondary level teachers with an age-appropriate reinforcer for modifying behavior.

The uses and availability of computers for exceptional students are increasing. While most of the educational applications of computers are based on the technical capabilities of computers, the motivational value of computers can also be employed to assist educators in modifying behavior in the classroom.

CHAPTER
FIVE

Improving Academic
Performance

This chapter introduces strategies designed to motivate students to learn and teachers to teach. We address specific environmentally mediated, teacher-mediated, peer-mediated, and self-mediated classroom strategies. Now we turn to classroom-level strategies, beginning with environmental modifications.

ENVIRONMENTALLY MEDIATED STRATEGIES

Environmentally mediated strategies rely on changing the environment. Specific strategies include curriculum modifications, instructional time, the physical plan of the classroom, and scheduling.

Curriculum Modifications

First, the students' curriculum must be appropriate. For this to happen, the assessment of the students in your classes must be up-to-date and functional. Consult Chapters Two and Three for specific tips on how to use assessment tools and incorporate the findings into a comprehensive evaluation plan. Stowitschek, Gable, and Hendrickson (1980) offered these guidelines for selecting a curriculum:

1. Identify critical instructional variables important to the selection of instructional materials.
   a. What measurement variables help determine whether a material is appropriate for an individual prescription?
   b. What planning activities must be carried out before materials can be systematically selected?
   c. How do decisions about the types of teachers' formats to be used depend on the types of materials available or to be selected?
2. Select appropriate materials for an entire class of learners.

   a. What must I know about the curriculum I am responsible to teach before I can select materials for my class?
   b. What must I know about the materials I already have available before I can select materials for my class?
   c. Can I select appropriate materials sight unseen? What information sources are there?
   d. How do I go about thoroughly reviewing materials?
   e. Can I organize the information I accumulate about materials for easy access and later use?
3. Select materials that are appropriate for an individual prescription.
   a. Where do I get an individual prescription?
   b. How do I go about matching the information I have on the learner with the information I have on the materials? (p.21)

Curriculum Modification for Special Problems

You need certain **curriculum modifications** to support the student whose problem is dependency. Assisting a student by modifying assignments does not mean, however, that you should prevent the student from ever experiencing failures, as emphasized by Seligman (1975):

Creating shortcuts around [all] difficulties for children is not kind—depression follows from helplessness.

A sense of worth, mastery or self-esteem cannot be bestowed. It can only be earned: If it is given away, it ceases to be worth having, and it ceases to contribute to individual dignity. If we remove [all] obstacles, difficulties, anxiety, and competition from the lives of our young people, we may no longer see generations of young people who have a sense of dignity, power, and worth. (pp. 158–159)

The following guidelines for curricular modifications include ways to prevent a teenager experiencing repeated failure, which Seligman concludes can be demoralizing to a student's sense of self-worth achievement. We see the necessity of making the environment demanding but predictable, allowing the adolescent a sense of control and accomplishment.

1. Schedule ample time for a student working at a typical pace to complete the assignment.
2. Plan each student's task carefully to prevent students from complaining that a task is too long.
3. Place work materials in a designated storage area—off your desk—so that the student must take responsibility for picking up work.
4. Plan tasks that will challenge students but will occasionally allow them to experience some failure, so that they will learn how to handle frustration.
5. Let students know when an assignment is difficult or encompasses new knowledge or skills.
6. Do not keep students from knowing how they are performing. Help students to develop a sense of competence by sharing your evaluations with them.
7. Provide specific feedback on students' papers so that they can modify their performances accordingly. Use descriptive praise, too.
8. Do not assist students every time they request help. Establish guidelines for requesting help (perhaps a signaling device on the student's desk) and follow these guidelines.
9. Encourage students to help themselves by using the dictionary, reference books, or answer keys.
10. Encourage students to assist one another through peer monitoring or peer tutoring.
11. Give students lots of positive feedback on their performances. Encourage them to make positive statements about their own

work by asking questions ("How did you do in algebra today?" "Did you organize your study time well for this exam?").

Think of ways in which you can translate these guidelines into actual practice in your classroom or other school setting.

We all know, however, that by merely assessing, planning, and providing a curriculum we are not guaranteeing that students will work harder at their academic tasks. Let us consider some classroom variables that will promote productivity and a focus on schoolwork.

Instructional Time

The amount of time that students are engaged in active learning and instruction is the one variable consistently linked with academic achievement (Rosenshine, 1977). Reith, Polsgrove, Semmel, and Cohen (1980) manipulated the instructional time of a behaviorally disordered high school student with a long history of learning problems (functioning at the second-grade level on a standardized test). By merely increasing instructional time by 5 minutes, the student's acquisition and maintenance of reading words increased. By insisting that students get to class on time (see Chapter Four for some strategies for class attendance), starting right off with academics, and working "until the finish," you may significantly increase instructional time.

Arranging the order in which students receive their instruction is also an important learning variable. If a student is troubled with measuring up to the demands of the classroom because of failure to complete work, apply Premack's Principle (1959). Every student engages in certain activities more readily than others. These preferred choices, or high frequency behaviors, may be used to reinforce low frequency behaviors. In a study by Gallant, Sargeant, and Van Houten (1980), a student was allowed access to a highly preferred subject area (science) after accurately completing assignments in math and reading. This student's academic performance improved.

Placement of Work

Each student should be given a designated place to pick up daily work. For a secondary school student, a businesslike in/out filing tray may be suitable. Be sure to provide trays for all students so that you do not call attention to the student needing extra support.

Physical Plan of the Classroom

To maintain the "well-focused academic program" recommended in the alternative education literature, use the classroom environment wisely. Stop and take a look at the teaching setting. Is it interesting? Does it look well organized? Is it engaging to adolescents? Is it fresh, or has time lapsed since changing the visual displays that pertain to the academic material being taught that week? Here are some other suggestions to consider. In planning for handicapped adolescents, design a classroom environment that is highly predictable and orderly, but one that requires the student to be an active, responsible learner. Many of the ideas for changing the classroom environment have been presented in earlier chapters, but we review them here.

Scheduling. First, post a clear weekly schedule of class periods that accounts for time within 30-minute segments and accurately reflects how each student should spend her time. Many teachers have found it helpful to post a shorter daily schedule adjacent to the overall one for changeable aspects of the school day. For example, this schedule might include weekly sessions with a guidance counselor, special schoolwide events, or vacation days. Arrange a time to review the schedule with the student and

suggest that the student use a highlighter pen to mark special or important dates (when a term paper is due, when auditions for the school chorus are being held, when the deadline for ordering class rings is here).

Be sure the classroom has a large wall clock to help students who want to remain on schedule. It may also be useful in giving students some idea about how much time has elapsed during a work period and how much time remains for them to complete work. To assist teenagers in becoming independent in time management, announce *how much time is needed* in each assigned task. Because this task might vary from student to student, you might want to include a time range. In the following section, we describe strategies that build upon the environmental changes you have made. These teacher-mediated strategies are designed for classroom use.

TEACHER-MEDIATED STRATEGIES

First let us look at direct teaching activities to increase the students' productivity.

Teaching Academic Productivity: General Guidelines

Not all students have the skills to be academically focused during class time. You must *teach* the skills students need, and these include notetaking, listening to the main points of a lecture, reading for complete comprehension, setting academic priorities, and organizing work materials. We offered some tips for teaching school survival skills in Chapter Four. Here are some ideas for teaching academic skills:

1. The Association of American Publishers has published several superb pamphlets for college students. We believe that these booklets have very useful information for teens, too.
2. We suggest that you set aside at least 20 minutes each week (perhaps more time dur-

ing the first few weeks of school) to teach academically related skills. Although you may not find many materials for adolescents, we can recommend *College Study Skills* (Shepherd, 1983), a text written for college students.

3. Students tend to procrastinate. Try designing a teaching unit adapted from some of the excellent time-management books available. We recommend *Do It Now*. by E. C. Bliss (New York: Bantam, 1984). You might set aside special times during your classes to discuss sections of this or other goalsetting/ time-management textbooks.

4. Model the skills you want. Show students a sample page from your schedule book or lesson book. If you are a list-maker, share your ideas on organizing your daily tasks. Remember, if you are disorganized, you are not modeling the behaviors you seek.

5. Give students the opportunity to practice their skills. When directing a class activity or giving an assignment, mention the time limits. Ask students to respond to questions that tap their organizational planning (e.g., "About how long do you think it will take you to finish this assignment?" "How much of this chapter do you expect we'll finish before Friday?") Remind students to write things down, with deadlines. Have spot-checks on assignments books—a good habit to begin in the middle school years.

6. Reinforce students when they exhibit academic productivity. Give bonus points for students who demonstrate that they are using these skills (e.g., extra points for assignments turned in early). Incorporate these skills into your contingency management program (e.g., token economy, contingency contract).

7. Allow students to learn these skills from one another. Hold group discussions in which students are prepared to offer one another suggestions on study skills. Let teenagers tell how they might organize their academic tasks—you may be pleasantly surprised!

8. Spend time with students individually, when you can, to find out how they go about studying and doing classwork. Let them know that you are interested in them and their productivity. Listen to teenagers explain how they approach a task. See if you can gently offer better strategies.

Listening to and watching teenage students is a great way to alter the teaching pace and to be more effective. In the next section, we offer suggestions for adjusting the style in which you teach and the rate at which you cover materials.

Adjusting Teaching Pace and Style

After several years of teaching, you may find yourself in a rut. Having presented the same materials year after year, you may think your lectures are set in concrete! Perhaps you should take a look at a few simple observational strategies that give you clues about how your audience is reacting to your lecture:

1. Watch the pencils of the students taking notes. Focus on one writer who seems representative of the group. Can you pace the lecture so that, if the student appears to be having trouble keeping up, you pause, giving the student notetaker a chance to catch up? Or, is the student even able to take notes? Has the student already given up because he could not follow the outline? Ask students at the end of a class if they felt they were able to take notes. By checking students' notebooks, you can gauge whether the lecture's major points are being transcribed accurately. An award-winning professor at Duke University once commented that his criterion for a successful lecture was whether students' notes closely matched his lecture notes.

2. Select an "average" student to serve as an informal visual guide to the understanding

level of the students. Does this individual look puzzled? Or does the student appear interested, as though she is following what you are saying? You may choose to formalize this little signal, by having students give you a signal (thumbs up, for example) at periodic intervals, to indicate their understanding of the lecture.

3. Ask students to give feedback on aspects of your teaching style. To maximize the information you will get, focus your questions on a particular lecture, project, or assignment. Attach a brief rating form or questionnaire to the students' papers. Figure 5–1 shows one example. If this seems a little threatening, remember that you are in control of the feedback—what you do with it is entirely up to you. We think you will find the feedback not only interesting but helpful.

Motivating Student Performance with Grades

In both the effective schools' and the alternative schools' literatures, the theme of motivation is obvious. Grades are one of the most naturally and frequently occurring reinforcers at the middle and high school levels. Students receive grades on homework, quizzes, projects, tests, and periodic report cards. We usually judge students on academic performance, and we hope higher grades serve as stronger reinforcers than lower grades. Grades are sometimes overlooked as reinforcers, because professionals assume that students, especially those doing poorly, are disinterested in grades. However, a recent study by Rousseau, Poulson, and Salzberg (1984) examined a grade effectiveness package to increase academic productivity. They found two ways to make grades more powerful reinforcers:

1. Treat grades as conditioned reinforcers (as in a token program) to strengthen back-up reinforcers.
2. Enhance the contingent relationship between student performance and grades.

Translate these findings to help strengthen academic behaviors in your class. For example, provide grades more immediately and more

FIGURE 5–1

Student questionnaire (yes/no)

1. Could you follow my lecture?
2. Did you feel like you understood the main points?
3. Did you feel you had a sufficient amount of time to record the information?
4. Do you like having the lecture outlined ahead of time on the blackboard?
5. Did the lecture seem organized?
6. Did the lecture seem relevant?

Comments: _____
_____
_____
_____
_____
_____
_____
_____
_____
_____

often after appropriate academic completion of a lesson. Announce definite contingencies between grades and academic performance to motivate the class one step further. Also, if you assign a lot of homework that counts significantly toward a student's final grade, be sure to provide immediate feedback. Place emphasis on effort and ability. Always incorporate homework practices into the lesson plans and tests, so students see its importance. When grades look poor and skills seem deficient, offer support and clear instruction to help remedy the problem. Grades can indeed be motivating, even for those students with a poor track record, if the above recommendations are followed.

Public Posting

Public posting is another effective strategy that you can easily implement in your classroom. Students' academic behavior and productivity improves when performance feedback is publicly displayed on a daily or weekly basis (Fink & Carnine, 1975; Van Houten, 1979; Van Houten & LaiFatt, 1981). Display quiz and test scores, attendance, or number of academic units completed in the curricula. For example, your students might be independently pacing themselves. You can display visually the various check-off points along the way to ensure understanding as they move through their lessons. You may decide that students have to read so many sections of their social studies text, take a test, pass at a pre-established criterion level, and then go ahead. When they pass, give them a visible mark on the classroom poster. If they fail to reach the criterion level, give them remedial materials and later retest them. Having the various assignments task-analyzed and highlighted before them can be monitoring in itself. According to Van Houten and Van Houten (1977), public posting promotes peer comments that are motivating. Public posting, and its elements of program charting, communicates to your students that you have multiple

expectations of them that are to be achieved on a continuous basis. Recall from the literature on effective schools the importance of high academic expectations.

Assigning Homework

Characteristically, the secondary curriculum is based on content acquisition. That is, everyone expects students to have earned basic skills *prior* to their arrival in high school or middle school. However, many students simply have not met this goal. For these students homework is essential.

Before homework is assigned, there are three *M*s to consider.

Meaning. Do not assign work unless it is meaningful. To expect students to do their assigned work, the practice must be meaningful and challenging. Although common sense dictates this tenet, it is easily ignored.

Modeling. Do not assign new material for practice: instead, model the procedure first. If the model is confusing or incorrect, the lesson is lost. Model the behavior and reinforce it with practice examples.

Monitoring. Student homework should be consistently monitored to ensure that work is being practiced correctly. Do not introduce new concepts via homework, otherwise the students might practice errors. The following are guidelines for assigning homework.

1. *How much of a task?* The smallest amount of a task that retains the most meaning is all that should be practiced at one time. Break the instructional task into small, meaningful parts that relate to the large concept being introduced.
2. *How long is the task?* Short, intense, and highly motivated practice periods produce more learning that is better remembered than do long, drawn-out periods. In class, schedule short practice intervals.

3. *How often?* The answer depends on whether new learning or old learning is occurring. If practice is for reinforcement of old learning, then it should be distributed over longer periods.
4. *How well?* Always offer specific feedback, and do it immediately.
5. *How important?* It is a good idea to include homework problems on quizzes and tests to convey the message to the students that skill practice (or homework) is critical enough to be tested. (Material adapted from PRISM and writing of Madeline Hunter) (Pittsburgh Research-based Instructional Supervisory Model, PRISM Manual, Pittsburgh, PA, 1985).

Strategy Teaching

The work of Deshler and his colleagues at the Learning Disabilities Institute at the Univeristy of Kansas (1981) has much to offer the teacher of mildly handicapped adolescents. While space does not permit an in-depth coverage of the findings of this group, we would like to highlight some of their recommendations for teaching. (We urge you to consult the reports of the Institute for more details.) Deshler et al. have provided a good outline for selecting instructional strategies for learning-disabled youth. Here is a summary of the steps:

1. Analyze current learning habit. Ask your students to perform the first task requiring the target skill. Give the students feedback on their performance and allow them to be involved.
2. Describe the new strategy. Describe to your students the steps involved in the new strategy. For example, "First, you will listen to me read you a paragraph. Then, you will ask yourself some questions that you think I might ask. See if you remembered what you heard. I will then ask you some questions. Were our questions similar?" As you describe each step, explain its purpose so the

students will be more likely to want to learn the listening strategy.
3. Model the new strategy. Show the class the strategy that was just described. Encourage questions if the students look confused.
4. Verbally rehearse the strategy steps. Ask your students to repeat the steps involved. This will encourage self-instruction.
5. Give students practice in controlled materials. When the students demonstrate mastery of the steps, choose controlled materials (adapted materials) such as high-interest, low-vocabulary materials, for practice. A key component here is the repetition and practice you give the students.
6. Allow student practice in classroom materials. Teach students specifically how to translate skills learned in "special education" to "regular education." Refer to our section on **generalization training**. Obtain regular classroom materials for the purpose of teaching steps in generalization.

As you can see, you must first teach the strategies in isolation, practice them, and then try them in regular settings. In a study by Deshler et al. (1981), students were taught to detect and correct errors in passages written by their teacher. The following steps in Table 5–1 illustrate the use of strategies that were developed by Deshler and his colleagues. This error-monitoring learning strategy is easy to use, for the instructional sequencing is very clear and specific. You can adapt materials or generate your own writing passages. Have your students detect the errors and provide them with feedback. This instructional procedure appears to be effective in teaching error monitoring to mildly handicapped adolescents.

Most likely, your students need to acquire this learning strategy because it is one that offers practical and continued application. Again, the importance of modeling, feedback, and analysis is highlighted. As a teacher, you can use and adapt this strategy in a number of ways.

TABLE 5–1
Teacher instructional steps for teaching a monitoring strategy

Step 1: Test to Determine the Student's Current Monitoring Skills
The teacher tested the student's monitoring skills first in the teacher-generated materials at both ability and grade level and then in a passage written by the student himself. After testing, the teacher discussed the results with the student, affirming that the student exhibited a deficit in the way he monitored for errors and, as a result, left a number of errors in his work.

Step 2: Describe the Error-Monitoring Strategy
The teacher described the steps involved in the Error-Monitoring Strategy and contrasted them with the student's current checking habits. The steps included the specific behaviors in which the student should engage and the sequence of behaviors that should be followed.

Step 3: Model the Strategy
The teacher modeled the Error-Monitoring Strategy for the student. The teacher demonstrated the strategy by acting out each of the steps previously described to the student while "thinking aloud" so the student could witness all of the processes involved in the strategy.

Step 4: Verbal Rehearsal of the Strategy
The student verbally rehearsed the steps involved in the Error-Monitoring Strategy to a criterion of 100% correct without prompts. This instructional step was designed to familiarize the student with the steps of the strategy such that he could instruct himself in the future as to what to do next when performing the strategy.

Step 5: Practice in Ability-Level, Teacher-Generated Materials
The student practiced applying the strategy to successive passages written at his current reading level. This reduced the demands on the student such that he could concentrate on the application of the new strategy. As the student became proficient in monitoring, he was encouraged to progress from overt self-instruction to covert self-instruction while practicing the strategy.

Step 6: Feedback
The teacher gave the student positive and corrective feedback after he completed monitoring each passage. When the student received a criterion of detecting and correcting 90% of the errors in a given passage, the student went on to Step 7.

Step 7: Test on Teacher-Generated Passages
The student received two tests in teacher-generated passages, one at ability level and one at grade level. These provided measures of each student's progress in learning the strategy. If the student reached criterion on the ability-level test but not on the grade-level test, Steps 5 and 6 were repeated using grade-level materials. If the student reached criterion on both tests, the student progressed to Step 8.

Step 8: Individual Analysis of Common Errors
The teacher analyzed the types of errors the student commonly was making in his own written work. The student and teacher used products the student had recently written. The result of this analysis was a list of the kinds of errors the student should be specifically careful to monitor. The list was secured in the student's notebook.

Step 9: Practice in Student-Generated Paragraphs
The student was instructed to write a paragraph and to apply the monitoring strategy to that paragraph.

continued

TABLE 5–1
(continued)

Step 10: Feedback

Each time the student completed monitoring a new paragraph, the teacher gave the student positive and corrective feedback about his use of the monitoring strategy to detect and correct errors. Steps 9 and 10 were recycled until the student's final copy of a paragraph had fewer than one error for every 20 words.

Step 11: Test on Student-Generated Paragraph

The student was asked to write a paragraph and monitor the paragraph as a final test of his monitoring skills.

Source: From *Teacher Instructional Steps for Teaching a Monitoring Strategy* (pp. 6–8) by J. B. Schumaker, D. D. Deshler, S. Nolan, F. L. Clark, G. R. Alley and M. M. Warner, 1981, Lawrence, KS: Institute for Research and Learning Disabilities, Research Report #32. Adapted by permission.

Think about other skill areas in which you can apply this same approach.

The recommendations of Deshler and his colleagues focus on strategy teaching, including these areas:

1. Self-questioning—Teach students to question or judge their responses to academic and social situations. For example, "Jamey, you just finished writing a paper on the Guadalupe Mountains National Park in Texas. Does your paper answer the many questions you had on the park, prior to your researching the material?" Encourage them to give you reports on their perception of their performance to improve their self-awareness.

2. Questioning strategies—We encourage you to involve your students in the teaching process. Teach students to ask different kinds of questions to elicit various responses. Model the behaviors and teach them these four types of questions:
   a. Cognitive memory questions. This entails review, offering facts, labeling, defining, and describing. For example, "Can you name each type of questioning strategy for me?"
   b. Convergent thinking questions. Ask students to think in terms of relationships, which involves reasoning, principles, conclusions, or inferences, such as, "What important data do you think should be examined to discover the Challenger's problem with its solid booster rocket?"
   c. Divergent thinking. Ask them to create novel ideas to generate a number of varied answers, such as, "Describe the ways you would have students go to school for six months of the year and have them accomplish as much as they do in a nine-month period."
   d. Evaluative thinking questions. Have your students offer opinions, based on given criteria. For example, "Based on the information in the February 15, 1986, *Newsweek* article, describe the ways you would balance our country's budget?"

3. Visual imagery—Instruct students to think of a picture that might be associated with the reading passage. This should aid students in increasing their analytical skills and reading comprehension. For example, if the students are reading about the six moons of Uranus, have them visualize the earth and its moon and Uranus and its moons.

4. Paragraph writing—Essentially, students can be taught to organize their thoughts into complete sentences and write appropriate

transitions that form readable paragraphs. Besides improving the quality of paragraphs, the quality of the student's writing will also be positively affected. Sonntag and McLaughlin (1984) demonstrated that students could be trained to improve their organizational skills in paragraph writing.

5. Error monitoring—As teachers, we need to monitor constantly for errors and teach our students to monitor their own and their peers' errors. Corrective feedback is crucial at *all* stages of learning.

6. Notetaking—Deshler organizes notetaking into two categories, formal and informal, that should be taught. *Informal notetaking* refers to students' spontaneous writing of notes from lectures or oral assignments. Here, accuracy and order are key variables, inasmuch as the material introduced by the teacher may be mentioned only once. When students record information, in their own language, we call this *formal* notetaking. You can teach ways to organize, label, and outline textbook material. Show your students ways to abbreviate and use symbols, to make notetaking easier and more efficient. As we mentioned earlier, you can go over major points in your lecture or provide students with handouts prior to beginning the class. See Chapter Four to review other school survival skills.

Deshler and his colleagues also pay close attention to two important learning concepts, feedback and generalization.

Feedback

Offer feedback, especially when teaching students *new* material. Feedback, like praise, should be descriptive, as well as corrective. In a study by Kastelen, Nickel, and McLaughlin (1984) the efficacy of a feedback system was demonstrated for secondary students needing to improve their academic and on-task behavior. Besides emphasizing academic ability, focus on student effort. When skills *are* deficient, offer support and skill instruction. When a student makes an error, pinpoint its occurrence, correct it, and try to prevent it from recurring. Because words like yes, no, right, or wrong do not always have a strong impact on students, *always* provide feedback that is corrective or descriptive. When correcting a student, prevent the situation from becoming intimidating. Just remember you are correcting the student to help him just as you would with any other procedure used for learning acquisition. In the textbook *Applying behavior-analysis procedures with children and youth*, Sulzer-Azaroff and Mayer (1977) remind us to use a "corrective procedure" when students are solving problems or answering questions. They note the importance of pausing prior to introducing a correction, to prevent inadvertent reinforcing of the student's error. Also, have the teenager practice the correct response. Earlier, we noted both the importance of motivating students with grades and feedback and the efficacy of public posting because of the continuous performance feedback they provide. Feedback alone, or combined with other strategies, is vital in any learning situation!

Generalization Training

Successfully reintegrating your students into the mainstream of school life constitutes one of your most complex and difficult tasks. Not only must you evaluate and develop appropriate pupil behaviors, you must also coordinate a number of environmental variables including schedules, curricula, materials, school staff, and other pupils. A technology for achieving this change is sorely lacking; however, we can offer suggestions and guidelines based upon our experiences and those reported by others. We begin with the assumption that you have improved the student's academic and social functioning to the point where she is able to profit from a less restrictive environment. Once this assumption is met, the issue becomes one of generalization and maintenance of behavior change, which necessarily involves arrangements with other persons.

In general, the issue of movement to a less restrictive environment is referred to as generalization training, the transfer of skills from the student's present environment (e.g., a self-contained classroom) to a new environment (e.g., a regular classroom). You need to plan for these transitions. Therefore, we offer you the following guidelines to assist you in this important process.

1. Teach behaviors that will continue to be reinforced by the natural environment (e.g., teach the pupil to sit quietly after finishing an assignment, to raise his hand before speaking, to look at the person who is speaking to him, to ask for feedback or acknowledgement).
2. Train the person in the natural environment to deliver contingent consequences (e.g., to respond to your pupil only when she has obtained permission to speak, to praise a student for waiting her turn or for cooperating with another pupil).
3. Make the contingencies of reinforcement less clear and less predictable (e.g., by delaying reinforcement, by using intermittent schedules of reinforcement).
4. Use stimuli likely to be found in both settings (e.g., move students out of study carrels into group desk arrangements, write assignments on the board instead of in individual folders, fade out points in favor of social praise and grades).
5. Employ self-management training (e.g., ask students to check and evaluate their own work and keep track of their own progress, teach them to praise themselves—"I did a good job").

6. Provide opportunities for generalizations to occur within the special classroom and reinforce at least some of these (e.g., ask pupils to submit their papers to your aide for grading, use other students to prompt and reinforce target behaviors) (Kazdin & Bootzin, 1972; Kerr & Nelson, 1983; Stokes & Baer, 1977).

Let us examine each of these six principles and reflect upon how we might use them to plan the transition program.

1. *Teach Behaviors That Will Be Reinforced in Regular Education.* To begin this task of preparing students academically for regular education placement (or to help them bring their performance up as close as possible to regular education students' performances), several simple steps must be taken:
   a. Copies of relevant regular education textbooks must be available in your classroom. Instructors' guides must also be available.
   b. You should be involved in as many curriculum workshops and departmental meetings as is feasible, so that you remain aware of changes in the curriculum and of innovative teaching strategies within these basal areas.
   c. Emphasize those academic-related behaviors that you know regular educators view as critical.
2. *Train Regular Educators to Deliver Contingencies.* This principle refers to the importance of getting regular educators to give contingent reinforcement to your students in their classrooms. It is difficult for most teachers to stay abreast of their own verbal behavior without some assistance. It will be most important that you build into the program some specific activities to ensure that students who are trying out the mainstream get recognition for their efforts:

a. Self-contained classroom and regular classroom report forms allow the regular educator to report to you on a daily basis. We should select only a few target behaviors, define them carefully, and ask regular educators to communicate with us on them.

b. The feedback loop on a student's behavior in regular education should be continued in the home, giving parents feedback on which skills the student is learning in the new environment.

3. *Make Contingencies Less Predictable*. It is important that students not go "cold turkey" when they come into regular education. So often our classrooms are filled with tangible reinforcers, leading students to expect these and to be disappointed when they arrive in regular, less restrictive environments. As much as possible, the contingencies of reinforcment in your classroom should be on a variable schedule, and the items or activities used for reinforcement should pattern themselves as much as possible on regular education activities.

4. *Use Stimuli Found in Regular Education Settings*. This fourth principle is extremely important to keep in mind when planning the environment. Some portion of each day should be allocated to "acting like regular education," also. Asking a couple of regular educators for their ideas about "arranging" your classroom might give you some insights.

Keep in mind that one of the adjustments students must make in regular education is to a much smaller amount of one-to-one attention. This modification is an important aspect of making the special education environment have stimuli likely to be found in the regular education environment. Under group activities we discussed the importance of preparing students for all kinds of group situations.

5. *Employ Self-Management Training*. Self-management is a new strategy in special education, which we discuss later on in this chapter.

6. *Provide Opportunities for Generalizations within the Special Classroom*. This principle refers to the chance we all have to create generalization within our classroom. For example, let students interact with more than one teacher and receive some of their instruction from other students. Let students work in different settings.

We in special education are always torn between structure and sameness and the necessity to generalize across trainers, settings, and conditions. It is a real dilemma! Recommendations to consider to help with this dilemma are discussed under peer-mediated and self-mediated strategies.

Using Different Media

Deshler and his colleagues found that learning-disabled adolescents responded more favorably when three approaches to content instruction were used:

1. Audio-taped textbooks, which present content orally to students. (If you decide to focus on this approach, remember to train oral listening before you begin.)

2. Controlled texts, or adapted materials designed to facilitate learning. Features such as reading level, organization, and presentation of visuals are controlled.

3. Variety in classroom presentations, creating a more dynamic learning environment.

Contingency Contracting

Contracts can help adolescents improve their academic performance, as demonstrated in a number of studies (Kelley & Stokes, 1982). The special procedure is explained in Chapter Six, but we would like to illustrate how it can be used for academic targets. In our case study at the end of this chapter, the teacher used a contract. Here are some additional target behaviors for you to consider:

- Amount of time on task.
- Academic productivity (number of correct math problems, number of new foreign vocabulary words, and number of new words introduced in writing).
- Rate of work.

Kelley and Stokes (1982) summarized the advantages of establishing a contracting procedure as follows:

- Goal setting permits both parties to negotiate the amount of behaviors required to earn a contingent reward.
- This procedure has all of the advantages of a self-management strategy, without all of the responsibilities.
- Academic productivity can be directly targeted.
- Defining and achieving goals gives students a sense of accomplishment.

Token Economies

This important contingency management system is explained in detail in the next chapter. In a token economy students receive tokens (points, chips) for performance. In return, they may "spend" these tokens for back-up reinforcers they choose from a large menu. Deshler and his colleagues at the Learning Disabilities Institute found that motivating students within a token economy was a good way to enhance their learning. The same examples of target academic behaviors that you used for contracting can be used in a token economy.

Figure 5–2 shows a simple token economy chart for a resource room. Notice that each student is given a place to mark his own progress. Each space of the box (there are four spaces) allows one day's check— accomplished by coloring in the space as shown. In this program, no checking was done on Friday, the reinforcement day. This chart was designed for students who spend one period per day (the chart depicts names of students for one period) in the resource room.

Combining Strategies

In a study by Smith, Schumaker, Schaeffer, and Sherman (1982) students were trained to improve classroom participation. Positive changes occurred in a classroom previously troubled by disruptive behavior and poor group discussion. The key variables included teacher-posted rules for discussions, praise for student contributions, teacher restatement of the contribution, teacher-outlined discussion questions, graded student contributions, and public posting. Table 5–2 displays an expanded version of the steps used to promote classroom discussion.

We highlighted this study because it represents an excellent "combination intervention." Here students are given clear direction, feedback, reinforcement, praise, and public recognition. The teacher also helped students with their notetaking strategies, inasmuch as an outline or a list of questions was always provided before each discussion. Students took notes, previewed the material, and then prepared themselves for appropriate classroom discussion. We can assume that grades served as effective reinforcers, because classroom discussion and participation improved. A response cost was also included in a clear hierarchy of expectations. Think about all of the various strategies we have discussed. Some of these strategies work effectively alone, but combining strategies is a creative way of getting good results!

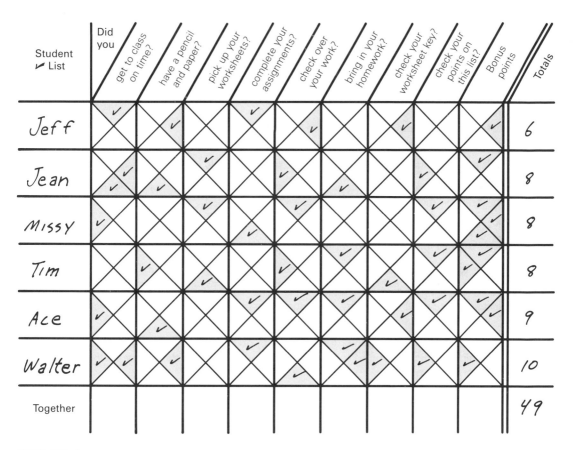

FIGURE 5–2
Token economy monitoring chart: Resource room

PEER-MEDIATED STRATEGIES

In this section, we describe strategies that involve a target student's classmates, who play a major role in improving that student's academic performance. Sometimes the entire class is involved in a peer-mediated intervention, helping one another in pairs. We offer you three peer-mediated strategies: peer tutoring, peer homework monitoring, and **peer-mediated task analysis**. All of these interventions work to involve students in each other's learning.

Structured Peer Tutoring

As teachers, we face the reality of limited time for individualized teaching, especially if we work in regular education with large classes. One option is to try peer tutoring. This intervention promotes reinforcement, modeling, immediate feedback, and teaching. A large body of research supports the benefits of peer tutors, who can be:

■ effective in increasing test and quiz performance and work completion of tutors and tutees (Maher, 1984);

TABLE 5-2
Ten steps to promote classroom discussion

Step 1. Hand out this list of rules pertaining to the discussion procedures. The rules for the students are as follows:
1. Raise your hand when you have something to say.
2. Speak only when you are called on.
3. If classmate is called on, put your hand down and listen quietly.
4. If you have something to add after your classmate is finished, raise your hand again.

Step 2. Explain to the class why you think classroom discussion is important.

Step 3. Designate a "recorder" to mark a point for student contributions that appear relevant. Contributions can be in the form of a question, answer, or comment.

Step 4. Give examples of relevant statements.

Step 5. Give examples of irrelevant statements.

Step 6. Explain to the class and the classroom recorder that one point will be subtracted for irrelevant statements and disruptions (e.g., out of seat, talking out, or hand waving).

Step 7. Discuss your discipline hierarchy. If anyone loses three points during one discussion period, she will be sent to the office and will have to attend an afternoon detention.

Step 8. Let the students know that their total number of points earned or lost will determine their daily grade. Explain the point system as follows (the difference between the number of points earned and the number of points lost):

Six or more = A
Five = A-
Four = B+
Three = B
Two = B-
One = C+
No points = C
Minus One = C-
Minus Two = D
Minus Three = F

Step 9. Post the weekly average of the discussion grades.

Step 10. At the end of the semester, average the weekly grades, and convert them to 25% of their final grade.

---

*Source: The material for this table was taken from "Increasing Participation and Improving the Quality of Discussions in Seventh-Grade Social Studies Classes" by B. M. Smith, J. B. Schumaker, J. Schaeffer, and J. A. Sherman, 1982, *Journal of Applied Behavior Analysis, 15,* p. 99.

- trained to reinforce tutees' on-task behavior with verbal approval (Greer & Polirstock, 1982);
- capable of influencing positive academic responses incompatible with deviant classroom behavior (Gable & Kerr, 1980);
- significant in providing instruction in basic skills (Ruffin, Lambert, & Kerr, 1985; Sindeler, 1982);
- effective in providing supplemental support to teachers and students during after-school hours;

- at least as effective as traditional teaching methods (Jenkins, Mayhall, Peschka, & Jenkins, 1974; Morrisey, 1981);
- change agents helpful in improving social goals.

Peer tutoring relies upon the principles of peer modeling and peer teaching. The peer tutor has to be a student who wants to do the tutoring, has the skills in the content area, can follow teacher directions, and can learn from a model. Use your judgment when pairing up students for tutoring. Do not select a tutor who may embarrass the target student (e.g., a regular class student who may criticize the special education student). When using a cross-age peer tutor (someone from another class), plan a schedule with the other that is mutually convenient and decide how to evaluate the tutoring student's involvement.

The selection of the task for peer tutoring is an important step. Give first priority to the subject area in which the target student has difficulty. Choose academic tasks that are best taught through a "model or prompt + feedback or praise" format. Good choices could include spelling, vocabulary, sight words, foreign language vocabulary, math facts, scientific formulae, dates and names in social studies. Select academic tasks that require discrete responses and simple evaluation procedures (e.g., written tally of corrects and errors: sorting flashcards into mastered and nonmastered piles). Plan tasks that require relatively brief 15- to 20-minute sessions. Guidelines for tutor training would include the following.

1. Select the task and analyze it before beginning.
2. Select and create the necessary materials.
3. Explain the goal of the tutoring.
4. Explain the tutoring task to the tutor.
5. Instruct the tutor in the use of materials.

6. Explain the monitoring and feedback form.
7. Spend sufficient time on record keeping.
8. Use many questions like, "After you do this, what do you do next?"
9. Instruct the tutor in the use of giving praise.
10. Explain the necessity of confirming correct response and correcting errors in a nonpunitive way.
11. Train students to avoid overprompting.
12. Explain that training should not exceed 1 hour. (This material was adapted from Jenkins & Jenkins, 1985; Kerr & Nelson, 1983; Morrissey, 1981.)

Monitoring, a key ingredient for a successful tutoring program, can be easily accomplished. Figure 5–3 shows a simple form that takes little time to complete.

The tutor records the name of the tutee and the amount of time tutored, rates tutee performance, and offers comments or suggestions (e.g., statements about attendance, behavior, and mastery).

Figure 5–4 offers a tutee evaluation form that can be used for secondary school students. This form provides the student with an opportunity to keep records on her own, and it allows you an opportunity to determine the amount of time the students are devoting to academic tasks, the subject areas to be reviewed, the number of objectives covered, and whether or not the students feel they have mastered their goals (Ruffin, Lambert, & Kerr, 1985).

Unstructured Peer Tutoring

In addition to structuring the peer tutoring sessions, encourage students to teach and monitor each other during unstructured times. Prevent students from wasting time in study hall, for example. In lieu of the typical independent study format, have students work together in dyads or triads. Good tasks for students who work

Tutee: _____ Time: _____ minutes

Subject: Math   Reading   Spelling   English
                Science   Foreign Languages
                Social Studies   History   Other

Mastered: _____ objectives (problem, pages, items)

Comments: _____
_____
_____
_____

FIGURE 5–3

Tutee evaluation form (Source: From "Volunteers: An Extraordinary Resource" by
C. Ruffin, D. Lambert, and M. M. Kerr, 1985, *The Pointer, 29*, pp. 30–38. Reprinted with
permission of the Helen Dwight Reid Educational Foundation. Published by Heldref Publications, 4000 Albemarle St., N.W. Washington, D.C. 20016. Copyright © 1985.)

together are calling out spelling words, quiz-
zing each other on names and dates in history,
drilling each other on new science vocabulary,
and proofreading a partner's writing.

Peer Homework Monitoring

Peer monitoring of homework assignments is
a straightforward procedure for students willing to help each other towards the goal of meeting homework due dates. As you may recall,
meeting due dates was considered a top priority
school survival skill. All homework should be
monitored, as we mentioned in the section on
teacher-mediated strategies. In this intervention, paired students remind each other about
homework completion on a daily basis. A
Homework Completion Checklist (displayed in
Figure 5–5) structures this 5- to 10-minute activity. Students initial their partners' checklists
when the assignments have been finished. You
can encourage students to remind each other
about significant deadlines. Also, have them review written and oral directions to ensure understanding. (Following directions, you will recall, was another highly rated school survival

skill.) Here are some questions that students
can ask each other to check on accuracy of the
homework:

1. Did you complete your assignments?
2. Did you put your name on the paper, the
   class, the teacher's name, and the date?
3. Did you check your spelling and punctuation?
4. Did you take notes?
5. Did you bring your assignment, your
   assignment book, your notebook, and textbook?
6. Did you write down the assignment in your
   assignment book?
7. Do you understand the assignment for
   tonight?
8. Do you have your book and notebook for
   tonight's homework?
9. When are you doing your work tonight?
10. How long do you think your homework
    will take?

The monitoring/teacher role allows students to
take some responsibility for each others' learning. Our experience tells us that students rise
to the occasion and often pleasantly surprise
teachers with their results.

Tutee Name	Reading—Vocabulary	Reading—Comprehension	Reading—Word Attack Skills and Pronunciation	Math—Drill Review	Math—Homework	Phonics	Spelling	English—Review	English—Homework				Time Tutored in Minutes	Comments

Rating Score Guidelines

☐ = Tutee did not attend session at all

1 = Tutee attended but showed poor performance. For example:
   —tutee arrived too late, left too early to work
   —tutee refused to work
   —student forgot books and assignments

2 = Tutee worked hard but did not understand concepts or problems. For example:
   —tutee worked on 1 of 10 problems

3 = Tutee did not complete assignments or complete assigned work. For example:
   —tutee showed some interest; finished a few homework problems; needs to concentrate, easily distracted

4 = Tutee completed 90% of all homework and mastered all but the most difficult problems.
   —tutee completed English assignment and reading assignment, had difficulty with 5 of 15 problems

5 = Tutee had excellent session. Tutee completed all homework and/or all assigned work. (Tutee must also show mastery of all work to attain this score.) For example:
   —tutee finished math, social studies homework, and completed 2 review worksheets in long division

FIGURE 5–4

Tutor monitoring form (Source: From "Volunteers: An Extraordinary Resource" by C. Ruffin, D. Lambert, and M. M. Kerr, 1985, *The Pointer, 29*, pp. 30–38. Reprinted with permission of the Helen Dwight Reid Educational Foundation. Published by Heldref Publications, 4000 Albemarle St., N.W. Washington, D.C. 20016. Copyright © 1985.)

Directions: Please put an X in the right box.

This homework assignment is:

	YES	NO
1. turned in on time	☐	☐
2. complete	☐	☐
3. neat and easy to read	☐	☐
4. done according to directions	☐	☐

Student: _____

Date: _____

Class: _____

Checker: _____
(initial)

Did you call to remind your partner? ☐ ☐

This homework assignment is:

	YES	NO
1. turned in on time	☐	☐
2. complete	☐	☐
3. neat and easy to read	☐	☐
4. done according to directions	☐	☐

Student: _____

Date: _____

Class: _____

Checker: _____
(initial)

Did you call to remind your partner? ☐ ☐

This homework assignment is:

	YES	NO
1. turned in on time	☐	☐
2. complete	☐	☐
3. neat and easy to read	☐	☐
4. done according to directions	☐	☐

Student: _____

Date: _____

Class: _____

Checker: _____
(initial)

Did you call to remind your partner? ☐ ☐

FIGURE 5–5
Daily homework completion checklist

Peer-Mediated Task Analysis

Peer-mediated task analysis allows peers to help each other break major academic tasks into smaller, more manageable ones. School, after all, is a challenging place for adolescents, yet adults do not always have the time to help students individually sort out their academic headaches. These are examples of the academic situations that occasionally overwhelm even the best students:

- getting along with teacher
- taking the SAT or the GRE

- finishing homework assignments on time
- getting good grades
- finding enough time to meet academic deadlines
- getting into the "right" college
- preparing adequately for final exams

In this intervention, teenagers choose a partner and take turns listening (and advising) and talking (and worrying). Figure 5–6 displays the form used to structure this interview.

Your role is to encourage each "listener" to help his partner pinpoint challenging situations

---

1. Ask your partner to tell you *three* things that are stressful for him these days at school. Listen carefully, then write down what your partner told you.

    a. _____

    _____

    b. _____

    _____

    c. _____

    _____

2. Were you a good listener? Read to your partner what you wrote down about the stressful things he described. Did you get the main points? Is there something you missed? If so, write it down now.

    a. _____

    _____

    b. _____

    _____

    c. _____

    _____

3. Have your partner choose *one* academically related problem to work on later. Write it down.

    _____

    _____

4. Now, switch roles and do this exercise again.

FIGURE 5–6
Peer interview

and plan a sequence of problem-solving steps. Teach students to be supportive and not critical of their partners' academic dilemmas. Instruct the "listener" to record two or three things that seem stressful for the partner who is talking. The partner then checks to see if his main points were recorded accurately. In the final step, the speaker chooses one problem for the dyad to task-analyze. Then the pair works together to break the chosen problem into manageable steps. This sequence is depicted in Figure 5–7.

SELF-MEDIATED STRATEGIES

This portion of the chapter deals with strategies in which the target student learns and applies skills of self-control. Self-control techniques include *self-monitoring*, *self-evaluation*, and *self-reinforcement*. Self-monitoring, or self-recording, is a strategy in which students record their own behaviors. Self-evaluation, or **self-assessment**, allows students to judge their own performance as compared with a predesignated criterion. Self-reinforcement, as the name implies, gives a teenager the chance to reward himself for meeting a behavioral or academic goal (Kerr & Nelson, 1983). Perhaps one of the most significant reasons to employ self-mediated strategies in the secondary school stated can be summarized by Rueda, Rutherford, and Howell (1980):

Along with the transmission of information and acquisition of academic and social skills, the schools have as their primary objective the facilitation of children's learning to independently manage their own behavior. (p.188)

These strategies are the "new wave" in special education; most of the research supporting them has taken place only in the past decade or so. Nevertheless, the findings are promising, especially for mildly handicapped youth. These strategies can be applied for a variety of academic reasons ranging from increasing on-task behavior to increasing classroom participation.

Self-Monitoring

Such procedures are considered particularly appropriate for facilitating the educational success of handicapped students in mainstream environments, where resources for external management programs may be limited. One self-control procedure which has been proven effective for increasing on-task behaviors is self-monitoring. (Sabatos, 1986, p.23)

Chapter Four offered guidelines for using self-monitoring with teenagers learning school survival skills. To orient you to self-recording with *academic* target behaviors, here are a few examples:

- Marielena will record the number of problems she correctly solves in algebra on each daily assignment. (Mrs. Stuttman will provide an answer key.)
- Michel will record the number of new, foreign language vocabulary words he learned in a 15-minute sitting. (Mrs. deLaTorre) will give out flashcards before the drill session.)
- Sarah will record the number of spelling words learned each night.
- Carlos will write down the amount of time he caught himself off-task during his first study hall period.

Figure 5–8 illustrates the monitoring forms that would be used for each of these students. In a variation of self-recording, Kneedler and Hallahan (1981) conducted a series of studies in which students heard cues from a tape recorder to prompt their self-recording. Academic production and on-task behavior increased, and the cuing was faded easily. This procedure might work in a resource room, though it is probably too complicated for a regular classroom.

Encourage students to correct their own spelling. Materials should be readily accessible so students *can* correct their spelling without your help. You can provide other sources, like glossaries, so students can consult the appropriate terms and

Stressful Situation: A major test is coming up in Algebra next week, and I'm lost!

Goal: To pass the test with a C or better.

Steps	Who or What Can Help	Estimate of Time Needed	I Did It!
1. Borrow friends notes for days I missed.	Nakea can lend me her Algebra notebook.	1 hour	
2. Rewrite my class notes, using Algebra text to help.	myself and textbook	1 or 2 periods	
3. Review odd problems and check answers in back of book.	myself	1½ hours	
4. Make a sample study test with sample problems.	myself	30 minutes	
5. Work sample problems with partner.	Dean and/or after school tutoring sessions (2x)	3 hours	
6. Set up an appointment with Mr. Venesky to review confusing concepts.	Mr. Venesky (Algebra teacher)	1 or 2 periods	
7.			
8.			

FIGURE 5–7

Task analysis of partner's academic problems

FIGURE 5–8

Sample self-monitoring forms

Student: _____ Week of: _____
Record the number of problems you solved correctly. Use your answer key!
Monday ____ Tuesday ____ Wednesday ____ Thursday ____ Friday ____
(If you do not have algebra, then mark the line with X.)

---

l'etudiant: _____ l'institutrice: _____
les mots:
_____ : c e _____ : c e
_____ : c e _____ : c e
_____ : c e _____ : c e
_____ : c e _____ : c e
_____ : c e _____ : c e
Les directions:
_____
_____

Dear Sarah,
   Attached is your spelling list for this week. Please record below how many words you mastered each night. Don't forget that the spelling test is on Tuesday! Please have your parent sign this note at the end of the week.

Miss Carlisle

_____

Mon. = ____ Tues. = ____ Wed. = ____ Thurs. = ____ Fri. = ____
signed : _____ date: _____

_____
_____
_____

Give yourself a check each time you think you are off-task. Remember: off-task means doing something that does not help you finish your assignments!

ascertain the correct spelling of specialized reading—again without your assistance. If you discover that this tactic is not working, then an alternative strategy can be implemented. Perhaps students can exchange their papers and proofread each other's work. Many times we discover that students are unaware that they repeatedly misspell or misuse words. You will probably be surprised at how well certain students check or edit their classmate's work.

As mentioned earlier, students can be given answer keys to check their work and record their grades. We encourage you to perform an occasional spot check to discourage cheating. Assignments can also be exchanged, and students can monitor one another's errors and record the grades of their peers. Many of the principles behind these self-monitoring strategies can be applied to peer-mediated ones. Your system of self-monitoring can also be expanded by adding new components.

Self-Evaluation

After introducing self-monitoring strategies, your next step may be students' self-evaluation. Workman (1982) defined self-assessment as the systematic examination of a student's own behavior and the evaluation of whether or not he performed a targeted behavior or group of behaviors.

Many adolescents constantly evaluate their own behavior. For example, each time they receive a grade, they decide whether the grade was fair or not according to their evaluation of their work performance.

For fun, you might want to give your class the following quiz (Figure 5–9). This gives them an opportunity to evaluate their academic goalsetting, while providing you with some very valuable information. If you discover that the majority of your students are responding No to the questions, perhaps you can offer the guidelines for academic goalsetting that are discussed under teacher-mediated strategies.

Unfortunately, some teenagers are unaccustomed to evaluating their behavior, and it is necessary to train them directly to do so. Two simple procedures to facilitate self-evaluation are graphing and charting (or using a checklist). These two approaches allow the student to summarize the results of his self-monitoring (or your monitoring), then evaluate accordingly. Figure 5–10 illustrates a student graph, while Figure 5–11 shows a student's self-designed evaluation form. Tying self-evaluation to goals that you and the student have set for academic performance is a good combined intervention. Remember the importance of reinforcing students (or letting students reinforce themselves) when they reach their goals or master successive approximations to their goals.

FIGURE 5–9
Academic goalsetting, self-mediated

Give Yourself the Following Quiz   (Yes/No)
1. Do I have in writing a list of goals this semester (i.e., Do I know what kind of grades I'm trying to earn in each class)?
2. When I need help with my work, do I do something about it?
3. Do I plan enough time in my day to get my homework finished on time?
4. When studying, do I try to plan as much as possible in terms of importance (i.e., Do I record important due dates)?

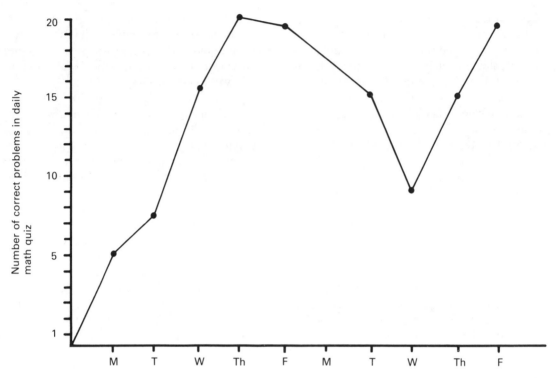

FIGURE 5–10
Gregory's self-monitoring graph

Self-Evaluation Combined with External Procedures

As we have mentioned before, you will often want to combine strategies. In a study by Cohen, Polsgrove, and Reith (1980), teenagers learned to evaluate their own academic performance (oral reading). To give you an idea of how self-management can be combined with other strategies (i.e., **token reinforcement**), here is an excerpt from the research study, showing the steps the students followed:

For each of the ten days [of the goalsetting phase], the teacher assigned one academic and one on-task goal per child at the start of each 15-minute period. These were written on computer cards fastened to each student's desk. The goals

assigned for the initial time period involved a description of the maximum number of oral reading errors allowable as well as a subjective description regarding the duration of on-task behavior; e.g., "try and stay on your work for the entire 15 minutes."

Academic goals for the latter period stated the number of problems to be completed correctly. [During the self-evaluation phase] the teacher continued to specify each student's academic and on-task behavior goals and then to rate their performance at the end of each 15-minute time interval. Each child was permitted to self-assign a maximum of 10 points on their goals cards—five each for academic and on-task behavior, per interval. The teacher kept private ratings of their behavior, giving only general feedback regarding the accuracy of their self-evaluations each day.

Classroom Discussion					
	M	T	W	Th	F
1:05					
1:20					
1:35					
1:55					

Each time the timer goes off, mark down whether or not you've been participating in our group discussion. Give yourself a " − " if you haven't been participating at all, a " + " if you've participated a little, and a " + + " if you've participated a great deal.

FIGURE 5–11
Tammy's self-evaluation form

[During an "external," token phase] the teacher assigned goals, rated students' performances, and informed each student of the number of points awarded for academic and social behavior following each 15-minute time interval. These points were exchangeable daily for back-up reinforcers.

[During a "matching" phase] the children were again required to evaluate their performance and to try to match the teacher's ratings of their behavior. (pp.144-145)

To fade the procedure, the teacher gradually introduced nonmatching days, so that students were required to match the teacher ratings on only two out of three, then one out of three days, and so on.

This illustration may give you ideas to consider in your own classroom, where you have already set up other forms of contingency management. In our case study, for example, self-management is combined with contingency contracting, a common practice.

Self-Reinforcement

The final strategy of the self-management group is self-reinforcement. This procedure helps students with the other self-control components, because it affords them rewards for their efforts. We urge you, therefore, to consider self-reinforcement whenever you adopt one of the other self-control procedures. Here are some steps for self-reinforcement of academic behaviors. These guidelines are taken from Workman (1982, pp. 76-77), a text that you might want to consult for more details.

1. Target the specific academic behavior you want. (See the list of examples for self-monitoring.)
2. Design a monitoring form (again, look at the examples in Figures 5–10 and 5–11).
3. Teach the self-monitoring steps to the student.
4. Select your back-up reinforcers (these may or may not be linked to a contingency contract or token economy).
5. Establish a level of desired performance (do not forget to shape the successive approxi-

mations to your ultimate goal). If the student performs at this level she will receive reinforcement. We would recommend that you start with a level 10 to 20% above the student's current level of performance.
6. Explain the program to the student. Be sure you tell students when they will have access to the reinforcers they earn.
7. Begin!

Reducing Teacher Assistance in Self-Management Programs

A critical feature of a successful self-management program is the fading out of your participation in your student's program. Once a student has shown consistent ability to self-monitor, self-evaluate, and self-reinforce, you can reduce your involvement in the program. Consider the steps outlined in Figure 5–12 for middle school students. For high school students, this "game"

1. For self-management programs that involve a group of students, divide the group into two teams. List students' names, according to teams, on the chalkboard.
2. Announce that only one group will be lucky and have their self-management records checked each day. The same group will be eligible for bonus points.
3. Flip a coin each afternoon, designating one group as heads and one group as tails. The winning team has self-monitoring cards checked for reliability with teacher records. If each member of the team has a reliable score, team members then win bonus points or reinforcers.
4. Remember, promote the idea that being checked is a privilege.
5. Continue this procedure for at least seven school days.
6. During the next stage of the fading program, announce that a new game is beginning.
7. Place all students' names, written on paper strips, into a jar. Draw two names each day. These two lucky students receive the opportunity to earn bonus points or reinforcers.
8. After a period of at least seven school days, adjust the program so that you draw only one name. Maintain this stage of the program for at least one school week.
9. At the completion of the final phase, checking is discontinued.

FIGURE 5–12
Guidelines for reducing teacher input in a middle-school self-management program (Source: From *Self-Management for Teachers* by F. Alford, 1980, Nashville, TN: George Peabody College for Teachers.) (Some of the ideas were based on Drabman, Spitalnik, and O'Leary, 1973.)

would not be appropriate. Instead, meet with the student to discuss termination of the self-evaluation activities and to recognize achievement of the student's goal. Figure 5–13 depicts one high school student's report to his parents and liaison counselor. He used this weekly form as a follow-up to a more systematic, daily self-monitoring.

Figure 5–14 displays a contract designed to promote independent classwork. Both strategies highlight ways you can involve the students in self-management strategies, while allowing you to fade your involvement.

As of Friday, Feb. 11 (Second week of second semester)

<u>Course</u>   Grade

French level three.. 70

comments *I was well prepared for the two small quizzes we had, one on grammar and the other on vocabulary.*

American Literature Advanced.. —

comments *no grades thus far: working on a short paper due Monday — will be our first grade*

History 85

comments *This is the same as last week. I expect a test next week.*

Elementary Physics... 41

comments *I was barely able to grasp a simple principle and did poorly on quiz. Afterwards I went in for HELP. I understand it now.*

Algebra and Trigonometry Advanced.. 90

comments *I am keeping up so it is not so bad as I might have expected.*

FIGURE 5–13

High school student's grade and progress monitoring form

This contract between _Janice_ and _Mrs. Gedekoh_
    (Student)   (Teacher)

and is effective on _2/17/86_ .
                    (Date)

I, Janice agree to try these behaviors.
    (1) to stop and think, "Do I really need help?", before calling
on the teacher.
    (2) to use at least one other source of help before calling on

Mrs. Gedekoh .

These other sources are:

textbook glossary
blackboard
partner (English and social studies)

_____

    (3) to check off on my "help" sheet which kind of help I tried
to use.

My goal is to have at least three (✓) per English period, showing that I
tried to use other kinds of help.

_____

If _Janice_ meets her goal, I, _Mrs. Gedekoh_ will
provide her with an extra 5 points on the assignment for that period. If
there was no graded assignment, she will be issued a 5 point credit to
be used when she chooses.

- -

Signed: _Janice Ruffin_ Date: _2/17/86_
                        (Student)
Signed: _Mrs. S. Gedekoh_ Date: _2/17/86_
                        (Teacher)
Signed: _M. Christopher Cantrel_ Date: _2/17/86_
                        (Principal)

We will review this contract on _2/21/86_ .
                                (Date)

FIGURE 5–14
Contract to promote independent classwork

SUMMARY

We introduced strategies designed to motivate students to learn and teachers to teach. This chapter addressed specific classroom level strategies—environmentally mediated, teacher mediated, peer mediated, and self-mediated. It has been our experience when teaching, supervising, or consulting that teachers are hungry for practical teaching strategies for academics. We included strategies for the classroom teacher as well as peer-mediated and self-mediated strategies, which can be teacher directed and can also take advantage of other resources available to you.

Some of the specific ideas included under environmentally mediated strategies were curriculum modification, instructional time, physical plan of the classroom, and scheduling. The section on teacher-mediated strategies included comprehensive coverage ranging from teaching academic productivity to the using of a token economy. Other areas targeted included adjusting your teaching pace and style, motivating student performance with grades, public posting, assignment of homework, strategy teaching (emphasizing information gathered from Deshler and his colleagues at the Learning Disabilities Institute at the University of Kansas), notetaking, feedback, generalization training, using different media, and contin-

gency contracting. We know that peers are also a viable resource, and we included strategies like structured and unstructured peer tutoring, peer homework monitoring, and peer-mediated task analysis. Lastly, under self-mediated strategies we included monitoring, evaluation, and reinforcement techniques to enable students to improve their awareness of their academic behavior.

We now present a case study with a self-recording program that combines self-mediated and peer-mediated techniques to improve the academic behavior of a specific individual and the entire classroom group.

RECOMMENDED READINGS

Deshler, D. D., Alley, G. R., Warner, M.M., & Schumaker, J. B. (1981). Instructional practices for promoting skill acquisition and generalization in severely learning disabled adolescents. *Learning Disabilities Quarterly, 4*, 415-421.

Morrisey, P. A. (1981). *A guide for teachers: How to set up a peer tutoring system in your classroom.* Series No. 4. Bloomington, IN: Center for Innovation in Teaching the Handicapped, Indiana University.

Rousseau, J. K., Poulson, C. L., & Salzberg, C. L. (1984). Naturalistic procedures for homework participation by inner-city middle school students. *Education and Treatment of Children, 7,* 1-15.

CASE STUDY

Using Self-Monitoring Procedures to Increase Academic Behavior

PROBLEM

As a teacher in a junior high class for socially and emotionally disturbed students, I decided that Thomas needed special attention. He was a very disorganized student who was quickly falling behind. The behaviors I was most concerned

about included accuracy of his algebra work (in-class assignment and homework completion). For the last two weeks, Thomas had been inconsistent in turning in homework. I suspected a rate of about 50%. I noticed other students in my class of fifteen were also experiencing "winter blues'' and appearing lackadaisical about their assignments. I would classify the majority of my classroom as capable, but disinterested.

While observing Thomas, I noted that he produced quality work when I gave him individual attention. I decided to write his regular classroom teachers to discover whether his behavior was any better in their classes. His science teacher, Ms. Ruffin, says he appears to be bright, but incapable of completing his work. There are times she knows he works on his assignment in class, but the work never makes it to the file. I wanted to be more directive and to establish a workable strategy. Before my zealous efforts got the best of me, I planned to assess accurately the problem behaviors. I wanted to focus on Thomas, and include the other class members because all needed to improve their work habits.

ASSESSMENT

The behaviors I targeted were work accuracy and task completion in algebra. My first concern was to go through the grade book and deduce the percentage of accuracy and assignment completion in algebra. I tallied the total numbers of assignments completed in the last week. The average percentage of accuracy was 64. (Accuracy ranged between 49% and 88%.) I then went through my grade book and averaged the percentages of work the students turned in. Of my students, 65% were turning in their homework on time.

INTERVENTION

I spoke with Thomas and explained to him that I was developing a self-recording program for the class to make everyone aware of their work performance. To strengthen his intervention, I decided to write up a simple contract to establish agreed-upon goals for algebra class. His mother had called me two weeks earlier, out of concern for her son. She wanted to be involved. We discussed his work and agreed on two behaviors. Figure 1 displays a contract between Thomas, his teacher, and his mother.

The next week I assigned algebra problems on a daily basis. I explained to the class the results I found from their last week's performance. I then described the monitoring system that our class was going to implement. I handed out self-recording forms for each student to fill out (see Figure 2). Each day my students were to check whether they turned in their homework. After I graded their papers, they were to record their scores. I was going to compare their recordings with my records in the grade book. I would also display the results daily. I was hoping the process of self-monitoring would serve as a prompt for work completion and accuracy. For an added incentive, I was going to award the students 5 extra points each for their next quiz grade, if the class met an average criterion of 90% homework completion with 80% accuracy for the first week.

Two sources of potential reinforcement as part of the intervention were used:

1. Social reinforcement—praise from myself and classmates.
2. Self-reinforcement—from the classroom recording.
3. Token reinforcement—from points added to the lowest grades if the class met a criterion level of performance.

OUTCOME

After one week of the student self-monitoring program, the students were completing their homework with a 90% turn-in rate. Thomas was receiving additional attention, as his mother supplied positive social reinforcement and reinforcement of extra television provisions contingent on his work contract. The first week he turned his homework in every day, and the second week he had a turn-in rate of 85%. I was also pleased to see that students were evaluating their daily work with my answer key. Self-monitoring promoted independence, which the students appeared to enjoy. Going through the grade book, I realized that everyone's homework performance improved. I was glad I targeted accuracy of assignments to encourage appropriate completion

This contract between _Thomas_ and _Mrs. Maola_
                              (Student)   (Teacher)

and is effective on _1/16_ .
                          (Date)

I, _Thomas_ agree to try these behaviors.
   (1) to complete my daily assignments in algebra
   (2) to check homework with an answer key
   (3) to ask for assistance when score is below 80% and ask
      for a remedial sheet.

   My goal is to have at least 4 out of 5 assignments turned in, with an average of 80%.

If _Thomas_ meets his goal, I, _Mrs. Maola_ will

provide him with 5 points on any assignment grade. I, _M. O'Rourke_ will provide Thomas with 30 minutes of TV.

Signed: _Thomas O'Rourke_
                          (Student)

Signed: _P. G. Maola_
                          (Teacher)

Signed: _Miriam O'Rourke_
                          (Mother)

We will review this contract on _1/25_ .
                                    (Date)

FIGURE 1
Contract to promote self-monitoring for work completion

of homework. Figure 3 demonstrates homework accuracy ranging from 76% to 89% during week 1 and 88% to 93% during week 2. (Recall that before the intervention accuracy ranged from 49% to 88%.)

The program was successful because everyone involved supported each other's efforts to improve academic behavior. I became aware of the importance of providing attention for priority behaviors. I was especially pleased that Thomas's work performance improved dramatically. According to his mother, Thomas began to take school more seriously with the added attention. I am happy that I did not single Thomas

Weekly Homework Monitoring	
Algebra I _____	Period _____
Name _____	Week of _____
Monday Turned in Yes ____ No ____ score _____	Tuesday Turned in Yes ____ No ____ score _____
Wednesday Turned in Yes ____ No ____ score _____	Thursday Turned in Yes ____ No ____ score _____
Friday Turned in Yes ____ No ____ score _____	Weekly Total # Turned in Average score _____

FIGURE 2

Self-monitoring form

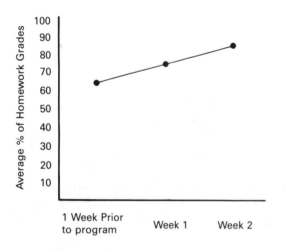

FIGURE 3

Average percentage of correct problems in daily algebra assignments

out, although implementing the contract seemed to be meaningful to him. The contracting system allowed the mother involvement with an already established classroom program. The contract, although successful, was discontinued after the two-week trial period because it was no longer necessary. The self-monitoring program with its self-evaluation component was easy to implement and successful in many ways. I plan to keep parts of the program constantly in motion. The targeted behaviors and reinforcers might vary, but the program will continue in some form.

CHAPTER
SIX

Decreasing
Behavioral Problems

This chapter addresses problem behaviors that interfere with learning and school success. The focus of the chapter is on strategies, or interventions. First, we describe school-wide procedures that prevent or deter management problems. After this initial look at strategies, you will find classroom-level recommendations for environmentally mediated, teacher-mediated, peer-mediated, and self-mediated interventions.

SCHOOL-WIDE INTERVENTIONS

This section describes behavior management approaches taken by districts or by schools, as compared with the classroom-level strategies illustrated later. Most all school districts have adopted some of the practices described here, including:

- discipline codes
- detention
- in-school suspension
- out-of-school suspension

We believe that your own personal disciplinary style is inextricably tied to the school's policies. Furthermore, you may have opportunities to improve your school-wide policies, so it is important to know as much as you can about the principles underlying them.

Discipline Codes

Nearly every school system operates under a general discipline code that individual principals revise to meet the particular needs in their buildings. To be maximally effective, be sure that you have a good working knowledge of the code in force in your building. To take an even more active role, join your building's discipline committee. One of the ways to assist your school is to help design effective rules of conduct. Let us review the "rules about rules" (Worell & Nelson, 1974).

Rules Should Be Reasonable. You may need to create different rules for different situations. For example, "no talking out" in the cafeteria would hardly be fair, although the same rule might facilitate class discussions in another setting. When rules are unfair, students are forced to test them, creating unnecessary power struggles. Whenever possible, include students' input for developing rules.

Rules Must Be Stated Behaviorally and Be Enforceable. For example, "Respect others" is ambiguous. Furthermore, it is difficult to enforce, because it invites different opinions about what constitutes disrespect.

Select the Fewest Rules Possible. Two problems arise when you state too many rules. First, students may find the rules too difficult to remember. Second, the rules may be so specific that students can easily find exceptions to them.

Be Sure That the Rules Carry Consistent Consequences. Research has shown that rules are virtually ineffective unless students receive clear feedback for following the rules (reinforcement) and for rule violations (negative consequences) (Madsen, Becker, & Thomas, 1968; O'Leary, Becker, Evans, & Sudargas, 1969; Walker, 1979).

In preparing a discipline code for the school, try to follow the guidelines generally accepted for classroom rules. You will also need to acknowledge the system-wide impact of your decisions. For example, recognize the issues in scheduling teachers for special disciplinary duties required to enforce a particular rule.

A successful discipline code represents a continuum of disciplinary alternatives. In contrast, teachers often face *limited* options when a student is disruptive. Check to see if your discipline code offers several levels of punishment before out-of-school measures are taken (e.g., home suspension).

Each component of the discipline code should be communicated to parents, staff, students, and administrators. Too often, discipline codes change without the proper communication to those close to the problems. Failure to communicate revisions in the discipline code may cause students to suspect "foul play"—capricious changes in the rules.

Successful discipline codes involve students. While students should never have the final say in a disciplinary action, it *is* important for them to be adequately and fairly represented in the development of rules and consequences. As an example, students may be surveyed about their opinions on discipline. Figure 6–1 displays sections from a middle school student interview. This questionnaire helped the authors study disciplinary practices in a large urban school system. Students agreed on several simple changes to improve the discipline code.

You can sample student opinions, too. (To get a good sample, we interviewed in-school suspension students as well as "average" students.) At least once a year, ask students to review the disciplinary codes. If an interview format takes too much time, then try this approach: Ask students during the homeroom period to vote on one particular issue. For example, "How many of you think we should have unidirectional traffic on the staircases ?" or "How many of you think that we should change the four-minute (between classes) rule ?" The outcome of this poll may enlighten the staff's review.

Even the best discipline code needs periodic revision. Many schools have formed discipline committees to offer questions and suggestions for disciplinary codes. These team approaches help, especially if the committee members do not use the meeting times solely to complain about individual problem students. Minutes of the meetings can be distributed to the rest of the school staff to maintain good communication about revisions in the rules. In turn, teach-ers can announce changes to students during homerooms or assemblies.

Underlying the discipline code should be a clear understanding of adolescent development. As an experienced middle school teacher defended her brief listing of rules, "Some battles are just not worth fighting!" The transition from elementary school to middle school represents major changes in the attitudes of both teachers and students. A discipline code must be sensitive to teenagers' increasing social sophistication, sense of situational ethics, and reasoning skills. For example, it is inappropriate to expect a teenager to walk silently down the hall or to ask the teacher for each and every trip to the restroom.

All disciplinary communications should be written as simply and clearly as possible, to ensure that the parents and students understand them. (For a reference on how to analyze readability, see Gilliland, 1974, pp. 100-101.)

Disciplinary Actions

Because school systems' discipline codes predominantly describe rules and the punishments that follow rule infractions, we would like to call attention to the guidelines for using punishment. First, let us review the typical continuum of disciplinary consequences, or aversives, found in a school system. This continuum is illustrated in Figure 6–2. Verbal consequences take place most often and allow you and the student to remain in a normal educational setting. Response cost (or the removal of privileges) is another relatively non-intrusive punisher. Detention, in-school suspension, and **home suspension** require changes in educational arrangement and change the student's regular schedule and setting for instruction. Finally, **expulsion**, or forcing a student to leave school altogether, is the most disciplinary consequence the school can issue.

Identifying Information
Name of child interviewed: _____
Grade: _____
Age: _____
Number of years in this school: _____
ISS: _____ Other: _____

Interview Questions
1. How do you like this school? Can you give us a rating on a scale of one to ten with ten being the best school possible?
   1 2 3 4 5 6 7 8 9 10

2. Do you think most kids seem to feel the same way you do about this school?
   Yes   No

3. Do you think that the kids in this school behave about the same as kids in other schools? Or would you say that they behave better? Worse?

4. What kinds of things do kids do here that get them into trouble with the adults? Can you think of four different things?
   1. _____
   2. _____
   3. _____
   4. _____

   Which of these problems do you think happens the most?

   Which one happens next most often? etc.?

5. What do you think makes these problems happen?

6. About how many kids at this school have these problems—for example, out of every ten how many would you say have these problems?

7. Do you think the rules at this school help children to behave?
   Yes   No

8. Are there any rules that you would change?
   Yes   No

   Which ones?

9. Would you say that teachers in this building stick by the rules?
   Yes   No

FIGURE 6–1
Student interview on disciplinary practices

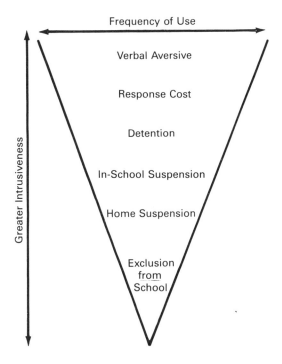

Frequency of Use

Greater Intrusiveness

Verbal Aversive

Response Cost

Detention

In-School Suspension

Home Suspension

Exclusion from School

FIGURE 6–2

Continuum of aversives (Source: From *Strategies for Managing Behavior Problems in the Classroom* (p. 87) by M. M. Kerr and C. M. Nelson. Columbus, OH: Charles E. Merrill Publishing Company, 1983. Copyright 1983 by Charles E. Merrill Publishing Company. Reprinted by permission.)

Table 6–1 gives guidelines for the use of punishment in school settings. This advice pertains to the more intrusive and severe punishments from our hierarchy.

Detention

Suspension in the in-school suspension room or at home ordinarily is preceded by a lesser punishment, detention. Detention may take place before or after school and usually involves a 30- to 90-minute period in which the students must complete assignments. These assignments may come from the regular class-room teacher or they may be specially assigned by the detention duty teacher.

Planning Detention. Here are some issues to keep in mind at the beginning of the school year when you are planning a school-wide or individual teacher's detention program:

1. Determine students' transportation options *before* you need to assign detention. At the beginning of each school term, contact parents to explain detention and work out transportation. Then make a list of students who are eligible if the occasion for detention should ever arise. This eliminates the awkward situation created when a teacher attempts to enforce an unworkable arrangement.

2. Establish certain days and times for detentions, rather than tying up precious time every school day that could otherwise be used for planning and conferences. This limited schedule also allows you to pay close attention to the detention students without having your time divided by other activities.

3. Think ahead about the assignments you want a student to complete. Directing students to complete the work they did not complete in class may not be feasible if the work requires your instruction, or special materials (e.g., film, lab equipment, reference books).

Implementing Detention. Once you have made the appropriate plans for detention, you may want to consider the following implementation guidelines:

1. Detention should be assigned through detention slips, written forms that explain to the student the rule violation and note the date of the assigned detention. These detention assignment forms should be simple to use, even in the hall between classes, when a teacher may stop a student for a hall violation. That is, the slips should be small and convenient for teachers who are

TABLE 6–1
Points to be considered before using aversive procedures

1. All reasonable positive alternatives should have been considered, if not actually tried, before decision is made to use an aversive procedure. Documentation of this exploration of alternatives is desirable.

2. Thorough knowledge of state and local regulation of the use of punishment and aversives should be sought. In addition, knowledge of recent local court actions and general public opinion is desirable. If there are state regulations that apply to noneducational agencies, for example, institutions supervised by the department of welfare, information about the standards they apply would be helpful in defining defensible practice for the schools.

3. Educators should be public about their intent to use punishing procedures and maintain careful records on the decision process followed as well as frequency of use, nature, and results. Discussion and criticism should be invited prior to use.

4. The line of authority and responsibility for decisions about the use of punishment must be clear, and a plan for continuing supervision and advice on policy by a committee of qualified persons, including an independent child advocate, should be implemented. Specific dates should be set for review of case material. As a further safeguard against abuse, the review should require that those planning the use of aversive procedures occasionally experience them themselves at a level of intensity similar to that being used in the program.

5. Be certain that all staff who will be using punishing procedures or observing their use understand the complex dynamics of punishment situations. Some important factors which have been more thoroughly discussed in the papers are:
   a. Certain student characteristics, mostly associated with low social status and antisocial, "acting out" behavior, put students having them more "at risk" of punishment than their classmates. Punishers should be on guard against any tendency to punish such students too quickly or severely.
   b. Individual continuums of aversiveness exist for any given set of punishing procedures. The reactions of the punished persons are the test, not those of the punisher.
   c. Punishing or aversive procedures must be adjusted to the characteristics of the individual student such as age, temperament, physical strength and sensitivity to pain, as well as to the nature of the behavior the punisher wishes to suppress.

Source: From "Punishment and Special Education: Some Concluding Comments" by F. Wood. In *Punishment and Aversive Stimulation in Special Education: Legal, Theoretical, and Practical Issues in Their Use with Emotionally Disturbed Children and Youth* (pp. 119–122) by F. Wood and C. Lakin, 1978, Minneapolis: University of Minnesota. Reprinted by permission.

on hall duty. Because others will need to know about the detention assignments, carbon-set slips or a perforated slip with a "receipt" work best. This allows you to make one copy of the important information for communications with parents and one copy for record keeping at school.

2. Parents must be notified in writing of the assigned detention, at least one day before the time is to be served. This allows parents to arrange for transportation in the event that the student cannot use the regularly scheduled school transportation. The parental detention notice should carefully explain the nature of the rule violation that warranted detention. The date and time for detention should be named. You may wish to include the telephone number of a

school staff person who can talk with the parent if the parent has a question about the discipline procedure. Figure 6–3 shows a detention slip that includes these features. Notice the clarity and easy reading level of the detention slip, designed for students as well as their parents to read. To revise your school's detention slips for a particular reading level, consult a readability formula (for example, Gilliland, 1974).

3. Plan the detention at a time when it will be enforceable. For example, if no teachers are required to serve an early morning duty period, then an early morning detention may have to be rearranged for an afternoon time, instead.

4. Be sure to have adequate work on hand for students. If students are to bring their own work, then apply a consequence for those who do not. For example, you might impose an additional day of detention for those students who fail to bring assigned work to detention. Or, you might require those students to do an additional assignment on their own time. Be sure you do not let students out of detention because they do not bring work—they will learn rapidly that they can beat the system.

5. Post and review firm rules for behavior during detention. These rules might resemble those you adopt for in-school suspension.

6. Establish firm rules for "excused" absences from detention. For example, require that parents contact you directly in the case of doctors' appointments that conflict with the detention schedule.

7. Consider having one individual coordinate detention schedules and parental contacts, if this will make the system more efficient. In some situations, it may be better for a dean or vice-principal to handle all of the parental phone calls, with a secretary tak-

---

Dear Parent/Guardian,
   Your child, _____ , broke a rule at school today. This is what s/he _____
did: _____
_____

   The school has a rule that your child must now go to a detention. In other words, your child will have to come to school at 3:00 P.M. on ___*January 16*___ to do school assignments. Your child will be able to go home at 4:00 P.M. To get home from school, your child can take the school activities bus for $0.50. Or, you may make other travel plans for your child.

   Please know that detention is serious. If your child does not come on time, with schoolwork, to the detention period, then we will have to keep your child in the In-School Suspension Room for one school day. This means that your child will have no regular classes for one entire day.

   We have told your child about the detention. If you have any questions, you may call Dean Whittaker at 556–9087 between 9:00 A.M. and 3 P.M. tomorrow. If you do not call us, we will look for your child at the detention.

                                                                                Mrs. Marsh, Teacher

January 15, 1987

FIGURE 6–3
Detention letter

ing care of detention (and in-school suspension) scheduling and make-up scheduling.

8. Teachers and other staff members who conduct the detention periods should receive reinforcement from their colleagues, whether the duty is assigned or voluntary. Managing a group of disgruntled adolescents before or after school is no picnic!

9. Make a conscious decision about where detention falls in the continuum of punishment in the building. Be sure that detention is assigned for lesser infractions, in-school suspension for more serious ones, for example. Naturally, students who cut detention should receive appropriate punishment: either a second detention or a day in in-school suspension.

10. Some teachers may wish to run their own detentions for infractions of their classroom rules. In this case, "central detention" is used exclusively for violations of school-wide rules. Moreover, central detention may be used for violations of the individual teachers' detentions (e.g., cuts).

11. As with all disciplinary programs, build into the detention system a regularly scheduled review. Some schools have created discipline committees that meet on a regularly scheduled basis for this purpose.

12. At the end of each school term (at least), review the list of students who have been assigned to central and to teachers' detentions. See how many are repeat offenders. Consider an alternative punishment for these students, or revamp the detentions so that they are viewed more negatively by students. If detention is working, students will think twice before committing a rule violation that incurs detention. Remember, however, that the classroom and school rules must be reasonable in the first place if the system is to work properly.

13. More spontaneous, specific detentions may help with highly disruptive times and sit-

uations, such as lunch or recess. In this instance, the detention is for a briefer period (the rest of the lunch period, 15 minutes of the recess time) and is applied to the particular violation of rules during the targeted period. In one school, for example, a highly successful daily lunch detention curbs lunchroom disruptions. Students who violate cafeteria rules are required to finish eating and then proceed to a lunch detention classroom, where work assignments are kept on hand. Adding to the power of this intervention is the fact that well-behaved students are entitled to earn one of a limited number of gym passes, enabling them to spend the remainder of the lunch period in the gym, playing organized sports. An alternative to the gym passes is also available: Students may earn time to play board games in a designated area of the cafeteria.

Because in-school suspension is relatively new, guidelines for its use may change as we gather effectiveness data. Perhaps we all should heed the advice of Garibaldi, who wrote on the topic of in-school suspension:

School personnel should seriously consider all the ramifications before setting up an in-school detention center. They should consider whether a teacher's expectation of a pupil is negatively affected by the student's participation in the program. Do students become labeled or stigmatized by their peers when they return? How informed is the regular teaching staff about the program and do they offer to work collaboratively with the [ISS] staff on the serious problems of some students? Will the [ISS] room be viewed only as a method of punishment? Will the program staff make a valiant effort to get at the heart of the student's behavioral difficulties? Once again, before putting the onus exclusively on the disruptive student and excluding him, other possibilities must be explored. These include the teacher's inability to manage the class, inflexibility in the school rules, and a lack of interest by school administrators to work with particular students. When the school staff is willing to modify its educational climate to better deal with disruptive youth, then an in-school alternative can indeed help it serve its purpose more effectively. (Garibaldi, 1982, p.312)

In-School Suspension

In-school suspension (ISS) varies widely in its applications, but we will discuss it here in terms of an ideal execution and translation of the behavioral concept, **Time Out** from **Reinforcement**. (Detention is another form of time out from [before or after school] reinforcement.) The crucial elements of time-out programs include:

- A reinforcing environment from which the student is removed, either partially or entirely,
- A nonreinforcing environment to which the student is assigned, and
- A carefully articulated set of contingencies that govern the student's passage from one environment to the other.

In the special case of ISS, the room serves as the nonreinforcing environment, the regular (or special education) class should be the more reinforcing environment, and the rules governing ISS should outline the contingencies, or consequences, for entry to and exit from ISS. Specific guidelines for this important school-wide program appear in Table 6–2.

TABLE 6–2
Guidelines for in-school suspension

1. Be sure that the individual in charge of ISS can manage misbehavior. Preferably, teachers should be hand-picked for this assignment. If one individual is not in charge all day, then rotate teachers through the ISS duty, with perhaps a permanent paraprofessional on duty.

2. Do not allow students to enter ISS any time except the beginning of the school day. Mid-day entries are disruptive and create additional problems (e.g., parents who are not notified in advance, failure to get enough appropriate assignments from regular teachers, etc.).

3. When students check into school on the day of their ISS, have them meet in a central location. In one successful program, students meet in the dean's office, where they receive a brief orientation to the ISS policies and a reminder of the infraction that earned them ISS. Students then go to ISS in a group, accompanied by the dean.

4. Have students' work already organized when they arrive to serve their ISS day. Do not allow students to circulate throughout the building collecting assignments—this may turn into a reinforcer!

5. When students go to the restroom, do not let them go in groups. One or two students per trip should be the rule.

6. ISS students probably should have lunch in the ISS room. The alternative, allowing them to eat with other students, may earn them vocal recognition from their peers and create cafeteria disruption.

7. Students who misbehave in ISS should be required to return for an additional day.

8. Time spent in ISS should be work time—no talking to one another or to the adults unless the talk relates to assignments. You may choose to set up carrels to facilitate this atmosphere.

9. At the end of the student's ISS time, an adult should review with the student alternatives to the behavior that warranted ISS placement. Somehow, the ISS teacher should communicate to the regular staff the student's compliance with the punishment.

Because in-school suspension is misused so often, we offer some troubleshooting ideas:

- Do communicate the rules for ISS to *all* staff members, students, and parents.
- Do inform students' parents about each instance of ISS.
- Do select ISS teachers with care, ensuring that they possess good behavior management skills.
- Do not let ISS become just another study hall or tutorial program.
- Do not allow students to misbehave in ISS without firm, negative consequences.
- Do not allow teachers to overrun the ISS room with students who have engaged in only minor infractions.
- Do monitor referrals for ISS and give teachers feedback on their referrals.
- Do check to see if ISS is reducing behavior problems. If not, review the guidelines and adjust the ISS program accordingly. Remember, a disciplinary consequence is not punishing, by definition, unless it reduces the behavior you designate!
- Do keep all staff informed on the ISS program and any revisions made in it.

Home Suspension

Closely tied to the concept of in-school suspension is home suspension, or sending a student out of school for a designated time period. This strategy differs considerably from expulsion, in which a student is sent out of school indefinitely (a strategy that we do not endorse for handicapped students). While the classroom teacher does not usually handle home suspensions, you may still be interested in the guidelines cited by Safer (1982), an expert on disruptive youth:

Suspensions are actions of the principal to exclude a student from school for periods up to 10 days pending a parent conference. With the Goss

decision (*Goss* vs. *Lopez*, 419 US, 565, 1975) principals or their designates are required to conduct an informal hearing on the charge without undue delay. The mini-hearing is set up to: 1) present the nature and basis of the charge against the student, 2) hear the apprehended student's version, and 3) obtain additional information on the offensive act if necessary. (p.43)

We now close our section on school-wide strategies and turn to classroom-level strategies.

ENVIRONMENTALLY MEDIATED STRATEGIES

This section describes strategies that call for a change in the classroom or school environment. While you may not always be able to change your classroom's or school's physical environment, you may play a role in revising aspects of that environment, including rules, curriculum, class size, groupings, schedule, and traffic paths. Little research in these areas has been reported, but we would like to share what is available with you.

Traffic Patterns

In a recent consultation program conducted by one of the authors, traffic patterns were determined to have an effect on the level of noise and disruptive behavior (often leading to aggression) in hallways. The school staff concluded that directional traffic might alleviate the problems. Students were given specific stairways to use for upwards traffic, with others reserved for downward traffic. Density of students in a given location in the corridors also seemed to be tied to disruptive behaviors. Consider altering the traffic pattern in your school to decrease the number of crowded areas.

Related to this issue is the need to consider the reasonableness of rules dictating how long students have to change classes. Students given four minutes to come from a gym in the farthest corner of a very large urban high school may arrive at class late and irritable, setting the occasion for a confrontation with the teacher. Consider flexible rules for class changes that require more time.

Visibility of Authority Figures

Visibility of persons in charge of discipline is important. Our recent survey of teachers in a large urban middle school indicated that disruptions in the hall were far less frequent when deans and faculty members remained visible in the halls during the changing of classes. This all-out effort also gives students a clear message that staff support each other in a consistent program of discipline.

Levels Program

Occasionally we encounter a student whose misbehavior is so severe that our traditional schedule does not work. These chronically disruptive students may not handle an entire day's schedule satisfactorily, or they may act out any time they are surrounded by their peers. Their behavior usually earns them home suspension or expulsion. When dealing with such a student, consider a variation of the levels program reported by Chambers, Sanok, and Striefel (1980). Under this arrangement, a student earns increasingly less restrictive alternatives for his instruction (Because this program is so restrictive, follow the guidelines for getting approval of a punishing event.) Here is an illustration of the program:

1. Craig was expelled from school for chronic fighting. The school team wanted to expel him permanently or have him placed in a private school. The assessment for this alternative placement, however, could not take place for three weeks. Craig's is a rural school district with limited services. The alternative program, in another state, would require residential status.

2. In order to provide Craig with some education during the interim period, three of Craig's teachers agreed to teach him individually after school, one hour a day. Craig responded very well to this arrangement, showing up on time and completing all of his assignments. His parents, relieved that their son was receiving *some* instruction, were very supportive. To show their support, they transported him to his daily tutorials.

3. The school psychologist realized that the interim plan might be the basis for a more long-range plan. That is, she proposed that Craig be allowed to continue the after-school instruction, gradually supplementing the tutorial model with one additional period of instruction—the last period of the school day, then the next to the last period, and so on. If at any time Craig received a negative report for attendance in one of these classes, then he returned to the after-school program only. In other words, *Craig was required to earn back his rights to attend school*, something he dearly wanted to do.

   Craig's parents were intensively involved in this arrangement. They transported Craig to his earned class period at school. They remained at the school until the teacher sent a note stating that Craig had re-entered the class without disruption and been on-task for at least 15 minutes. This provision was necessary if Craig was to be reaccepted by the teachers whose classes he had disrupted previously. (Sweeney, personal communication, January 1986)

For some students this levels system would be ineffective (e.g., students who do not want to come to school). Nevertheless, you may consider this intervention for otherwise last-resort cases.

TEACHER-MEDIATED STRATEGIES

In this section we discuss strategies in which an individual teacher takes primary responsibility for behavior change. Many of these interventions may be familiar.

Keep in mind that your need for these interventions will be far less if you have practiced the strategies recommended in the previous chapters. Appropriately paced instruction, clear expectations, and individual attention go a long way to prevent behavior problems. Another good suggestion is to "ask before you intervene." Students often complain that teachers overreact simply because they do not understand the student's perspective. In other words, talk with students about their misbehavior before you develop a major intervention program.

In order to manage your interactions with students, you must first recognize what it is that you say to students. The following section offers suggestions for modifying verbal comments.

Monitoring Teacher Verbal Behavior

Your comments to students may help form your most powerful behavior management strategy. We have all known teachers who seemed to be "naturals" when it came to disciplining students. Think carefully about these individuals and you may recall that each one of them had a distinctive speaking voice—one that commanded students' attention without screaming. You, too, can develop an authoritative but courteous voice. First, ask a trusted colleague to role-play some situations with you. Pretend that you are stopping a rambunctious student in the corridor. Ask your colleague to tell you honestly how you sounded. Did you sound angry and out of control? Did you convey a sense of authority without flying off the handle? Were you meek or apologetic? Now, practice again. This activity might seem silly at first, but it helps teachers to become more aware of their verbal reactions, especially those they emit under stressful situations. Once you realize the way you sound, concentrate a role-play on your facial expressions. Ask your partner to give you candid feedback on how you look when you are speaking. This visual impression can be used to your advantage, if you know how.

Self-monitoring is a wonderful way to regain control of your own verbal messages to students. Table 6–3 offers steps in monitoring your own verbal statements in the classroom.

TABLE 6–3
Guidelines for modifying teacher verbalizations

---

1. Obtain at least 50 pennies.
2. Issue yourself the pennies in one pocket.
3. Each time you find yourself giving a designated verbal statement, move a penny to the other pocket.
4. At the end of the day, count the pennies in each pocket and record your score.
5. Tally the number of times you gave the designated verbal statement, and record this on an individual chart. Try to improve your record the next day.

---

1. Obtain a wrist counter or golf tally device.
2. Set the counter back to <u>000</u>.
3. Press the wrist counter whenever you find yourself giving the statement to a student.
4. Total the number of statements at the end of each day.
5. Record your daily score on an individual chart.
6. Try to improve your daily score.

Source: From *Strategies for Managing Behavior Problems in the Classroom* (p. 122) by M. M. Kerr and C. M. Nelson, 1983, Columbus, OH: Charles E. Merrill Publishing Company. Copyright 1983 by Charles E. Merrill Publishing Company. Adapted by permission.

Just as important as speaking to students is your capacity to *listen* to them. Too often, students report that no one listens to them; some teenagers tend to talk a lot, so everyone tunes them out on occasion. Nevertheless, you might want to tabulate how well you listen without interrupting or correcting students. The self-monitoring strategy can be applied to listening skills as well as talking.

Reprimands

Admonishing students who misbehave, one of our oldest strategies, is a part of the teaching tradition, Let us examine the reseach on reprimands. Studies have shown that you can make your reprimands more effective by:

1. Making your reprimand private, not public (O'Leary, Kaufman, Kass, & Drabman, 1970),
2. Giving the target student direct eye contact while you are scolding him (Van Houten, Nau, MacKenzie-Keating, Sameoto, & Colavecchia, 1982), and
3. Standing near the student while you are talking to her (Van Houten et al., 1982).

While we generally recommend that you pick a different way to handle misbehavior (e.g., a contingency arrangement that will not lead to a power struggle), you should try to follow these rules when you do scold.

Praising and Ignoring

Most of us have tried to ignore problem behaviors, only to be disappointed in the results. Our failure to control behavior with this strategy may be traced to a misunderstanding of the basic principles that underly this intervention. Often, teachers attempt to ignore the problem behavior, not realizing that praise for the preferred behaviors must take place, too (hence, the ignoring becomes a time out from the praise). Without this recognition, the student is virtually ignored; but ignoring by itself does not constitute a solid intervention. Here are four guidelines for conducting an effective praise-and-ignore program.

1. Remember that an ignoring procedure will not work unless the reason for student's behavior is to gain your attention. To determine this, use an antecedent-behavior-consequence analysis (see Chapter Two).
2. Remember that disruptive behavior will increase before decreasing, when an ignoring intervention is successful. Do not give up!
3. Develop ways in which other adults present can distract you from the student who is being disruptive, so that you do not find yourself giving the student attention. Let others present know that the student's disruptive behavior is to be ignored.
4. Be sure to praise the student and provide attention for appropriate behaviors. Ignoring as a single behavior management strategy will not work.

Just remember: This is not one of our most powerful strategies, so it may not reverse "hard core" behavior problems.

Differential Reinforcement of Low Rates of Behavior

You may be familiar with a strategy very similar to praise-and-ignore, **Differential Reinforcement of Low Rates** of behavior (DRL). This relatively simple strategy has been applied to swearing (Epstein, Repp, & Cullinan, 1978), talking out (Dietz & Repp, 1973), inappropriate questioning, and negative verbal statements. Teasing and name-calling were identified as the problem behaviors in a successful intervention study reported by Zwald and Gresham (1982). Here are the steps taken in this intervention:

1. The teacher posted and discussed class rules, telling the group the maximum number of teasing/name-calling occurrences allowed to still obtain reinforcement for that day.

2. A mark was made on the blackboard for every teasing/name-calling verbalization. These vebalizations were not discussed or reprimanded: a mark was merely placed on the board.
3. Positive reinforcement was selected by each boy from a reinforcement menu mutually decided upon by the teacher and class members. The reinforcement menu for each day consisted of a hot drink (hot chocolate, tea, or coffee), free reading, or listening to radio.
4. In order to prevent the number of teasing remarks from getting out of hand if the students went beyond the limit set for the day (thereby losing that day's reinforcement), a larger reward was given at the end of the week if the group had five or fewer "extra" recorded teasing remarks for the week. The large reinforcer was 20 minutes of free time on Friday.
5. A line graph was posted so that class members could graphically see their progress. The extra teasing remarks (the number of remarks that exceeded the imposed limit) were recorded on a bar graph so the students could observe whether they would obtain free time at the end of the week. (p. 430)

Trice and Parker (1983) reduced the use of obscene words in two adolescents in a resource room by using DRL and a response cost. *Specific words* were targeted for these interventions which were compared with one another. Each time a student said one of the six targeted words, he was given a colored marker. At the end of the class period, these markers were tallied and the students' behavior was posted on a graph. A 5-minute detention (the response cost) was required for each marker the students earned. Under the DRL condition, students received praise at each class period tally that fell below the mean tally for the day before: students whose tallies were higher received no comment. The

authors recommended the response cost procedure as more immediately effective than the DRL procedure.

Physical Interactions with Students

You may have noticed that we have focused almost entirely on verbal interactions with students. Most of the interactions around problems will be, and certainly should be, verbal, not physical. Often, however, we are asked about physical interventions or about the less serious casual touching, hugging, or handshakes that are common in everyday school life. Our advice is that you not engage in any physical interactions that you would deem inappropriate with an unfamiliar adult. While a handshake may be appropriate and courteous, touching a student of the same or opposite sex in any other way may lead to problems, especially with students who have a history of acting-out behaviors. Naturally, there will be good exceptions to this rule, but a conservative stance is usually best. Adolescents are developing their own sexual identities and are often confused about physical affection of any kind. Hypersensitive to these initiations, they may misunderstand your intentions. This likelihood increases in situations when the teenager is under special stress, angered, or likely to be embarrassed.

Physical interventions for aggressive students create their own problems, as we have noted earlier in the sections on punishment. Our advice is to avoid physical confrontations whenever possible, taking precautions to protect yourself and others.

Contingency Contracting

A written explanation of contingencies to be used by a student's teacher or parents is termed a contingency contract (Homme, 1970). Contingency contracting is a useful procedure when there are only one or two disruptive students in a classroom. General guidelines for implementing a contingency contract would include the following:

1. Explain to the student what a contract is. Your explanation will depend upon the conversational level of the child, but it may be helpful to use examples of contracts that the student will encounter.
2. Give the student an opportunity to discuss what a contract is, sharing examples.
3. Ask the student to suggest some tasks that might be be included in a contract between student and teacher. Write these down.
4. Suggest some tasks that you would like to see the student accomplish and write these down.
5. Decide on mutually agreeable tasks. If a third party is to be involved in the contract, be sure that party also agrees on the selected tasks.
6. Discuss possible activities, items, or privileges that the student would like to earn. Write these down.
7. Negotiate how the student will earn the reinforcers by accomplishing portions or all of the tasks.
8. Identify the criteria for mastery of each task (time allotted, achievement level, how the task is to be evaluated).
9. Determine when the student will receive the reinforcers for completing tasks.
10. Determine when the contract will be reviewed to make necessary revisions or to review progress.
11. Make an extra copy of the contract. Give this copy to the student. If a third party is involved, give that party a copy of the contract, also.
12. Sign the contract, get the student to sign the contract, and if there is a third party involved, ask the third party also to sign the contract.

Figure 6–4 displays a contract that includes parent involvement. Note that the *review date* for the contract is included. This allows everyone a chance to discuss problems with the contract, before these problems get in the way of success. Also note the parent involvement, reflected by the signatures. While it is not always possible for you to secure parents' cooperation, it is advisable to include them, especially with teenagers. After all, parents generally control the reinforcers that teenagers want most (e.g., car keys, allowance, free time, telephone privileges).

Contracts are often used to supplement or explain another behavior management strategy, such as self-monitoring. The contract specifies the contingencies for a student's performance under another strategy. In this way, a contract is similar to a token economy, the strategy discussed in the next section.

Token Economies

If you are a special education teacher, you will undoubtedly want to try a **token system** for classroom behavior management. Token economies have earned a great deal of respect for their capacity to handle a wide variety of behavior problems.

Literature on the management of behavior problems in the classroom is filled with references to token reinforcement or token economy systems. A token economy program has many uses in managing student behavior problems, particularly when a system is needed to serve a large group of students.

Token economy programs have been used in numerous schools and clinics, including special education classrooms (Broden, Hall, Dunlap, & Clark, 1970); regular classrooms (McLaughlin & Malaby, 1972); and even the school cafeteria (Muller, Hasazi, Pierce, & Hasazi, 1975). Token economies have also been successful in decreasing disruptive behavior such as jumping out of seat and in increasing attention and academic performance. The resources you will need before initiating a token economy program are:

I, _____ *Jeff* _____, agree to do the following at school:
    (student)

1. Stop making noises during my

science and social studies

classes;

2. Stop playing with things on

my desk during these classes

----

on this schedule: _every day – 1st & 3rd period_

I, *Mr. Navarsky*, agree to provide help as follows:
    (teacher)

1. Look at Jeff when he is making

noise or playing with things.

2. Not say anything to him at

these times.

3. Give Jeff a "scorecard" for each

class to show him how he did.

FIGURE 6–4
Home-based contingency contract

We, ~~Mr. and Mrs.~~ Arnaud, agree to provide privileges
(parents)

as follows: ~~If~~ Jeff brings home a
"scorecard" showing eight out of
ten classes a week in which
he didn't make noise or play
with things, he will be able
to go to the movies with a
friend on Sunday.

We have read and discussed this contract in a meeting

on _10/24_. We hereby sign as a way of making our
commitment to this program.

We agree to meet again on _11/6_ to re-evaluate the contract.

Signed: _Jeff Arnaud_

Mr. + Mrs. J.J. Arnaud

Mr. Navarsky

Witnessed: _Dr. McClean_

Date: _10/24_

FIGURE 6-4

(continued)

165

1. Back-up reinforcers appropriate for your classroom group.
2. Tokens appropriate for your group (e.g., points).
3. A kitchen timer, if you plan to reinforce behaviors by measuring their duration.
4. A monitoring sheet on which to record tokens or points earned.

These items are described on the following pages.

You will need a couple of hours to gather the materials and to duplicate the monitoring sheets. Once you have materials ready, plan to spend about 30 minutes a day for the first week of the program in introducing the tokens and orienting students to the program. After the first week, the program should require no more than 20 minutes a day in addition to the time spent delivering tokens. (Note: programs may differ in the amount of time required.)

To begin the program, select target behaviors for your class. Some of the behaviors you list should be ones you take for granted presently. Select easy behaviors to be sure all students can earn a few tokens from the beginning of the program. Try to select target behaviors compatible with the classroom rules. Sample target behaviors developed for a high school classroom token economy could include the following:

1. Go promptly to homeroom when you arrive at school.
2. Keep your coat in your locker at school.
3. Throw away your chewing gum before you get to school.
4. Pick up your work for the day and take your seat.
5. Eat lunch within the allotted area.
6. Walk in the halls when you are outside the room.

To ensure that the target behaviors selected are appropriate, ask yourself the following questions:

1. How can I describe this behavior in words the student(s) can understand?
2. How can I measure this behavior when it occurs? If the behavior is measured in terms of time (on-task for 10 minutes, no outburst during a 15-minute period, solving a certain number of math problems within a specified amount of time), then assign the tokens or points on a token:time ratio basis.

   If the behavior is measured in terms of frequency (percent correct on a worksheet, number of positive verbal comments to a peer, number of independent steps in a project), then award tokens or points on a token:frequency ratio basis.
3. How will I know when this behavior is exhibited?
4. How important is this behavior? You will not be able to initiate the program with all of the behaviors you identify, so you may have to rank them. Try to start with some behaviors that you can modify successfully.
5. Is the behavior one that you wish to reduce or eliminate? You can handle this behavior in two ways. First, determine incompatible, desired behaviors for which the student will be rewarded. Second, apply a fine or response cost to the student for engaging in this behavior.
6. Does this behavior occur in other settings? If so, you may want to extend the token economy program to include other classes or in the halls. To do this, you will need to monitor the behavior in those settings, so include space on your monitoring form or develop a different form for those settings. Record your findings as briefly as possible, however. For example, a behavior statement might be, "Get no detention slips in the hall." This would eliminate an extra form, for if the student has gotten a detention slip, then he has "missed" the behavior.

Selecting reinforcers and fines is the next step. If your students can help, let them develop a reinforcement menu for the class. Think of items or events that will be enjoyable and can be obtained within the school. Some ideas for involving students in identifying their own reinforcers might include the following:

1. Allow students some free time, and observe what they choose to do. (HINT: watch the vending machines and pay phones!)
2. Allow students to "sample" reinforcers by placing them in an accessible place and noting which items the students select frequently.

Remember that you can identify a reinforcer by noting what students dislike doing and then allowing them to forego that event as a reinforcer. For example, some teachers issue homework cuts or allow students to rearrange their seating.

When selecting a reinforcer, ask yourself these questions:

1. For whom is this a powerful reinforcer? If an item or event has appeal for only one adolescent, it may not be worth the trouble it takes to use it.
2. Are several students interested in this reinforcer? If so, go ahead!
3. Can I justify the use of this reinforcer? Consider educational value, nutrition, possible danger, possible misuse.
4. Can I obtain this reinforcer? Consider replacement, since handicapped students are sometimes hard on play equipment and games. In other words, could you get a duplicate item without much trouble or delay?
5. Is this reinforcer convenient to this situation? Do not promise reinforcers that you cannot deliver! Think of your own convenience in providing this item or event.
6. Do you have some long-range and short-range activities on your list? To help students learn to delay reinforcement, try to plan some events that will take place later.

Token systems should be adjusted constantly to avoid some pupils collecting too many tokens (which diminishes their value as conditioned reinforcers) or other students hoarding them. You can have sales, reduce the price of items that are not selected, or eliminate them. In the early stages, it should be fairly easy to obtain tokens for small amounts of work or behavior. Later, as student performance improves, contingencies should be increased gradually (Walker & Buckley, 1974).

You are ready now to draw up a task/reinforcer or wages/earnings list for your program. Depending on the reading level of your students, develop a listing that can be posted in the classroom, a catalog of pictures, or an individual student checklist. Figure 6–5 is an example of a token economy in a special education classroom.

The fines or response cost are listed on the same poster, but they are listed separately. Figure 6–5 displays a response cost list in the right-hand column. Remember to keep the ratio of target behaviors ("earners") to response-cost behaviors ("losers") large enough to prevent any student from "going in the hole" on a typical day. In other words, there should be more behaviors that earn points than those that lose points. We recommend a 2:1 ratio.

To determine how many tokens or points to assign to each "earner" or "loser," we suggest that you begin with this simple system:

1. Rate each of the positive behaviors according to its importance. Give each "earner" a 1, 2, or 3, with 3 for the most important behaviors (the ones that should earn the most points or tokens).
2. Rate each "loser" similarly. This time, however, assign a 2, 4, or 6 (for the behaviors that should lose the most points.)
3. Assign each behavior the number you gave in the rating exercise.
4. The number now denotes the number of points or tokens earned for each behavior.

Student: _____	Date: _____
Level: _____	Started Level on: _____

Behaviors which earn points/ points earned today:				*Points lost today:*			
Good bus report	3	3	3	Complain/moan	4	4	4
Say hello to teacher	1	1	1	Make weird noises	4	4	4
Put up coat/lunch	2	2	2	Hit/kick others	6	6	6
Answer questions appropriately	1	1	1	Destroy something	6	6	6
Follow a direction	3	3	3	Laugh in silly way	4	4	4
	3	3	3	Leave without permission	6	6	6
Tutor a peer	3	3	3	Swear	4	4	4
Look at person/while talk	3	3	3				
Finish work on time	3	3	3				
Good music, art class report	3						
Talk in pleasant voice	1	1	1				
Work without disturbing others	3	3	3				
Good gym report	3						
Say goodbye	1	1	1				

TOTAL POINTS EARNED TODAY = _____   TOTAL POINTS LOST TODAY = _____

Comments:
Once Juan reaches 50 points as his average daily score for five consecutive days, he can move to Level II. Then he receives credit, not tokens, for the items starred.

FIGURE 6–5
Token economy monitoring chart: Level I

To see how this system works, look at the token economy listing in Figure 6–5. You will see that each behavior is listed with numbers after it. Depending on how many *opportunities* the teacher believes she will be able to award points or tokens (not how many times the behavior could possibly occur—this would place impossible demands on the teacher's time!), the number is repeated from two to six times. A "good music, art class report," then, is noted once per day, while following directions may earn tokens up to six times per day.

One of our major problems with token economies is our failure to move the student through (and eventually off) the system, as they develop better skills. To overcome this problem, create a levels system within your token economy. Figure 6–5 showed a Level I token economy, while Figure 6–6 shows a more advanced Level III system.

Note the comment at the bottom of Figure 6–6, indicating that the student receives credit for items that he has previously demonstrated in an earlier level. This is a very important con-

Student: _____					Week: _____				
Level: _____					Started Level on: _____				
Points "Earners":					*Points "Losers":*				
Finishing classwork in a	3	3	3	3	3	Fighting		6	6	6
mainstream class:	3	3	3	3	3	Swearing		4	4	4
	3	3	3	3	3	Destroying something		6	6	6
Scoring an "A" or "B" on						Suspension offense		6	6	6
a test	3	3	3	3	3	(not named above)				
Getting a good mainstream	3	3	3	3	3	Detention offense		4	4	4
class report	3	3	3	3	3					

Points "Earners":

Finishing classwork in a mainstream class: 3 3 3 3 3 / 3 3 3 3 3 / 3 3 3 3 3

Scoring an "A" or "B" on a test 3 3 3 3 3

Getting a good mainstream class report 3 3 3 3 3 / 3 3 3 3 3

Getting to class on time 3 3 3 3 3 / 3 3 3 3 3 / 3 3 3 3 3

Going all day without swearing (self-monitored) 2 2 2 2 2

Walking (not running) in hall 2 2 2 2 2 / 2 2 2 2 2

Taking hat and coat off in school 1 1 1 1 1

Contributing in a successful group contingency 3 3 3 3 3

Bringing in homework on time 2 2 2 2 2 / 2 2 2 2 2 / 2 2 2 2 2

Taking materials to class 1 1 1 1 1 / 1 1 1 1 1 / 1 1 1 1 1

Helping someone 3 3 3 3 3

Meeting group goalsetting 3 3 3 3 3

[REMEMBER TO ADD 50 POINTS EACH WEEK FOR PREVIOUS LEVEL CREDITS!]

FIGURE 6–6
Token economy monitoring chart: Mainstreamed, level III

cept! Without this credit arrangement for a student, he is punished by receiving no tokens for the skills he has been demonstrating consistently. Moreover, this credit arrangement allows you to "wean" students from the actual tokens, since none are distributed for "credit"

items. If a student backslides on previously "credited" behaviors, he returns to the conditions of the previous level.

Selecting tokens is usually a fairly straightforward procedure for older students, most of whom will respond satisfactorily to points (if the rest of the token economy system is well designed). If you decide to use actual tokens, however, be sure that they cannot be duplicated. This will curb cheating. Consider also the expense, convenience, and durability of the tokens, and do not forget to consider your token *container* before making your final token selection!

Maintaining Flexibility and Humor

Finally, we address a strategy you may not have considered: maintaining your own flexibility and sense of humor on the job. Studies have shown that teachers who are under stress become irritable, tired, bored, and even depressed. In the later stages, stress may lead teachers to resist change and to become inflexible (Weiskopf, 1980). Such traits would make interacting with disgruntled teenagers difficult. On the one hand, being flexible will increase your chances of managing and coping with problem behaviors on the job. On the other hand, not handling the stresses of your job may lead you to be irritable, short-tempered, and less able to handle potentially difficult interactions with teenagers. Adolescents, especially those with a history of behavior problems, often provoke adults into conversations or interactions that lead to bigger problems, such as aggressive behaviors (Strain & Ezzell, 1978). Learn to cope with the stresses of working with adolescents.

Weiskopf (1980) offered these suggestions for reducing the stress of your job:

1. Know in advance what the job requires in terms of emotional stress.
2. Set realistic goals for yourself and for your students.
3. Delegate routine work, such as paperwork, to aides or volunteers.
4. Avoid becoming isolated from other staff members.

5. Break up the amount of direct contact you have with students through team teaching, the use of learning centers, etc.
6. Remain intellectually active off the job.
7. Get physical exercise.
8. Interject newness and variety into your day to counterbalance routine.
9. Participate in hobbies and activities not related to your job.

In the next section of the chapter we offer you help in the classroom, through an often untapped resource: peers.

PEER-MEDIATED STRATEGIES

In this section we describe several strategies that allow classmates or older students to take an active role in behavior change. A group contingency is a peer-mediated strategy in which several peers and the target student work with the teacher to modify behaviors. Other peer-mediated interventions include peer contingencies within a token economy and group goalsetting and feedback.

Group Goalsetting and Feedback

This intervention relies on a group discusssion in which peers "vote" on a fellow student's behavior. Each student receives a behavioral goal, specified in clearly observable terms. Daily or twice a week, students meet in a highly structured 20-minute group discussion to vote and give one another feedback on their goals, under adult direction. Here are a few target goals for your consideration:

- Martin will not tease another student during fifth period biology lab.
- Mario will go from fourth period class to fifth period class without getting a detention slip.

- Theresa will not swear during her morning classes.
- Alexa will not fall asleep in classes after lunch.
- Bruce will not cut his last class.

You will notice that the goals are very specific. You may wonder why they are not more ambitious; after all, would we not want Alexa awake all day? Should Bruce not attend all his classes? Two reasons support this type of goal. First, the behavior may be specific to a particular class, perhaps one that the student finds boring. Second, the goal should reflect the behavioral principle of shaping successive approximations. This important principle tells us that we will be more successful in changing behavior if we break the goal into smaller, more attainable target behaviors and reinforce students for mastering them.

The specific steps in directing group goal-setting and feedback are outlined in Table 6–4.

You may find that your group of students is not together for the entire day, or even one period. This creates an obstacle to accurate feedback, because peers are not able to observe behaviors firsthand. As long as at least two students can observe each other, you might try the variation of group goalsetting and feedback mentioned in Chapter Four. In that version, two or three students monitor one another and vote on each other's behavioral goals. Moreover, goal mastery can be incorporated into a contingency contract (students earn privileges for meeting their goals during the week, according to their partner's feedback) or to a group contingency (students are required to earn a percentage of total possible "yes" votes each week for certain privileges).

Using Peers within a Token Economy

When you create a token economy, strengthen it with the "power of peers" by having students earn extra points or tokens when they work in partnership with another student or within a group project. In other words, incorporate a group contingency arrangement within your token economy. Students lose points when they deliberately get one another into trouble.

Another way to use the peer group in a token economy system is to consider interactions and time with peers as privileges that must be *earned*, not taken for granted. Too often we allow students free access to their favorite reinforcer: their friends. Consider removing these peer-oriented experiences from a student who misbehaves. For example, take away the privilege of changing classes with his friends, and require him to change classes alone.

Group Contingencies

Closely linked to the concepts underlying a token economy is the strategy we call group contingency. The basic characteristic of a group contingency is group reinforcement. Litow and Pomroy (1975) described three types of group contingencies: dependent, independent, and interdependent.

In a **dependent group contingency** the performance of certain group members determines the consequence received by the entire group. This arrangement works best when the behavior of the large group is better than that of the target student or students (Hayes, 1976). Therefore, this arrangement may not be the best one for a group of behaviorally disordered teenagers whose behavior is generally disruptive. To be sure that a group-oriented contingency does not result in negative peer pressure with such a group, follow these two rules: Use a group reinforcement rather than a response cost, and be sure that the behavioral target and criteria are within the students' range.

The identifying characteristic of **independent group contingencies** is that the same con-

TABLE 6–4

Strategy for conducting group goalsetting and feedback

1. For each student in the group, develop a social behavior objective that is written in language the student can understand. Typical goals might be "To speak up in the class discussion times." "To share materials with others on the playground." "To play baseball without teasing my classmates." "To play with at least one other child at recess."

2. Write each student's name, goal, and the date on which the goal was announced on a separate sheet in the group notebook. Record the feedback of the student's peers each day during the group session.

3. Schedule a fifteen- to twenty-minute daily session for the group goalsetting and feedback session.

4. Ask everyone to sit in a circle for the group session. Instruct students that this is a time when everyone will speak and that no one is to speak out of turn. Explain further that each student has some behavior that warrants improvement and that the time will be spent talking about our behavior goals.

5. Explain to each student on the first day of the group goalsetting session what his or her goal is for the next week or two. It is recommended that individual goals be maintained for at least ten school days.

6. On subsequent days of the group goalsetting session, turn to the first student sitting next to you in the group, announce that student's goal, and state either "I think you made your goal today," or "I don't think you made your goal today." Then provide limited feedback in the form of a statement to support your evaluation. A typical evaluation statement might be, "I like the way you cooperated with Charlie on the playground," or "I don't like the way you took the baseball away from Jane."

7. Request that the student sitting next to the target individual now evaluate that individual's progress towards the goal. Reinforce eye contact with the target student and other constructive feedback. Be certain that each student in the group provides not only an evaluation but a feedback statement. Repeat this process until each student in the group has provided the target individual with an opinion and a feedback statement.

8. Tally the votes of making the goal or not making the goal and announce the result. If the student has made the goal, invite others in the group to give the student a handclap or other reinforcement you have chosen. If the student has not made the goal, there is no group response.

9. Repeat this process until all members of the group have received feedback on their goals.

10. If the group has developed a consistently productive performance you may decide to allow one of the students to be the group leader. This student will then read each student's goals and request feedback from members of the group. These goals could still be teacher-assigned, or in the case of an advanced group, the goals could be self- or peer-assigned.

Source: From "PowWow: A Group Procedure for Reducing Classroom Behavior Problems" by M. M. Kerr and E. U. Ragland. *The Pointer,* 24, pp. 92–96, 1979. Reprinted with permission of the Helen Dwight Reid Educational Foundation. Published by Heldref Publications, 4000 Albemarle St., N.W., Washington, D.C. 20016. Copyright © 1985.

sequence is applied to individual group members (Litow & Pomroy, 1975). Contingency contracting is a good illustration of an independent group contingency. This arrangement is less likely to produce negative peer pressure.

In an **interdependent group contingency**, students must each reach a prescribed level of behavior before the entire group receives a consequence. You may recall from Chapter Four an interdependent group contingency for teaching school survival skills. Students were entitled to earn points through their individual performance in the regular, mainstreamed classroom. These points were then pooled for the group (hence an interdependent group contingency). Criteria for reinforcers were based on the ratio of points earned to points possible. Criteria began with 50% (to get students initially interested in the self-monitoring) and progressed to 80%.

Table 6–5 illustrates the three types of group contingencies.

Our final section describes self-mediated strategies involving the target student in his own behavior change program.

TABLE 6–5
Group contingency arrangements

Type of Group Contingency	Examples
Interdependent	If each student meets his self-monitoring goal on Tuesday, the whole class can skip one homework.
	As soon as each student teaches his lab partner this week's vocabulary wordlist in earth science, we will launch our weather balloons.
	As soon as each student makes it through one home economics class without one reprimand for disruptive behavior, we will prepare lunch for the class and our guests (one per student).
Independent	Each students who finishes his homework on time during the allotted 15-minute homework drill time will receive a food coupon for a fast food restaurant.
	Each student who meets her group goalsetting and feedback goal may have an extra gym period for the week she met her goal.
	Each student who goes for an entire English class without a reprimand will receive 5 extra grade points.
Dependent	If a student who returns to the regular classroom from the in-school suspension room has a good day (i.e., no warnings and classwork completed), all students will get to drop their lowest daily classwork grade. This recognizes the supportive role that classmates can play a student's re-entry.
	Three students in this class got detention last week for pushing in the class. If these three students do not get detention for two weeks, then the entire class will get popcorn during the Friday film.

SELF-MEDIATED STRATEGIES

The strategies described in this section focus on the target student's abilities to work on his own behavior problems. Although this does not sound very promising for disruptive students, studies have documented the effectiveness of the three major self-mediated strategies: self-monitoring, self-reinforcement, and self-assessment (Glynn, 1970). Rueda, Rutherford, and Howell (1980) underscored the importance of teaching self-control strategies:

Along with the transmission and acquisition of academic and social skills, the schools have as their primary objective the facilitation of children's learning to independently manage their own behavior. . . . However, self-regulation is rarely approached as a skill to be independently and systematically taught. (p.188)

For mildly handicapped students entering mainstreamed settings, self-control skills are essential, if transfer of learning from the specialized setting to the "regular" setting is to happen. Some of the disadvantages of behavior management systems that rely exclusively on teacher-mediated strategies are that (a) behavioral skills may not generalize outside the setting in which they were first learned, (b) adults who "controlled" behaviors may become inextricably associated with appropriate behavior, lessening the chance that students will act appropriately in their absence, and (c) teachers busy with a number of students may not notice the behavior of students.

Self-Monitoring

In Chapter Five we demonstrated a self-monitoring intervention for academic improvement. For inappropriate social behaviors, the procedure is essentially the same, although you would substitute behavioral targets. Here are a few examples:

- Thomas will decrease his talk-outs by 10% over his baseline self-record level.
- Eileen will increase her positive verbal interactions 25% each week, over her baseline level. These interactions must be verified in writing by the adult to whom she spoke.
- Lewis will receive not more than three reprimands per week for being off-task during science. In addition to his record of off-task, his performance will be concurrently measured through Mr. Kauffman's written report.
- Cynthia will record on her self-report form at least six instances of "kindness to other students" each week. On a random basis, these claims will be verified with the other students.

Notice the attention we paid to the measurement of these self-recording goals. You will want to incorporate other sources of confirming data, at least in the initial phases of the program.

Many students will alter their own behavior simply as a function of becoming more aware of it. This approach may be helpful for minor behavior problems (mannerisms, blurting out during class discussions, standing too close during a conversation, teasing, talking too loudly or for too long a time, failing to accept criticism, fidgeting, touching others, moving excessively, daydreaming). While these behaviors may not be at the top of your priority list, remember that they may be the very behaviors that lead to more serious infractions.

Figure 6–7 shows a self-monitoring form completed by a target student, Tommy.

As we have mentioned before, behavior management strategies are often most effective in combination. When you use a self-monitoring intervention, describe the intervention within a contingency contract. Figure 6–8, a contract for Tommy, shows you how. Notice how specifically the target behaviors are named.

Monday: swear: _____   tease: _____   silly: _____

leave: _____   TOTAL:[   ]

Tuesday: swear: _____   tease: _____   silly: _____

leave: _____   TOTAL:[   ]

Wednesday: swear: _____   tease: _____   silly: _____

leave: _____   TOTAL:[   ]

Thursday: swear: _____   tease: _____   silly: _____

leave: _____   TOTAL:[   ]

Friday: swear: _____   tease: _____   silly: _____

leave: _____   TOTAL:[   ]

POINTS TRADED IN: [   ]   [   ]   [   ]

POINTS LOST: [   ]

Date: _____

FIGURE 6–7
Tommy's self-recording form

Tommy agrees to engage in this intervention:

1. I will self-record my disruptive behaviors in class. Here they are: swearing; teasing; being silly; leaving my desk. Swearing means saying a cuss word, including: damn, shit, hell, and fuck. Teasing means calling someone an insulting name or laughing when they do something wrong. Being silly means giggling or laughing when work is going on. Leaving my desk means that I go to the back of the classroom or out into the hall when the teacher has already started the lesson.

2. I will self-record every period. I understand that Miss Gross may record, too, on certain days. If my tally does not match hers (at least 80% match), then I lose two points.

3. I have set my own baseline. It is on my graph. My goal is to improve my behavior by reducing it at least one tally each day. If I do this, I earn ten points a day. I can then trade these points in on my own schedule, as long as I do not use classroom time to do it.

4. I can trade points for study hall cut (with permission to play computer games during that time) = 30 points, extra gym period during early lunch time = 40 points, a "second chance" for detention (I don't have to go the first time I am sent) = 50 points.

5. This contract is in effect for two weeks. Then we review it.

Agreed: _____
      (teacher)

Agreed: _____
      (principal)

Signed: _____

Date: _____ Witness: _____

Review Date: _____ Time: _____

FIGURE 6–8
Contract for Tommy

This is an important feature of self- monitoring for behavior problems. Avoid the difficulties that come with ambiguous definitions ("but you said." "I *did* it—you just didn't see me!" "I thought you said ... "). The contract itself will clarify target behaviors: putting them in writing helps.

Self-Assessment

While we naturally assume that students will pay attention to their own self-monitoring data and evaluate themselves, this is not necessarily the case. Self-assessment, or self-evaluation, provides a clear opportunity for adolescents to reflect on how well they are meeting their goals. Self-assessment usually involves graphing or charting one's performance. This visual summary makes it easier for teenagers to see their improvement. Figure 6–9 displays a self-graph designed by Tommy.

Self-Reinforcement

Self-reinforcement, as you learned in Chapter Five, gives teenagers a chance to reward themselves for a "job well done." This strategy may be used on its own. For example, a student might be allowed to take his own tokens, or to schedule himself into the privileges he has earned. Or, self-reinforcement can be used in combination with self-monitoring or self-assessment. Once a student has mastered the basics of self-monitoring, try to expand the intervention through self-reinforcement. Notice

the self-reinforcement clause included in Figure 6–8.

Self-control procedures are very important in the classroom, especially if you work with students whose behavior problems prevent them from entering less restrictive settings. In addition to increasing a teenager's self-control, these strategies require less of your time than do teacher-mediated strategies, giving you more time for instruction. Another advantage, in our experience, is that adolescents actually enjoy these interventions and the autonomy they represent.

SUMMARY

This chapter focused on decreasing problem behaviors and improving classroom decorum. Research has shown that discipline problems hinder students' school success, sometimes leading to truancy and dropping out. School-wide disciplinary programs, if effective, must be based on sound behavioral principles. We have offered guidelines for setting up rules, detention, and in-school suspension. Taking behavior management one step further, we highlighted interventions that have been validated empirically: token economy systems, contingency contracting, teacher feedback, and group contingencies. These strategies share a common theme of recognizing and rewarding good classroom deportment, while punishing poor behavior. Moreover, we have tried to address the importance of the expectations, attitudes, and affects that color the teacher's approach to behavior management. Finally, we call upon the peer group as well as the target student, whose roles in resolving behavioral difficulties often have been overlooked.

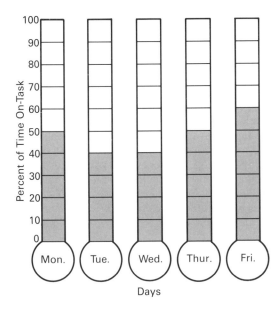

FIGURE 6–9
Tommy's self-assessment graph

RECOMMENDED READINGS

Kauffman, J. M. (1985). *Characteristics of children's behavior disorders* (3rd ed.). Columbus, OH: Charles E. Merrill Publishing Company.

Kerr, M. M., & Nelson, C. M. (1983). *Strategies for managing behavior problems in the classroom.* Columbus, OH: Charles E. Merrill Publishing Company.

Walker, H. M. (1979). *The acting-out child: Coping with classroom disruptions.* Boston, MA: Allyn and Bacon.

Wood, F. H., & Lakin, K. C. (Eds.) (1978). *Punishment and aversive stimulation in special education:* *Legal, theoretical and practical issues in their use with emotionally disturbed children and youth.* Advanced Institute for Trainers of Teachers for Seriously Emotionally Disturbed Children and Youth, Department of Psychoeducational Studies, University of Minnesota. (Grant from the Division of Personnel Preparation, Bureau of Education for the Handicapped, United States Office of Education, Department of Health, Education and Welfare.)

CASE STUDY

Reducing Inappropriate Language in a Secondary Level Learning Disabled Student

An important component of the behavior change process is the Antecedent-Behavior-Consequences analysis (ABC analysis) (Kerr & Nelson, 1983). An ABC analysis allows educators to identify the events and stimuli that precede and follow a behavior. Information from the ABC analysis can be instrumental in planning the intervention strategy.

Frequently, the ABC analysis will reveal that a student's peers are exhibiting behaviors that maintain inappropriate behavior (Buehler, Patterson, & Furness, 1966; Solomon & Wahler, 1973). When an inappropriate behavior of a student is reinforced by peers, an effective management strategy should include peers in the behavior change process.

Our ABC analysis revealed that Johnny's cursing was being reinforced by his peers. When Johnny used inappropriate language, his classmates usually responded by laughing and giving Johnny attention. Therefore, to decrease Johnny's cursing we had to involve his peers in the remedial process.

Source: From "Using Peer Mediated Extinction Procedure to Decrease Obscene Language" by F. J. Salend and D. Meddaugh. *The Pointer,* 30, pp. 8–11, 1985. Reprinted with permission of the Helen Dwight Reid Educational Foundation. Published by Heldref Publications, 4000 Albemarle St., N.W., Washington, D.C. 20016. Copyright © 1985.

The purpose of this case study is to examine the use of a peer-mediated extinction system to decrease Johnny's use of obscenities. An obscenity was defined as any conventional verbal statement related to: "(a) body parts designed for sexual activity or waste elimination, (b) sexual or eliminative behavior or the products of such behavior, or (c) uncomplimentary references to someone's 'parentage'" (Epstein, Repp & Cullinan, 1978, p. 420).

METHOD

Subject. Johnny was a 14-year-old male eighth grader. He was classified as learning disabled and received his academic instruction in a departmentalized, self-contained special education program. He was mainstreamed for art, music, and vocational instruction. His IQ was 90 as assessed by the *Wechsler Intelligence Scale for Children* (WISC-R). He frequently cursed in math class.

In addition to Johnny, this math class was composed of five other male students. The five students' IQs ranged from 79 to 90 with a mean of 84. Their ages ranged from 14 to 15. All of Johnny's peers had been labeled learning disabled.

Setting. This case study took place during the class's daily math period, a 42-minute session where the class learned basic math skills (e.g., division, multiplication, decimals, and fractions). The classroom was typical of most remedial math classes, with students receiving small group instruction and working individually on independent seat work.

Experimental Design. An AB design with a follow-up phase was employed to evaluate the effectiveness of the intervention. While the limitations of this design in establishing the degree of experimental control were recognized, a reversal design or a multiple baseline design was not feasible. A reversal design was not possible because the peers continued to apply spontaneously the intervention procedures in the follow-up phase when reinforcement for appropriate responding to Johnny's obscenities was removed. Ethically, we could not encourage the peers to exhibit the initial baseline behaviors that served to reinforce Johnny's cursing. Additionally, because peer attention only followed one behavior of one of the students, the prerequisites for employing a multiple baseline design was not available and thereby precluded its use.

Baseline. Before implementing the intervention, event recording was used to count the number of obscenities Johnny used. The teacher and students responded to his cursing in their usual way. This baseline period was maintained for seven days.

Intervention. During the baseline period, an ABC analysis was conducted. As previously mentioned, the ABC analysis showed that Johnny's inappropriate language was being reinforced by his peers. Therefore, the teacher enlisted the support of Johnny's peers in reducing the inappropriate behavior. She told the students that if they ignored Johnny's cursing, they would earn 10 minutes of free time.

Prior to initiating the peer extinction system, the teacher solicited the support of peers by asking for their assistance in helping Johnny improve his school behavior. Additionally, she discussed with them the negative effects of Johnny's behavior. After all the peers consented to participate in the peer extinction system, the teacher reviewed with them the target behavior and the intervention procedure, including their roles as behavior-change agents. Johnny was not present during this introductory discussion.

Because peer attention during the implementation of the intervention system can serve as intermittent reinforcement and interfere with the success of the system, the teacher monitored the group's adherence to the extinction procedure. The peers adhered to the proper procedures in all the intervention phase sessions. The intervention phase lasted for 10 days.

Follow-up. In this phase, reinforcement for ignoring Johnny's inappropriate behavior was withdrawn. However, the peers continued to ignore Johnny's obscenities. On day 2 of the follow-up, one of Johnny's obscenities was followed by peer laughter, which appeared to lead to a resultant increase in Johnny's use of obscenities. The follow-up phase lasted 6 days.

Reliability. Interobserver agreement was accomplished by having the teacher and a second trained observer independently record the target behavior. Reliability checks were made on 87% of all possible sessions and were distributed across the experimental phases. Reliability was calculated by dividing the smaller number of obscenities recorded by the larger for each observation and multiplying by 100. Reliability measures were 100% for each session.

RESULTS

The results of the case study are presented in Figure 1. The results revealed that the intervention caused a marked decrease in the targeted subject's use of obscenities. During the baseline period, the number of obscenities engaged in by the subject ranged from 5 to 8, with a mean of 6.7. During the intervention phase, the number of obscenities decreased to a mean of 2.4, with a range of 0 to 11. Data collected during the follow-up phase revealed a mean of 1 and a range from 0 to 4.

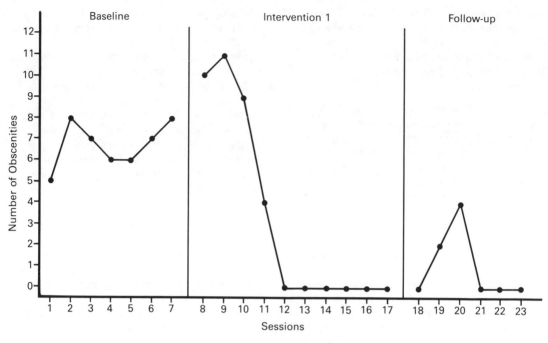

FIGURE 1

DISCUSSION

The results of this case study suggest that a peer-mediated extinction procedure can be an effective strategy for reducing the use of obscenities in a special education classroom. However, while the results indicated that the treatment conditions were successful, experimental control was not conclusively demonstrated. Nonetheless, Johnny's use of obscenities appeared to vary with the introduction and removal of the peer extinction system. For example, when a peer reacted to Johnny's obscenity on day 2 of the follow-up phase, a sudden rise in Johnny's cursing occurred. Furthermore, the initial increase in the rate of cursing and subsequent gradual decrease following the implementation of the intervention, which is characteristic of extinction data indicate the effectiveness of the intervention procedure.

The failure of the peers to return to their baseline behavior during the follow-up phase may be related to the effectiveness of the technique and its ease of implementation. The peer extinction procedure provided the students with a practical and positive system for dealing with inappropriate behavior. Therefore, instead of reinforcing Johnny's obscenities, the students had an effective strategy for dealing with inappropriate behavior. Thus, it appeared that the students had acquired constructive skills for coping effectively with peer-related disruptive behavior. Training students to deal constructively with peer-related inappropriate behavior makes the peer extinction procedure a particularly relevant and viable remedial strategy for learning disabled students.

CHAPTER
SEVEN

Helping Adolescents
with Psychiatric and
Interpersonal Problems

This chapter is about teenagers with inadequate interpersonal skills or psychiatric problems. The problems we address in this chapter include depression, suicide, eating disorders, school refusal, truancy, and social skills deficits. This chapter will help you identify, refer, and/or intervene with students who have special problems. This information is especially important to secondary school personnel, as the rate of certain psychiatric disorders dramatically increases in adolescence (Rutter, 1985). For example, depressive conditions as well as suicides are much more likely to occur in adolescence than in earlier years (Eisenberg, 1980; Shaffer & Fisher, 1981). We begin with information that may help you identify a problem.

IDENTIFYING PSYCHOLOGICAL PROBLEMS

When you are concerned about a student, consider these 10 general warning signs:

1. a sudden, unexplained change in behavior or attitude
2. a sad, unhappy mood that seems to persist
3. unexplained fatigue and lethargy
4. a disinterest in activities that once were pleasurable
5. a change in sleep habits (either being sleepier or having difficulty sleeping)
6. a change in appetite (either direction) or a remarkable weight loss
7. a failure to establish and maintain friendships with peers
8. a tendency to have accidents or to make statements about hurting oneself
9. a sense of hopelessness or extreme self-depreciation
10. a sudden decline in academic performance

We will go over these symptoms in our discussion of specific problems. But first, let us offer some assessment strategies. Interviewing is perhaps the best way to gather information about a teenager's psychological problems.

Interview Strategies

Perhaps the very best way to identify some of these warning signs is to have a conversation with the student about whom you are worried. Arrange to see the student privately, and allow enough time (no less than 20 minutes). Begin by telling the student that you are concerned about him and want to know if there is anything you might do to help. If the student seems confused or reticent, gently offer an example of the behavior that concerns you: "You seemed to have lost your interest in the class science projects." Or, "I've noticed that you seem more tired than usual. . . ." Or, "You seem a little down on yourself these days." Or, "I notice you've been sick a lot lately.")

Resist the urge to explain the symptom. Here are some examples of explaining the symptoms just-named: "I guess the science class hasn't been too interesting after all." Or, "Maybe you should go to bed earlier." Or, "Cheer up—your grades are better than you give yourself credit for!" Or, "Are you eating a balanced diet?"

Instead, be a quiet, accepting listener, so the student will feel comfortable enough to talk. After all, your guess may be wrong, throwing the conversation off the track.

Do not badger! Here are some ways in which we might badger a student: "I took important time out of my schedule to talk with you and you're just going to sit here like a clam?" Or, "Why don't you want to face reality—*something* is going on with you!" Or, "Okay, if that's the way you want it, that's the way you'll get it. If you don't take this opportunity, then don't ask for my help again." Or, "This is your last chance—you either tell me what's going on or you snap out of it and get your work done."

If the student does not feel comfortable, offer an alternative to talking with you. For example, you might say, "Perhaps this is not a good time for you. If you would like, we could talk another time." Or, "I know you and Mrs. Parron are rather close—do you feel you might want to talk with her? I could check to see when she is free." Or, "I know it is not always easy to talk. If you ever want to write me a note, I will be glad to help in any way I can.

Listen! Students experiencing interpersonal or psychological problems are not always articulate. It may take a little while for them to explain themselves. Be patient and do not interrupt. Show the student that you are listening, by looking directly at him and occasionally nodding your head.

Avoid judgments. This is not the time to offer a snap judgment of the student's perception of the problem. "Well, that isn't anything to worry about." Or, "Is that all you're worried about?" Or, "How did you ever get into such a mess anyway?" Or, "That was pretty stupid. . . . I hope you've learned your lesson."

Once you have heard the student's concerns, name some action that you can take together. Do not worry if you cannot immediately think of a solution. The important thing here is to show your real support and willingness to help. Here are some ideas: "I am not sure how to solve this problem, but I am willing to think it through with you, anytime you want to." Or, "Gee, this *is* a real problem. But two heads are better than one. Let me give this some thought. We'll talk tomorrow after science, okay?" Or, "Now I understand. Do you mind if I share some of this with Mr. Cavalesky, the counselor? I have a feeling he could help." Or, "I want to help you see your way through this. How would you like to leave it ?" Or, "Well, I may not be the very best person to help you, but I will help you find the right help."

Do not close the conversation until you have offered some reassurance (even if you cannot genuinely show *acceptance* of the student's views). Sometimes all a student really needs is

some information to help him see things differently. If this is the case, offer it. For example: "I see why you were so worried about the biology quiz. You may feel better knowing that *everyone* did poorly. I have decided to give a new, easier exam." Or, "Being in in-school suspension *is* serious; but no, it does not mean you go for the entire week. Only one day." Or, "I know the tenth graders said *they* could keep you off the team. But that decision is made only by the coach. The students do not have a vote." Or, "I guess you *would* be worried if you thought you were going back to the resource room again for math. Let me explain. The *only* reason you are going back is because your math class is taking a standardized test that you don't need. You are returning to the resource room just for these two days. After that you will return to Mr. Williams' math class."

Follow through with your commitment. Even if you have promised just to listen, be sure that you follow through on your promise of help. If you offered specific assistance, be sure to make this a priority.

Know how to help. Working with teenagers obligates you to know the proper referral procedures and sources, to understand how the mental health services in your community function, to know hotline phone numbers, and so forth. Most communities and some schools have all this information in a directory.

You should also know how to handle confidentiality. Do not promise total confidentiality to a student if you cannot uphold this—and often you should not, as, for example, in the case of a student who talks about suicide or serious psychiatric symptoms. Get some help from your school psychologist, counselor, or supervisor on this issue.

In some instances, you may notice a behavior pattern, one the student may not even have noticed. Directly watching for the behaviors and giving yourself and the student an estimate of how often they occur may be a good idea. The information you gather can help to convince the students that there is a problem. This might also be the basis for an IEP goal. The next section tells you how to gather this information.

Other Assessment Strategies

An alternative or supplement to interview strategies is direct observational procedures, as we described in Chapter Three. For mild behavioral problems, including social skills deficits, these direct observations are very helpful. Recall that one of the biggest problems with social skills assessment is the influence of different persons' perceptions of skills and problems. With an objective direct observational record you may be able to overcome the difference of opinion that often delays services to behaviorally handicapped students.

Sociometric measures, as described in Chapter Three, allow us to estimate students' friendship patterns and general popularity. They have proven enormously helpful, although many classroom teachers do not have the opportunity to include them in their assessment program. In part, this problem is attributable to the informed consent sometimes required from parents whose students are involved in a sociometric measurement activity.

Once you have gathered a little information (or even before you do, if you are really concerned), you will probably consider a referral. In some instances you will play a role in the **intervention**, or treatment, of the problem, too. The next section may help you to understand the referral and intervention process more thoroughly.

REFERRAL AND INTERVENTION STRATEGIES

This section covers the special psychological problems you would most likely see in a middle or senior high school program: depression, suicide, eating disorders, school refusal, truancy,

and social skills deficits. In every case, we also illustrate the problem behaviors.

Depression

Recall the symptoms of depression included in our list of general warning signs. What should you do if you suspect that one of your students is depressed? First, talk with the student, as we described earlier. Second, let another professional know about your concern. Third, inform the students' parents. Finally, follow some of the guidelines later in this chapter for working with students who exhibit depressive or suicidal behaviors or moods.

Suicide

Most of us have become painfully aware of the rising death toll from adolescent suicides in the United States. The adolescent suicide rate has increased 40% from 1970 to 1980, making suicide the third leading cause of death among adolescents (Holinger, 1979).

While depression is a factor contributing to suicide, the picture is not entirely that simple. Until research efforts produce a more definitive picture of the teenager who is likely to attempt suicide, we cannot offer you steadfast guidelines for the identification of students "at risk." However, we can suggest some characteristics that place students at risk for this tragedy, and we can offer some general approaches to the problem. First, there are the risk factors, which increase the chances for a suicide attempt. These include acting-out behavior, school refusal, social withdrawal, decline in school grades, suicidal threats or behavior, signs and symptoms of depression, substance abuse, or psychosis.

Both family members and friends of adolescents who have completed suicide are themselves at higher risk for completed suicides. Similarly, the children of parents with major psychiatric disorders, particularly the depression disorders and alcohol abuse, appear to be at particularly high risk for suicidal tendencies and for subsequently committing suicide (Brent & Kerr, 1986). Additional high-risk groups in adolescence include teenage girls who are pregnant (Gabrielson, Gabrielson, Klerman, Currie, Tyler, & Jekel, 1970) and runaways (Shaffer & Caton, 1984). According to recent studies, one-third of these teenagers will make a suicide attempt.

What does this mean to you, a professional working in schools? First, you should increase your general knowledge of the risk factors. Try to learn something about the family backgrounds of your students. Build your knowledge about handling teenage pregnancies: Chapter Eight is a good place to begin. Secondly, become familiar with your school and community mental health resources and drug rehabilitation agencies. Third, talk with a drug rehabilitation specialist to find out specific signs of intoxication or drug use, so that you can recognize these signs in your students. Fourth, read Chapter Nine.

Next, for a better understanding of depression and its signs, review the information we have just presented and refer to some of the additional readings listed in the references for this chapter.

Warning Signs. Keep the warning signs for suicide in mind as you interact with your adolescent students. These warning signs include:

- Changes in eating or sleeping habits
- Increasing isolation from friends and family
- A tendency to become more active and aggressive than usual, unlike suicidal adults, who tend to become apathetic when severely depressed
- A drop in academic achievement
- Giving away a valued possession, or an increased interest in getting his or her "life in order"
- Talking about suicide
- A sudden and intense interest in religious beliefs and the afterlife

- A recent loss, such as a divorce or death in the family, or a close friend moving away

Help strengthen the teenager's support network, that group of family members, friends, and adults whom the student views as supportive. "Help in strengthening the [individual's] support system will be beneficial, as it is with all other psychiatric problems: with suicidal [individuals] it may be lifesaving." (Strayhorn, 1982, p.480)

Specific steps to take with a teenager who talks about suicide follow:

1. Listen! Follow the guidelines outlined above for talking with students who are having difficulties.
2. Try to encourage the student to view his general situation as hopeful, by offering real assistance in the ways we have described.
3. Offer to help the student reach a mental health service, even offering to accompany the student there.
4. Contact the student's family.
5. Try to get the student to agree to call you before making any serious decisions.
6. Do not make light of the student's situation or expressed intent to end his life or hurt himself.
7. Let other professionals know of your concern, so that they might help in the ways mentioned and so that awareness of the student's behaviors might be increased and shared.

Eating Disorders

Individuals working with adolescents, especially girls, should be aware of the two major eating disorders: anorexia nervosa and bulimia. The following vignette describes an anoretic teenager:

Katherine states that in February she went on a diet. At that time she was 127 pounds at 5'8". She decided to cut down because she felt she didn't look good at that weight. She was surprised that she had so much willpower and was able to get down to 100 pounds. Katherine reports that her mother became uncomfortable with the dieting around April. By the end of April her mother was really getting angry about her diet. She said that she did about a half-hour of exercise each night and wouldn't eat sweets. She did find herself being too occupied with counting calories. Katherine currently does not see herself as being too thin, so she does have a distorted body image. Katherine has always felt herself to be different from the other kids. She has always been tall and was especially bothered by this in the seventh and eighth grades. When she was in ninth grade her periods began. Her mother told her about periods and talked to her about sex. She also viewed some informational movies at school. Katherine was somewhat uncomfortable talking about this area. She reports that her periods stopped several months ago. Katherine reports a change in her personality since going on the diet. Before February she would become depressed only if her mother yelled at her, and her mother often became angry and upset. Now she becomes depressed over nothing, or so she feels, and just wants to be by herself. However, she does no excessive crying. She does not feel that her current problems have had any effect on her friendships, though she has only one close friend, Natalie. (Kerr & Nelson, 1983, p.169)

The three criteria for anorexia nervosa cited by Russell (1985) include:

1. Marked loss of weight that is self-induced, usually through a systematic avoidance of 'fattening' foods (e.g., high-carbohydrate foods) and excessive exercise. Self-induced vomiting and purging are less frequent (cf. bulimia nervosa).
2. A specific psychopathology: an overvalued idea that fatness is a dreadful state to be avoided at all costs.
3. A specific endocrine disorder. In the female: amenorrhoea is an early symptom. In the male: there is loss of sexual interest and potency. (Russell, 1985, pp. 629-30)

The parallel criteria for bulimia, which often follows anorexia nervosa, are:

1. Preoccupations with food associated with episodes of gross overeating.
2. Devices aimed at counteracting the 'fattening' effects of the food ingested: especially self-induced vomiting or purging or alternation with periods of starvation.
3. The psychopathology of anorexia nervosa: fatness is so dreadful as to be avoided at all costs.
4. In 'true' bulimia nervosa there is a history of a previous episode of anorexia nervosa, possibly of minor severity. However, other forms of bulimic disorder may arise *de novo*. (Russell, 1985, p. 631)

Keep in mind that "the very nature of the illness [is] that the [individual] tries to avoid measures that are aimed at inducing a gain in weight" (Russell, 1985, p. 632). Therefore, you will probably not be successful if you merely encourage or admonish the student to eat a more nutritious and caloric diet. Rather, consider your role to be one of informing parents and mental health professionals of your concerns. Above all, do not ignore your concerns. The mortality rate for eating disorders has been estimated as high as 25% (American Psychiatric Association's Diagnostic and Statistical Manual of Mental Disorders, 1980).

School Refusal and Truancy: An Introduction

School refusal (sometimes triggered by depression) and its sister problem, truancy, are problems you undoubtedly have encountered. To prepare a referral or intervention for one of these problems, delineate the differences between these two worrisome behavior patterns. To help in making this discrimination, consider this vignette describing a school refuser:

In older children and adolescents, there is often no abrupt or definite change in personality but a gradual withdrawal from peer group activities formerly enjoyed, such as scouts or guides or youth clubs. The youngster ceases to go out, clings to and tries to control his mother, and may express a general fear or dislike of the world outside home. He may also become stubborn, argumentative, and critical in contrast to his earlier compliant behavior: often this anger is directed against his mother. Very often there is no clear precipitating factor other than a change to senior school which may have occurred as long as a term ago. . . .

Very often the school refusal is one indication of the young adolescent's general inability to cope with the increased demands for an independent existence outside the family, and entry into normal peer group relationships.

. . . complaints may take the form of loss of appetite, nausea, vomiting, syncope, headache, abdominal pain, vague malaise, diarrhea, limb pains, tachycardia (Schmitt, 1971). These complaints occur in the mornings before school or even at school without any overt expression of fear about school, which is only elicited on careful enquiry. At times the somatic symptoms are not actually experienced but fearfully anticipated, so that the child may avoid school in case he might faint or vomit in situations such as school assembly. . . . (Hersov, 1985, p. 384)

Hersov added that these somatic complaints may require the input of a pediatrician or family.

The discrimination between school refusal and truancy is crucial, because the two behavior patterns require dissimilar management approaches.

School Refusal Interventions

If you suspect school refusal, you should notify the appropriate guidance counselor, school psychologist, mental health professional, and/or administrator for your program. Share with them the information in this chapter, as well as your concerns and observations about the target student. Just as in the case of suicide or major depression, yours will be an indirect intervention or referral role at first. Later, after the student (and his family) is seen by a mental health professional, you will probably be asked to help arrange the student's return to school, a step that should occur as soon as possible (Hersov, 1985). To give you an example of how the student's entry might take place, consider this vignette:

Once back to school, on the first day contact must be maintained with child and parents by means of telephone calls to or from parents to gauge their own and the child's reactions to this first school attendance. Suggestions are made on how to deal with any new anxieties or attempts to manipulate parents to avoid school. If parents can manage unaided on successive mornings, they are praised and encouraged to take total responsibility for this, but support from clinic or school must be available if there are signs of faltering or loss of resolve in either child or parents. The child should be interviewed again after one week at school to sort out any existing or potential sources of stress and anxiety in the school or home situation which can then be discussed with teachers and parents. All concerned should be warned that the times of potential danger of breakdown of school attendance are after a weekend, after an illness requiring more than a day or two at home, the beginning of a new term, family illness or bereavement, and change to a new class or school. (Hersov, 1985, p. 395)

We hope that this brief overview of school refusal will assist you in your handling of this problem. Now let us turn to a more common problem, truancy.

Truancy

According to a recent study (National Coalition of Advocates for Students, 1985), one in four high school students in the United States drops out of school before graduation. Blacks and Hispanics drop out twice as often as whites, according to the same study.

Truancy, a serious problem, is made even more troubling when it appears, as it often does, with other, antisocial behaviors (violence, delinquency) (Ferguson, 1952; Hersov, 1960; Scott, 1966; Douglas et al., 1968; Tennent, 1971; Belsen, 1975; May, 1975; Farrington, 1978). The long-term consequences of truancy are upsetting, too: individuals who were truants may be at risk for poor employment experiences, criminal convictions, and addictive behaviors (Farrington, 1980; Gray et al., 1980; Robins & Ratcliff, 1980). Truancy also has a cross-generational effect: Truants often later have truant children (Robins, Ratcliff, & West, 1979).

What should school personnel do about truancy? The first rule is to identify the problem early and begin to handle the problem in its early stages. A second guideline is to gain parental co-operation—not always a simple matter. You should at least attempt to notify parents about their truant children and secure whatever level of assistance they are willing to provide. Unfortunately, parents typically are notified *and* punished (fines, court appearances), a strategy that fails to engender a cooperative attitude. A related third guideline is to make staying home from school as unpleasant as possible—a task that obviously requires parental help. Finally, published reports of truancy-prevention programs tend to recommend that the school take a hard look at itself, doing what it can to create relevant, interesting curriculum offerings—otherwise dubbed "holding power."

Realistically, an individual educator can do little to change a pattern of chronic truancy, but you may be able to participate in a school- or system-wide program. Consider the steps taken by Schloss and his colleagues (1981, p. 178):

1. **Increase the amount of satisfaction the adolescent gains from going to school.** Typical events included reducing academic demands on the student to increase the likelihood of success, monitoring and intervening on peer relations to reduce peer tensions, providing more frequent social reinforcement for completed work, frequently communicating successful school experiences to the parents and encouraging the parents to equate favorable reports with special after-school and weekend activities, encouraging the parents to send the adolescent to bed at a reasonable time, and engaging the adolescent in frequent conferences with the teacher whereby he or she can openly express concerns toward the school program.

2. **Decrease the amount of satisfaction the adolescent gains by staying home from school.** If the student did not arrive at school at the appropriate time, the home interventionist would immediately make a home visit. If the adolescent was ill, the day's schoolwork would be brought to the home. If the adolescent was not ill, the parents and home interventionist escorted the adolescent to school. If the adolescent physically refused to accompany the home interventionist and parents to school, prearranged sanctions were placed against the adolescent, including removal of television privileges for the day, confinement to his or her bedroom, dockage of allowance, etc.

3. **Actively teach skills which enhance the adolescent's ability to benefit from going to school.** The teachers were asked to provide small group activities for the purpose of developing socially skillful behavior. In addition, special interest areas in which the adolescents were highly motivated to achieve were included in the academic program. These included shop classes, art classes, and athletics.

In a program recently proposed for the New York City schools, a "dropout prevention coordinator" and a "family assistant" were named to work in each of the project schools. The latter individual was

a person drawn from the surrounding community who helps resolve family-related problems that affect a student's school work or contribute to decisions to drop out.... The family assistants, people with high school diplomas who will be paid about half the salary of a teacher, are also supposed to work outside the school, finding out why students are missing from classes and seeking the help of parents to keep them in school. (Christian, 1985, p.14)

As another illustration of a dropout prevention program, an urban high school program for high-risk ninth graders included these components:

1. High-risk ninth graders were identified from their attendance records from the eighth grade. In May, letters were sent to "feeder" schools sending their eighth grade graduates on to the project high school. Through this correspondence, the group of 30 new ninth graders were chosen as "high risk" for dropping out. These students then were assigned to a special homeroom.
2. Two teachers were assigned to the homeroom to act as co-homeroom teachers.
3. The homeroom teachers were given the period immediately after homeroom as a duty period. Their duty period consisted of making contact with parents regarding attendance, immediately confirming absence or reinforcing good attendance.
4. All tardies to school, class cuts, or other reasons for absence flowed directly and immediately to the homeroom.
5. During homeroom period the group received mini-lessons in school survival skills (see Chapter Four). The homeroom teachers were keys to providing support (to the targeted students).
6. The reward system for this group was revamped as follows:
   a. Students were encouraged to construct a form to keep a running account of their grades.
   b. Each student kept a daily assignment book. Parents signed each day that they assisted with or checked homework.
   c. A system of rewards was worked out individually through contracts. (D. Mackey and S. Ruta, personal communication, October 11, 1983)

If you are involved in planning a truancy prevention program, keep in mind the general principles these successful programs have illustrated.

SOCIAL SKILLS DEFICITS

This section focuses on social skills deficits. First, we remind you of assessment strategies you can use to pinpoint a student's social skills problems. Second, we offer several curriculum ideas and teaching strategies.

Before turning to assessment, let us put the problem of social skills deficits in some perspective for you.

Defining Social Skills

We define social skills as the capacity to develop and choose from a variety of actions when faced with an interpersonal situation (cf., Goldfried & D'Zurilla, 1969).

Sheldon, Sherman, Schumaker, and Hazel (1984), who wrote an excellent social skills curriculum for mildly handicapped adolescents, named the social skills listed in Table 7-1.

The Significance of Social Skills Deficits

Research has shown that mildly handicapped teenagers do not enjoy the good social skills of their nonhandicapped peers (Mathews, Whang, & Fawcett, 1982; Schumaker, Hazel, Sherman, & Sheldon, 1982). We know also that poor social skills may have a negative impact on achievement. For example, a socially unskilled teenager may not exhibit the interpersonal school survival skills discussed in Chapter Four. Social skills also play an important role in how a teenager gets along in his community (Sheldon, Sherman, Schumaker, & Hazel, 1984). Consider this statement:

TABLE 7–1

Target social skills

Accepting Compliments	Giving Help
Accepting Criticism	Giving Rationales
Accepting "No"	Goodbye Skills
Accepting Thanks	Greeting
Active Listening	Interrupting Correctly
Answering Questions	Introducing Yourself
Apologizing	Joining Group Activities
Asking for Feedback	Making Friends
Asking Questions	Negotiation
Body Basics	Persuasion
Conversation	Problem Solving
Following Instructions	Responding to Teasing
Getting Help	Resisting Peer Pressure
Giving Compliments	Saying Thanks
Giving Criticism	Starting Activities with Others

Source: From "Developing a Social Skills Curriculum for Mildly Handicapped Adolescents and Young Adults: Some Problems and Approaches" (p. 110) by J. Sheldon, J. Sherman, J. Schumaker, and J. S. Hazel, 1984. In S. Braaten, R. Rutherford, Jr., and C. Kardash (Eds.), *Programming for Adolescents with Behavioral Disorders*, Reston, VA: Council for Exceptional Children. Reprinted by permission.

A number of studies have indicated that, although the type of behavior (offense) is critical, a youth's interaction skills are a major determinant of police dispositional decisions (Black & Reiss, 1970; Goldman, 1963; Piliavin & Briar, 1964). Also, once a youth is labeled, especially "delinquent," his/her ability to get along with teachers, social workers, probation officers, and judges often has a major bearing on whether the youth remains in the community or is institutionalized (Cohn, 1963: Gross, 1967). Thus, engaging in appropriate social behavior may mean the difference between institutionalization and being allowed to live in the community.

Social skills also appear to be related to obtaining a job and successful job performance (Fulton, 1975). Goldstein (1972), for example, found that employers tend to view vocational adjustment problems as related more to social behavior than to the actual job or task performance. Thus, it may be just as important to follow instructions properly, accept criticism appropriately, and negotiate conflict situations as it is to perform the job well. (Sheldon, Sherman, Schumaker, & Hazel, p. 106)

The student with social skills deficits is at risk, according to research, for other problems later in life. Students with poor social skills are more likely to drop out of school, become juvenile delinquents, and have adult mental health problems (Asher, Oden, & Gottman, 1977).

As you can see, social skills deficits are a very serious problem. Moreover, the school setting may not be the ideal or practical place for social skills training, especially if you are a classroom teacher of large regular education classes whose focus is academics. Nevertheless, we offer specific interventions for two reasons. First, you may want to know what kind of training a student is receiving in a mental health facility that offers him social skills training. Second, you may be involved as a counselor, psychologist, or classroom teacher in a social skills training program.

We begin with teacher-mediated strategies for improving social skills.

Teacher-Mediated Strategies

You can do a great deal to improve the interpersonal skills of your students. Begin with choosing a curriculum for social skills, then move to a skill that is important for both social *and* academic instruction, working in a group. Then move to role playing, teaching social skills, and group goalsetting and feedback. One of your first decisions as the leader of social skills training may be to choose a curriculum for social skills. Until very recently, you would have faced few alternatives, even fewer of which had been validated in classrooms. The picture today is brighter, offering several well-evaluated curricula. Table 7-2 displays a list of some of these curricula.

To give you an idea of the teaching strategies used in these curricula, here are the components of steps you would follow in the structured-learning approach that underlies the skillstreaming curriculum developed by Goldstein, Sprafkin, Gershaw, and Klein (1980):

1. *Modeling.* Teaching a skill begins by exposing groups of youngsters to vivid examples (live on video or audio tape, films or filmstrips) of the skill being used well. This constitutes the modeling component. Modeling displays present scenes or vignettes in which the protagonist handles potentially troublesome situations successfully by employing the skill being taught. One skill is taught at a time, so that the modeling vignettes depict several examples of a single skill being used

TABLE 7–2
Annotated bibliography of social skills curricula

---

(1) **Simulation Materials**

a. Goldstein, A. P.; Sprafkin, R. P.; Gershaw, N. J.; and Klein, P. *Skillstreaming the adolescent.* Champaign, Illinois: Research Press, 1980.
   Target population. This program was developed for adolescents, and can be utilized with intermediate level elementary students.
   Description of materials. The text provides the educator with 50 lesson plans for 50 social skills, two different homework report forms and instructions for implementing the program.
   Format. The teacher selects one of the 50 skills to be taught. Each lesson follows the same format: (1) define and discuss the skill to be learned, (2) distribute skill cards containing the steps for the skill, (3) model appropriate use of the skill, (4) organize role-plays during which students practice the skill, (5) give and invite feedback, (6) provide social reinforcement, and (7) assist students in planning homework assignments.

b. Hazel, J. S., Schumaker, J. B.; Sherman, J. A.; and Sheldon-Wildgen, J. *Asset: A social skills program for adolescents.* Champaign, Illinois: Research Press, 1982.
   Target population. Designed for adolescents grades six through 12, this program functions best when used with groups of five to eight members.
   Description of materials. The Asset manual provides the leader with training procedures, nine lesson plans, skill sheets outlining the steps for each skill, home notes, checklists, consent forms and various questionnaires. The program includes nine video taped sequences modeling appropriate and inappropriate social interaction skills. The leader is encouraged to utilize appropriate props for role-plays.
   Format. Each session follows the same format: (1) review of home notes, (2) review of previously learned skills, (3) presentation and discussion of positive and negative examples of the target skill on video tape, (4) distribution and examination of skill sheets containing the steps in the target skill, (5) verbal rehearsal, (6) role-play or behavioral rehearsal, (7) feedback, (8) criterion role-plays and (9) home notes assigned.

Source: From ''Teaching Social Routines to Behaviorally Disordered Youth'' by R. Neel. In *Social/Affective Interventions in Behavioral Disorders,* edited by J. Grosenick, S. Huntze, E. McGinnis, and C. Smith, 1984. Washington, DC: U.S. Dept of Education.

continued

TABLE 7–2
continued

---

c. *MARC: Model affective resource curriculum.* Orlando, Florida: Orange County Public Schools. **Target population.** This program is designed for adolescents.
Description of materials. The manual provides the teacher with lessons for skills in four areas: self-control, interpersonal problem solving, communications and behavioral interactions.
Format. Each lesson teaches a specific skill or component of a skill. The leader (1) facilitates discussion, (2) models appropriate behavior, (3) assists students in practicing the skill through role-plays, (4) provides feedback, (5) summarizes the lesson and (6) gives a practice assignment. Several lessons involve practicing the skills in natural environments, as well as simulation.

d. Stephens, T. M. *Social skills in the classroom.* Columbus, Ohio: Cedars Press, Inc., 1978.
Target population. This program can be used with student groups of all ages.
Description of materials. The manual provides the educator with instruction in a variety of directive teaching techniques: social modeling, social reinforcement and contingency management. The manual also provides three lesson plans (one for each teaching technique) for each of the 136 skills. The teacher selects the skill to be taught and the teaching technique most applicable to the student's needs.
Format. When teaching a new skill, the educator uses the social modeling strategy: (1) set the stage through discussion, a story, a film, etc., indicating the value of learning the skill, (2) draw out of discussion the specific steps which make up the skill, (3) model correct behavior, (4) set up role-plays in which the students practice correct behavior, and (5) plan and implement reinforcement strategies for the skill throughout the day. The teacher may use social reinforcement or contingency management techniques if needed to continue to maintain the skill once learned.

(2) **Supplementary Activities**

a. Ball, G. *Interchange.* San Diego, California: Human Development Training Institute, 1977.
Target population. Separate kits are available for junior high and senior high students.
Description of materials. Each kit is packaged in a storage box for easy access to leader's manual and cards for discussion sessions. The discussion topic cards are organized into approximately 40 units, each with six to 10 discussion lessons outlined.
Format. The leader facilitates a supportive, open-ended style discussion session which focuses on one of the discussion topics.

b. *Project Transition.* Seattle, Washington: Seattle Public Schools, Dept. of Student Services, 1981.
Target population. This comprehensive program is designed for use by counselors at the senior high level. Use by classroom teachers is encouraged as well.
Description of materials. The materials are organized into six booklets, each one a separate unit. The six content areas are introduction, communication, self-assessment, goal setting/ decision-making, career exploration and long-range planning.
Format. The leader follows the manual for each discussion session or activity lesson. Activities include paper-pencil tasks, group tasks, art, etc. Discussion following the activity is directed by the leader.

---

in different situations. To make a skill presentation as concrete as possible, the skill is broken down into its component behavioral steps, each of which is illustrated in the modeling vignette. Youngsters' skill deficits are assessed via self-reports, observers' reports, and for research purposes, situational behavioral tests.

2. *Role Playing.* Following the presentation of the modeling display, a group discussion ensues. Youngsters are urged to comment on what they have seen and heard, and to relate the modeling of the skill to times in their own lives when use of the particular skill has been difficult. From the material generated in these discussions, role plays are developed. Each youngster is given an opportunity to role play or practice the skill as a rehearsal for a situation that might actually occur in a real-life circumstance.

3. *Performance Feedback.* Following the enactment of the role play, the trainers elicit performance feedback (approval, praise, constructive criticism) from the other group members. In general in this phase, the main actor is given support as well as helpful suggestions on how his or her performance might be made even more effective. At times the trainer may have the main actor replay the scene immediately so that the feedback from the other youngsters (and/or the trainers) may be incorporated without delay.

In addition to these steps, transfer of the adolescents' social skills to other situations is addressed. This emphasis on what we call **generalization** and **maintenance** is created through approaches such as teaching students the general principles that guide a social encounter, having students practice interactions until they "overlearn" them, using real-life didactic examples and situations (especially in the videotapes for modeling) and having students practice through "homework" on real-life encounters, changing trainers to improve generalization across trainers, and reinforcement of new social skills (Goldstein et al., 1983).

You will notice that these same basic components make up the social skills curriculum, ASSET (Hazel, Schumaker, Sherman, & Sheldon-Wildgen, 1982). Here is the sequence from that curriculum:

1. *Awareness*, in which students read booklets depicting common situations, complete workbook exercises, discuss their answers to questions with a teacher, and complete written practice on the steps of each social skills,

2. *Practice*, during which students participate in role-plays, and

3. *Application*, during which the students might play simulation games with each other, use home notes, complete homework assignments, and receive feedback from parents or others.

We believe that these components (i.e., didactic instruction, pencil-and-paper activities, practice through role-playing, and homework activities for generalization and maintenance) are common to successful social skills training programs. Although we do not suggest that you "reinvent the wheel" and create your own social skills programs, these are good guidelines to follow in the event that you choose to work with a student on one or two particular social skills. The generalization or transfer-of-learning component is especially important for mildly handicapped students as demonstrated by Schumaker and Ellis (1982) and Kelly et al. (1983). Self-monitoring has been an essential feature of this transfer-of-learning phase. We discussed self-monitoring in Chapters Four, Five, and Six. Later in this chapter, we will offer examples of self-monitoring as it applies to social skills.

As you review curricula for your students, consider their group participation skills. Some curricula require considerable sophistication on the part of the students who will function as a working group for each lesson. Other curricula require fewer group participation skills. Our next section discusses the assessment of group skills.

Assessing Group Skills

One of the most important obligations we have to handicapped adolescents is to teach them interactional skills. Too often we offer only one-to-one teaching, preventing students from learning how to interact during academic discussions or group work. In this section we offer a plan for assessing students' group interaction skills and deficits and for matching them to appropriate group and dyadic activities. Figure 7–1 displays a hierarchy of skills for use in assessing students. Let us examine each of the levels proposed in Figure 7–1.

Level I describes students who really do not have the skills to function successfully in even a small group. These students may get along all right in a highly structured, teacher-directed group instructional activity, but their capacity to function without so much teacher direction is minimal. A group discussion, class meeting, or project would present difficulties for these students, who have deficits in the areas of self-disclosure, socially appropriate initiations towards others, and self-control within a group activity.

Level II students could benefit from highly structured dyadic activities under adult supervision (interviews of one another, structured peer tutoring that follows the same format each day). These students can participate in a minimal way in group discussions, if the teacher calls on them. These students exhibit generally better self-control than do Level I students (can listen to others, can begin to self-evaluate their own contributions to the group).

Students at Level III begin to enjoy some unsupervised group activities. They can function for short periods without constant adult supervision, so they can maintain peer tutoring or small group projects, as long as these activities are planned by an adult and follow a fairly predictable format. While everyone may not be enamored with their style, they are usually tolerable (e.g., they may be long-winded and irritating, but not abusive towards others). You may recognize these skills and deficits in some of your adult colleagues!

Level IV students can easily function in groups without adult supervision. They can actively participate in a group decision-making activity, peer tutoring, group goalsetting and feedback directed by a classmate, or "brainstorm" sessions.

Level V describes students who are good group participants and leaders—definitely great candidates for regular education classes. In fact, these students may tire of highly structured activities and prefer student-run sessions and projects. These students have another good skill: They can criticize their own group interactions and modify them accordingly.

Matching Group Skills with Group Activities

Assessing your students' group interaction skills is only half the problem, of course. Next comes the difficult task of deciding which group activities to organize for which students. We hope that the checklist in Figure 7-2 will facilitate this task for you. To review this checklist, begin with the first three items. The reason to include these basic information items is to help you recall the nature of the activity, once you have recorded the other information. This facilitates your sharing activities with other teachers or colleagues.

The variable, *direction/adult involvement*, describes how much structure the activity offers. Recall that students at Levels I-III require a great deal of structure and supervision. To make an activity more structured, you can do these things:

- Increase the ratio of adult to students,
- Have an adult direct the activity, and
- Let the adult group leader be a familiar classroom figure, rather than an outsider.

Predictability refers to the amount of newness and change to which students must adjust. To make a group activity (or a dyadic activity) more predictable, try these changes:

Level I Skills/Problems:
1. Will answer specific teacher-directed questions.
2. Has minimal listening skills.
3. Needs lots of attention (e.g., must be called on).
4. Refuses other than highly directed responses.
5. Has poor self-disclosure skills.
6. Has few prior group experiences that were successful.
7. Generally does not get along well with others.
8. Has poor self-evaluation skills for group participation.

Level II Skills/Problems:
1. All of Level I Skills exhibited consistently.
2. Can make appropriate contributions with teacher calling on him/her.
3. Has a few classmate friends or can interact singly with others (e.g., converse).
4. Occasionally volunteers personal information.
5. Has high attention needs but can give others attention, also (e.g., can conduct short interview).
6. Requires adult direction; does not function well without supervision (e.g., engages in problem behaviors if activity is not teacher-directed and involves a group).
7. Responds well only in groups that practice previously learned skills.
8. Weak but improving self-evaluation skills.

Level III Skills/Problems:
1. All Level I and II Skills shown consistently.
2. Can interact in structured activity with one or two other students, without adult supervision and direction (e.g., structured peer tutoring).
3. Shows beginning leadership skills in a group activity (e.g., makes suggestions for projects, assists others in articulating their ideas).
4. May still require help with personal style in group (e.g., drones on and on, dominates conversation); can self-evaluate with help.
5. Exhibits irritating style, perhaps, but is not essentially disruptive to group.
6. Can learn new content or adjust to a *slight* change of format or topic within a group (e.g., structured lessons on different topics).

Level IV Skills/Problems:
1. All above skills are exhibited.
2. Can function successfully in peer-run groups with minimal adult direction (e.g., half-hour brainstorm with peers).
3. Can disclose personal information with relative ease.
4. Can peer tutor, peer monitor without adult supervision.
5. Can participate in group decision-making.
6. May still require contingent reinforcement.
7. Can self-evaluate in certain activities, without help.

Level V Skills/Problems:
1. Can serve as a group leader or co-leader.
2. Makes useful suggestions to others in the group regarding their participation (e.g., complimenting, revising, using their ideas).
3. Can succeed in a spontaneous, unstructured group.
4. May tire of structured groups or lessons.
5. Devises own peer tutoring strategies to enhance existing program.
6. Can accurately self-monitor own group participation skills.

FIGURE 7–1
Assessment of the teenager for groups and dyads

Name of Activity _____

Purpose _____

_____

Time Required (per school day) _____

Proposed Level pre-I   I   II   III   IV   V

Direction/Adult Involvement

Adult:student ratio _____ Number of students _____

Adult directed _____ Peer-mediated _____ Both _____

Who selects the goals? _____

Is the adult leader a familiar classroom figure? _____

For what portion of the activity is the adult involved?   100%   60%   40%   0%

Level of Predictability/Structure

Is activity highly structured _____   Structured _____

   Somewhat structured _____   Without structure _____

Is the activity a peer tutoring activity? _____

Does the activity follow the same format every session? _____ Or does the format change? _____

Does the topic change with every session? _____

Does the activity allow students to practice old skills? _____

   Learn new skills? _____ Both? _____

Do students know the topic in advance? _____

Are students asked to disclose personal information? _____

Do students volunteer for the activity? _____ Or, are students called on? _____

Is the activity in a familiar environment? _____

Does it take place in the classroom? _____ In the community? _____

Name the academic skills this activity requires _____

_____

_____

_____

Name the social skills this activity requires _____

_____

_____

_____

_____

_____

Comments _____

_____

_____

_____

_____

FIGURE 7–2

Analysis checklist for group activities

- Offer a firm structure for each session,
- Have the same format each time,
- Keep the same topic for each session,
- Incorporate a number of skills students have learned previously (The last two items on the checklist allow you to list skills that serve as prerequisites for participants.),
- Do not require students to disclose highly personal information,
- Call on students, and
- Hold the activity in a familiar environment.

Remember that students will not learn important group participation skills simply sitting in groups. Many of our students must begin at the beginning: learning to work and interact with only one or two other classmates. You must design group activities with your students' needs in mind, if your students are to improve their interactions and proceed to less restrictive, highly group-oriented environments.

Combining Group Skills with a Token Economy. Recall the "levels system" described in the discussion of token economies in Chapter Six. You could incorporate group levels at each of the levels of your token economy system. Students would then be reinforced for working on their group participation skills.

Group Goalsetting and Feedback

This strategy for helping students master their individual goals through a group context was described in Chapter Six.

To illustrate how you can develop individual goals from each of these areas, here are some examples:

- Janette will offer a comment in each class discussion.
- Walt will offer to help at least one other student each day.
- Derek will ignore teasing on the bus.
- Annette will compliment at least one student each afternoon.

- Dick will participate in one group project each science or social studies class.

Be sure to review carefully the guidelines for group goalsetting before you begin. Group goalsetting and feedback have much in common with self-monitoring of target behaviors, the topic of our next section.

Self-Monitoring

We know that adolescents need good social skills to be successful in their jobs (Adams, Strain, Salzberg, & Levy, 1979). Warrenfeltz and his colleagues (1981) found that behaviorally disordered adolescents transferred their learning more effectively when they used self-monitoring. Of particular importance is the fact that their study addressed social skills in the workplace. Students were asked to self-monitor whether their responses to their employer were appropriate or inappropriate, on a simple two-column recording form. This additional aid helped students to transfer their social skills learning to the vocational training site. Without the self-monitoring, students tended not to make the transfer. Here are the definitions of "appropriate" and "inappropriate" as reported by Kelly et al. (1983):

Appropriate response to instruction. The supervisor's instructions were defined as direct commands requiring the student to perform simple tasks which could be accomplished easily within 1 minute. Examples include: "Please close the door," "Put away those tools," "Return this book to Terry," and "Put this on the shelf."

An appropriate response to instructions first required that the student discriminate an instruction from other verbal interactions of the vocational supervisor. Second, upon receiving an instruction, the student had to verbally acknowledge it in a moderate tone of voice. Third, the student had to begin to comply with the instruction within 5 seconds. Appropriate student verbal responses could include requests for clarification or a restatement of the instruction.

A response was scored as inappropriate if the student did not begin to comply within 5 seconds, made no attempt to comply, or complied insufficiently. Further, a response was considered inappropriate if there was no verbal response or if the verbal response contained abusive language, rude or threatening gestures, whining, complaining, or refusing: or if it implied, by tone or inflection, a negative affect.

Appropriate responses to critical feedback and conversation. Critical feedback from the work supervisor included remarks that expressed dissatisfaction with some aspect of the student's performance and implied that a corrective action should be taken. Examples include: "All the tools haven't been put away yet," "That part of the bench is still dirty," and "This form is not complete." Conversational initiatives by the supervisor consisted of statements or questions which were unrelated to the vocational training program and did not call for a compliant motoric response. Examples of conversational initiatives included: "It's a nice day today," "What did you do this weekend?" and "I saw 'Elephant Man' last night, did you see it?"

An appropriate response to the supervisor's critical feedback required a polite verbal acknowledgement from the student that the criticism had been heard, and that corrective action be taken within 5 seconds. An appropriate response to the supervisor's conversational initiative was defined as a polite, topic-related verbalization by the student indicating that the supervisor's comment had been heard.

Inappropriate responses included failure to comply (in the case of critical feedback), absence of a verbal response by the student, or the student's making a rude or content-inappropriate statement or a statement with negative affect in tone or inflection. (p. 20)

To create a self-monitoring component for your social skills training program, just select specific targets and design some kind of recording form as suggested in Chapter Five. Our case study for this chapter describes an intervention for a student with social skills deficits.

SUMMARY

This chapter has covered a variety of special problems that you may encounter in your work with adolescents. We have offered several general guidelines for you to follow for recognizing problems before they become serious—and in some cases, life-threatening. Unfortunately, several of these problems are on the increase in our society, resulting in a need for increased awareness on the part of all who work in schools.

Although specific interventions may be outside your professional realm, we have tried to indicate ways in which you can promote positive mental health, especially in remediating social skills deficits. We urge you to consult the bibliography on social skills and the recommended readings for additional help. Furthermore, we encourage you to share information on warning signs and referral practices with others in your schools who may be able to support your efforts. This dissemination is especially important in large, comprehensive high schools, where students may share many teachers. By informing your colleagues, you improve the chance of early identification of psychiatric and interpersonal problems—the key to successful intervention and treatment.

RECOMMENDED READINGS

Asher, S. R., & Gottman, J. M. (Eds.). (1981). *The development of children's friendships*. Cambridge: Cambridge University Press. A collection of views, in 12 chapters, emphasizing research. Part I, "Group processes," includes assessment and social skills, with respect to popularity, social structure of friendships, and within or between group

This reading list was reprinted (in part) from "Social Skills and Children: An Annotated Bibliography" by P. W. Dowrick and C. A. Gilligan, 1985, *The Behavior Therapist*, 8(10), pp. 211-213. Copyright 1985 by the Association for Advancement of Behavior Therapy. Reprinted by permission of the publisher and author.

differences (interracial, mental retardation). Part II, "Social-cognitive processes," contains one chapter analyzing social skills training, others analyzing naturally occurring processes.

Buss, A. H. (1980). *Self-consciousness and social anxiety.* San Francisco: W. H. Freeman. Examines the theory of self-consciousness, relevant research and implications. Basic components illustrated with examples are provided for social skills training with children, adolescents, and handicapped children. Major components include the selection of social skills, assessment, teaching process, generalization and maintenance. One chapter specifically addresses "shyness."

Cartledge, G., & Milburn, J. (Eds.). (1980). *Teaching social skills to children: Innovative approaches.* New York: Pergamon. Oriented towards social skills training as part of a school curriculum. Part I (120 pp.) sets out general assessment and teaching procedures. Part II, in chapters by different authors, focuses on specific populations: behavior disorders (aggression, withdrawal): handicapped: young children: adolescents.

Curran, J. P., & Monti, P. M. (Eds.). (1982). *Social skills training: A practical handbook for assessment and treatment.* New York: Guilford. Contains one chapter focusing on children. The book is in three parts. Part I—Social skills training with schizophrenia and related variables, such as family influences, maintenance, and generalization. Part II—Other populations: including children with peer relationship difficulties. Part III— Social skills assessment.

Eisler, R. M., & Fredriksen, L.W. (1980). *Perfecting social skills: A guide to interpersonal behavior development.* New York: Plenum. A theoretical framework encompassing the development of social skills, their effects, and the basic principles of training. Research examples illustrate specific components and emphasize practical application. The book is in three parts: research, assessment, and application. Chapter 8: "Skills training with children."

Elardo, P., & Cooper, M. (1977). *AWARE: Activities for social development.* Menlo Park, CA: Addison-Wesley. A book of procedures, emphasizing the development of empathy and social problem solving for school-age children. Over 60 (2-page)

modules covering recognition of feelings (e.g., anxiety), appreciating individual differences (e.g., learning difficulties), and developing social behavior (e.g., "A stealing dilemma," & "What can you do about teasing?").

Goldstein, A. P., Sprafkin, R. P., Gershaw, N. J., & Klein, P. (1980). *Skillstreaming the adolescent.* Champaign, IL: Research Press. A packaged program of "structured learning" with adolescents. Initial chapters outline the development of procedures and their basic principles, including assessment (checklist). Later chapters (c. 100 pages) give details of target skills, with trainer notes, and example dialogues between trainers and trainees.

Journal of Pediatric Psychology. (1981). (Special section on children's social skills), *6,* 335-434. Six articles covering normative and developmental issues, learning disabilities, and peer intervention strategies.

Kelly, J. A. (1981). *Social skills training: A practical guide for interventions.* New York: Springer-Verlag. Divided equally between chapters on general principles and procedures, and chapters on specific skills. One chapter on social skills for children (describes components, procedures, and some studies).

Lahey, B. B., & Kazdin, A. E. (Eds.). (1981). *Advances in clinical child psychology* (Vol. 4). New York: Plenum. Chapter 4—"Social skills assessment of children," reviews and highlights theoretical, conceptual, methodological, psychometric, and programmatic issues. Chapter 5—"Peers as behavior change agents for withdrawn classmates," reviews procedures and research findings on systematic and incidental influence by children on their shy peers. Other chapters have some relevance to social function.

Lahey, B. B., & Kazdin, A. E. (Eds.) (1983). *Advances in clinical child psychology* (Vol. 6). New York: Plenum. Chapter 1—"Social relationship problems in children: An approach to intervention." A review of social skills training for children who have problems interacting with their peers.

Mash, E. J., & Terdal, L. G. (Eds.). (1981). *Behavioral assessment of childhood disorders.* New York: Guilford. Chapter 8— "Social skills deficits." Several other chapters are relevant to assessment in social problems of children. Topics are presented in four major divisions; Externalizing disorders (e.g., conduct problems); Internalizing disorders (e.g., fears, social skills deficits); Developmental disorders (e.g., gender problems); Health-related disorders (e.g., obesity).

Michelson, L., Sugai, D. P., Wood, R. P., & Kazdin, A. (1983). *Social skills assessment and training with children: An empirically based handbook.* New York: Plenum Press. Emphasis on assessment and program implementation details for social skills training with aggressive or withdrawn children. Briefly reviews relevant findings on social development and empirical studies of intervention. Two hundred pages detailing 16 training modules and associated materials.

Patterson, G. R. (1982). *Coercive family process.* Eugene, OR: Castalia Publishing. Extensive and detailed review of childhood aggression. Substantial theory and research, focusing on reciprocal effects within the family, are presented. One chapter describes family treatment (emphasis on behavioral parent training), and one relates aggression to other antisocial behavior.

Patterson, M. L. (1983). *Nonverbal behavior: A functional perspective.* New York: Springer-Verlag. Examination of the social function of nonverbal behavior. The book reviews the goals or purposes served by patterns of nonverbal behaviors, discusses the role of nonverbal behavior in social exchange.

Rubin, K. H., & Ross, H. S. (Eds.). (1982). *Peer relationships and social skills in childhood.* New York: Springer-Verlag. Examines a variety of social skills and peer relationships in the study of infants, toddlers, preschoolers, school-age children and adolescents, and several special populations. Part I—social skills in infants through the development of prosocial behavior. Part II—predominant focus on peer relationships. Part III—individual differences in peer relationship and social skills.

Schinke, S. P., & Gilchrist, L. D. (1984). *Life skills with adolescents.* Baltimore: University Park Press. A behavioral counseling approach to the life skills a child should acquire before independence from parents. Areas addressed include interpersonal relationships, sexuality, stress and health, work and society.

Social skills training for children [special issue]. (1983). *Child and Youth Services, 5* (3,4). Eight articles on a variety of topics. Issues: early development; applicability of research. Approaches: cognitive-social-learning; classroom settings. Populations; withdrawn children; adolescents: court-adjudicated youths; emotionally disturbed adolescents.

Spence, S., & Shepherd, G. (Eds.). (1983). *Developments in social skills training.* New York: Academic Press. A variety of issues and interventions (over half of which are institution based). Section II—"Social skills training with children and adolescents," includes three chapters focusing on school children, adolescent psychiatric outpatients, and adolescent offenders.

Strain, P. (Ed.) (1981). *The utilization of classroom peers as behavior change agents.* New York: Plenum. Ten contributed chapters review peer relationships, and their incidental and programmatic influence on children's educational and social development. Two chapters have procedures for withdrawal and aggression; others address methodology and specific populations.

Zimbardo, P.G. (1977). *Shyness: What it is, what to do about it.* Menlo Park, CA: Addison-Wesley. Examines different types of shyness, problems faced by shy individuals, and the origins and analysis of shyness. Different chapters relate shyness to alcoholism, criminality, and sexual disorders. Chapter 9— "Building your self-esteem," Chapter 10—"Developing your social skills." The book presents, in lay terms, simple tactics and strategies for better social effectiveness, oriented to both children and adults.

CASE STUDY

Reducing Attention-Getting Behaviors and
Increasing Appropriate Social Interaction

PROBLEM

David, age 13, recently transferred to the Mill Run School from a middle school in another county. His current 25-student classroom is located in a small rural school which is served by an itinerant consultant.

Since David's coming to Mill Run School, his teacher has become concerned about mild but persistent "attention-getting" behavior. She has also noted David has problems making friends. During the day, many of David's classmates complain about his disruptions. Peers also avoid him on the playground during lunch break.

The classroom teacher and the consultant met. Together they selected a structured intervention that the teacher could implement easily. In addition, the specialist decided to participate in a short-term intervention program designed to improve David's social functioning.

ASSESSMENT

The first step taken was to objectively define what the teacher meant by "attention-getting" behavior. In this case, "attention-getting" referred to interruptions when the teacher was engaged in instruction and asking frequent, off-topic questions. To get a baseline measure of the level of David's attention-getting behavior, the consultant recorded the number of "attention-getting" incidents per 20-minute observation performed by David and by a teacher-identified "average" classroom peer (see Figure 1). The peer was observed to obtain a comparison measure of "average" levels of the same classroom behaviors. Both David and the peer were observed concurrently and observations were collected over several days.

Because the teacher felt David may have reacted to being observed by the consultant, his teacher covertly observed David on two other days. It was found David's level of attention-getting was more frequent when he was covertly observed. In contrast, David's behavior occurred about twice as frequently as the peer behavior.

Because David's behavior was best described by the teacher-collected counts of "attention-getting," it was decided that the teacher would keep regular tallies of these behaviors during randomly selected 20-minute periods during the intervention phase. The average peer also would be observed to provide a way of monitoring average levels of the target behaviors.

David's social interactions during lunch time were assessed by simply counting initiations to and from David and responses to and from peers following initiations. The duration of interactions (when David was talking with a peer after an initiation-response start) was also estimated by running a stopwatch continuously during the interaction and stopping the watch while David was alone. Since no negative or hostile behavior was observed, only positive initiations and responses were recorded (see Figure 2).

Observations by the consultant during lunch suggested David was initiating to peers much more than peers initiated to him during lunch. When David initiated, peers tended to ignore rather than respond. Occasionally, some peers did respond to David's initiations. However, those initiations were very brief. It was decided to help David increase the duration of interactions with those peers who responded to initiations. This was done by targeting conversational skills David needed to keep receptive peers "engaged" in longer interactions.

INTERVENTION AND OUTCOME:
ATTENTION-GETTING

A teacher-directed intervention was implemented for David and classroom peers to re-

---

This case study was written by Tamara S. Hoier, Department of Psychology, West Virginia University.

202

Subject(s): *David + Peer*

Setting: *Attention Getting*

RAW DATA SHEET

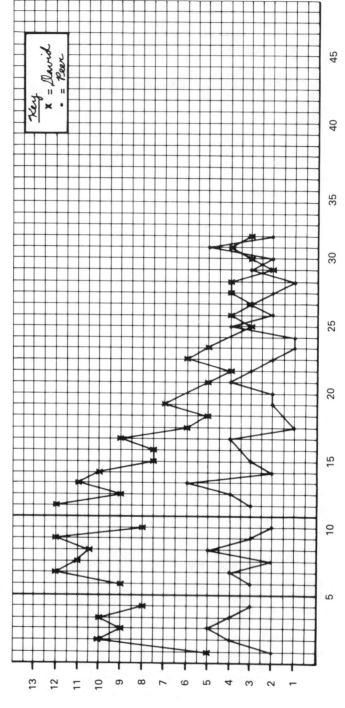

FIGURE 1
Graph of David's progress

	Baseline				Intervention						
	Day 1	Day 2	Day 3	Day 4	Week 1	Week 2	Week 3	Week 4	Week 5	Week 6	Week 7
Initiations to Peers by David	卌 III	卌 卌 II	卌	卌 卌	卌 卌 IIII	卌 卌 II	卌 III	IIII	卌 II	卌 I	卌 卌
Positive Responses to David's Initiations	II	I	I	III	III	III	卌	IIII	卌	卌	卌 III
Intiations to David by Peers	I	I	I	II	III	卌	IIII	II	卌 I	卌 II	卌
Responses to Peer Initiations	I	I	I	I	III	卌	IIII	I	卌 I	卌 II	卌
Estimated Duration of Interations (in seconds)	10 sec.	10 sec.	5 sec.	10 sec.	30 sec.	60 sec.	127 sec. (2 min., 7 sec.)	350 sec. (5 min. 20 sec.)	540 sec. (9 min.)	580 sec. (9 min. 40 sec.)	800 sec. (13 min. 40 sec.)
Average Peer*				893 sec. (14 min. 53 sec.)	735 sec. (12 min. 10 sec.)						935 sec. (15 min. 35 sec.)

*Collected on another day from data obtained for David.

FIGURE 2
Social behavior at lunch

duce David's attention-getting behavior. Every day, David and three to four other students were given a set of counters that were to be used to trade in for the opportunity to ask or answer questions. David and his classmates worked as a group to "plan" questions so there were counters left over. If the team managed to have a certain number left over at the end of the day, they earned free time as a group. This "game" involved David and different peers in a cooperative planning activity. After a few rough days, David and different teammates managed to plan questions such that they averaged less than five per child. David's data as collected by the teacher indicated the intervention had reduced his "attention-getting" to the "average peer" level (refer to Figure 1).

INTERVENTION AND OUTCOME: SOCIAL INTERACTION

David was seen individually by the consultant for two sessions per week. During those visits, David was taught how to ask open-ended questions (to keep someone talking), how to talk about his own experiences as follow up to a peer's conversation, and how to alternate asking questions and making comments about himself in conversation. After the second week, training involved having David ask rapid-fire questions and give rapid-fire descriptions of relevant experiences so that he could "think on his feet" when anxious with peers. David also learned to identify and initiate to those peers who were *most* likely to reciprocate his initiations.

Data collected by the consultant one day per week during intervention indicated that peers responded to David's initiations more over time (as he began to seek receptive peers). Peers also began to initiate to David much more often, and David consistently responded to those initiations. The time he spent in interaction, as indicated by stopwatch data, increased significantly over time. By week 7 of the intervention David spent almost as much time in interaction as the average peer from his classroom.

PART
THREE

Special Issues for
Adolescents

CHAPTER
EIGHT

Sexual Maturation in
Adolescents

This chapter was written by Dr. Robert Gedekoh.

The psychological and emotional consequences of sexual maturation have a tremendous impact on an adolescent's ability to function in an academic environment. Puberty represents the most stressful, perplexing stage of development, filled with conflicts and confusion. Dealing with sexual maturation is a difficult task, even for a normal teenager. The difficulties of making this transformation are compounded for a youngster with special needs. Educators must play an active role in helping mentally and emotionally disturbed children deal with their developing sexuality.

Because handicapped students are sexual beings and because we live in a time of great turmoil regarding sexuality, we cannot simply ignore the issue of sex education. But it is hard to imagine a more controversial topic. Everyone agrees that our school systems should prepare our children to balance a checkbook, follow a road map, write an intelligent letter, look up a telephone number, and read a newspaper. Our children are taught to operate computers, swim, speak French, drive cars, twirl batons, and kick field goals without the least bit of controversy. Yet, the mention of sex education still strikes terror in the hearts of many ministers, parents, teachers, and school boards across the land.

But is the moral majority really a majority? A recent study by the Guttmacher Institute (1981) revealed that eight out of ten Americans believe that sex education belongs in the schools. Nine out of ten parents of teens believe that birth control and sexuality should be included in academic curricula. A recent government-sponsored study demonstrated that 98% of parents said they needed help in discussing sexuality with their children. Yet, a recent Gallup Youth Survey reported that only 43% of American teens reported receiving any sex education, and only 31% said they were taught about contraception.

Meanwhile, nearly one-half of males ages 15 to 17 and one-third of females of the comparable age are sexually active. Eight in ten males and seven in ten females report having intercourse while still in their teens. More than one million teenage girls become pregnant in the United States each year; nearly 40% of these undergo abortions. Forty percent of our female children become pregnant during their teens.

Too often it is assumed that the purpose of sex education is merely to teach the mechanics of sexual intercourse. The purpose of sex education, however, is to teach the individual to deal positively with his or her developing sexuality, to understand the physical manifestations of sexual maturation, and to cope with the psychological stresses that accompany this process. Finally, we need to provide the information our students need to be responsible, caring, sexual beings.

Sexual education comes from many sources. Children are exposed to information and misinformation about sex continuously from television, radio, magazines, and their peers. Yet, straightforward information about venereal disease and contraception is almost never given to adolescents; in fact, it has been banned in many communities.

The parents of handicapped children are generally aware that some information regarding sexuality needs to be provided to their children. Those with learning handicaps may be more vulnerable to sexual exploitation because they are taught to be obedient and do what is asked of them without question. Anxious to please and receive attention, adolescents with special needs may offer little resistance to sexual predators. Some have poor judgment and lack impulse control; thus they may commit inappropriate sexual acts unless they receive adequate instruction regarding sexual matters. Handicapped adolescents may find themselves at odds with society in terms of their own sexual behavior for this reason.

Adolescents with special needs have less opportunity to glean information from their peers, may find it difficult to seek out information from written sources, and have fewer chances to observe the interaction between the sexes at social functions. Yet, the consequences of ignorance regarding sexual matters can be profound, and the teacher who avoids the subject may be doing irreparable harm.

Sol Gordon, a pioneer in sex education, has suggested that "the retarded do not need to know many facts about sex. The information that needs to be imparted to them can be given in a few minutes, though it must be repeated many times and for different levels of understanding" (1974).

He stresses that the following points need to be made:

1. **Masturbation is a normal sexual expression no matter how frequently it is done or at what age. It becomes a compulsive, punitive, self-destructive form of behavior largely as a result of suppression, punishment, and resulting feelings of guilt.**
2. **All direct sexual behavior involving the genitals should take place only in private.**
3. **Any time a boy and a girl who are physically mature have sexual relations, they risk pregnancy.**
4. **Unless both members of a heterosexual couple clearly want to have a baby and understand the responsibilities invovled in child rearing, they should use an effective method of birth control.**
5. **Until a person is about 18 years old, society holds that he or she should not have intercourse. After that age, the persons can decide for themselves.**
6. **Adults should not be permitted to use children sexually.**
7. **The only way to discourage homosexual expression is to risk heterosexual expression.**
8. **In the final analysis, sexual behavior between consenting adults (regardless of their mental age and whether their behavior is homosexual or heterosexual) should be no one else's business—provided there is little risk of bringing an unwanted child into this world. (Gordon, 1974, p. 69)**

We believe that special-needs adolescents should also be taught to recognize the signs and symptoms of venereal disease and pregnancy and should know how to obtain medical attention. They must also be prepared for the emotional and physical changes that accompany sexual maturation.

PHYSICAL MANIFESTATIONS OF ADOLESCENCE

During adolescence, important cognitive, psychosocial and physical changes occur. **Puberty**, by definition, occurs when an individual is capable of reproduction. **Pubescence** is defined as the span of time during which the sex characteristics appear.

The biological changes that characterize adolescence are mediated by the endocrine system, composed of a number of ductless glands widely separated from one another in the body. These glands secrete messenger substances, or hormones, into the bloodstream. The activity of the endocrine glands is integrated through neuronal and hormonal mechanisms.

The pituitary gland, located at the base of the brain, serves as the master of the endocrine system. Through its hormonal messengers, the pituitary regulates the function of the adrenal glands, the thyroid gland, the parathyroid gland, as well as the ovaries and the testes. The pituitary also secretes growth hormone, which regulates physical growth and skeletal development; prolactin, which mediates the production of milk from the breast; as well as other hormones integral to kidney function and the initiation of labor. The pituitary operates under control of the hypothalamus, a portion of the midbrain. Pituitary function is also mediated by the hormonal feedback from the target endocrine glands.

Although the activity of the thyroid and the adrenal glands is important in sexual maturation, it is the gonads—the testes in the male, the ovaries in the female—which are perhaps most integral to the development of sexual characteristics. These organs are also the source of the gametes—the sperm in the male, the egg in the female.

No one organ can be singled out as being responsible for the sexual maturation and function of an individual; rather, it is the integrated function of several organs, known collectively as the hypothalamic/pituitary/gonadal axis, that coordinates this monumental task. The detailed biology of the endocrine system goes beyond the scope of this book; indeed, to date, it is incompletely understood. The system is, in fact, sufficiently complex that it seems almost miraculous that puberty occurs at all. Yet, in most individuals, sexual maturation, at least in the physical sense, occurs smoothly, even in the face of various environmental and emotional insults.

The process of sexual maturation in the male is reflected by the appearance of pubic and axillary hair; the enlargement of the penis, scrotum, and testes; the development of the male habitus: and finally, the production of semen containing sperm capable of fertilizing an egg. In the female, the development of pubic hair, breast enlargement, the development of the female habitus, and menstruation are observed.

Special-needs educators must be aware of the normal sequence of events that occur during adolescence so they may reassure and educate their pupils, who may be puzzled and disturbed by the dramatic transformations in their bodies. They need to understand that there is a wide range of variability in the onset and progression of puberty among adolescents. Teachers should also recognize those rare instances when the normal process of sexual maturation is significantly disturbed, so that appropriate medical evaluation and intervention can be initiated.

Girls usually mature about two years sooner than their male peers, but because of the wide range of variability, an occasional boy will complete puberty before the first signs of sexual maturation appear in some of his female cohorts. Because girls generally undergo the adolescent growth spurt 1½ years sooner than do their male counterparts, many 11- and 12-year-old girls will be taller than their counterparts.

Females

Breast budding, or **thelarche**, is the first sign of puberty in most girls, occurring at a mean age of 10.5. This may happen as early as 8 or as late as 13 years of age and still be considered within normal limits. The appearance of pubic hair, **pubarche**, usually occurs about six months later, at 11 years of age. However, in approximately 25% of girls, pubic hair development precedes breast development. The appearance of pubic hair between the ages of 8 and 14 is considered normal.

The peak of the adolescent growth spurt in girls occurs at a mean of 11.6 years of age; the normal range is from 9.5 to 14.5. **Menarche**, which is the first episode of menstrual bleeding, occurs at a mean age of 12.8, with a normal range from 9.5 to 16 years.

In nearly all instances, this sequence of events proceeds in an orderly fashion. Variations from this sequence may be a signal of trouble, particularly if vaginal bleeding occurs before breast development or the appearance of pubic hair. In these instances, a tumor, foreign body placed into the vagina, or child abuse must be suspected.

Evaluation for delayed puberty is indicated if a girl has not menstruated by age 16, has not had the onset of breast development or the appearance of pubic hair by the age of 14, or has not menstruated within three years of the appearance of breast budding.

The appearance of breast budding or pubic hair before the age of 8 also merits medical attention, as does the appearance of vaginal bleeding without other signs of puberty. About 80 or 90% of girls with precocious puberty will have no identifiable pathology, but the remainder will have some disease state that may respond to therapy. In some instances, precocious puberty may be tracked to accidental exposure to medications containing steroid hormones, such as birth-control pills.

Menstruation

Because the first episode of menstrual bleeding may occur as early as age 9, it is important to prepare female children *before* this occurs. The child who experiences vaginal bleeding for the first time without preparation is likely to be confused, frightened, and embarrassed.

Many girls will be aware of menstruation from observation of their older siblings or mother. Family members should be encouraged to take a positive position regarding menstruation, emphasizing that it is a normal sign of growing up and that is need not disrupt daily living patterns. The cultural myths and taboos surrounding menstruation may be particularly disturbing to suggestible youngsters. Educators should attempt to demystify menstruation. It is important to establish that menstruation is not dirty and that it is not a cause for guilt or shame. Menstruation should *not* be treated as a sickness.

Details of personal hygiene must be reviewed in class prior to the onset of menstruation. Youngsters should be told to notify a responsible individual when menstrual bleeding first appears. They should be taught how to use sanitary pads, and they should be told how to obtain these supplies. Some handicapped individuals can be taught to use tampons, but others will lack the manual dexterity and confidence to manage this skill. If a youngster cannot be trusted to change tampons regularly, she should not be encouraged to use them inasmuch as **toxic shock syndrome**, a life-threatening medical emergency, may occur if a tampon is left in place for an inordinate period of time.

Males

The first sign of puberty in males is the enlargement of the testes and the appearance of straight hair at the base of the penis, usually around the time of the 12th birthday. Later, the hair becomes coiled and profuse, eventually forming an inverted triangle extending towards the umbilicus. Axillary hair generally appears about two years after the first pubic hair is seen, although dense axillary hair does not usually become evident until about age 16-18. The appearance of the beard and indentation of the anterior hairline is a late change, occurring in most individuals after age 16.

The growth of the larynx, or voicebox, leads to lengthening of the vocal cords, and in most males the voice drops about one octave in pitch. Pitch changes and roughness may occur until about age 18, when the mature male vocal quality is generally attained.

The growth spurt in males generally occurs between 13 and 15.5 years of age; during this time there is usually an increase in height of about eight inches. After age 18, most males will grow less than one additional inch. The development of the masculine habitus occurs during the growth spurt.

The first ejaculation of semen may occur as early as age 12, but in most males this will be seen at age 13½. In many individuals, it will occur during sleep in the form of a wet dream. At age 11, male adolescents should be told to anticipate nocturnal emissions. It is important to emphasize that this is a natural occurrence and just another sign of growing up. Most commonly, nocturnal emissions may be accompanied by vivid dreams of a sexual nature. Wet dreams should not become a source of guilt or shame for the child.

The appearance of signs of puberty in males under the age of 10 warrants medical evaluation. In 50% of such cases, no causative factor can be identified, but in the other 50% a pathologic condition may be diagnosed. Likewise, if no testicular enlargement or pubic hair has developed by the age of 13.5, a physician should be consulted, although in most instances normal development will occur.

SEXUAL BEHAVIORS

Masturbation

Although many people consider any form of self-stimulation to be masturbation, it is best defined as an attempt to achieve orgasm through manual stimulation of the sexual organs exclusive of intercourse. In the past, masturbation was a behavior that was universally practiced while being universally condemned. Today, we understand that masturbation is a normal form of sexual expression and not a cause of impotence, insanity, brain damage, blindness, tooth decay, or any other malady that may have been attributed to it in the past.

There are many reasons for an individual to choose to masturbate. It is a means to relieve sexual tension; it is a means of dealing with anxiety, depression, or boredom; for some, it is a compulsive behavior; it may be a way to attract attention. But the simple fact is that most people masturbate because they find it a pleasurable experience.

Those responsible for the education and supervision of the adolescents with special needs must understand that masturbation is normal and is, in itself, harmless. In some instances masturbation is potentially beneficial: it relieves sexual tensions that otherwise might lead to disruptive behaviors, and it familiarizes the child with his/her own body and patterns of sexual response. Masturbation may be the main outlet for sexual expression for many mildly handicapped adults and children.

All kinds of people masturbate, irrespective of age, race, marital status, religion, or cognitive ability. The myth that mentally handicapped people masturbate more frequently is, in part, a function of the social and occupational deprivation that characterized their care in the past. Without guidance, the retarded are more likely to masturbate in inappropriate places and times.

Most small children discover that handling the genitals is enjoyable. As children grow older, they usually continue to masturbate, irrespective of the wishes of their parents and teachers. Most children learn quickly that it is best to masturbate in private, at a time and place when adults are not likely to intercede. Children living in institutionalized settings under close supervision may find this problematic.

It is not enough to admonish special-needs children to masturbate only in private. It is necessary to establish what constitutes privacy. For those living at home, the bedroom or bathroom are likely to be private places. Children living in institutions may need a broader definition, particularly if they share their sleeping quarters with others.

Not infrequently, a child may be discovered handling the genital area at an inopportune place or time, for instance, in the classroom. It is important for the teacher to assess what might have led to this behavior. The child with an infection, allergic rash, or inordinately tight clothing might not actually be masturbating. In other instances the teacher might observe that the child masturbates when anxious or under stress. Identify the source of anxiety, and offer the child alternative methods of coping. Unusual or harsh punishment may traumatize the child. Make the child understand that such behavior is not acceptable in public, and establish specific guidelines for intervention should the behavior recur.

Those responsible for the care of a child with special needs may believe that the child masturbates so excessively as to interfere with social and educational activities. Such individuals might be spending a great deal of time by themselves in their rooms or in the lavatory. Persistent masturbation to the exclusion of other activities may result from loneliness or diminished self-esteem. Individual counseling, encouragement, and a careful reevaluation of the student's environment and educational program may be in order in these instances. The problem of excessive, inappropriate masturbation may not respond to negative reinforcement, especially when the student is masturbating to attract attention. In this case, a student could be rewarded for not engaging in masturbatory behavior during a predetermined period of time. Such a student might also be encouraged to engage in other types of appropriate behavior.

It may be necessary to involve the parents in dealing with this situation. Discussions with parents must be handled with tact, with consideration and respect for their moral and religious views. Parents may be unduly repressive and punishing in regard to masturbation, or, at the other extreme, may choose to ignore excessive masturbation. A conference with an appropriate counselor or therapist may help the family to understand and deal with this sensitive issue.

Homosexuality

At the outset we must distinguish between homosexual behavior and **homosexuality**. Homosexual behavior is sexual activity or play between members of the same sex. Many individuals engage in homosexual behavior at some time in their lives, but most of these individuals are not homosexual. A homosexual is an individual who feels a strong sexual attraction to members of the same sex. This attraction predominates over the individual's attraction to members of the opposite sex; that is, the homosexual prefers sexual partners of the same gender. Before an individual is labeled ho-

mosexual, this pattern of behavior must be established as longstanding and the sexual activity should be overt.

Most homosexual behavior in adolescents will not persist. Transient homosexual behavior usually represents childhood experimentation. A child experiencing the increased libido that accompanies puberty may feel uncomfortable in directing interest towards members of the opposite sex, with whom he or she is less familiar. Instead, this sexual drive may be directed towards members of the same sex.

"At this age, homosexual behavior may be viewed as a temporary defense against the fears associated with the move toward full homosexual relationships. Since the handicapped child may be rather inept in his dealings with the opposite sex, he or she may persist in exhibiting homosexual behavior" (Kempton, 1975, p. 113). Individuals who are restricted in their exposure to members of the opposite sex may often exhibit circumstantial homosexual behavior. Handicapped and disturbed youth restricted to an environment that discourages heterosexual interaction may turn to same-sex sexual expression for gratification. Some institutional staffs have not actively discouraged homosexual activity, believing that to do so might increase the likelihood of heterosexual activity and pregnancy.

Homosexual behavior that continues past the age of 16, involves an intense "love" relationship, is longstanding, and is not explained by environmental restrictions, may represent true homosexuality. If the homosexual behavior is frequent, nearly all sexual fantasies are directed towards members of the same sex, and the individual preferentially seeks out those of the same gender at social functions, the individual may be considered homosexual.

Homosexuality is no longer considered a form of psychopathology, but rather is considered an alternative life-style. Unfortunately, society as a whole is somewhat less tolerant of gay people than are psychologists. Efforts to divert sexual interest from a homosexual to a heterosexual orientation have met with questionable success and should be utilized only by those wishing to attempt such a transition. Increasing numbers of homosexuals have decided that they are satisfied with their own sexuality and do not desire any change.

But adolescents need to understand that there are important rules regarding homosexual behavior, just as there are rules regarding heterosexual behavior. Homosexual behavior that is forced upon another individual, that involves an adult and a child, or that occurs in public cannot be tolerated. Male homosexuals making sexual contact with a number of partners run the risk of acquiring **AIDS** (Acquired Immune Deficiency Syndrome), a disease that is not treatable and is nearly always fatal. Disturbed and retarded youngsters must be admonished against homosexual prostitution, which can, of course, have devastating psychological and physical consequences.

When transient homosexual behavior is observed in adolescents, several strategies might be utilized. Counseling regarding sexuality may help alleviate the fears that an individual might harbor regarding the opposite sex. Adequate social exposure to members of the opposite sex should be assured. Exposure to appropriate role models may be helpful, allowing the child to observe normal interactions between men and women. Hysterical or punative attitudes must be avoided, although, out of consideration for other students, close scrutiny of the individual's behavior is indicated. It may be important to reassure the family that such behavior is usually temporary and not a cause for panic.

In summary, while we agree that homosexuality is not, in itself, pathological, we also recognize that in our society homosexuals still may be subjected to discrimination and ridicule. Because emotionally and mentally handicapped youngsters are already vulnerable to stigmati-

zation, the additional burden of being labeled homosexual should be avoided if possible. Homosexual behavior should be gently discouraged, and alternative forms of sexual expression should be encouraged. In some instances the homosexual orientation may persist. In these cases, those responsible must teach the individual to deal with his or her sexuality in a way that will maximize personal development while preventing psychological or physical harm.

Unacceptable Forms of Sexual Behavior

We have already emphasized that special-needs adolescents may be prone to inappropriate sexual behavior for a number of reasons, not the least of which is diminished impulse control. We have also suggested that some exceptional youth may be vulnerable to sexual abuse and exploitation because of their trusting and obedient natures. It is important that these adolescents learn that certain types of sexual expression are unacceptable and that engaging in them may have serious physical, social, and even legal consequences. Like other children, children with special needs must learn to avoid these activities, and they must know what to do if another individual attempts to lure them into inappropriate sexual activity.

Handicapped children must learn that nudity is not acceptable in public. **Exhibitionism**, either as a form of sexual expression or a means of gaining attention, must be discouraged. Children must be made to understand that such behavior will make them targets of ridicule and could lead to incarceration.

They should be told that it is wrong to give or receive money or material possessions in return for sexual favors. Such activity constitutes prostitution, a dangerous situation, which can result in serious physical or emotional harm.

Special-needs students must be taught that it is not acceptable to force or cajole another individual into any form of sexual behavior against that person's will. Reinforce the idea that it is wrong to kiss, fondle, or touch another individual who does not desire such attention and that is is very wrong to force another individual to have intercourse, be it homosexual or heterosexual, against his or her will. Students should know that such activity constitutes rape and that it is regarded as one of the most serious forms of crime.

It is also important to explain that adults are never to engage in sexual activity of any kind with those under the age of 18. This may be troublesome for some handicapped adults, who, because of their own cognitive and social limitations, may feel more at home in the company of younger individuals. Exceptional individuals need to understand that sexual experimentation must never take place with children and that they should never touch the genital organs of a child. Nor should they permit any adult to handle their genitals inappropriately.

Handicapped children should be warned to avoid situations in which they might be abused. They must learn not to trust strangers who offer assistance or gifts. They should be instructed to travel in groups whenever possible. And, perhaps most importantly, they need to know that it is okay to say no to an adult whose behavior seems suspect. Sexual offenders are rarely strangers to the child; family members, friends, neighbors, and even those responsible for the child's care are the most common instigators of sexual abuse. A specific authority figure should be designated to the child as the appropriate source of help should such abuse occur. This individual should not be frightening or intimidating to the child; he or she must be approachable.

When sexual abuse has occurred, it is important to avoid hysteria. Handled correctly, a single episode of sexual abuse need not have serious psychological consequences to the child. The child must be reassured that he or she was not to blame and that no permanent, irreparable physical damage has occurred. By law, sus-

pected sexual abuse must be reported to the proper authorities.

When incestuous activity is suspected, the situation is explosive. Incest most commonly occurs between an adolescent female and her father or stepfather. Usually the adult involved in such activity is manifesting arrested psychosexual development. The other parent will often go to great lengths to deny that which must surely be suspected. Intensive family counseling is imperative, for incest is rarely an isolated event, but rather a symptom of a profound familial pathology.

Occasionally, a child may exhibit crossdressing and assume the clothing and affect of the opposite sex. Most commonly seen in boys, cross-dressing is usually transient and is best handled by gently discouraging or ignoring the behavior. In girls, it is less problematic inasmuch as many female children are routinely permitted to wear male attire. When crossdressing becomes persistent, psychological counseling is imperative, as this may be an indication of **transvestism** or **trans-sexualism**.

A transvestite knows and accepts his gender identity, but seeks sexual gratification by affecting the attire and mannerisms of the opposite sex. A trans-sexual believes that he or she is, in fact, a member of the opposite sex, trapped in an inappropriate body. Transsexualism is manifested by persistent, intransigent cross-dressing. Both transvestism and trans-sexualism are manifestations of profound disturbances in gender identity and are best handled by knowledgeable and experienced professionals.

THE SEXUALLY ACTIVE ADOLESCENT

Contraception for the Mentally and Emotionally Handicapped

Although the fertility of some handicapped individuals is limited, most are biologically capable of conceiving a child. Of course this does not mean that they are ready or able to accept the responsibilities of childrearing. In the not so distant past, those responsible for the education and supervision of the handicapped assumed that the best course of action was to discourage sexual activity. Of course, many handicapped individuals engaged in sexual activity anyway, and unintended pregnancies were common. Attempts to restrict the sexual activity of handicapped people led to anxiety, embarrassment, and guilt—all serving as obstacles to personal development.

When faced with a special-needs individual who may be sexually active, a counselor or physician must first ascertain whether there is really a need for contraception. Some mildly retarded individuals may be openly affectionate or even flirtatious, but may not intend to engage in intercourse. It may take subtle questioning to ascertain whether they are really sexually active.

Merely asking whether intercourse has occurred may not be sufficient. The student may not understand this terminology, and some may not distinguish between hand-holding, kissing, or petting and actual intercourse. After all, these can all be considered to be "making love." Frequently, it may be necessary to resort to the vernacular to ascertain the degree of sexual involvement.

Once the educator has concluded that sexual intercourse has occurred or is likely to occur, counseling regarding birth control is indicated. Adolescents with special needs deserve factual information regarding the risks and benefits of various contraception. In many instances, they need some gentle guidance in choosing an appropriate method.

Barrier Methods. It has been our experience, as well as that of others, that barrier methods such as diaphragms, sponges, and condoms are not always the best choice for teens.

Some handicapped women never master the technique of placing and removing tampons, so it is difficult to teach them to utilize a diaphragm or sponge correctly. And because teens may be forced by circumstance to have intercourse at odd times in out-of-the-way places, barrier methods are likely to be inconvenient. A final concern is that handicapped individuals might forget to remove the diaphragm or sponge at the appropriate time, and an infection or even toxic shock syndrome could follow. *Some* handicapped women engaged in a stable relationship, however, can learn to use diaphragms effectively.

Condoms. Condoms are only 80% effective, inasmuch as they may tear or come off if improperly placed. It may be difficult for the adolescent male with special needs to obtain condoms. However, any male who has intercourse with a number of partners should be taught to use condoms, the only birth control method that offers any protection against the transmission of venereal disease. Vaginal contraceptive suppositories or foam placed concurrently with condom use can theoretically increase the level of effectiveness to 95%, but this tends to be messy, and many teens do not cope well with the inconvenience.

IUDs. Prior to 1986, the intrauterine device, or IUD, had been a popular choice for mentally retarded individuals requiring birth control. These small plastic devices were produced in a number of shapes and sizes and placed within the uterine cavity by an experienced physician. In some instances a portion of the IUD contained copper to enhance its effectiveness (Copper-7, Tatum-T). Those containing copper were to be changed every three years. Plastic IUDs (Saf-T-Coil, Lippes Loop) could theoretically be left in place indefinitely, although some physicians felt they should be changed at three-year intervals to minimize the risk of serious pelvic infections such as **pelvic inflammatory disease** (PID).

Due to the medicolegal liability crisis, these IUDs are no longer available in the United States.

However, patients who already have one of these IUDs in place may continue to use them. Only the Progestasert, a progesterone-containing IUD, remains on the market. It must be changed at yearly intervals.

Although it is known that IUDs are safer than oral contraceptives under certain medical circumstances, it is not clear at this time whether they will be available to American women in the future.

IUDs are not without risks, and these must be understood by both the patient and those responsible for her supervision. Almost every woman who uses an IUD will note an increased menstrual flow, and her period may last several additional days.

Most physicians who place IUDs encourage their patients to check their vaginas once a month, after the menstrual period, to confirm the presence of the IUD string. Occasionally IUDs are spontaneously expelled into the vagina, and in rare instances they may be passed from the vagina without the patient's knowledge. If this happens, pregnancy can occur.

Pregnancies may also occur in patients with an IUD still in place; these instances are medical emergencies. Intrauterine pregnancies associated with an IUD may lead to life-threatening infections, and a pregnancy associated with an IUD may not be located in the uterus at all, but rather in the fallopian tube (ectopic pregnancy). For this reason patients who use IUDs should be able to identify the signs of pregnancy (missed periods, morning sickness, breast tenderness). When the question of pregnancy rises, a simple blood or urine pregnancy test should resolve the issue.

Another serious complication of IUD usage is pelvic inflammatory disease. Most commonly caused by gonorrhea and/or chlamydial infections, PID in some instances is caused by microorganisms that are not generally associated with venereal infections. In any case, such infections may lead to sterility due to scarring of the fallopian tubes. Such infections may be se-

vere enough to require hospitalization and intravenous antibiotic therapy. In some instances major abdominal surgery is needed to resolve these infections.

Individuals using IUDs should know that lower mid-abdominal pain associated with a foul vaginal discharge and/or an elevated temperature may be signs of infection and that prompt medical attention is necessary. Because IUDs potentiate the consequences of venereal infections, they are not a good choice for patients with several sexual partners or for women with a single sexual partner who is promiscuous.

IUDs have been popular with handicapped people because they are very effective (98%) and because they do not require much patient compliance. The removal of IUDs from the market is particularly unfortunate for handicapped women inasmuch as an acceptable substitute may not be available. It is important to understand, however, that while IUDs were a good choice for many, they were never a panacea, and that they may not be the best method for all retarded individuals.

Oral Contraceptives. During the past decade, oral contraceptives (the Pill) have been utilized with greater frequency by handicapped individuals. Taken correctly (every day) it is the most effective form of contraception, aside from sterilization. It is convenient, easy to use, and requires no manual dexterity. Much has been said about the risks associated with oral contraceptives, but physicians have become increasingly aware of certain benefits as well.

Most patients on oral contraceptives have very regular, 28-day menstrual cycles with minimal cramping and reduced flow. The risk of ovarian and uterine cancer, iron deficiency anemia, and PID is diminished by oral contraceptive use.

There are definite contraindications to pill use, including hypertension (high blood pressure), a history of thrombophlebitis (clotting within the veins), a history of cerebrovascular accident (stroke), and serious liver disease (hepatitis). Oral contraceptives may increase the frequency of seizures in some epileptics. But the risk of life-threatening complications with pill usage is actually quite small for a patient who is young (under age 30), does not smoke, and is in otherwise good health.

The pill is a good contraceptive choice for a patient with several sexual partners because it is very effective and may reduce the risk of serious PID. It is also a good choice for a patient with irregular, heavy, or painful menstrual cycles. Patients must be educated regarding the need to take the pill at the same time each day, otherwise irregular bleeding or pregnancy can occur. They must also be instructed to report unusual head, chest, or leg pain promptly.

Some physicians prescribe Depo-Provera, an injectable hormonal contraceptive, that is effective for 90 days. This method requires no compliance on the part of the patient, which makes it an attractive method for the sexually active patient who cannot be relied upon to use other methods effectively. Although this medication is frequently utilized in the treatment of other gynecologic disorders and has been used widely overseas as a contraceptive, it has not been cleared for use as a birth-control method in the United States by the Federal Drug Administration. For this reason, Depo-Provera may not be available to many handicapped women.

Because adolescents with special needs may not have the financial resources to see a private gynecologist, many will need to obtain contraceptive counseling and supplies at a public health facility. Planned Parenthood has been a leader in developing educational and medical programs for the handicapped. Many Planned Parenthood clinics are staffed by individuals specially trained to deal with handicapped patients.

Venereal Disease

Adolescents who are likely to engage in sexual activity need to know about the risks, symptoms, and treatment of venereal disease (VD). It is not necessary to offer a detailed discussion of each disease entity (syphilis, gonorrhea, herpes). Rather, specific symptoms should be reviewed so that the individual will recognize when medical attention is needed.

Emphasize that VD is transmitted through direct genital-genital or oral-genital contact and not through inanimate objects. The use of condoms should be encouraged when an individual may have multiple sexual partners. Students must be told that it is wrong to have sex with another person when untreated VD is present.

Males should be cautioned to look for a purulent discharge from the penis (not semen), burning in the penis, and any sore or ulcer on the genitals (painful or not). Females should be vigilant for ulcers or sores around the labia or vagina, unusual vaginal discharges, and pain during intercourse.

Emphasize that sometimes VD can only be diagnosed through special cultures or blood tests, so that if an individual suspects that he or she might have had intercourse with a partner with VD, medical attention is warranted.

Finally, it is important to stress that an individual with VD should not fear punishment or embarrassment. A sensitive, convenient source of VD testing and treatment must be identified so that a special-needs adolescent will know where and how to obtain help.

Marriage and the Emotionally and Mentally Disturbed

Now that most special-needs adolescents no longer reside in institutions, the opportunity for interactions with members of the opposite sex is enhanced. Intense relationships between such individuals may develop, and eventually the issue of marriage will be raised. Traditionally, marriage has been considered a fundamental milestone in an individual's life; those who choose not to marry are considered, at best, curiosities and, at worst, incomplete, unfulfilled persons. Although the sexual revolution and the women's movement may moderate this attitude somewhat, the cultural impetus to marry is still great, and retarded as well as normal children learn early on that society considers marriage an important institution.

The subject of marriage is important and one that should be dealt with early in the education of the exceptional child. Otherwise, the child may reach maturity without realizing the complexity and magnitude of the marital commitment and may have unrealistic expectations regarding his or her potential to engage in a marital relationship. Because many emotionally disturbed children come from broken homes and because many mentally handicapped children have spent years in institutionalized settings, they may know little about the day-to-day interaction between husband and wife.

Because such children tend to spend more time with their mothers than their fathers and because many of their caretakers are female, some exceptional children may have difficulty in traditional gender-role identification. These children know whether they are male or female, but they may have problems identifying the jobs, responsibilities, interests, and pastimes traditionally considered appropriate to their sex. While purists might argue that such distinctions between the sexes are no longer necessary or valid, it is no secret that our society still makes distinctions between masculine and feminine behavior, and the young adult who is unaware of these distinctions may well find himself the subject of ridicule in the real world. The child deserves to know that, while there may be exceptions, most construction workers are men and most secretaries are women.

Because some individuals may never marry, it is important for them to understand that this does not represent a failure on their part and that it is possible to find personal satisfaction and happiness as a single person. Families of the handicapped and those responsible for their care should refrain from good-natured teasing

regarding marriage. Asking a 16-year-old girl with a cognitive disorder when or whom she plans to marry might seem an innocent jest, but it raises a loaded issue for the child, placing before her another social milestone that she may never attain. In our society, where nearly 50% of marriages are unsuccessful, marriage is a difficult and serious proposition, even for those of normal intelligence. Surely it is no less serious a matter for those with significant mental handicaps.

Although many would argue that the marriage of mentally handicapped individuals is unwise, in some instances such long-term commitments can be successful. Michael and Ann Craft (1978) argue convincingly that many handicapped people can find happiness, stability, and personal satisfaction in a marital relationship.

They wisely observed that "giving and receiving love, including physical satisfaction, is not the prerogative of those above a certain IQ level; being incapable of anything more than a superficial relationship is not an inherent feature of mental handicap. Love can raise some from apathy, others from despair and loneliness and give meaning to life to many who have lost it" (Craft & Craft, 1978, p. 49). Their study of 25 Welsh couples, in which at least one partner was considered mentally handicapped, revealed surprising findings. There seemed to be no correlation between the severity of the handicap and the overall success of the partnership. In some instances, marriage seemed to increase the individual's determination to succeed, and often, by pooling their individual strengths, these couples were able to overcome their individual weaknesses.

Kempton (1975) suggested that marriage of the mentally handicapped must be considered from four angles—that of the handicapped couple, that of their parents, that of their unborn children, and that of the community. Advantages of such a marriage include companionship with someone of the same intellectual abilities, broadening of the individual's horizons via exposure to the spouse's extended family and acquaintances, the need for less supervision, the complete expression of sexual needs, and the sense of love, security, and self-confidence that comes from being loved and sharing responsibilities in the care of the home.

Kempton also noted the following disadvantages of such a match: the sharing of problems, which may be overwhelming to the spouse; the constant testing of emotional stability, which the individual may lack; the individual weaknesses (be they emotional or physical), which may be too great for the spouse to deal with in a peer relationship (Kempton, 1975).

Certainly an important consideration in such a marriage is the availability of support from the families and the community. If such a match is opposed by both families and if the community offers no supervision or support to the married couple, the marriage is likely to fail. Individuals unable to deal with the routine demands and responsibilities of life are poor candidates for marriage. Likewise, those who lack emotional stability and are incapable of maintaining a lasting, giving relationship will surely not succeed in marriage.

Handicapped children must understand that marriage entails commitments on a number of levels. In the discussion of marriage the teacher might raise the following issues:

1. How does a married couple find a place to live?
2. How do they get money to support themselves?
3. How do they share the responsibility for household chores?
4. What happens when one of the individuals gets sick?
5. What happens if the woman has a baby? How can this be prevented?
6. What happens when one individual gets tired of living with the other?

Confronted with such concerns, most handicapped individuals will make appropriate decisions regarding the advisability of marriage.

Pregnancy

All too frequently unplanned and unwanted pregnancies occur in emotionally disturbed and mentally handicapped young women. The young woman may have voluntarily had intercourse with one of her peers, but pregnancy may also result from exploitation by strangers, acquaintances, or family members. Educators must be aware of the early signs and symptoms of pregnancy, and these should be discussed with handicapped students who may be sexually active. These include a missed menstrual period, morning sickness or persistent nausea, breast tenderness, and lassitude. If the suspicion of a pregnancy is raised, prompt medical attention is important. A simple blood or urine test will quickly resolve the issue.

The handicapped individual and her family may exhibit remarkable denial towards an obvious pregnancy. We have seen several handicapped teenagers brought to the hospital for the evaluation of abdominal pain who were, in fact, in labor. Both the parents and the patient denied any knowledge of the pregnancy. An observant teacher may be the first to note the changes of pregnancy in an exceptional child and should not hesitate to suggest a medical evaluation.

Once a pregnancy is recognized, several questions must be raised. Does the patient wish to continue the pregnancy or does she wish to terminate it? Is she capable of rearing a child? If not, will her family accept responsibility for the child? Can or will the father of the baby be of any assistance? Is the mother's and/or father's handicap likely to be transmitted to the baby?

In helping an emotionally or mentally handicapped individual decide how to handle an unplanned pregnancy, make certain that the individual has a realistic knowledge of what child-rearing will entail. Many adolescent youth may express initial excitement regarding parenting, naively believing that caring for a baby will be like caring for a special doll. In these instances, the educator is obligated to encourage the individual to consider the responsibilities and drawbacks of child rearing seriously. Through questioning and role playing, the patient may be asked what she will do when the baby is sick; how she will provide appropriate food, shelter, and clothing for the child; how she will cope with another individual who may often be willful, disobedient, and unpleasant. After such an exercise, the excitement may give way to sorrow and dismay as the teen realizes that she is ill-equipped to deal with the realities of parenting. Of course, we believe that such questions ideally should be raised before such a pregnancy has occurred, in an effort to motivate the handicapped individual to avoid unprotected intercourse.

There are three courses of action available to a pregnant individual. She may choose to undergo an abortion. She may continue the pregnancy and place the baby for adoption. Or she may attempt to raise the child, perhaps with the assistance of her family or the baby's father.

Abortion

Although controversial, abortion is now legal in all states and available in most areas of the country. When performed prior to 12 weeks' gestation, the risks and costs to the patient are minimal as hospitalization, and general anesthesia can be avoided. The risks of such a pregnancy termination are less than that of carrying a pregnancy to term. When the pregnancy has progressed past 12 weeks' gestation, the risks increase, and some physicians may insist on hospitalization. Abortions may be performed as late as 24 weeks' gestation in some states, although there should rarely be a need for such

delay. Because handicapped women, especially teens, may deny or fail to recognize their pregnancy, the more difficult procedures may sometimes be necessary. By the time the pregnancy is diagnosed, it may be too late to terminate it at all.

The adolescent's family, the father of the baby, and those responsible for the mother's care may have some input into the question but the final decision must be made by the adolescent herself—providing of course she is legally competent. A minor's parents may attempt to prevent their daughter from undergoing an abortion; on some occasions the courts have ruled in favor of the parents, in other instances they have ruled in favor of the minor. Such a situation is usually best resolved outside the courts. We believe that it is a mistake to force a minor to complete a pregnancy against her wishes. Expert family therapy and counseling is indicated under such circumstances so that the young woman's decision will not lead to estrangement from her family.

Adoption

Before a mentally retarded person decides to continue a pregnancy, some consideration must be given to the likelihood that the parental handicap might be transmitted to the child. The likelihood that this will happen depends on the specific etiology of the parent's learning disability. Genetic counseling may be invaluable in helping the potential mother to make an appropriate decision.

Because of the availability of abortion, the number of adoptable infants has diminished in recent years. In general, there should be little difficulty in placing a normal, healthy infant in a good home. Children with handicaps may be more difficult to place, though there are some who are willing to accept a special-needs infant.

Careful counseling regarding adoption is essential during and after the pregnancy. When the issue is handled improperly, the mother may fail to resolve the sense of loss that inevitably accompanies giving up an infant. The mother-infant bond is a strong one, and there is nearly always some degree of ambivalence on the part of the infant's mother. Reassurance that the child has been placed in a good, loving home may do much to alleviate the mother's concerns.

Childrearing

Rearing a child is difficult even for parents of normal intelligence. Those with moderate or severe mental handicaps are not equipped to function as parents, and their children must be raised by others. The mildly handicapped individual may attempt to raise a child, under some circumstances, but such a situation must be closely supervised. In general, the prognosis is better if the parent's handicap is minimal, if the spouse is of normal intelligence, and if the extended family is actively involved in the care of the child.

An emotionally or mentally handicapped teenager who is isolated may not provide adequate stimulation to her infant to ensure normal intellectual development. In fact, retarded or emotionally disturbed parents may lack the judgment and stability required for parenting; they may not be capable of providing for the physical needs of an infant. The potential for child abuse is great when one parent (or both) is emotionally disturbed or handicapped.

When a handicapped individual attempts to raise a child, the infant's physical and psychosocial development must be carefully monitored. Child welfare services should be consulted. In some locations, special programs are available for those who may have difficulties with parenting. These programs couple day care with education in parenting skills and psychological support. Unfortunately, in some instances, the handicapped parent may be over-whelmed by the responsibility of childrearing, and in these cases the infant must be removed from the home and placed in foster care.

SUMMARY

Dealing with the developing sexuality of special-needs adolescents constitutes one of the greatest challenges facing educators. Not only must the teacher contend with the often perplexing and unpredictable behavior of the students, he must also do so in a fashion that is acceptable to parents, administrators, and society at large.

Both the physical and emotional aspects of sexual maturation must be addressed in a straightforward and accurate manner. Teachers must be well informed regarding these matters. Educators must also be comfortable with their own sexuality and should be prepared to deal calmly with situations that might be awkward or embarassing.

Some of this material should be incorporated into the formal curriculum, but a great deal of education regarding sexuality is best covered through role modeling and providing students with appropriate, supervised opportunities to interact with the opposite sex.

The task is not an easy one, but it is important. The failure to provide appropriate information to teens regarding their developing sexuality may have serious consequences, including embarrassment, loss of self-esteem, inappropriate sexual behavior, abuse, venereal disease, and unplanned pregnancy. A conscientious and knowledgeable instructor of special-needs adolescents may do a great deal to help students avoid these pitfalls of sexual maturation.

RECOMMENDED READINGS

Alan Guttmacher Institute (1981). *Teenage Pregnancy: The problem that hasn't gone away*. New York: Alan Guttmacher Institute.

Kempton, W. (1975). *A teacher's guide to sex education for persons with learning disabilities*. North Scituate, MA: Duxbury Press.

Ory, H., Forrest, J., & Lincoln, R. (1983). *Making choices: Evaluating the health risks and benefits of birth control methods*. New York: Alan Guttmacher Institute.

Tyrer, L.B., & Duarte, J.E. (1984, January). Guiding teenagers' choice of a contraceptive. *Contemporary Obstetrics and Gynecology, 23*, 171-186.

Wagner, C. A. (1980). Sexuality of American adolescents. *Adolescence, 15*, 275-280.

CHAPTER
NINE

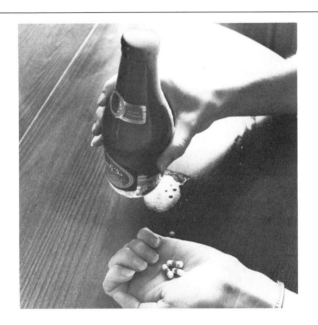

Drug Abuse
Management in
Adolescent Special Education

This chapter was written by Steve Miksic, Ph.D.

Drugs have been used by many different cultures for hundreds of years. During the early 1980s, there has been increasing alarm about the continuing drug use by youth when social agencies are investing more and more resources in prevention and treatment. On September 21, 1986, President and Mrs. Reagan appeared on national television to announce a revived "national crusade" against drugs. In October, the Senate and Congress enacted new legislation to increase the mandatory penalties for drug-related crimes. *Time* magazine (1986) featured a cover story about "America's Crusade" against drugs. Drug abuse problems are not a new development; however, our society has changed over the past few decades in general attitudes about drug use and in the increased variety and availability of psychologically active chemicals. There are also many conflicting messages about drugs with which we now must cope. First, some drugs are mysterious, miracle medical tools, and panaceas for most of our discomforts. Others are used openly by many responsible adults for entertainment and recreation. Youth are also sensitive to attitudes that drugs are illegal, immoral, and poisonous vices, depending on the drug and the context in which it is used. We should not be surprised that youth (especially youth with special needs) are bewildered and confused about an experience they are denied, while they witness others using drugs without apparent harm. For example, consider these contradictions: the legal use of a known **carcinogen** (tobacco) and a dangerous depressant (alcohol) is often accepted, while other drugs are forbidden even though they appear harmless (marijuana, "pep" pills). Thus we can understand the problems a young person faces in making difficult choices regarding drug use. The same decisions are difficult enough for adults who have achieved a stable, mature life-style. The adolescent is faced daily with developmental hurdles of identity crises, sexual awakening, establishing a self-image, joining a peer group, and searching for a satisfactory role in society.

This chapter presents drug-abuse facts and information as addressed in an educational setting, with attention to the adolescent's special developmental concerns. For the adolescent in a special education placement, whether due to perceptual/intellectual deficits or emotional needs, the developmental hurdles and concerns, including vulnerability to drug abuse, are magnified.

The chapter will begin with a brief discussion of essential terminology. This is followed by a presentation of the special developmental characteristics of adolescents that may be associated with drug use patterns. The next section provides information about major drugs and classes of chemicals that are most likely to be abused. The last three segments deal with classroom techniques for crisis intervention, detection of abuse and management of drug-abusing students, prevention programs and educating youth about drugs and drug use.

TERMINOLOGY

A list of basic concepts, accompanied by brief, commonly used definitions is provided below. These concepts serve as a foundation for understanding drug-related behavior and dealing with drug issues.

Drug refers to any chemical that is consumed and is present in abnormal concentration in the body. This includes substances such as hormones found naturally in the body as well as artificial and naturally occurring chemicals. Even substances produced within the body can dramatically influence emotion and behavior if their concentrations are not kept within normal limits.

Drug abuse is more difficult to define. This chapter is concerned with the voluntary intake of chemicals and their adverse physical and social consequences.

Addiction is the compulsive use of a drug, characterized by a behavior pattern centering on drug use, procurement, and continued use. Evidence of physical tolerance and dependence is not necessary for establishing that a person is addicted.

Tolerance is physical adaptation to the effect of a drug so that, with repeated use, more of the drug is necessary to produce the same effect.

Dependence is indicated when physical or emotional discomfort or both result when drug use is discontinued. The person "depends" on the drug to prevent withdrawal or abstinence-related stress.

Physical and psychological dependence are distinguished on the basis of overt and predictable physical withdrawal symptoms. Drugs such as narcotics and barbiturates, when discontinued after prolonged use, cause a spectrum of physical reactions and accompanying emotional distress. This is the same for everyone and is directly related to the duration and amount of drug use. Psychological dependence is inferred by the degree of emotional distress associated with the discontinued use of a particular drug.

It is clear that drug abuse and tolerance (and physical dependence) are not synonymous. Drug abuse, then, occurs when a chemical continues to be ingested in spite of extreme disruption of physical well being, psychological integrity, social functioning, or a combination of these. Although narcotics, depressants, and marijuana are commonly regarded as abused drugs because their nonmedical consumption is illegal, this definition would include diuretics, aspirin, alcohol, tobacco, caffeine, and dietetic stimulants.

A useful categorization of patterns of drug use has been put forth by the National Institute on Drug Abuse (1982). Refer to Table 9–1 for a synopsis of behavior patterns associated with progressive drug use.

Experimental Use. This includes short-term use, up to 10 times, of one or more drugs. Curiosity, sometimes bolstered by peer pressure, represents the primary motivation for this type of use, and such use does not occur on a daily basis or for the purpose of escaping or avoiding personal problems.

Social/Recreational Use. Such use is noted to take place within a specific and relatively small social context. Highly addictive drugs, such as **heroin**, are usually not found in this context. The primary motivation appears to be the facilitation of the limited social interaction situation. Frequency or intensity of drug use is not usually seen during the period between social interactions.

Circumstantial/Situational Use. In this case, a drug is used to obtain a certain emotional effect. Drinking alcohol to come down after a taxing exam, taking stimulants to stay awake and study, or sedatives to aid sleep when sleep is difficult are some common examples. This type of drug use can easily become habitual and then intensified.

Intensified Drug Use. At this stage, drug use normally occurs on an almost daily basis. It becomes an integral part of the drug user's self-image and his social and community life. At the same time, it may still be used to alleviate the emotional impact of personal problems or stressful events.

Compulsive Drug Use. At this point, the use of the drug becomes the center of the individual's life-style. Most daily activities are designed for purposes of acquiring, ingesting, and experiencing the drug effect. Both physical and psychological dependence have occurred and have persisted over a relatively long period of time.

Of primary concern to the special education teacher, as well as to any concerned adult, is the point at which the drug-use pattern changes from experimental or social/recreational to cir-

TABLE 9-1
Patterns of progressive drug abuse

Stage of Use	Behavior	Frequency of Use	Emotional State
Experimentation	Little effect Denial of negative consequences	1 to 5 times (total)	Excitement/daring Mild euphoria Possible discomfort Mild guilt
Social/situational	Decreased academic performance Loss of interest in hobbies Loss of interest in special activities Begins to seek out drug-using friends Changes in clothing habits Some uncharacteristic behavior	2 to 4 times per week	Excitement Being "in" with the crowd Feels better with drug than without it Less guilt-"Drugs are OK, I can handle them"
Habitual	Most friends use drugs Beginning of family problems due to drug use Major loss of interest in school and other activities Impulsiveness Erratic mood swings Uses drug alone	Daily use	"Need" for euphoric state Highs are very high, and lows are very uncomfortable More guilt and depression
Obsessive/dependent	Skips school regularly Weight loss or gain Messy, unclean appearance Loss of ability to concentrate Severe paranoid or depressed thoughts Dangerous aggression Suicidal thoughts Pathologic lying Stealing to obtain drugs Family chaos	Multiple times per day depending on drug	Needs drug to feel "normal" Severe discomfort if drug not available Disorganized thoughts Erratic behavior May become psychotic or suicidal

cumstantial/situational, intensified, or compulsive. It is at the point of circumstantial/situational use that the individual's social and academic performance may first show a notable change.

ADOLESCENT DEVELOPMENT

The period we refer to as adolescence, approximately ages 14 to 21, is an important transition period physically and emotionally. During these years, children become, physically, adults. Observing the adolescent in the context of this transition, we can identify factors that affect the student's vulnerability to drugs.

Adolescents are part of a system they do not fully understand. Drugs, too, are a part of that system and can influence development indirectly—through alcoholic parents, for example, or drug-using peers—or directly—through personal experimentation and addiction or abuse. A greater understanding of adolescent development processes can help us reduce the detrimental effect of drugs in their lives.

School experiences are particularly important influences. They can have an intense impact on vulnerability, either positive or negative, depending on how they are managed by teachers and administrators. An outline of some important elements of the adolescent's development as it relates to vulnerability follows. Keep in mind that the special education teacher will be dealing with "special" adolescents.

Psychophysical Development

Adolescence represents the final development of habit-setting processes. During this period there is stabilization of hormonal secretion and final nervous system and brain function integration, including eating, sleeping, hostility/passivity, anxiety, and emotional reactivity. All these attributes are molded by physical developmental forces. The younger the individual is,

the more vulnerable are his body's developing physical/psychological systems to drug effects. Motivation, judgment, decision making, and memory are all highly dependent on the smooth completion of these developmental processes. Any or all of them can be altered by direct and residual effects of drugs ("Marijuana and Youth," 1982). During the ages of 12 to 14 (grades 7-9) these developmental phenomena are more dynamic, and disruption is more serious than in the adult system (Milman, 1982; Brill & Christie, 1974; Heath, 1976; Soveif, 1976). In developmentally disabled students this process is further confounded.

Social Development

The adolescent is constantly moving through different stages of social turmoil and challenges to healthy social development. The major issues are changing relationships with family members and other adults, general peer groups, and peers of the opposite sex. Much of this socialization process involves need satisfaction, or learning how to channel drives through healthy behaviors to achieve gratification. The primary influences on adolescent social behavior are, in order of the degree of their impact: peers, family, school personnel, general newsmedia, and literature. In fact, school and family influences may be equal at times, or school may be more important.

Major changes are taking place within the family system as the child reaches and passes through adolescence. During this period, the individual separates psychologically from the family and forms a sense of self-identity outside the family system (Freedman & Kaplan, 1965). Relationships with parents may engender positive or negative coping behaviors in adolescents. Those who use drugs may be emulating their parents (Kandel, 1974) or rebelling against their parents' values (Jessor & Jessor, 1980). The greater the restrictiveness of the home setting, the greater the rebellion reaction is likely to be. A large proportion of problem drinkers come from homes where alcohol is forbidden (National Institute on Drug Abuse, 1975). If the family climate is stressful, drugs may be an escape (Stern, Northman, & Van-Slyck, 1984). Environments filled with conflict or parental abuse are particularly traumatic and are more likely to be linked to drug abuse (Wright, 1985). The absence of a father figure is highly associated with alcohol and marijuana use and sexual acting out. In one study, teenagers reported an average of three stressful family events (such as arguments between parents and financial crises) during the first year before drug abuse became a serious problem (Duncan, 1978). Family bonds are more important in decreasing vulnerability to drug use in females, while peer relationships have the most weight with adolescent males (Ensminger, Brown, Hendricks, & Sheppard, 1983).

The family separation process is paralleled by increased importance of peer relationships. This involves a comparison and modification of personal values. The values of the family and those of the peer group may be consistent, at odds, or entirely new and different. The stress and effort required to reconcile these value systems is highly significant. The resolution of this struggle will have a profound influence on the drug-use habits of the adolescent and developing adult.

Many examples of peer-pressure influences related to drug use can be found. Adolescents acquire a vast majority of their drugs from friends who are peers (O'Donnell, Voss, Clayton, Slatin, & Room, 1979). In close-knit groups, such as gangs and fraternities, drug use is more consistent and heavier than in the general population of that age (Maddox, 1970). Primary social factors related to the onset of drug abuse listed in the National Institute on Drug Abuse Monograph *Adolescent Peer Pressure* are competition, escape, and pressure to conform (1983). Levitt and Edwards (1970), and Kandel,

Kessler, and Margulies (1978) put it more strongly: onset and maintenance of drug use of all types are linked directly to peer interactions with friends; in larger groups, this pattern is dependent on sociocultural setting. Blount and Dembo (1984) have found that in concentrated urban areas, nonusers and heavy users of drugs may mix freely as friends without transfer of use habits.

Social relationships with the opposite sex, or psychosexual development, is a further process ongoing in adolescence. Adolescents in their early teens are experiencing drastic changes in hormonal status that affect emotional stability. They must learn to manage the satisfaction of physical/emotional needs in a manner society deems acceptable. These teens experience increased sexual awareness, which is often acted out in masturbation, flirting, and short-term emotional attachments, or "crushes." When adolescents reach their midteens, they increase their exploration and experimentation, experiencing longer periods of attachments, or "going steady." During the late teens there should be a maturing of the emotions and behavior associated with sexual gratification combined with a mutual concern and confident intimacy. Drug use or abuse may interfere with both physical and emotional development. The drug may stimulate or inhibit sex hormone activity and may alter the emotional experience. Drugs may serve as a crutch for the development of intimacy or lead to a premature intimacy through a loss of judgment, a development with which an adolescent is not prepared to cope. At times, individuals may be introduced to certain drugs, aphrodisiacs, to aid their sexual experience. Marijuana, alcohol, narcotics, stimulants, and depressants may reduce social anxiety, lower inhibitions, distort thoughts, and stimulate sexual interaction when used acutely (one time). With chronic use (regularly) these same drugs inhibit or suppress sexual motivation and activity.

During adolescence, the personality is in a state of flux, constantly searching, focusing, and reevaluating. Trying to find a stable image of the self and the environment is an ongoing activity. Part of this process is a result of the adolescent's desire for exploration. Two of three drug users in one survey gave this as their reason for initiating drug involvement (Mizner, Barter, & Merne, 1970). In addition, if the adolescent is experiencing personality problems, drug use is often seen as a related factor or a causal agent. Because adolescents as a group have lower impulse control, drug use may cause some severe antisocial or risk-taking behavior (aggression, dangerous showing off, stealing, sexual permissiveness), and this may lead to more stress, depression, and alienation (Severson, 1984). An adolescent already experiencing a problem may see drugs as a relief or distraction. Schaeffer, Schuckit, and Morrissey (1976) have shown that low self-esteem is highly related to heavy drinking. Moderate marijuana users are more unconventional, introspective, and rebellious than are nonusers (Khavari, Mabry, & Humes, 1977), and chronic users show more psychopathology than nonusers (Brecher, 1975). Special education students may be experiencing difficulties with self-image, resulting in a high vulnerability to peer pressure.

Other changes noted with the onset of drug use are self-destructiveness, depression, insecurity, aggression, and withdrawal. Even cigarette smokers in high school are seen as being more frank and extroverted, as well as less agreeable than nonsmokers (Smith, 1980; Chassin, 1984).

There is a wealth of information that indicates culture, ethnicity, social class, religion, and educational status are also related to the vulnerability of the adolescent to drug use and abuse (Pandina & Schuele, 1983). It is of interest that the number of moderate and heavy drinkers rises with both education and social class (Harris and Associates, 1981), and within-city neighborhoods have become an additional area of study (Blount & Dembo, 1984). Specific neighborhoods have their own perceptions of the role of drug use.

MAJOR CLASSES OF ABUSED SUBSTANCES

Abuse of drugs by adolescents is the primary topic of this section. Discussed are several major drug classes likely to be abused as well as multiple drug abuse. Let us keep in mind, while reading this section, that a 1984 study of high school student drug use, nationwide, shows that 62% try an illicit drug before finishing high school, and 40% will have used illicit drugs other than marijuana (Johnston, O'Malley, & Bauchman, 1985). A summary table (Table 9–3) is included at the end of this section.

Alcohol

Our culture, like many others throughout the world, is one in which alcohol is both used and accepted as legal. Many youth are exposed to alcohol at home because it is used by other people in the household. For this reason, alcohol is the first recreational drug to which youth are exposed. It is the drug that young people abuse most heavily and with the greatest frequency. This means that it is tried first at an earlier age than are other drugs and that it also becomes used habitually earlier. A report by Abelson and Fishburne (1976) found that in a sample of 14- and 15-year-olds, 31% said they were current drinkers. In a similar report (O'Donnell et al., 1976), 47% of 16- and 17-year-olds and 90% of 19-year-olds reported similar alcohol usage. Patients as young as age 7 have been involved in alcohol abuse rehabilitation programs (Rosenthal, 1970). Alcohol use continues to appear to be increasing in preteen and teenage children, with reports of students coming to school significantly intoxicated

(Solleder, 1974; Nemy, 1974). There is evidence that between 50 and 70% of all youth have tried both alcohol and cigarettes by age 12 (McIntosh, Fitch, Staggs, Nyberg, & Wilson, 1979). Mayer and Filstead (1979) note that between 5 and 23% of seventh through twelfth grade students can be categorized as "problem drinkers" because they report being drunk at least one to four times per year. Adolescent alcohol use has remained relatively stable in high school populations since 1975, but at a high level (Johnston et al., 1985). Alcohol use in high schools has remained steady at 90 to 93% having reportedly used alcohol each year from 1975 to 1984. Of those reporting alcohol use, 72% had used it in the past 30 days. Reports of occasional heavy drinking are at 39%, currently.

Only ethyl alcohol is of a low enough toxicity to be able to be consumed regularly, compared with other forms of alcohol. Subjective descriptions of the effects of alcohol include relaxation, calming, drowsiness, talkativeness, sedation, moodiness, well-being, irritability, and combativeness. These effects are highly individualized for different people. They can depend on many different factors, including the person's mood when the alcohol is consumed and any prior experiences with alcohol or other drugs.

Alcohol is absorbed into an individual's bloodstream through the stomach and the small intestine. The result is gross impairment of both motor function and the senses; emotional stability is affected as are learned inhibitions, which are decreased, and there is a much higher likelihood of inappropriate or poor judgment (Ritchie, 1980). Speech becomes slurred at moderate to high doses, balance is also highly affected. There is a lowering of blood pressure, and one may experience apathy and sleepiness, with a significant slowing of breathing, as with an anesthetic. If the amount of alcohol consumed reaches a high enough level, the person will slip into a coma and die from over-sedation. Many such deaths occur each year in chil-

dren, adolescents, and adults (Berger & Tinklenberg, 1977; Weisman, 1972; Leavitt, 1974).

Both physical and psychological dependence result from regular consumption of large amounts of alcohol. A severe withdrawal reaction occurs if alcohol use is curtailed. The withdrawal behavior, when mild, is trembling, sometimes termed *the shakes*. This may begin during the first 12 hours after the last drink of alcohol and may last for three days. In more severe withdrawal reactions there may be violent seizures, sweating, fever, increased heart rate, general agitation, paranoid thoughts, hallucinations, mental confusion, and possible death from vascular or circulatory collapse. Death is likely to occur in 10 to 20% of severe cases (Victor, 1974). The teacher may at times observe students in different stages of withdrawal ranging from a mild hangover through tremors to mental confusion and hallucinations.

Depressants

Students are exposed to many types of **depressant** drugs. The types of chemicals that make up these depressants are barbiturates, minor tranquilizers such as **Librium** or *Valium*, and antihistamine sedatives. The barbiturate drugs are usually prescribed by physicians for inducing sleep or for seizure control. Minor tranquilizers are used medically for control of anxiety. Antihistamines are agents prescribed for relief of allergy symptoms and respiratory problems; they may be used as sedatives, too. Certain types of minor tranquilizers are also used in the control of seizures and for muscle relaxation. There are other types of muscle relaxants and sleeping preparations that may be abused. These different kinds of drugs are very different in terms of their chemical composition; however, they produce many similar subjective effects. Their effects also mimic those of drinking alcohol (Barry, 1974; Overton, 1966; Wallgren & Barry, 1970). As with alcohol, all of these drugs can produce both physical and psychological dependence. Specific effects of the drugs depend upon the amount taken. These effects include, at low doses, drowsiness, sedation, and loss of inhibition; at moderate doses, loss of balance, coordination, and judgment; and, at high doses, nausea, loss of consciousness, and coma. An extremely severe withdrawal reaction, which is very similar to that seen after alcohol, occurs when these drugs are used chronically and then discontinued (Rachal, Williams, Brehm, Cavenaugh, Moore, & Eikelman, 1975; Pascarelli, 1973).

Adolescents are introduced to depressant drugs through three different sources: contact with drug-using peers at school or parties, through medical prescription, or through unsupervised access to parental drugs that have been prescribed for specific medical conditions. Abuse develops in susceptible individuals who progress beyond the experimental or social use stage (Berger & Tinklenberg, 1977).

The documentation of depressant use in adolescent populations is relatively well established. An indicative study done by Jasso and Wolkon (1978) found that 57% of adolescents admitted to a free clinic in Los Angeles said that they had used **barbiturates**. A Colorado study by Braucht and Berry (1971) found a range of barbiturate use across age groups from 3% of 13-year-olds who were studied up to 12% of the 17-year-olds who were sampled. In a similar study, 25% of 12- to 18-year-old students reported mild to heavy barbiturate use, and barbiturates were reported as the most frequent drug of abuse after alcohol, marijuana, and stimulants (Jalalai, Jalalai, Crochetti, & Turner, 1981). Currently, 5% of a nationwide sample of high school students report barbiturate and tranquilizer use, compared to a high of 11% in 1975.

Marijuana

Since 1976, marijuana has been the illegal substance used by the most people in this country (O'Donnell, Voss, Clayton, Slatin, & Room, 1976).

In 1975, the National Youth Drug Survey (NYDS) found that 90% of all youth had used marijuana, with 12.8 years the average age of first use for males, and 13 years the average age of first use by females (O'Donnell et al., 1976; Abelson & Atkinson, 1975). Alcohol was the only drug that was used at a lower average age. In high school, marijuana use is generally second only to that of alcohol and is about the same as that of cigarettes (Steffenhagen, Polich, & Lash, 1978). Jasso and Wolkon (1978) observed that 96% of patients entering a free clinic in the youth age-range reported having tried or regularly using marijuana. In a 1985 report (Johnston et al., 1985), a nationwide sample of high school students shows that 25% currently use marijuana, compared to 37% in 1979.

Dried leaves, flowers, and a purified resin (**hashish**) of the hemp plant, otherwise known as *Cannabis sativa*, are the preparations most commonly used by youth. The hemp plant grows throughout the world and has been used by many cultures for the subjective, pleasurable, and euphoric experiences that it produces. The reasons for marijuana use given by students include "getting high," "feels good," "to get away from problems," "because friends use it," and "boredom" (Leavitt, 1974; Jasso & Wolkon, 1978).

Marijuana is used most commonly through the smoking of various parts of the plant; the active chemical (THC) that causes the physical and psychological effects of marijuana is rapidly absorbed into the bloodstream in this manner. Marijuana-containing foods may be eaten to produce a psychological effect (Weisman, 1972). The full effect of marijuana, when smoked, is attained in approximately 30 minutes and can last an hour at full intensity, usually with little effect after 3 hours. When marijuana is eaten, the onset of the drug effect is longer, and the effect may last up to 6 hours. Physical effects of marijuana include a rapid heart rate; reddening of the membrane of the eye; and, psychologically, relaxation, increased appetite, and sleepiness. At higher doses, the effects include hilarity, confusion, loss of concentration, anxiety, restlessness, distortion of space and time senses, and, finally, if the dose is high enough, a psychotic reaction or prolonged coma (Jaffe, 1970; McMillan, Dewey, & Harris, 1971; Soveif, 1967; Watson, 1977).

Marijuana has been reported to produce both tolerance to and dependence on its effects. Severe or readily observable physical dependency is rare, and psychological dependence is a primary factor in marijuana abuse (McMillan, Dewey, & Harris, 1971).

Stimulants

Stimulants have been described as having the ability to alleviate fatigue, to produce a subjective euphoria, and to increase both mental and physical performance. To experience a combination of these effects is the usual reason for abusing these drugs. **Amphetamine** (speed) and **cocaine** are the stereotypical stimulants. **Nicotine** (found in tobacco), **caffeine**, **PPA** (phenylpropanolamine, used for weight reduction), and several other drugs are also in the class of stimulants.

Nicotine. The stimulant most heavily used among adolescents is nicotine, which is contained in cigarettes made of commercially grown tobacco. Nicotine-containing cigarettes are more addicting than either alcohol or marijuana, as judged by adolescent use. The psychological and physical dependence produced by cigarettes is more severe than that produced by either alcohol or barbiturates (Becker, 1972; Steffenhagen et al., 1978).

The effects of nicotine include nausea and increased salivation, and, in high doses, vomiting, diarrhea, cold sweat, headache, dizziness, confusion, convulsions, and respiratory failure. (Several commercially sold insecticides contain nicotine as an active ingredient.) Nicotine increases the body's metabolic rate, including heart rate, blood pressure, and hormones. The chain-smoking of 10 to 20 cigarettes by an inexperienced person may be enough to cause death.

Despite the adverse physical consequences of smoking, cigarettes are legally and socially acceptable and do not generally lead to agitation or loss of control, confusion, and other disruptive effects. During the past few years, however, the long-range health effects of cigarette smoking have become more widely publicized, and the amount of adolescent use of cigarettes has been declining. A 1984 high-school-student sample showed daily smoking at 19%, and use of half-a-pack per day or more, at 12% of the total sample (Johnston et al., 1985).

Caffeine. Caffeine is also a stimulant. However, it is not likely to be disruptive to the behavior of most students. It is felt that caffeine produces a mild euphoria (Ritchie, 1980; Weisman, 1972), increases endurance, augments motor activity, and facilitates thought processes. It should be noted that many children are susceptible to the effects of caffeine-induced nervousness, jitters, and stomach upset. Regulating of caffeine intake is rather difficult because it is often an ingredient in cocoa beverages, chocolate candy, soft drinks, and certain analgesics such as some forms of aspirin, as well as in coffee and tea. In 1984, 23% of a sample of high school students reported use of "stay awake" pills, whose major ingredient is caffeine (Johnston et al., 1985).

Cocaine. A drug that has received considerable attention and whose popularity among the young upper-middle class has drastically increased in recent years is cocaine. Cocaine is very similar to the amphetamines. Some South American native cultures have used cocaine for generations to increase alertness, decrease fatigue, and to bring about a feeling of euphoria. Cocaine in modern times has become increasingly more prominent as a drug of abuse of sports and entertainment personalities. In the past it was used by such historical figures as Sigmund Freud, with the objective of increasing physical and intellectual productivity. Cocaine use among adolescents is primarily recreational, experimental, and due to peer pressure. In 1981, a report found 14% of high school student populations surveyed had had contact with cocaine (Jalalai et al., 1981). It was predicted in a United States Government Drug Enforcement Administration report (Beschner & Friedman, 1979) that cocaine would continue to increase in use until such use approached near epidemic proportions in youth populations. This seems to have been largely accurate when we observe the amount of documented cocaine incidents in the news, nationally and locally. A comprehensive and historical account of the effects of cocaine and its use was published in *Time* magazine (1981). Cocaine use among high school students has remained at a relatively stable 12% since 1979 (Johnston et al., 1985).

The direct effects of cocaine on the nerves include anesthesia and the reduction of pain sensitivity. For these reasons it has long been used in both mouth and eye surgery. The commonly used anesthetics **procaine** and **lidocaine** are related to cocaine. These drugs are also often mixed with the cocaine sold illicitly on the street.

Cocaine use is primarily intranasal (snorting powder) or intravenous (by injection) and may be combined with heroin (hardballing). The onset of the drug's effects is rapid and is reported to produce an intense euphoria that has been described as more powerful than that seen with narcotics. Tolerance to and physical dependence on cocaine have not been reliably established, but psychological dependence on cocaine may be one of the most extreme forms of addiction seen with any drug of abuse. The effects of cocaine range from increased activity, an enhancement of mental and physical endurance, and a decreased appetite to toxic paranoid psychosis, coma, and, at higher doses,

even death from convulsions (Kosman & Unna, 1968). Death from cardiac arrhythmia may occur the first time the drug is used if the form is potent.

Amphetamines. Amphetamines are a class of chemicals with a history of being abused by many different groups within our culture. They also have a long history of medical use for treating children with hyperactivity problems, for reduction of obesity, and for treating **narcolepsy** (a disorder in which an individual may fall asleep without warning).

Amphetamines are generally ingested as pills, but may be injected intravenously or subcutaneously, or used in combination with depressants such as barbiturates and alcohol or heroin. Amphetamine tolerance develops rapidly, with an accompanying tendency to use higher and higher doses of the drug. When such use is discontinued there is irritability, excessive fatigue, psychological depression possibly leading to suicide attempts, and intense drug craving (Patrick, Snyder, & Barchas 1975; Weisman, 1972). As can be seen from these withdrawal symptoms, physical dependence is quite low; however, the psychological dependence factor is extremely significant. In a 1981 assessment of adolescent school students by Jalalai et al., 26% of those surveyed had either used or come in contact in a social situation with amphetamines. When a clinic population was studied (Jasso & Wolkon, 1978), it was found that 69% of those adolescents seen in a clinic had used amphetamines, and this was the most frequent use of any drug after marijuana. Use of amphetamines by high school students has been declining as measured by a nationwide study, from 20% in 1982 to 18% in 1984 (Johnston et al., 1985).

Other Stimulants. There are several other drugs with stimulant properties that are abused by adolescents. These drugs are commonly called "look alikes" because they are sold to users in a form that resembles an amphetamine or other stimulant drug. One example is phenylpropanolamine (PPA), an active ingredient in many over-the-counter weight-loss pills. PPA has been used as a decongestant in capsules prescribed for colds and flu. The side effects of PPA and other look-alike stimulants are restlessness, aggressiveness, confusion, irritability, sleep disturbance, paranoia, mania, or hallucinations (Norvenius, Widerlov, & Lounerholm, 1979). Johnston and colleagues (1985) reported that 33% of seniors, primarily females, had at some time used over-the-counter diet pills with such ingredients as PPA.

Hallucinogens

The **hallucinogen** class of abused drugs contains many compounds that are very different from each other in both their chemical structures and their physiological effects. The characteristic that these drugs share, which allows them to be classified together, is their alteration of both sensory perception and mood. **LSD** (lysergic-acid-diethylamide) is the stereotypical hallucinogen. Because of the wide range of behavioral disturbances these drugs can cause, they have also been described as *psychotogens* or *psychotomimetics*, terms that equate their effects with extreme mental illness. Some examples of the most common hallucinogens are **psilocybin**, **dimethyltryptamine** (DMT); **2,5-dimethoxy-4-methylamphetimine** (DOM or STP), **mescaline** (peyote), **phencyclidine** (**PCP**), **scopolamine**, and even marijuana. Many of these hallucinogens are found in plants and have been used throughout the course of history in religious ceremonies and/or for recreational purposes. Other hallucinogens are manufactured synthetic drugs.

The experiences induced by these drugs, allowing their classification as hallucinogens, include euphoria and sensory distortions. Reported examples describe vivid awareness, disturbance of attention, loss of ability to distinguish both time and place, disturbances in body concept, illusions of movement, and distorted touch, hearing, taste, and smell. Mood changes may be sudden and intense: laughing can change to crying within a very short period of time, there can be feelings of power, control, and omnipotence, or one can experience profound religious and philosophical revelations.

Because of their differing chemical natures, the side effects of hallucinogens are varied. LSD enhances reflex activity and produces dizziness and nausea. Phencyclidine (PCP) can trigger highly aggressive behavior and increased physical vigor. Scopolamine produces confusion and can cause amnesia, along with arousal or excitement.

There is little evidence that this class of abused drugs produces significant tolerance or physical dependence or causes withdrawal symptoms. The greatest problem is the loss of control in both behavior and emotions. An additional documented danger is the continuing confusion, psychotic-like emotional states, panic experiences, and recurring hallucinatory experiences (flashbacks) that can continue long after the drug itself is no longer used. LSD and PCP represent the most frequently abused hallucinogens causing these types of disorders (Caracci, Migone & Dornbush, 1983). They are abused most frequently simply because they are chemically synthesized at relatively low cost and can be produced in large quantities. PCP is a drug to which users of marijuana are frequently unwillingly exposed, as it may be added to weak street samples of marijuana to give it a more intense impact (Peterson & Stillman, 1978; IMS America, 1975).

Those between ages 10 and 19 have been documented as having the highest use of hallucinogens. Hallucinogen use also appears to be steadily declining; this has been noted since 1979 (Schnoll, 1979; Johnston et al., 1985). LSD prevalence of use has dropped to 5% in 1985, compared with 6.5% in 1981. PCP use dropped by 67% between 1979 and 1981 and has been steady at 2.3% since.

Inhalants and Volatile Solvents

The classification of **inhalants** and **volatile solvents** is based on a method or technique of use rather than the chemical attributes or physical effects of the drugs. These substances mix easily with surrounding air and are inhaled to produce the drug effect desired (Jalalai et al., 1981). There is a rapid and intense impact because they are absorbed very rapidly into the bloodstream through nasal and pulmonary membranes and reach the brain quickly in high concentrations.

A general public awareness of vapor inhalation as a form of drug abuse can first be noted after 1959 (Kupperstein & Sussman, 1968). Examples of the types of techniques commonly used for administration of these solvents includes spraying aerosols directly into the mouth, climbing inside a plastic garment bag with an open chemical container, shutting oneself into a small area such as a bathroom or a closet in which the chemical is released, inhaling fumes from a paper/plastic bag (huffing), inhaling directly from a solvent container, or placing a cloth soaked with the desired chemical directly over the nose and face. Barnes (1979) and Cohen (1979) list such products as spray aerosols, fingernail and other polishes, household cements, lacquer thinner, gasoline, lighter fluid, and cleaning fluids. In the past, model cement was frequently cited.

Solvent abuse appears to decrease with increasing age (Braucht & Berry, 1971; Elinson, 1975). Abusers start in their mid-teens, and abuse is generally associated with younger adolescents from low socioeconomic or disadvantaged backgrounds (Tinklenberg & Berger, 1977). From 1970 to 1981, the estimates of school children engaged in solvent abuse increased from 5% to 13% (Berg, 1970; Jalalai et al., 1981). In the study by Jalalai et al. (1981), 35% of the students sampled had reported using inhalants during school hours. A longitudinal study of inhalant use by high school students found a decrease in use between 1979 (9%) and 1981 (6%), with an increase again in 1984 (8%) (Johnston et al., 1985). Inhalant use is one of the most hazardous forms of substance abuse, as indicated by the number of fatal or debilitating cases seen, compared with the total number of users sampled. In 12- to 17-year-olds, the drug abuse early warning network (DAWN) reported inhalants ranking second in the total number of coroner reports, having a higher proportion of fatal accidents associated with their use than any other drug.

The variety of effects that are experienced with inhalation of different substances is extremely great, due to the many different chemicals that may be used in this manner. Reported effects include alcohol-type euphoria and intoxication, exhilaration, confusion, disorientation, loss of self-control, lack of pain sensitivity, drowsiness, and, at higher doses, unconsciousness and death due to central nervous system toxicity, lack of oxygen, or cardiac **arrhythmias**. The variety of physical side effects is also extremely large, including visual and auditory disturbances, dizziness, respiratory problems, gastrointestinal upset, muscular incoordination, reflex disorders, and seizures (Barnes, 1979; Cohen, 1979; Lawton & Malmquist, 1961; Press & Done, 1967). Short-term and long-term debilitating effects of inhalants are a result of the various toxic components included in the product, which are inhaled along with the active ingredient itself.

Most inhalant abuse begins through curiosity and/or peer pressure. Tolerance to and physical dependence on the specific active ingredient may become a major factor in addiction. It is interesting that the two most frequently reported effects of inhalation were "got high" and "got sick," and these often occurred together

(Clements & Simpson, 1978). Recent literature is directed to identifying demographic characteristics of inhalant abusers (Santos de Barona & Simpson, 1984) and describing current cases (Crawshaw & Mullen, 1984).

Narcotics/Opiates

There are two types of **narcotic** drugs: synthetic and natural (those derived from plants). There are many different drugs with different chemical makeup that fall into this classification; however, the stereotypical narcotics are morphine and heroin. The original narcotics were derived from the opium plant, hence the term *opiate*, which is still applied to this drug category. These drugs are the primary treatment for specific types of pain conditions. They reduce pain: however, they do not seriously alter the ability of the individual to function quite normally in other ways and do not reduce sensations in general, as would an anesthetic (Akil, 1979). The drugs in this classification also have attributes other than reducing pain. They may also lower sex drive, decrease depression, and reduce aggressiveness. They are used in hospital settings throughout the world and have a long history of use without subsequent addiction after the patients are released from hospital treatment.

When the use of the narcotic is tied to a social structure that rewards its use, certain individuals become so compulsively devoted to procuring and using narcotics that they neglect all other aspects of self-care, development, and social relationships. Narcotics have been used for medicinal and nonmedicinal purposes throughout history. The Greeks first noted that opium could be used to alleviate pain; the Arabs introduced narcotics into China in the ninth century, and throughout the world, there is evidence of the use of narcotic drugs by the early 1800s. In 1805, the first purification of the drug morphine from opium was recorded, and the more refined form of the drug known as heroin was first produced in

1874. The Harrison Narcotic Act of 1914 was the first legal restriction of opiates for use exclusively by physicians (Becker, 1972).

The National Institute on Drug Abuse and the Alcohol, Drug Abuse and Mental Health Administration were formulated during the 1960s and, in the early 1970s, began a program of intensive educational activities to raise public awareness and social consciousness of the process and problems of drug abuse in the United States. It was during this same time that a so-called heroin epidemic occurred in the U.S., with an estimated addict population of 560,000 (Greenwood & Crider, 1978). The current addicted population is somewhat less today but remains at a high level, and the number of addicts in our society will continue to be dependent on the cost and availability of this drug. It has been suggested that the age of first use of narcotics has been on the increase. In a 1977 report (McCoy, McBride, Ruse, Page, & Clayton, 1979), a sample of Dade County Narcotic Treatment Center admissions revealed a decrease in the number of patients below the age of 21 from 30% in 1973 to 12% in 1977. It has also been documented that only 12% of addicts are in the 10- to 19-year-old age range, while the majority are older than 18. However, a 1981 survey by Jalalai et al. found that nearly 10% of high school students had had contact with narcotics, and 18% of these reported using the drug during school hours. Heroin use by high school students was reported by 0.5% of a nationwide sample in 1984 and has been stable since 1979 (Johnston et al., 1985). Use of other narcotics has declined only slightly, from 6% in 1980 to 5% in 1984. The nationwide drug abuse survey (Drug Abuse Early Warning Network III) completed in the mid-1970s ranked heroin as the third leading drug of abuse. The inner city, urban black neighborhoods, with their high density of population, demonstrates the highest use of narcotics across all ages. Sociometric factors also play a larger role in the tendency to narcotic use and are probably more important than race or ethnicity.

The most prominent effect of the narcotic, which is linked to its abuse, is its intense euphoria. Other effects of narcotics include analgesia and cough suppression, which are its medicinal components; drowsiness; slowed respiration; suppression of other reflexes; constipation; nausea; hypotension or low blood pressure; at high doses, pulmonary edema (fluid build-up in the lungs) and, at toxic doses, seizures (Weisman, 1972). Primary instinctive drives such as hunger, sex, aggressive drives, and other basic responses are reduced by these drugs. Narcotic withdrawal symptoms can be intensely severe and debilitating, usually beginning to appear 8 to 10 hours after the last dose. Depending on the dosage, the withdrawal reactions, identified as the withdrawal "syndrome," range from restlessness, sleeplessness, increased respiration, tearing of the eyes, a runny nose, yawning, and sweating to the pimply goose flesh that gives rise to the term *cold turkey*, the name applied to this withdrawal reaction. Because physical and psychological tolerance and dependence develop rapidly and intensively, the addict usually experiences a second stage of the withdrawal syndrome; these symptoms include increased agitation and anxiety, fever, vomiting, chills, loss of appetite, muscle and joint pain as with flu viruses, abdominal cramps, diarrhea, and increased blood pressure (Berger & Tinklenberg, 1977). Death by overdose usually occurs as a result of an addict, having built up to two, three, or more times his beginning dose of drug and having been unable to acquire the drug for a few days, beginning his habit at the same dosage at which he left off, which is now high above his tolerance level. This loss of tolerance in the interim is what makes him vulnerable to the overdose. In addition, the social and material circumstances surrounding the usual use of a narcotic (environmental influences) can act to produce

a euphoric-like feeling without the drug or stimulate withdrawal symptoms in a drug-free former addict (Lal, Miksic, & Drawbaugh, 1978; Miksic, Smith, & Lal, 1976a,b). Death from narcotic overdose is primarily the result of suffocation because the drug paralyzes the respiratory system at high doses.

Designer Drugs

Designer drugs are chemicals produced in illegal laboratories. They are not covered by legal sanctions against manufacture because they have not been identified by the Food and Drug Administration. When a chemical is found to have a euphoric effect in a street addict, the chemist makes a large quantity of the drug, sells it to a dealer, dismantles or abandons the laboratory, and can make hundreds of thousands of dollars. Designer drugs may surface on the market and soon disappear as the only supply is used up. They are not detected by standard drug-screening tests and may be misrepresented to buyers as a more well-known drug. The problem of designer drugs is a major new threat to the stability and control of the drug market.

Abuse of Multiple Substances

Abuse of a single drug or class of drugs is uncommon. In fact, drug abusers are usually described more accurately as substance abusers. These people have a personality trait that leads them to seek some kind of an altered emotional state because the one that they are presently experiencing is unhappy or otherwise undesirable. Table 9–2 shows the typical pattern of multiple drug use in a sample of hospital and clinic patients under the age of 18.

In a study in 1970 (Chambers & Moldestad) sedative/hypnotic drugs such as alcohol and barbiturates were found to be used by 54% of the adult opiate abusers admitted to a federal

TABLE 9–2

Multiple drug use in clinic patients*

Drug	Percent of Total Patients Using the Drug
Valium	9
Quaalude	9
Heroin	9
Volatile solvents	13
Barbiturates	26
Hashish	26
Hallucinogens	35
Stimulants	35
Alcohol	60
Marijuana	100

*Sample of 200 from private files and hospital records, ages 14 to 18.

treatment program in Lexington, Kentucky. From 1969 to 1971, 11,380 persons who entered drug treatment programs across the U.S. showed a profile of approximately 45% being multi-drug abusers (Curtis & Simpson, 1976). The most commonly used mixtures included heroin, cocaine, marijuana, and barbiturates.

A report of addicts under the age of 18 in federal drug treatment programs between 1976 and 1977 found that only 25% of those sampled used a single drug and described it as the problem. The interpretation is that 75% of the sample were multiple-substance abusers. At least three drugs were used by 44% of the sample, and 33% of the sample abused at least two drugs. This study was derived from the Client Oriented Data Acquisition Process (CODAP). A separate report, the National Youth Poly-Drug Survey (NYPS) found that each client reported using an average of five drugs during the abuse history and were using, at the time of the report, at least three substances (Abelson et al., 1977). Only 16% of those abusers whose information was included in the report had a regular use pattern of fewer than two drugs. Many recent studies found that three-drug combinations were

most common, and of these the most widely used are alcohol-marijuana-hashish, alcohol-marijuana-amphetamine, alcohol-marijuana-inhalants (Cohen, 1979; Jalalai et al. 1981; Jasso & Wolkon, 1978; McIntosh et al., 1979). When Jalalai et al. (1981) studied reports of 40,320 possible drug combinations, compared to those actually reported by students in two days immediately prior to the report, 185 different combinations were found. After further analysis, it was determined that there were 18 specific combinations that were primarily representative of multi-drug abusers.

From the preceding material, we see that drug abuse is different from the abuse of *a* drug. A substance abuser is just that, a person who is vulnerable to the effects of chemicals that can change mood and/or perception. Just when it seems that a student has overcome a drug habit, she may switch to another substance. It is not surprising, then, that teachers, parents, and friends become confused when the abuser's mood shifts unpredictably and physical effects change with phases in abuse combinations. One principle can be extracted from multi-drug use behavior: drug combinations are used with the goal of enhancing the euphoric mood or perceptual effects of a primary drug or to try to alleviate withdrawal or side effects when an addictive drug is no longer available through an abuser's supplier.

If you suspect that a student may be under the influence of a drug, use caution. The student may be using a therapeutic drug that can cause effects in behaviors similar to those seen in students using illicit drugs. Particularly in special education populations, the students may be taking stimulants, anxiolytic agents, and antipsychotic drugs prescribed by physicians as aids to behavioral control. That these students use these drugs may not always be known to the teacher. So, keep an open mind and withhold impulsive judgments about drug use when working with special education and other student populations. Table 9–3 provides an over-

TABLE 9–3
Major drugs of abuse and their prominent effects

Drug Class	Representative Drugs	Prominent Effects	
		Intoxication	Withdrawal
Depressants	alcohol phenobarbital Valium Quaalude	relaxation sedation drowsiness irritability	tremulousness fever hallucinations psychological dependence
Marijuana	cigarettes (joints) hashish (resin)	relaxation sleepiness poor concentration confusion anxiety distortion of perception	psychological distress
Stimulants	amphetamines cocaine nicotine caffeine phencyclidine (PCP)	pupil dilation restlessness loss of appetite paranoia hallucinations	mental and physical depression fatigue
Hallucinogens	lysergic-acid-diethylamide (LSD) mescaline psilocybin cannabis (marijuana) scopolamine	pupil dilation disturbed attention hallucinations altered body concept distortions of time perception emotional fluctuations	inconsistent evi- dence—little or none noted
Inhalants	aerosols glue paint thinner cleaning fluid	exhilaration confusion loss of balance drowsiness depression hallucinations frequent coughing	inconsistent
Narcotics	morphine Darvon methadone codeine Dilaudid	analgesia slurred speech drowsiness constricted pupils poor coordination	fever vomiting cramps sweating "goose flesh" chills irritability running nose tearing

Source: From *Strategies for Managing Behavior Problems in the Classroom* (p. 255) by M. M. Kerr and C. M. Nelson, 1983, Columbus, OH: Charles E. Merrill Publishing Company. Copyright 1983 by Charles E. Merrill Publishing Company. Reprinted with permission.

TABLE 9–4

Therapeutic drugs and their side effects

Drug Class	Representative Drugs	Therapeutic Application	Side Effects
Psychotropics (psychiatric)	Tranquilizers Librium Valium	anxiety reduction muscle relaxation	intoxication physical dependency drowsiness
	Antipsychotics chlorpromazine (Thorazine) Mellaril haloperidol	reduced irritability control of hallucinations control of delusions control of thought process	lethargy social withdrawal sedation restlessness muscular spasm altered muscle control
	Stimulants amphetamine methylphenidate (Ritalin) pemoline	improved concentration reduced acting out increased behavior control	anorexia toxic psychosis
	Antidepressants imipramine	reduced depression decreased anxiety bed wetting (enuresis)	loss of balance visual disturbance restlessness dry mouth
Antiseizure	Barbiturates phenobarbital Phenytoin (Dilantin) Tegretol	seizure control seizure prevention	intoxication physical dependence
Tubercular	isoniazid Seromycin	tuberculosis	anxiety paranoia confusion
Hormonal Agents	Corticosteroids	hormone imbalance	hallucinations confusion delirium
Anticholinergics	scopolamine	Parkinson's disease asthma sleep disturbance	dry mouth blurred vision fever increased heart rate
Antihypertensives	methyldopa (Aldomet) guanethidine	high blood pressure	depression fatigue
Levo-dopa	L-Dopa	Parkinson's disease	paranoia restlessness delusions
Cardiovascular agents	digitalis propranolol (Inderal)	heart failure chest pain arrythmia	depression confusion fatigue hallucinations
Contraceptives	estrogen preparations	pregnancy prevention other gynecologic reasons	depression

Source: From *Strategies for Managing Behavior Problems in the Classroom* (p. 265) by M. M. Kerr and C. M. Nelson, 1983 Columbus, OH: Charles E. Merrill Publishing Company. Copyright 1983 by Charles E. Merrill Publishing Company. Reprinted with permission.

view of the effects on behavior of a sample of drugs of abuse; table 9–4 lists a sample of therapeutic drugs these students may be taking.

In the following two case studies, examples will be presented about drug use in students with personal problems, and with different outcomes depending upon their experiences within the school system.

CASE STUDY I

Ben was the only child of an intact lower-economic-status family, in an inner-city urban area. He first began using alcohol when suspended from school at age 14 for unauthorized absences. While he was out of school on suspension he began experimenting with pills— both stimulants and depressants. By age 17 he was introduced to narcotics by some friends, at first in pills and then by intravenous injection. At this time he was able to limit its use to weekends; he attained and held a menial job and was married, subsequently fathering two children. His wife was an alcohol abuser, but was able to abstain after the birth of the first child. As is typical of the narcotic abuser, Ben's use gradually became more frequent, and his marriage and employment-related behaviors deteriorated by the time he reached his early 30s. By age 35, Ben was unemployed, separated from his fam-

ily, and stealing daily to obtain the $300-$500 needed to support his extreme habit. He had a record of several shoplifting convictions, but was released on his own recognizance each time when he began attending methadone programs. During the programs, he used narcotics while receiving methadone. Ben also had been hospitalized for heart problems related to infections from dirty injection needles and from injecting the coating of pills along with the drug into his veins. His arm veins were too scarred to be used at the time he was seen, and at last contact he was injecting the drug into veins in his feet and legs. Ben described the feeling produced by narcotics as "better than sexual orgasm." He was caught in a compulsive cycle of use that was likely to cause premature death through infection, severe withdrawal, overdose, or a drug-related crime or argument.

CASE STUDY II

James came from a middle-class suburban family with chronic parental conflict. He had a learning disability and was maintained in elementary school in a socially and emotionally disadvantaged (also known as a learning and adjustment problem) classroom. As a junior high and high school student, James was continually on the verge of serious juvenile justice involvement and used alcohol heavily. He also frequently "sampled" other substances. In his junior year, James came to school late one morning, and on

his arrival the teacher felt he was behaving strangely. He looked unkempt, his eyes were "funny looking" and bloodshot, and he appeared "distracted" or "dreamy." During first period, he could not concentrate on his work but was not drowsy. At two different times the teacher noticed James giggling and smiling to himself. The teacher walked to his desk after the second episode and stood looking down at him. At this time she saw a suspicious looking plastic bag in his shirt pocket with some greenish looking material inside. Without confronting him, she made arrangements for another person to supervise her room while she took James to the principal's office. While James sat in the waiting area, the teacher described her concern to the principal, and the security officer was called. When James came into the office he was confronted by the principal and security officer, not his teacher, who remained an observer. James turned over the marijuana he possessed and admitted that he used the drug before, during, and after school most days. Juvenile justice authorities and James's parents were contacted, and in a meeting James was given the choice of alternative consequences, with participation in the school's drug program being the most lenient in other respects. The major program interventions involved were: (a) a parent-student-administrator or counselor conference; (b) application of appropriate discipline—usually suspension (in school if possible); (c) a 10-week (two hours per week) counseling program focusing on life-skills development—self-concept, peer relations, adult relationships, responsibility, and communication (This program used a group format with an adult facilitator and a peer leader and co-leader.); (d) a counseling program of the same time and duration for James's parents; (e) an ongoing peer support group which served as a resource for James at times of increased stress; or (f) referral with parental support to a mental health or drug abuse program for further evaluation and treatment.

Entry into the counseling was difficult for both James and his parents, who were initially resistant, but they became more involved as the program progressed. In this context James's parents became more aware of the effect their relationship had on James's behavior, and James began to feel supported and more in control of himself. He was able to complete the school year and get through the summer without a serious drug-use incident, largely because of support from peers who had been involved with his support group through the past school year. In his senior year, James was able to avoid drug use during school hours, and became more receptive to vocational training. He eventually graduated and was able to find an acceptable job relatively soon. At this time, James was using marijuana on weekends but seldom during the week.

James will continue to be susceptible to increased drug use during times of stress but will be able to develop more healthy attitudes towards drug use. He experienced peer support and gained in living skills while finishing high school. All of these experiences will help provide him with a more positive attitude toward life and aid him in dealing with stress and frustration, thus counteracting his impulses to substitute drug use for other methods of coping.

PREVENTION AND EDUCATION

How can drug use/abuse be prevented? The answer is that it cannot be, entirely. However, we can help prevent the senseless wasting of a highly significant proportion of lives. Education and intervention can prevent the type of chemical use that often progresses to uncontrolled and compulsive use.

The observation that drug abuse is, in reality, a symptom of basic social and psychological problems is important. Prevention, therefore, must deal with drug abuse in the context of these problems. The National Institute on Drug Abuse held a series of meetings in the mid-1970s to define "drug abuse prevention" and determine strategies for accomplishing such a goal. Their definition: "a constructive process designed to promote personal and social growth of the individual toward full human potential, and thereby inhibit or reduce physical, mental, emotional, or social impairment which results in or from the abuse of chemical substances."

This is a somewhat demanding goal. Realistically, the effective school prevention program first needs the support of a few key administrative and teaching personnel. The main elements to be included in a successful program are identified as follows:

1. Establishing a clear, well-defined policy for teachers and students that spells out the way the teacher and administration will deal with apparent or substantiated drug use or possession while in school. This will be further discussed under "Detection and Management" and "Crisis Intervention."
2. Encouraging the teachers to establish a basic drug education curriculum for their grade level. This should be kept simple, brief, and presented in a nonjudgmental style that emphasizes the concern of the teacher for the student's physical and psychological welfare.
3. Helping teachers increase their awareness of local drug problems and community service agencies.
4. Provide an atmosphere in which the teacher can develop skills to be able to be sensitive to the need to resolve classroom and individual problems, and lead group discussion about topics such as adolescent development and drug use.
5. Developing an intervention program that involves families as well as students by offering both one-to-one and group counseling and by utilizing community resources, such as community counseling centers and drop-in centers within the school. Such a drop-in center could be staffed by an education counselor with some training in drug abuse counseling.
6. Try to get each teacher to review her perception of her role. If she feels that her job is basically unfulfilling, and she is unable to empathize with the students and deal with their feelings as well as cognitive training, this may lead to some constructive career reorientation.
7. Peer-group approaches can be developed with the involvement of positive role models for group or individual support. Different types of peer programs are discussed in the National Institute on Drug Abuse publication, "Adolescent Peer Pressure" (see Table 9–5).
8. Promote an understanding of the emotional structure and perceptions that often accompany drug use. Many of these students feel they are incompetent and unreasonably rejected by adults and peers. They need an understanding approach, rather than a disciplinary attack and a judgmental attitude that simply confirms their belief that the teacher and school are only concerned with keeping things in order, rather than with helping students.

DETECTION AND MANAGEMENT

Early detection of drug-related problems is important. The earlier the intervention, the higher the probability that a crisis in the classroom or in the life of a student and his or her family can be averted. The teacher can be considered as the first line of defense against substance use and abuse (Collaboretta, Fossbender, & Bratter, 1983).

Psychological and Psychosocial Indicators

One of the primary indicators of initiation of drug abuse, the change from recreational use or experimentation, is moodiness. This is a chronic change in the style or character of a particular student's emotions. It may be seen as increased elation, stimulation or hyperactivity, depression, or rapid changes from one state to another. When this is accompanied by other indicators such as a sudden change in the student's grade or achievement level or other aspects of school performance, this is also significant. Often there is a loss of interest in extracurricular activities and in general participation in the classroom. Also indicative of drug abuse is complaining of problems with parents

TABLE 9-5

Drug-related peer programs

Objective	Program and Source	Developmental Level
Listening skills Group interaction Social attitudes	Magic Circle Discussion Groups (Schaps and Slimmon, 1978) Ombudsman (Charlotte Drug Education Center, 1980) Tribes (Gibbs and Allen, 1979)	Elementary
Self-esteem Value of school Mutual respect	SPARK (New York Office of Drug Abuse Services, 1977) PEDE (Adolescent Peer Pressure, 1983) Operation Snowball (Carlson, 1979)	Secondary
Communication skills Problem solving Leadership skills	Positive Peer Culture (Vorrath and Brendtro, 1974) Gang Programs (Gold and Mattick, 1974)	Junior high and high school
Empathy Support Positive role modeling	Peer Counseling Programs (Samuels and Samuels, 1975) Student Service Centers (Myrick and Erney, 1979) Peer Facilitation Programs (Myrick and Erney, 1975)	High school and college
Tutors and adult aids Youth perspectives for decision making Counseling co-therapists Program co-planning	Something More Than Survival (Bennett, 1979) Channel One (Adolescent Peer Pressure, 1983) Urban Youth Teams (Adolescent Peer Pressure, 1983)	High school and college

		Junior high and high school
Knowledge Support Information sharing Peer relationships Self-esteem Academic performance Positive role modeling	Youth Action Teams (Sundlee and Stapp, 1979) Youth Tutoring Youth (Gartner, Kohler, and Riessman, 1970) Jigsaw (Aronson et al., 1978) Teen Involvement (Resnick and Gibbs, 1983) Teen Age Health Consultants (Jordan and Valle, 1978) Planned Parenthood (Verhoeven, 1980)	
Health attitudes Self-esteem Information Social attitudes	Houston Smoking Prevention Program (Evans, Roselle, Helmark, Hansen, Bane, and Davis, 1976) Project CLASP (Perry, McAlister, and Farquhar, 1978) Saying "NO" (National Institute on Drug Abuse, 1980)	

247

or juvenile authorities. Students may make statements about parents' marital problems, which may be accompanied by changes in self-care and appearance, attitude changes, and excessive nervousness or anxiety. An additional indicator is a change in speech characteristics and usage of jargon. The moodiness mentioned earlier may increase into outbursts of anger or severe social withdrawal. There are often changes in peer-group affiliation; the student may spend much more time with a different group of friends than previously. Depression can also be an important indicator.

All of these indications must be taken into consideration in the context of the student's life and should not immediately be interpreted as the onset of drug abuse. These changes can often accompany other difficulties a student may be encountering; however, they are indicative of the student's difficulty, which the teacher can help the student to resolve.

When there are negative changes in performance or extracurricular involvement, your first impulse may be to apply discipline. Often firm limits are necessary to help a student improve her performance, but the important ingredient is a caring and empathic response. Expressing concern along with discreet mention of available sources of help and support, both in and out of school, evokes a much more positive response, although the initial reaction may be hostility or a denial. The simple question stated privately, "Are you having a problem with drugs?" can be very effective, depending on your attitude and relationship to your students. Again, it is very important to use discretion and not to come to premature conclusions. It may be just as important to ask, "Are you having a problem? I would like to help you." (For a synopsis, refer to Table 9–1.)

In the special education population, the task of detection may be more difficult as the student will have a high degree of variability in achievement levels, ability, and personality characteristics that may be easily misread as a drug problem, or that may obscure drug-abuse-related behavior.

Physical Indicators and Side Effects of Drug Abuse

There are many physical indicators of the effects of a drug. Unfortunately, these are difficult to classify by drug-type because many drugs produce similar behavioral effects. An additional difficulty is that the student may be taking a legitimate therapeutic substance. Some examples of drug influence indicators follow (see Tables 9–3 and 9–4 as well).

Alcohol. When there is intoxication, indicators may be anger, combativeness to seemingly insignificant situations, depression, and of course, smell. Additionally there may be poor physical coordination and slurred or confused speech. When a student who is dependent on alcohol has been deprived, this withdrawal state may produce intense anxiety and physical shaking as with chills.

Marijuana. When marijuana has been used or is abused, the specific indicators may be emotional apathy and lack of motivation, drowsiness, unexplainable silliness, and a reddening of the membranes of the eyes.

Stimulants. The stimulant drugs produce several overt effects. Amphetamine is a classic, producing agitation, paranoia and excessive suspiciousness, hyperactivity, an inability to stop talking about a subject, and flushed skin. When an individual who is dependent upon a stimulant no longer can obtain it, the most likely response is significant depression.

Hallucinogens. Abuse of hallucinogens may produce the following effects even when the drug is not present: mental confusion; disorientation as to time, place, or person; and an inability to make sense.

Narcotics. Narcotic drugs, when an individual is intoxicated, are likely to induce drowsiness and sleepiness, slurred speech as with alcohol, and sometimes an unusual walk as though the person were dancing. When an abuser is deprived of a narcotic, there is excessive anxiety, often accompanied by nausea, "gooseflesh," and a general sleeplessness and insomnia.

If you review the effects of these drugs you will notice that many of the overt behavioral effects are similar; for example alcohol and narcotics both produce depression and drowsiness. For this reason, it is very difficult to determine from his emotional behavioral responses which specific substance an individual may be using. This determination is usually performed by some medical personnel at the direction of a legal organization that has intervened in a situation.

Management of Drug Abuse Episodes

There are some implicit rules in dealing with an individual you believe to be a drug abuser who is either under the influence of a drug or is in a withdrawal condition. These are as follows: Do not directly confront the individual in front of a group or in a group setting. Remove the individual from the group setting and/or from your classroom to a more private place like the principal's office. Always try to seek assistance from the school psychologist, guidance counselor, or other, similar individual. Next, notify school authorities (Principal, Vice-Principal, Security Department). It will not help the student to try to deal with his problems on an individual basis without involving the school counselor and others who may be able to get community support for the student and/or parents. Not involving the appropriate authorities is likely to cause more difficulties for you and the student than it will solve. The next step will depend on the philosophy and approach of the individual school or school system. Parents may

be contacted immediately or after a period of time. Police and/or juvenile authorities are likely to be contacted. If there is an appropriate *therapeutic* response to the problem, the individual will be referred for counseling and/or treatment. There is usually an accompanying disciplinary consequence, even if the individual is amenable to counseling and/or treatment. This communicates that drug use is a serious disruptive factor for the whole school and is not excused.

It is important to define the role of the teacher, which is to deal with education for prevention of drug abuse, identification of problem students, and possibly, identification or discovery of drug use, possession, or abuse. This responsibility does not include counseling or treatment. That role must be left to the professionals in order to prevent problems between teacher, school administration, and the student.

An important element in any school is its drug policy for teachers, students, parents, and administrators. Having this policy ensures that all who are involved with the educational system know which behaviors will lead to which consequences within that system. This establishes a common understanding. A part of this written drug policy should include a philosophic statement. Such a statement of philosophy indicates the reason the school has a drug policy, and usually states that such behavior affects the individual's education and other students within the school system. The policy must have a very clear definition of terms. In this way the meaning of key words such as *drug*, *small amount*, and *distribution amount*, are clear to all.

The team approach is an important concept in drug abuse interventions. Ideally, the team will consist of the family, student, teacher, counselor, and community agencies that can provide support. The first step is identification and awareness of the student's "problem." When the parents, and most importantly the student, admit that a drug problem exists, the team can work effectively through shared goals and interventions.

It is important within a school drug policy to have clearly spelled out stages of disciplinary actions. An example of a system that has ranked serious offenses can be seen in that of the Pittsburgh Public School System. The examples are as follows:

1. Possible use, no concrete evidence
2. Obvious symptoms of drug use
3. In possession of small amount of drugs
4. Caught second time with a small amount
5. Caught with possession of a distribution amount
6. Caught with drug use equipment or "paraphernalia"
7. Non-student violators at the school on school property

Within the policy are also clearly defined actions to be taken with respect to any of the above eventualities or violations.

1. Immediate action
2. Investigation
3. Notification of parents
4. Confidentiality
5. Disposition of substance
6. Discipline
7. Notification of police

Each of the above actions may differ with respect to the specific violation that occurs. What is important is that all who read the policy of the school system will know the consequences for specific violations of the school drug code. An important effect of such a policy is that it may be a primary deterrent to inappropriate behavior and provides a system for immediate resolution of an anticipated problem. Schwartz (1984) lists the practices of a large sample of public schools across the country in terms of their reactions to each of the above-listed con-

ditions. A primary conclusion of this study was that student rights must be respected and a firm disciplinary policy must be balanced by a means of getting therapeutic interventions for students with drug abuse problems. If all these elements are not present, both the schools and the students suffer. If the school system in which you provide services does not have such a clear drug abuse policy, you may be able to be instrumental in developing such a system for the benefit of the school and the students. If there is a clearly stated drug and alcohol policy, it is very important to be aware of it and its contents. This may help you to deal with a potentially dangerous or disruptive episode in the future.

CRISIS INTERVENTION

The types of drug crises you are most likely to encounter are physical and/or emotional. Severe intoxication with a drug may result in convulsions, hypertensive crisis, loss of consciousness, or other reactions where immediate medical attention is necessary. In such cases, you would follow the school's established procedure for any severe physical reaction. This is similarly true for withdrawal reactions, where an addicted individual no longer has access to the drug. Such reactions can cause nausea, trembling hands (alcoholics and heavy smokers), cold sweat, stomach cramps, and dizziness. Such symptoms do not always indicate drug abuse. Medical treatment will discover the cause; if drug abuse is indicated, it will be dealt with by school administration and legal authorities.

When there is no clear physical crisis, you may have to deal with an emotional-behavioral reaction. This reaction can take the form of extreme anxiety, depression, hyperactivity, or aggression. Both drug intoxication and withdrawal can produce increased impulsivity. A student's loss of control can best be handled by remaining calm, nonconfrontational, and placing a higher priority on the safety of other students and yourself than on taking disciplinary actions or demonstrating who is in control. Resources should first be directed to defusing a crisis, rather than subduing it. Remember that tone of voice and physical stance or position are important factors that may stimulate or reduce aggressiveness in an out-of-control individual.

Recent Trends in Adolescent Drug Use and School Programs

Literature in the field of adolescent drug use from 1980 to the present suggests that the problem is not declining. There are changes in types of drugs emphasized and publicized, but overall, drug abuse continues at a high rate and may even be increasing in adolescents (Crippen, 1983; Reagan, 1984). There is a greater emphasis on educational awareness of the health-related effects of commonly used drugs, notably alcohol, tobacco, and caffeine. This contemporary trend is very positive, because alcohol and tobacco are still the primary drugs most likely to cause long-term physical and psychosocial problems (Stephenson, Moberg, Daniels, & Robertson, 1984). Marijuana continues to be regarded as a generally "safe" drug (as compared to others) by a large cross-section of the population. This attitude often lures a student into believing that use of marijuana is okay and promotes the use of this drug by juveniles. The barbiturates and depressants are still abused, but have taken a secondary role to the new "status" drug of the 1980s—cocaine (coke, crack), which is being used by more younger individuals than ever before. Similarly, the stimulant methamphetamine, "speed," is being used by increasing numbers of the youth population because it can be produced so inexpensively in large quantities in makeshift laboratories and thus floods the street market. During early 1985, several illicit amphetamine production facilities were discovered in the Philadelphia area, labeled by some as the methamphetamine capital of the United States. Narcotics usage has generally not increased, and their popularity is overshadowed by cocaine. Significant levels of narcotic use are still found in youthful inner-city populations, however. Inhalation of volatile solvents also remains a problem of low frequency but high severity and toxicity when it does occur (Parker, Tarlow, & Milne-Anderson, 1984; Sourindhrin & Baird, 1984). Hallucinogen use is becoming less popular and apparently was a fad of the late 1960s and early 1970s in terms of widespread use. The unpredictability of the effects of hallucinogens, even in the same individual, from one administration to another has kept them from becoming extremely popular. Hallucinogen use is still an experimental phenomenon with which to be reckoned, however.

New chemical compounds called "designer drugs" and new forms of existing drugs are primary developing problems. An example is "crack," a relatively inexpensive, short-acting form of cocaine that has become the "in" drug virtually overnight in many drug subcultures. Drugs developed in "underground" laboratories for use as potential money-makers on the street are called *designer drugs*. They are not illegal to make because they have not been banned by the Drug Enforcement Agency (DEA). If the DEA does not know of their existence, it cannot outlaw their manufacture. These drugs are not detectable in routine drug tests and are cheap to produce. A major problem is that their toxicity is unknown until enough users (the guinea pigs) experience it, and they are easily substituted for other drugs (cocaine, heroin, amphetamines) without the user being aware until it is in his body. Two specific examples are MDMA (ecstasy), reported to have the subjective effects of cocaine and LSD combined, and MPTP, a euphoric stimulant. For further discussion, see "Drugs, the Enemy Within" (*Time*, 1986).

It is clear that adolescent drug abuse in general is not going to go away or be cured, and the thrust now is prevention through education, along with control, and a system to provide treatment and rehabilitation where needed (Thorne & DeBlassie, 1985). School systems generally provide education, identification, and referral when necessary. Some schools include individual or group counseling, a quasi-therapeutic component designed to provide support and reinforcement for positive behavior. It is emphasized that this component must be planned and carried out very sensitively. If the teacher spends too much time, or has an approach that is too strong, the program may backfire and have adverse effects (Malvin, Moskowitz, Schaeffer, & Schaps, 1984). School programs have come under increased scrutiny as the role of the school in the student's life is clarified and the school's impact on nonacademic social behavior is more strongly acknowledged.

An element that has been shown to be very effective in the adolescent, but continues to be underutilized, is peer counseling and peer-group process (Biase, 1984; Dembo, 1983). Stern et al. (1984) found that adolescents are more likely to discuss sexual, alcohol, and drug problems with peers than with parents or any other people. In addition, it has been found that most drug education curricula are perfunctory or ineffective (Crippen, 1983). Several authors feel that viable drug education programs can and should be developed that will have a demonstrated impact on substance use and abuse in pre-teens and teenagers. (Please refer to Table 9–5 for peer-involved programs.)

These concerns are reflections of an increasing interest in outcome in school drug abuse programs (Sexter, Sullivan, Wepner & Denmark, 1984). There have been attempts to describe the "model" school-based comprehensive alcohol/drug abuse program (Holsaple & White, 1984; Smith, 1980). Schwartz (1984) suggests that many school policies, practices, and procedures are more punitive than those of juvenile justice authorities. A recommendation for changing emphases is: to consider students' prior behavior and the amount and type of drug use more sensitively in disciplinary policies. Also, alcohol should receive more emphasis as a dangerous drug, in-school alternatives to suspension should be developed more fully, and substance abuse practices and policies should more effectively recognize student's legal rights to due process.

The National Institute on Drug Abuse can provide a list of regional drug-abuse education coordinators. The address is 5600 Fishers Lane, Rockville, Maryland 20857. The Addiction Research Foundation, at 33 Russell Street, Toronto, Canada M5S 2S1, provides a highly varied selection of drug education curricula that are specific for grade level. The National Institute on Drug Abuse has also published a monograph entitled *Treatment Services for Adolescent Substance Abusers* (Friedman & Beschner, 1985). The contents describe the characteristics of the adolescent drug-user and the most effective intervention strategies. Chapter 12 of the monograph is directed toward the treatment of drug-abusing adolescents in schools and alternative school settings.

SUMMARY

We are very concerned about the problem of drug abuse afflicting teenagers today. Because adolescent drug abuse is on the rise, our educational awareness must be increased as we tackle issues around drug management within our school systems. Today there are multiple classroom techniques and prevention programs designed for crisis intervention, the detection of drug abuse, and the education of youth about drugs. We are aware of the need for effective school prevention programs that receive support from the administration and teaching personnel. The role of the school in a teenager's life has been strengthened, and the school's impact on both academic and social behavior is strongly acknowledged.

We cannot write a textbook on mildly handicapped adolescents without including a chapter on the management of drugs. Special education students are as vulnerable as other teenagers—coping with academic stress, family problems, peer pressure, and other concerns. We have a responsibility to educate and re-educate each other and our youth population. This chapter included a special glossary, the developmental characteristics associated with drug-use patterns, a listing of major drugs and classes likely to be abused, classroom techniques, and prevention programs.

The two case studies illustrated instances of drug use and the various outcomes within different school systems.

RECOMMENDED READINGS

There are a number of books currently on the market and readily available that deal very intensively with drug terminology and drug culture jargon. A few examples are:

Leavitt, F. (1974). Effects of drugs. In *Drugs and behavior* (pp. 48-50). Philadelphia: Saunders Co.

Lingeman, R. (1974). *Drugs from a-z*. New York: McGraw-Hill.

Malvin, J., Moskowitz, J., Schaeffer, G., & Schaps, E. (1984). Teacher training in affective education for the primary prevention of adolescent drug abuse. *American Journal of Drug and Alcohol Abuse, 10,* 223-235.

CHAPTER
TEN

Understanding the
Juvenile Justice
System

Throughout this text we have emphasized that the needs of handicapped adolescents pose unique challenges to special educators. The need to deal with the juvenile justice system is one such challenge. In 1981, 1,383,380 juveniles were arrested for crimes (Zawitz, Mina, Kuykendall, Greenfield, & White, 1983). Half of the persons arrested for serious crimes in the United States are under the age of 20 (Cantwell, 1983), although juveniles account for only 20% of the population (Ryan, 1983). An estimated 1.5% (455,000) of all juveniles aged 10 to 17 are under some form of correctional care, custody, or supervision (Zawitz et al., 1983). Approximately 117,000 offenders in adult institutions are under 21 years of age (Gerry, 1985). As these data suggest, a substantial number of the nation's young people are involved in criminal activity.

Even more alarming is the fact that handicapped youths are overrepresented in these statistical reports on crime. For example, in a national survey, Rutherford, Nelson, and Wolford (1985) found that the estimated prevalence of handicapped offenders in state juvenile correctional facilities was 28%, or 33,190. Santamour and West (1979) reported that the proportion of retarded offenders in correctional institutions is at least three times that of retarded persons in the general population. Learning-disabled youths appear to be similarly represented (Coffey, 1983; Keilitz & Miller, 1980). These data do not indicate that handicapped youths are more *prone* to criminal behavior, only more likely to be caught, convicted, and sentenced (Santamour & West, 1979). However, a relationship between learning disabilities and juvenile delinquency has been demonstrated (Keilitz & Dunivant, 1987). This relationship is complex and suggests that learning disabilities may increase an adolescent's susceptibility to delinquent activities and may contribute to a greater likelihood of arrest and adjudication. Because law enforcement personnel and juvenile court officers often do not understand or recognize mildly handicapped adolescents, they tend to respond prejudicially (Keilitz & Miller, 1980). For example, a judge may think a youth who fails to answer her questions or who provides ambigous or irrelevant answers is being disrespectful. Murray (1976) observed that the likelihood of adjudication is 220% greater if a youth is learning handicapped.

Unfavorable treatment of handicapped youths extends also to correctional institutions, where such persons have been observed to be more frequent targets of physical, sexual, and economic abuse by fellow inmates than are nonhandicapped offenders (Santamour & West, 1979; Snarr & Wolford, 1985). Moreover, they apparently receive differential treatment by corrections staff; Santamour and West (1979) observed that the sentences served by mentally retarded inmates average two to three years longer than those of nonretarded inmates. Retarded offenders also more often fail to meet parole criteria, and so must serve out longer sentences. Santamour and West suggested that the explanation for this fact is that such inmates do not understand prison rules and guards' directions; therefore, they more often are the targets of disciplinary reports and actions. Furthermore, the lack of special vocational training and life-skills programs for handicapped offenders means that such persons are not provided with employable skills. Typically, having a job is a prerequisite for parole from adult correctional programs. The unemployability of retarded offenders thus further contributes to their serving longer sentences (B.I. Wolford, personal communication, December 1983).

Thus, the probability that adolescents with learning and behavior disorders will run afoul of the juvenile justice system is perhaps greater than that of their nonhandicapped peers. These young people also are overrepresented in correctional programs. In contrast to adult correctional institutions, juvenile programs often contain mandatory educational components, which include special education. Correctional education programs are under the same obligation (P.L. 94-142) as public and private schools to provide a free and appropriate educational program for handicapped youths 21 years of age and under, although, as we shall see later, the adequacy of many correctional special education programs can be questioned.

The previous observations contain a number of implications for special educators at the secondary level. First, the likelihood that handicapped students will have contact with the juvenile justice system means that their teachers, counselors, and school administrators also are likely to become involved with this system. Some pupils will commit offenses, some will be arrested, some will appear before the juvenile court, some will be sentenced, and some will return from correctional programs to their public schools and communities. Each of these events signifies an occasion in which the support, advocacy, or intervention of a special educator may be required.

Second, that handicapped youths often are insensitively or prejudicially handled by the juvenile justice system indicates a need for advocacy by professionals with information and skills to help law enforcement and court personnel understand these youngsters and how they can best be served. Special educators, because of their general expertise in these areas, as well as their specific knowledge of individual pupils, are in a unique position to provide such advocacy.

Third, professionals in the juvenile justice system need information and training regarding the characteristics and needs of handicapped youths. This goes beyond advocacy on behalf of an individual client because special educators should want to ensure that all handicapped offenders are fairly and humanely treated by the juvenile justice system. Such a goal requires that professionals in the latter system possess the information and skills neces-

sary to determine whether a youth has special educational needs and to respond appropriately when such is the case, without a special educator being present. Available evidence indicates that the special educational needs of juvenile offenders are not considered by law enforcement agencies or courts (Wolford, 1983), which reduces the likelihood that they will receive "appropriate" handling or educational programming while under the supervision of the juvenile justice system. Inappropriate handling or educational programming means no gains (or worse) by the handicapped adolescent, which decreases his chances of successful reentry into the cultural mainstream.

Finally, employment opportunities exist for special educators in the juvenile justice system. For example, while an estimated 81% of incarcerated handicapped juvenile offenders are in correctional special education programs, only 28% of the teachers in these programs are certified in special education. Currently, only about 10% of state correctional agencies are in compliance with P.L. 94-142. However, the pressures of litigation and administrative sanction, as well as the desire to better serve educationally handicapped offenders, are prompting states toward greater compliance (Rutherford et al., 1985). As correctional special education programs increase in number and sophistication, more special educators may find professional opportunities in this field attractive.

The purpose of this chapter is to present information about the juvenile justice system and its clients to assist secondary special educators in dealing with it. We describe the broader criminal justice system and point out the differences between the ways juvenile and adult offenders are handled. Then we describe the procedures and interventions of the juvenile justice system in greater detail, followed by a discussion of some of the problems and issues regarding interactions between the juvenile justice and educational systems. Next, we present

strategies for working on behalf of students under the supervision of the juvenile justice system. The chapter concludes with a brief discussion of employment opportunities in the
juvenile justice system. However, because the
definition of seriously emotionally disturbed
(SED)[1] 1 in the implementing regulations for
P.L. 94-142 specifically excludes the *socially
maladjusted* (a term generally considered synonymous with juvenile delinquency), we first
address the issue of eligibility for special
education.

ARE SOCIALLY MALADJUSTED YOUTHS HANDICAPPED?

As just mentioned, the socially maladjusted are
excluded from the P.L. 94-142 definition of SED.
Presumably, the motivation for this, as also suggested by the term *seriously*, was to exlude from
eligibility those students who do not manifest
significant underlying emotional pathology and
whose behavior does not deviate from the
norms of their reference (i.e., peer) group. We
also presume that the federal government
wished to avoid a repetition of the fiasco associated with the discrepancy definition of
learning disabilities, a definition that permitted
any student to be eligible for special education
if her achievement was two or more grade levels below her educational capacity. This "loose"
definition resulted in some schools identifying
40% or more of their student population as
learning disabled. Such practices would only
be embarrassing to the educational system, were
it not for the fact that state and federal special
education funds are allocated on the basis of
the number of handicapped pupils identified
in a specific category. The link between pro-

gram funding and the number of handicapped
pupils identified means that the identification
of large numbers of handicapped students is
expensive for taxpayers as well as embarrassing
for school districts. A "tighter" definition would
reduce the tendency to identify any student exhibiting behavioral difficulties as SED. The Office of Special Education and Rehabilitative Services estimates the prevalence of serious
emotional distrubance at between 1.2 and 2.0%
of the school-age population (Comptroller
General of the U.S., 1981), in spite of the pre-
ponderance of research showing that the prevalence of educationally significant behavioral
disorders is 4-7 or even 10 percent (Bower,
1983; Nelson, 1985).

Socially maladjusted is a term used to identify students whose antisocial and frequently
illegal behavior conforms to the standards or
norms of their deviant cultural or peer group
(Neel & Rutherford, 1981). *Juvenile deliquency*
is a legal term applied by a court of law to
identify a person under the age of majority (under 18 in most states) who has been found
guilty of a criminal offense (i.e., adjudicated).
It also is used to refer to juveniles found guilty
of "status offenses," i.e., behaviors not considered criminal when committed by adults, such
as truancy, disobedience, running away from
home, and sexual promiscuity. It is difficult to
see how either group could be logically or practically separated from the population of SED or
behaviorally disordered students, because their
behavior does violate the norms of the larger
social order and is not considered normative
or tolerable by the schools. Moreover, the author of the definition of SED used in the federal
regulations has objected to this false dichotomy,
pointing out that, regardless of etiology, the
emotionally disturbed child as defined in his
study had to be socially maladjusted in school
(Bower, 1983).

Because they are available for study, the
characteristics of incarcerated offenders have

---

[1]The term *behaviorally disordered* is preferred over *seriously emotionally disturbed* by the Council for Children
with Behavioral Disorders, the major professional organization for educators working with such youngsters (see
Huntze, 1985).

been extensively monitored. The data suggest a strong relationship between the lack of education and crime. For example, only about 40% of male inmates in jail and prison have completed high school, compared with 85% of males aged 20 to 29 in the U.S. population. There also is a statistical correlation between educational attainment and the severity of crime; offenders with less education tend to account for more crimes and for a greater proportion of violent crimes (Cantwell, 1983). The average adult inmate functions two to three grade levels below the actual grade level he completed (Snarr & Wolford, 1985). The prevalence of learning handicaps among juveniles has been found to range between 28% (Rutherford et al., 1985) and 42% (Morgan, 1979). Some states (e.g., Delaware, Kansas, Massachusetts) have declared virtually all of their incarcerated juvenile population as handicapped for educational purposes.

The demographic characteristics of incarcerated persons also show marked similarities to those of students with behavior and **learning disorders**. The backgrounds of offenders include turbulent home life, lack of family ties, and a relationship between violent behavior and neurological abnormalities and abuse as children (Cantwell, 1983).

The view we have taken in this text is that socially maladjusted and delinquent youth, as a group, should be considered educationally handicapped for two reasons. First, most of them manifest serious learning handicaps, according both to national studies of their educational and social performance and to administrators' estimates. Second, most have not responded well to traditional school curricula and practices, as attested to by records of truancy, low achievement, disciplinary actions, and dropping out. They need individualized, functional educational experiences, not a repetition of teaching approaches to which they became alienated early in their school careers.

THE CRIMINAL JUSTICE SYSTEM

The juvenile justice system is a subcomponent of the larger criminal justice system, represented schematically in Figure 10–1. The criminal justice system constitutes society's organized response to crime. This response is a complex process, involving many agencies, levels, and branches of government. There is no single criminal justice system in the United States; instead, there are many subsystems which, although similar, are individually unique (Zawitz et al., 1983). In this section, we describe the criminal justice system and point out differences in the handling of adults and juveniles. The juvenile justice system will be described in the following section.

The criminal justice system is composed of three major units: law enforcement (police), the courts (prosecutors, defense attorneys, and judges), and corrections (probation, institutions, and parole). From the perspective of the offender, there are three basic tracts: adult felony (serious offenses, such as armed robbery, assault, or murder), adult misdemeanor (relatively minor offenses that generally do not result in incarceration), and juvenile offense (crimes committed by persons under the age of majority, as well as status offenses). Each tract involves different philosophies, laws, procedures, courts, and personnel (Wolford, 1985).

The commission of a crime marks the usual entry point into the criminal justice system. However, the majority of crimes are not responded to by the system because they are not discovered or reported (Snarr & Wolford, 1985; Zawitz et al., 1983). Juveniles may enter the system through referrals by school officials, social service agencies, neighbors, parents, or law enforcement officers, as well as through arrest (Zawitz et al., 1983). The criminal justice system responds to reported or detected crimes through the following pro-

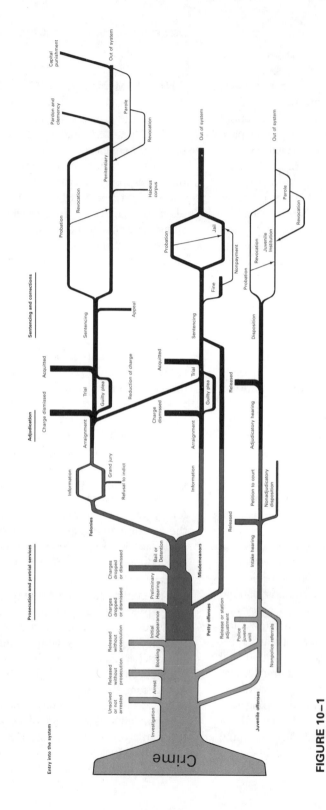

FIGURE 10–1

The criminal justice system (Source: From "The Response to Crime" by M. W. Zawitz, T. R. Mina, C. M. Kuykendall, L. A. Greenfeld, and J. L. White, 1983, in *Report to the Nation on Crime and Justice*, Washington, DC: U.S. Department of Justice, Bureau of Justice Statistics.)

cesses: investigation, arrest and booking, initial court appearance, preliminary hearing, filing charges, arraignment, trial, sentencing, and appeal (Snarr & Wolford, 1985). Correctional services are provided at the sentencing level and include, for adults: probation, jails and lockups, institutions, and parole. Juvenile correctional services include detention, probation, institutions, and aftercare. Each state and territory administers its correctional programs at the level of state government. Some states have one administrative agency for adults and juvenile corrections, while others administer juvenile programs separately (Rutherford et al., 1985; Snarr & Wolford, 1985).

As Figure 10–1 illustrates, there are multiple exit points from the criminal justice system. Relatively few persons arrested on suspicion of committing a crime are sentenced to a correctional facility; for example, of every 1,000 felony arrests, 300 are juvenile cases. Of the remaining 700, about 440 will be convicted and receive some type of sentence. Approximately 300 of these represent felony convictions, of which 200 receive probationary sentences and 100 receive a prison term (Snarr & Wolford, 1985). Similarly, only about 10% of juveniles apprehended are committed to institutions (Zawitz et al., 1983). Juveniles are processed through an intake hearing, where the intake officer decides whether the case warrants filing a petition requesting an adjudicatory hearing or a request to transfer jurisdiction to adult criminal court. The juvenile court may reject the petition, or the juvenile may be diverted to other agencies or programs. If the petition is accepted, a *hearing* (the term used instead of trial) is conducted (in most states without a jury), and if the youth is found guilty, he is adjudicated as delinquent, rather than being convicted of a specific crime (Snarr & Wolford, 1985). Should the youth be adjudicated, the juvenile court typically exercises far greater discretion than do adult courts. *Dispositions* (the term used to designate sen-

tencing of juveniles) include probation, commitment to a correctional institution, restitution, fines, removal from the home to a foster home or a treatment agency, participation in special schools, or referral to adult criminal court (Zawitz et al., 1983). The juvenile court may waive *jurisdiction* (authority to hear a case and render a decision) and transfer a youth for trial as an adult if the offense is serious, if there is extensive prior record, and/or if the juvenile is older. The minimum age for waiving juvenile court jurisdiction varies among states, from 16 to no specific age given (Zawitz, 1983).

Although a very small proportion of persons apprehended receive sentences or dispositions, it is estimated that over 2.4 million individuals are under some form of correctional care, custody, or supervision. This includes nearly 2 million adults (1.2% of all adults over 18) and 455,000 juveniles (1.5% of youth aged 10-18). Approximately 1.2 million adults are on probation and another 200,000 are on parole or some other form of prison aftercare. About 330,000 juveniles are on probation, and another 50,000 are on parole or aftercare. Of the remainder, nearly 530,000 adults are incarcerated (i.e., confined in a federal or state prison or a jail to serve a court-imposed sentence). Approximately 72,000 juveniles are housed in detention centers or juvenile correctional institutions. There are 3,493 local jails in the U.S., and 521 state and 38 federal prisons. The number of public and private juvenile correctional facilities in 1979 was 2,550 (Zawitz et al., 1983). The cost of incarceration for all prisoners (adults and juveniles combined) is more than $6 billion a year, or $13,000 per inmate (Snarr & Wolford, 1985). Correctional programs for juveniles are even more expensive—$20,000 to $30,000 per year for each incarcerated youth (Abt Associates, 1980) because of their lower inmate-to-staff ratio and the existence of expensive treatment programs.

Community-Based Correctional Programs

The majority of correctional services are operated at the local level and include jails and lockups, work release programs, halfway houses, parole, and employment assistance. Community correctional programs are especially important for juveniles, due to the prevailing deinstitutionalization movement, and include parole to the home, group homes, foster homes, day treatment programs (e.g., alternative education, court schools), and probation. Juvenile or adult offenders may become involved in such programs at several points:

1. Prior to court conviction, they may be placed in secure detention (e.g., jails, lockups, or detention centers) or diverted to other programs, such as alcohol or drug counseling, driver education, or psychiatric therapy. Diversion programs are used regularly with juvenile offenders.
2. After conviction, as an alternative to incarceration (e.g., probation).
3. During incarceration (e.g., study and work release programs).
4. After release from incarceration (e.g., parole or aftercare) (Snarr & Wolford, 1985).

Jails differ from prisons in that they are locally administered and are designed to hold prisoners for brief periods (between 48 hours and 1 year). (Lockups are designed to provide secure detention for less than 48 hours.) Jails provide secure custody for persons charged with but not convicted of crime, as well as detention for individuals sentenced by the courts. An estimated 3 million persons enter jails in the United States each year. Because most jails are small and provide short-term detention, only slightly more than a third offer meaningful educational, vocational, recreational, or other programs. However, jails frequently house youthful offenders: 22% of all persons arrested for vio-

lent crimes are under 18 years of age, and nearly 50% of all arrestees for property offenses are juveniles (Snarr & Wolford, 1985).

Prisons

Federal and state correctional facilities are designated by their level of security. State prisons typically are designated as maximum, medium, or minimum security, while the Federal Bureau of Prisons includes six security levels, with level six being the most secure.[2] When an offender is given a prison sentence, usually she is sent to a classification and reception center, where she is examined, interviewed, and tested and where attempts are made to obtain other documentation useful for classification and making institutional assignment decisions. Such decisions are largely based on custody and security needs, as well as on length of sentence and bed space, rather than on the type of program best suited to the offender. After classification, the offender is transferred to the institution where she will serve her sentence. Classification in juvenile institutions is somewhat different for three reasons:

1. Many juvenile systems are too small for a separate reception and classification center. Classification is done by a field worker, or the youth is sent to the nearest juvenile institution and classified there.
2. Classification often is much less formal, as juvenile institutions are relatively small and educational or treatment programs tend to have precedence over custody considerations.
3. The same committee that makes classification decisions may also make parole and release decisions.

---

[2]Women's prisons are too few in number to permit separate facilities at each security level. Different levels of security are provided within a single women's institution. Co-ed prisons are all classified as minimum security (Snarr & Wolford, 1985).

The movement to deinstitutionalize juvenile offenders has been somewhat counterbalanced by an increase in the number of juveniles sentenced to adult institutions, the call for tougher penalties, and the efforts of some jurisdictions to have juvenile offenses count toward adult career criminal statutes (traditionally, a juvenile's court record is expunged when she reaches the age of majority). Juveniles are incarcerated in public or private programs, which may be designated as open or closed. Private programs tend to be smaller, more specialized (e.g., serving only chemically dependent offenders), and more selective in whom they accept. Closed facilities or programs are more secure and include detention centers, training schools, and some camp programs, whereas open programs include shelters, group homes, ranches, or camps (Snarr & Wolford, 1985).

Release from adult correctional programs generally is preceded by a parole process. In many states, inmates in adult prisons may earn substantial amounts of "good time" (time off sentence for consecutive periods of time served without trouble, or for heroic or meritorious service). Good time credits chracteristically amount to 1/3 to 1/2 of the inmate's sentence. Conversely, good time is lost for rule violations, and such punishments as loss of privileges or solitary confinement may be imposed as well. A formal parole hearing is conducted by a parole board. Sometimes a preliminary hearing precedes the parole hearing. Parole may be granted or denied, depending on the inmate's record in prison as well as other factors. If parole is granted, a local parole officer in the jurisdiction where the offender plans to reside investigates the community to verify the inmate's parole plan (anticipated employment, place of residence). If no discrepancies or problems are revealed, the individual is released on parole (Snarr & Wolford, 1985).

In contrast, the release process for juveniles is far more informal. Many juvenile programs operate on a highly structured reward system where offenders earn increasing levels of freedom and privileges as they progress. Release decisions are made by program personnel in a staff meeting rather than in an official hearing. The juvenile often is not present. An increase in sentence length is a frequent punishment technique for rule infractions; this decision also tends to be made in informal staff meetings. Responsibility for working with both adult and juvenile released offenders rests with parole officers, although both groups may participate in community aftercare programs (e.g., employment assistance, group home, halfway house) after their release from detention.

THE JUVENILE JUSTICE SYSTEM

In the previous section we described the juvenile justice system in terms of how juveniles are processed in comparison with adults. This section will provide a more detailed examination of the juvenile system, including **juvenile law**, the rights of juveniles, and case processing.

Juvenile Law

Jurisdiction for juveniles is based on age and behavior. In most states, once a youth has been adjudicated by a juvenile court, he is considered under that jurisdiction until reaching the age of majority, which varies from state to state. Most states have not established a lower age limit for juvenile court jurisdiction, but the common law presumption is that a child under age 7 is not capable of criminal behavior. A youth's juvenile court record typically is expunged when he leaves the juvenile court's jurisdiction except in rare cases in which the youth is remanded into the custody of adult corrections upon reaching the age of majority. The practice of expunging juvenile records protects young persons from entering adulthood with a public criminal record; however, it also interferes with the early identification of career criminals (individuals who have been committed of repeated felony offenses). The identification of such persistent felony offenders is important to criminal justice professionals, as approximately 45% of the total adult inmate population may be classified as career criminals (Snarr & Wolford, 1985). The majority of crimes appear to be committed by a small group of career criminals. For example, in one study chronic offenders account for 23% of all male offenders, but they had committed 61% of all crimes (Cantwell, 1983). Some jurisdictions (e.g., Ohio, New York) have attempted to make juvenile offenses count toward habitual offender status (Snarr & Wolford, 1985).

In terms of behavior, juvenile law is concerned with three major areas: criminal (illegal) behavior, status offenses, and neglect/dependency cases. Criminal or nonstatus offenses are illegal behaviors by juveniles. Status offenses are behaviors forbidden only to juveniles (i.e., are based on the status of age), and neglect/dependency cases are those in which parental behaviors or circumstances that adversely affect children are subject to juvenile and/or adult court jurisdiction (Snarr & Wolford, 1985). Because status offenses are considered delinquent activity, the number of girls in this population is greater than the adult female prison population: Females make up 6% of the adult population of jails and prisons, whereas they make up 20% of the population of juvenile institutions (Cantwell, 1983).One-third of juveniles in custody are held for reasons other than a criminal offense (Zawitz et al., 1983). This fact underscores the tremendous discretionary power of the juvenile justice system, which raises the important issue of protecting a young person's legal rights through due process safeguards.

The Legal Rights of Juveniles

Juvenile courts were established in the United States to protect children and to look after their best interests. They were not designed as a forum for deciding innocence or guilt but were viewed as advocates for children. Therefore, the provision of constitutional guarantees of due process was given little attention. This proved to be a serious omission, and in the 1960s and 1970s, the Supreme Court, after hearing the case of a 15-year-old boy who received a sentence of six years for making an obscene phone call, outlined due process procedural requirements for juvenile hearings. These include the following:

1. The child and parents must receive a written notice of charges.
2. The child and parents have the right to legal counsel.
3. The child has the right to remain silent under the Fifth Amendment's self-incrimination clause.
4. The child has the right to confront and to cross-examine any witness against him (Snarr & Wolford, 1985).

The Supreme Court also set forth due process safeguards for waiver procedures involving the transfer of a juvenile case to adult criminal court. These are as follows:

1. The juvenile is entitled to a hearing on the question of waiver.
2. The juvenile is entitled to representation by counsel.
3. The juvenile's attorney must have access to the juvenile's social records on request.
4. If jurisdiction is waived, the juvenile is entitled to a statement of reasons (Snarr & Wolford, 1985, p. 85).

Thus, juveniles now are afforded most of the same due process safeguards as adults, except for the right to a trial by a jury. The Supreme Court ruled that juries are not essential at juvenile hearings; therefore, most states do not provide for juries at juvenile court proceedings (Zawitz et al., 1983). Also, the majority of juveniles are not represented by counsel. On the other hand, it has been established that juveniles have a right to treatment, whereas adults do not (Snarr & Wolford, 1985).

How Juveniles Are Processed Through the System

Our description of the criminal justice system included information regarding the processing of juveniles. In this section, we take a closer look at how youthful offenders are processed through the juvenile justice system. Figure 10–2 represents the portion of Figure 10–1 pertaining to juvenile offenses, shown in greater detail. As the data we reported previously suggest, crime is largely a young person's game (Snarr & Wolford, 1985). Half the arrests reported in national crime indices were of persons under 20 years of age; furthermore, the highest rates of offending occur among black males, aged 18-20 (Cantwell, 1983). Violent crime appears especially to involve youths: juveniles and youthful offenders account for more than 40% of the violent crime in the United States (Snarr & Wolford, 1985). The characteristics of violent juvenile offenders resemble those of violent adult offenders. These youths are predominantly male, disproportionately black and Hispanic, economically disadvantaged, likely to exhibit interpersonal difficulties and behavior problems, and from single-parent families or families with a high degree of conflict, instability, and inadequate supervision. Violent juvenile offenders appear likely to become violent adult offenders. Age of first offense also appears to predict future offenses: Youths who had their first encounter with the police in their early teens have a greater number of subsequent police contacts than do those whose first encounter occurred later (Cantwell, 1983).

Figure 10–2 shows cases entering the juvenile justice system through a police-juvenile encounter. However, not all such encounters are occasioned by the commission of a crime, and a substantial number of juveniles do not enter the system through contact with law enforcement officers. Particularly in the case of status offenses and dependency/neglect, they enter through referral to the police juvenile unit or to the juvenile court. Black and Smith (1981) reported that of the more than 2.5 million cases handled annually by the juvenile justice system, 75% are referred by community agencies, including schools, probation officers, and other courts. Schools rank high on the list of complainants. Other referrals are made by parents and relatives, as in cases of incorrigibility, sexual misconduct, or running away from home. Figure 10–3 represents the portion of referrals (including police arrests) to juvenile court for various categories of offenses. Crimes against property account for almost 50% of juvenile offenses, but status offenses make up an estimated 20% of referrals (Zawitz et al., 1983).

Figure 10–2 illustrates the considerable discretionary power exercised throughout the juvenile justice system, in that juvenile cases may be diverted from the system or within the system or may be dismissed, or the disposition may be adjusted (e.g., a youth may be transferred from one program to another, referred to as a *station adjustment* in Figure 10–1) at numerous points in the case processing sequence. The exercise of this discretion may begin with a youth's initial police contact. For example, of 1,383,380 arrests of juveniles in 1981:

- 34% were released without referral to any court or welfare agency.
- 58% were referred to juvenile courts.
- 5% were referred to adult criminal courts. Less than 2% were referred to welfare or secondary police agencies (Zawitz et al., 1983).

Juveniles who are not released or diverted from or within the system at this point go through intake proceedings. These may be informal or may involve a formal intake hearing (Zawitz et al., 1983). Most states have a court

266

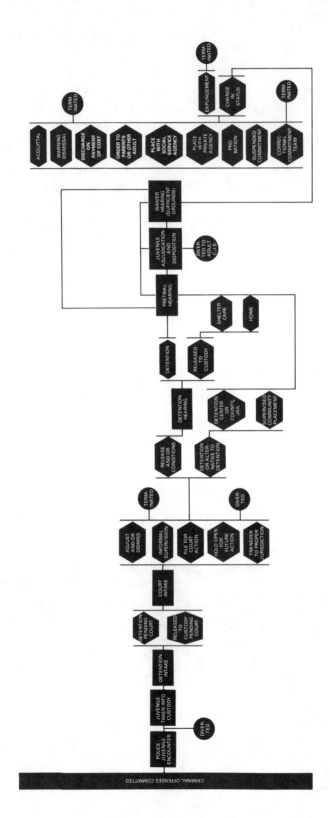

FIGURE 10-2

The juvenile justice system (Source: From "Educational Interventions in the Juvenile Justice System" by B. I. Wolford, October 13, 1984, Paper presented at the National Adolescent Conference, Pensacola, Florida. Reprinted by permission.)

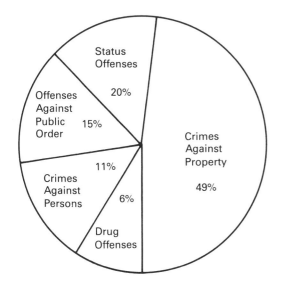

FIGURE 10–3
Prevalence of juvenile offenses

gether. Fewer than 20% of juvenile cases are placed in secure detention prior to adjudication (Zawitz et al., 1983). Thus, much discretion is practiced here, also. Table 10–1 illustrates the range of intake decisions for a sample of juvenile offenses. It shows that the proportion of cases dismissed was greatest for status offenses, approximately equal to those informally or formally handled (i.e., an adjudicatory petition filed) for misdemeanors and property offenses, and that the proportion of cases formally handled was greatest for offenses against persons.

If the intake unit decides to hand the case over to the juvenile court, a petition for an adjudicatory hearing is filed. As we stated previously, the juvenile court may accept or reject the petition. If the petition is rejected, the court can dismiss the case, refer the youth to a diversion program, or waive jurisdiction and bind the juvenile over for trial in an adult criminal court. Nearly 70% of juvenile cases in which jurisdiction is not waived are dismissed. Should the petition be accepted, the youth may be held in detention, placed in a community program or foster home, or remanded to the custody of her parents. Such a decision may or may not entail a detention hearing.

Should the case be prosecuted this far, the next step is a pretrial hearing, where a decision is made whether to conduct a juvenile adjudicatory hearing or hold a waiver hearing and handle the case through the adult criminal justice system. If jurisdiction is waived, the youth

intake officer under the administration of a juvenile court judge. Depending on the state, juvenile court intake personnel may include a clerk of the court, the court probation intake officer, an intake officer or youth services program officer, or the district attorney. In addition to beginning formal court proceedings, intake officers may release the juvenile in the custody of her parents; place her in protective custody; admit her to a detention facility, refer her for psychiatric evaluation, for informal probation, or for counseling; or may close the case alto-

TABLE 10–1
Intake decisions by type of offense charged

Offense Charged	Dismissal (%)	Informal Handling (%)	Formal Handling (%)	(N)
Status	26	36	38	77
Misdemeanor	33	34	33	123
Property	29	34	35	132
Person	16	32	51	37

Source: From *Juvenile Justice: Policy, Practice, and the Law* by H. T. Rubin, 1979, New York: Random House. Copyright 1979 by Random House. Reprinted by permission.

is tried as an adult and, if found guilty, convicted of a specific crime (e.g., armed robbery) instead of being adjudicated as deliquent. Although the conviction rate of juveniles tried as adults is high (more than 90%, compared to less than 40% for adults), over half of the juveniles convicted receive sentences of probation or fines (Zawitz et al., 1983).

As Figure 10–2 illustrates, the number of disposition alternatives subsequent to juvenile adjudication is large. Naturally, these options are considerably affected by the programs and services available in the area. The majority of adjudicated youths are issued warnings, made to pay fines, remanded into the custody of their parents (who are given orders from the court regarding their child's behavior and supervision), or placed on probation. Others are referred to diversion or community-based correctional programs or are placed in juvenile correctional institutions, which vary in size and type; some are small, private facilities, others are large public facilities, some specialize in one type of offender or treatment, others are open or closed in terms of security and access to community programs (Snarr & Wolford, 1985). Nearly all juvenile correctional institutions offer education and/or treatment programs. State juvenile correctional agencies report that more than 80% of handicapped incarcerated youth are receiving special education services, but the quality of these services varies tremendously from program to program and from state to state (Rutherford et al., 1985). Juveniles leave the juvenile justice system following parole or aftercare, and juvenile court jurisdiction is terminated in most states when youths attain the age of 18 or 21 (Snarr & Wolford, 1985).

SPECIAL EDUCATION AND THE JUVENILE JUSTICE SYSTEM

As we pointed out earlier, handicapped youths are more likely to be dealt with harshly by the juvenile justice system. Moreover, although correctional education programs are under the same mandate as public and private schools to provide an appropriate, individualized education to handicapped students, the implementation of P.L. 94-142 in many such programs is far behind that of public education agencies. It is important for special educators who become involved with the juvenile justice system to understand the problems involving handicapped offenders and the areas in which they are likely to occur, because this knowledge may help them serve as better advocates for handicapped adolescents, in general, and their students, in particular. Therefore, in this section we briefly review the educational programs available to juvenile offenders and discuss two related clusters of problems: those involving the implementation of special correctional education programs and those concerning the effective transition of handicapped youths into and out of correctional programs. The following section presents strategies and considerations for special educators who deal with the juvenile justice system.

Educational Programs in the Juvenile Justice System

Wolford (1985) described four stages in which educational interventions can occur in the juvenile justice system. The first consists of preventive or predelinquent interventions, which span a large portion of the sequence depicted in Figure 10–2. The educational interventions at this stage include alternative schools, which may be operated by the public schools, juvenile court, or a combination of the two; parent education programs, aimed at improving parenting skills and parent-child relations; and the efforts of individual teachers, who may include law-related content in their curricula or who may serve as advisors and youth advocates in the courts.

The second stage consists of diversions from and during adjudication, in which the youth is diverted to a program outside the juvenile justice system. Educational options outside the system include referral to court and alternative schools, and job training or work-study programs. Detention education programs are offered for those offenders not qualifying for diversion or those living in areas where diversion programs are not available.

The third stage includes dispositional options, such as probation, community residential placement, and institutional confinement. Conditions of probation usually include mandatory school attendance. Achievement Place (Phillips, Phillips, Fixsen, & Wolf, 1971), now called the Teaching Family Program, is an example of a community residential program. It is a highly structured group-home environment, in which youths experience clear expectations and systematic contingency management of their behavior, including their performance in local community schools. Education programs also exist in most juvenile institutions.

Educational programs available at the fourth stage, reentry, are fewer in number because many youths leaving correctional supervision do not choose to return to school. In addition, the conditions of parole often mandate full-time employment (Rutherford et al., 1985). Youths who do return to school may seek readmission to their local public school, enter a vocational training program, training school, or institution of higher education, should they be qualified.

Implementing Correctional Special Education

The difficulties experienced by correctional educators attempting to provide individual education programs for handicapped offenders have been widely discussed (Coffey, 1983; Gerry, 1985; Rutherford et al., 1985; Wolford, 1983, 1985) and begin with the juvenile court. Judges

and court officers are not trained to recognize handicapped youths, nor do they understand their unique needs and how these affect court decisions and dispositions (Schilit, 1983). Furthermore, in many cases, juvenile courts do not have youths' school records when making adjudicatory decisions; thus, handicapped students are not identified early enough to be directed to programs where their special learning needs can be met. As a consequence, many handicapped offenders pass through the juvenile (or adult) justice system unidentified and, as far as their educational needs are concerned, inadequately served. For example, probation officers, who are responsible for supervising the majority of adjudicated youths, usually are not familiar with the special learning needs and problems of the handicapped (Wolford, 1985). The special education needs of handicapped offenders assigned to institutions often are not identified when they arrive at a correctional facility for classification. Their identification depends on how sophisticated the classification instruments and personnel are and whether public school records are obtained at this point. Often, classification involves group testing and rapid screening, especially in adult facilities (recall that more than 100,000 persons incarcerated in adult institutions are under 21 years of age). School records often do not reach correctional personnel until after classification is completed and may not catch up with the youth at all (Edgar, Webb, & Maddox, 1987).

Even if handicapped offenders are identified prior to or during classification, there is no guarantee that they will receive an adequate special education program while serving their sentences. The reasons are numerous. First, P.L. 94-142 was not designed for implementation in correctional settings (Coffey, 1983). For example, the small size of many juvenile programs reduces the number of optional educational environments, which makes the **least restrictive environment** clause extremely difficult to implement. Second, the transitory nature of correctional populations complicates the planning and delivery of IEPs. The average sentence for juveniles is between 4 and 7 months (Gerry, 1985) and just over 20 months for adults (Zawitz et al., 1983).

Third, especially in adult facilities, a conflict exists between custody and program functions. Corrections personnel see their chief priority as the protection of society from offenders. Programs such as education are viewed as far less important. Education is mandatory in most juvenile facilities, but even here there is need for security; disciplinary practices such as solitary confinement and the need of some inmates for administrative segregation (e.g., to protect them from fellow inmates' abuse) seriously interfere with special education programming (Snarr & Wolford, 1985).

Fourth, many correctional education programs lack the financial resources to support a continuum of regular and special education services. Typically, education accounts for the smallest portion of correctional institutions' budgets (Coffey, 1983). Although some state correctional agencies receive P.L. 94-142 flow-through monies, many do not qualify or do not apply for funds (Rutherford et al., 1985). The shortage of trained special educators in correctional education programs constitutes a fifth reason and is, of course, related to the lack of financial resources to support such programs.

Finally, correctional special education programs find the issue of parent involvement very difficult. The frequent separation of correctional programs from offenders' home communities makes it hard to locate or involve parents, and finding and training legally acceptable parent surrogates has proven to be a significant problem (Coffey, 1983).

It is unlikely that these issues will be adequately addressed unless two steps are taken simultaneously: (1) improve the special education services provided handicapped youthful offenders and (2) provide training to professionals at all levels of the criminal justice system. Increasing pressure from litigation and the threatened withdrawal of federal education funds have spurred efforts by correctional education agencies to develop special education programs, and training programs for correctional special educators are multiplying (Rutherford et al., 1985). However, appropriate educational planning for handicapped youth under the supervision of the criminal justice system will depend upon the advocacy and hard work of concerned professionals on a case-by-case basis. Public school special educators whose students are affected by the criminal justice system should attempt to find out which programs and agencies are providing services and establish communication with the appropriate professionals. Ideally, this communication will lead to interagency planning and collaboration, so that a handicapped adolescent's special education experience is not curtailed when he enters the criminal justice system.

Transition of Handicapped Youths

Many of the problems described above may be attributed to the geographical and/or political isolation of correctional programs from other human service agencies, especially education (Rutherford et al., 1985). Correctional programs are separate administrative entities, with purposes, goals, and philosophies vastly different from those of public education. It is not surprising, therefore, that a smooth and coordinated transfer of information and individuals between correctional and community settings seldom occurs. Most citizens recognize that governmental bureaucracies find it extremely difficult to interact cooperatively, and the juvenile justice and educational systems are no exception. Problems involving the transition of handicapped youth from one jurisdiction to the other begin at this level. Neither agency has accepted responsibility for **transition services**, and most states lack mechanisms for effective interagency collaboration (Grosenick & Huntze, 1980; Keilitz & Miller, 1980). The consequences of this bureaucratic separation include limited mechanisms for the exchange of information (Rutherford et al., 1985) and the lack of transition services for facilitating the successful return of offenders to school or work (Edgar et al., 1987).

The traditional isolation of correctional education programs also has reduced the usefulness of the training they provide. Whereas many inmates, handicapped or not, lack functional survival skills for successful employment and community living, most regular or special correctional education programs provide training in basic academic tool subjects. Transition programs have been the most neglected component of correctional education efforts, but their absence is particularly detrimental to handicapped youths, for whom systematic generalization and maintenance training has been shown to be critical (Rutherford et al., 1985). As Wolford (1985) emphasized, "The continuum of educational services should not be broken, whether *by entering or leaving* the correctional environment" (p.15). Specific issues and strategies regarding the transition of handicapped youths between public school and correctional education programs, as well as to community settings, are discussed in Chapter Eleven.

STRATEGIES FOR WORKING WITH THE JUVENILE JUSTICE SYSTEM

We hope the information provided in the preceding sections will give educators a useful basis for interacting more effectively with juvenile or adult law enforcement officers, courts, and correctional programs. Knowledge of these systems is essential in the effective advocacy of and cooperative planning for the educational needs of handicapped youth. Such knowledge, however, is not enough; it must be augmented with a repertoire of strategies and skills for working with a variety of agencies, professionals, and lay persons. Those inexperienced in dealing with the criminal justice system are prone to making two errors. The first is being intimidated by the system. This is a natural enough reaction; most citizens are somewhat fearful of involvement with the police, and the formality, technicality, and seemingly esoteric proceedings of courts can be quite threatening. Moreover, most of us are familiar with the stereotypic glib attorney who renders witnesses incredible and juries gullible with his eloquent and pointed discourse. No one wants to appear a fool, and no one wants to be accused of perjury or contempt. However, the second error is in assuming that one will single-handedly beat the system and exonerate the accused. Such an attitude not only may work to the detriment of your student, but also may rob you of your credibility. This balance point between activism and credibility need not be precarious: we suggest that you be secure in your professional role, and provide input and advocacy within the boundaries of that role. Furthermore, you should be willing to take as well as to give. If proceedings are conducted in the spirit of trying to help the adolescent, all professionals can contribute. You should recognize that outside of the schools, special education is not necessarily viewed as the salvation of pupils with learning and behavioral handicaps (Kerr & Nelson, 1983).

Professional correctional educators have suggested a number of ways in which special educators can help overcome the problems of handicapped persons in the criminal justice system. For example, Coffey (1983) indicated that special educators can (a) offer training and assistance to law enforcement, court, and correctional personnel; (b) help correctional administrators understand P.L. 94-142 and its implementation; (c) lobby for the resources needed for compliance; (d) become expert witnesses; (e) help develop program models and disseminate these through correctional and special education channels; (f) join the Correctional Education Association (CEA) and invite CEA members to join special education professional organizations; and (g) lobby for needed legislation. Wolford (1983) added that special educators can provide input regarding special education student needs and instructional methods in correctional institutions. The major benefits of these activities involve crossing the traditional boundaries between disciplines and learning to help one another. Achieving such a goal probably will take much time and many professionals; however, the special education training needs of criminal justice personnel have been recognized and are beginning to be addressed (Rutherford et al., 1985). In the following sections, we will describe specific strategies for working with students and with the juvenile justice system.

Working with "High Risk" Students

"High risk" students are those whose demographic and behavioral characteristics predict a high probability of encounters with the criminal justice system. They tend to come from economically disadvantaged homes and neighborhoods; to live in single-parent or unstable families; to be black or Hispanic and male; to be frequent truants; to have committed previous offenses; and to do poorly in school (Cantwell, 1983). Although none of these characteristics, either singly or in combination, should be viewed as perfect predictors of delinquent behavior, you probably do not need a recitation of them to know whether your students are high risk or not; observation of their behavior and examination of their records will tell the story. If you teach in a community with a high youth crime rate, and/or one in which youth gangs are active, you can be fairly certain that at least some of your pupils are high risks. This is not to say that adolescents who do not match these characteristics will not commit juvenile offenses. White, middle-class males and females also commit crimes; therefore the following strategies may be useful in any teaching situation.

The strategy over which you, as a classroom teacher, can exert most control involves the curriculum that you teach. It has been observed that many incarcerated youths, especially those with learning handicaps, lack functional living skills (Rutherford et al., 1985). Furthermore, handicapped adolescents may lack basic social skills (Goldstein, 1987). Finally, these youths may lack skills critical to getting along in school settings (Zigmond, Kerr, Schaeffer, Brown, & Farra, 1986). Special educators should consider the relative merits of providing instruction in such **functional skills** as avoiding fights, expressing feelings, interacting appropriately with others, responding politely to teachers and adults, being on time, interviewing for a job, dressing appropriately, planning within a budget, and so on. At the secondary level, a predominant curricular emphasis on improving basic academic performances by a grade level or fraction thereof should be weighed against the need to provide instruction in skills that have more immediate application to adolescents' lives and may help to keep them in school. Specific suggestions regarding functional curricula are provided in Chapter Eleven.

A particularly important strategy is to learn the characteristics of the juvenile justice system in your local area. Recall that although we have described this system in general, actually it encompasses many variations (Zawitz et al., 1983). To work with it most effectively, therefore, you should learn how it operates in your area, how juveniles are processed, to which programs and facilities they are referred or sentenced, and the persons who make the major decisions regarding their progress through the system. Toward this end, Figure 10–4 represents a form

1. Persons making referrals to local police juvenile unit

   Name, Title, or Agency   Telephone

   _____   _____

   _____   _____

   _____   _____

2. Contacts in police juvenile unit
   Name   Telephone

   _____   _____

   _____   _____

   _____   _____

3. Juvenile court intake officer(s)
   Name, Title, or Agency   Telephone

   _____   _____

   _____   _____

   _____   _____

4. Juvenile court judges
   Name   Presiding (Days)   Telephone

   _____   _____   _____

   _____   _____   _____

   _____   _____   _____

5. Community diversion and correctional programs
   Program   Contact Person   Telephone

   _____   _____   _____

   _____   _____   _____

   _____   _____   _____

6. Juvenile detention and correctional institutions
   Institution   Contact Person   Telephone

   _____   _____   _____

   _____   _____   _____

   _____   _____   _____

FIGURE 10–4
Juvenile justice system contacts

7. Parole officers

Name   Agency   Telephone

_____   _____   _____

_____   _____   _____

_____   _____   _____

8. Aftercare programs

Program   Contact Person   Telephone

_____   _____   _____

_____   _____   _____

_____   _____   _____

9. Adult criminal court contacts

Name   Title   Telephone

_____   _____   _____

_____   _____   _____

_____   _____   _____

FIGURE 10–4
(*continued*)

for recording information about personnel at each contact point in the juvenile justice system. This form should be modified to reflect the idiosyncrasies of your community, of course. The information on it should be revised and updated as you make new contacts or personnel are replaced. We encourage you to keep a copy of this form at home also, as the need for this information is not likely to arise only when you are at school.

Another important strategy is to monitor students who encounter the system at some point, as well as the juvenile justice professionals with whom you have contact. Figure 10–5 is a student contact log. Note that it is organized in the sequence the justice system uses to process youths. Again, this log should be modified to reflect local variations. Logging student contacts serves two purposes: it summarizes data you may need for interactions with your local juvenile justice personnel, and it prompts you to

keep up with students who are under the temporary supervision of juvenile justice programs.

Figure 10–6 is provided to help you evaluate the persons and agencies with whom you deal on behalf of students. It should prove useful for making decisions about whom to contact for a specific youth or purpose. Of course, we recommend that you keep evaluative information to yourself.

While monitoring student progress through the local juvenile justice system and maintaining records of your most and least useful professional contacts will help you keep abreast of the system, it essentially is a passive process. The next set of strategies are more active, in that they put the special educator in an advocacy or collaborative role. One such strategy concerns parent involvement. Parents of youths chronically in trouble with the law are not known for their openness and zeal; often, they have given up and are defensive, if not antagonistic, especially toward law en-

Student's name ——————————————— Telephone ———————————————
Date of birth ——————————————— Parent's name(s) ———————————————
Address ———————————————
——————————————— Work phone ———————————————
Employer ——————————————— Phone ———————————————
Date arrested or referred ———————————————
Arrested or referred by ———————————————
Offense or reason for referral ———————————————
———————————————————————————————————
———————————————————————————————————
———————————————————————————————————
Action ———————————————
Detention facility ———————————————
Contact person ——————————————— Telephone ———————————————
Intake
Intake officer ——————————————— Telephone ———————————————
Intake hearing date ——————————————— Place ———————————————
———————————————
Outcome ———————————————
———————————————————————————————————
Detention facility ———————————————
Contact person ——————————————— Telephone ———————————————
Educational information requested or sent ———————————————
———————————————————————————————————
Date sent ———————————————
Adjudicatory hearing
Court ——————————————— Judge ———————————————
Date ———————————————
Educational information requested or sent ———————————————
———————————————————————————————————
Date sent ———————————————
Action/disposition ———————————————
———————————————————————————————————
Transferred to ———————————————
Date IEP, records provided ———————————————
To whom ———————————————
Conference scheduled (date) ———————————————
Correctional special education assignment ———————————————
IEP committee ———————————————
———————————————
——————————————— ———————————————
Contact person during incarceration ———————————————
Telephone ——————————————— Address ———————————————
Date paroled ——————————————— ———————————————
Parole officer ——————————————— Telephone ———————————————
Date released ——————————————— Comments ———————————————
———————————————————————————————————

FIGURE 10–5
Student contact log

275

Personnel/Agencies	Have worked with you previously?	Knowledgeable re: needs of students?	Knowledgeable re: P.L. 94-142?	Will require training?	Willing to be trained?	Acted upon training received?	Use or contact again?	Comments (phone numbers, etc.)
Law Enforcement Officers								
Court Intake Officers								
Attorneys								
Child Advocates								
Judges/Court Officers								
Probation Officers								
Parent Surrogates								
Employers								
Social Agencies								
Others								

FIGURE 10–6
Juvenile justice system resource checklist

forcement and juvenile court officers. However, they may be willing to work with their child's teacher, if they believe that she is an earnest advocate for the child. They may need to be encouraged to inform police or the court about their child's functional limitations and needs. They also should be strongly encouraged to insist on their child's legal and educational rights and to participate actively in adjudicatory hearings and IEP meetings.

As the student's teacher, you also may know persons in the community who could serve as resources for the juvenile justice system. For example, the willingness of a youth's employer to provide daily or weekly feedback regarding work performance to a probation officer might influence a judge's disposition in favor of a less restrictive alternative than incarceration. You also may know of educational resources, such as an interested guidance counselor or principal, who could help the court construct an alternative to secure detention.

Your role as a teacher also places you in an ideal position to help the court and/or correctional agency develop an appropriate educational program for handicapped students under juvenile justice supervision. Assuming that you have the legal right to do so, you can provide IEPs and other student records containing information that otherwise might not be known or heeded. You also can ask to serve on IEP committees for students in local correctional education programs. You can facilitate their transition from public school to corrections and back to public school by supervising the transfer of records and ensuring that school officials do not adopt an "out of sight, out of mind" attitude with regard to incarcerated students. In short, your active involvement in case management can help both the student and the juvenile justice system. Keep in mind that the latter exists to *serve* youth, not just to punish them. Juvenile justice professionals are as interested as you in meeting adolescents' needs; therefore, your ability to serve as a resource for the system will increase your effectiveness as an advocate for your pupils.

Providing Information and Training for Juvenile Justice Professionals

Earlier, we mentioned some of the needs for information and training in the juvenile justice system. It may surprise you to know that many judges, court officers, attorneys, and law enforcment officers do not know about P.L. 94-142, as such information typically is not part of their training, although correctional education programs are specifically included in the implementing regulations for the law. The training you can provide regarding the law may range from answering questions to providing informal or formal workshops. We suggest that you obtain copies of the law and its implementing regulations (from your state department of education) and one of several instructional booklets (e.g., Abeson, Bolick, & Hass, 1975) to have on hand.

It also would be wise to maintain an up-to-date professional special education library to assist you in responding to questions and to provide resources concerning the nature and needs of handicapped adolescents. We have noted that, in general, the courts appear not to know the characteristics and needs of handicapped persons, and this lack of knowledge may be responsible for their differential and sometimes harmful treatment. If you approach juvenile justice officials as resources and not as adversaries, you should find that your information and services are welcome. Incidentally, you need not provide all this information by yourself. The Council for Exceptional Children maintains a clearinghouse on information regarding the handicapped, as well as a call- or write-in informational service (Ask Us). Moreover, they support an active political action network, including a governmental relations unit. You can request information from these offices for your own resource files or refer your juvenile justice colleagues to CEC's information services. Write to the Council for Exceptional Children, 1920 Association Drive, Reston, Virginia 22091 for further information.

As you establish credibility with the system, you may have the opportunity to serve as an expert witness in litigation involving handicapped offenders. An expert witness is a professional who provides technical information to a court. You may be called by the prosecution or the plaintiff, and you may be asked to visit programs that are the subject of the litigation and to make depositions (written or oral statments) for either or both sides. The adversarial nature of such proceedings can be somewhat disturbing, but if you stay within the limits of your professional role, the experience should be positive as well as beneficial to handicapped offenders.

We want to remind you again that the issue is not necessarily serving the student *versus* serving the system. If a youth has committed a criminal offense, she should face the consequences. However, the student is entitled to an appropriate and effective treatment program aimed at helping her become a productive member of society, and that program includes special education. Your job is to help design the most appropriate and effective individualized educational program possible, given the constraints imposed by necessary juvenile justice supervision, and to coordinate this program with community educational and vocational opportunities to facilitate the student's transition to her local community (more about this in Chapter Eleven).

Preventing Delinquent Behavior

For many years sociologists, psychologists, criminologists, and educators have pondered the complex problem of delinquent behavior and its prevention. It is far beyond the scope of this text to attempt a thorough discussion of this issue, nor do we wish to suggest that special education has the technology and strategies to deter youth from involvement in crime. However, we can provide a few observations from the work of Jerome Stumphauzer and his colleagues (Aiken, Stumphauzer, & Veloz, 1977; Stumphauzer, Aiken, & Veloz, 1977) regarding the characteristics of nondelinquent males in a

high juvenile crime community. For example, two nondelinquent brothers were extensively interviewed (Aiken et al., 1977). These brothers apparently chose not to follow local gang models of dress or behavior, they maintained a persistent goal orientation, developed skills (e.g., bicycle repairing, restoring cars) valued by the community, attended school regularly, valued strong family relationships, had a strong sense of cultural and ethnic pride, had nondelinquent role models, and avoided gang activities and police encounters. These observations point out that alternatives to delinquent behavior do exist, even in high-crime areas. What young persons need are people who will teach them alternative skills and provide support for and modeling of a nondelinquent life-style. We are not suggesting that you should spend all your free time in your students' home or neighborhoods. However, we do believe that you can become one support person and role model and perhaps join forces with others who wish to help high-risk adolescents.

EMPLOYMENT OPPORTUNITIES FOR SPECIAL EDUCATORS IN THE JUVENILE JUSTICE SYSTEM

At the beginning of this chapter we pointed out the shortage of trained special education teachers in correctional education programs. These shortages exist at all levels, from community-based programs such as alternative or court schools to secure detention facilities. The range of salaries and working conditions is wide; the pay scales of some states are lower than for public school teachers, and many programs lack the materials and other resources available in the public schools. In addition, most correctional facilities have 11- or 12-month employment periods, which may be a deterrent to teachers accustomed to a 10-month contract. However, correctional educators are working to improve such conditions. In several states correctional educators' salaries are higher than those of their public school counterparts. Efforts to improve correctional education programs have been boosted by former Chief Justice Warren Burger's strong position supporting correctional education as a key to the successful rehabilitation of criminal offenders (Burger, 1981). Many educators find the flexibility of working conditions in correctional programs a refreshing change from the atmosphere of some public schools.

As working conditions and teacher salaries improve in the criminal justice system and as employment opportunies in this system increase, more special educators will find positions in correctional education programs desirable. If you are intrigued by the challenge of working with adolescents exhibiting multiple problems in a system that is striving to improve itself, you may find correctional special education to your liking. Contact your state department of corrections, department of human resources, department of education, or your local youth services office for more information.

SUMMARY

The information presented in this chapter is designed to assist secondary special educators in dealing with the juvenile justice system. Because a substantial number of the teenage population is involved in criminal activity and because students with learning and behavioral problems are overrepresented in correctional programs, we feel a strong need to describe procedures and interventions of the juvenile justice system in detail. Chapter Ten began with a discussion as to whether or not socially maladjusted youth are in fact handicapped. We included a discussion of problems and issues regarding the interactions between the justice system and the educational system. Also presented are strategies for working with students under the supervision of the juvenile justice system and employment opportunities.

You, as teacher, are in an ideal position to help the courts and/or the correctional program. There is a need to develop appropriate educational programs for special education students under the juvenile justice supervision. Recall that correctional educational programs are under the same P.L. 94-142 obligation as your public or private school to provide a free appropriate education for handicapped youth 21 years of age and under. Your ability to serve as a resource and an advocate for your students will help the system increase its effectiveness. This chapter included practical suggestions to aid you in your involvement.

RECOMMENDED READINGS

Black, T.E., & Smith, C.P. (1981). A preliminary national assessment of the number and the characteristics of juveniles processed in the juvenile justice system. *Report of the National Juvenile Justice Assessment Center*. Washington, DC: Office of Juvenile Justice and Delinquency Prevention.

Keilitz, I., & Miller, S.L. (1980). Handicapped adolescents and young adults in the juvenile justice system. *Exceptional Education Quarterly*, *2*, 117-126.

Kerr, M.M., & Nelson, C.M. (1983). *Strategies for managing behavior problems in the classroom*. Columbus, OH: Charles E. Merrill Publishing Company.

Nelson, C.M., Rutherford, R.B., Jr., & Wolford, B.I. (1987). *Special education in the criminal justice system*. Columbus, OH: Merrill Publishing Company.

Snarr, R.W., & Wolford, B.I. (1985). *Introduction to corrections*. Dubuque, IA: William C. Brown.

Zawitz, M.W., Mina, T.R., Kuykendall, C.M., Greenfield, L.A., & White, J.L. (1983). The response to crime. In *Report to the nation on crime and justice: The data*. Washington, DC: U.S. Department of Justice, Bureau of Justice Statistics.

CHAPTER
ELEVEN

Post-Secondary
School Adjustment

Until recently, many special educators have assumed that the school's responsibility for handicapped students ends when youths exit secondary education programs. However, P.L. 94-142 mandates that free and appropriate educational services be available for such pupils through the age of 21. Surveys of the post-school status of handicapped young adults indicate that 40-75% of this population are unemployed (Hasazi, Gordon, & Roe, 1985; Wehman, Kregel, & Barcus, 1985). A follow-up study of special education graduates in Colorado by Mithaug and Horiuchi (1983) revealed that although 60% were working, many were underemployed and earned low wages. Given that 250,000 to 300,000 handicapped pupils leave publicly supported education programs each year (Will, 1984), it is apparent that a large portion of these young persons are contributing to this country's unemployment problem. The Office of Special Education and Rehabilitation Services (OSERS) has responded to this problem by assigning a high priority to **transition** programs and **services** for handicapped students preparing to leave school (Will, 1984). A major section of **Public Law 98-199**, the Education for Handicapped Children amendments, is concerned with funds and support for secondary education and transitional services (Wehman et al., 1985). Transition may be broadly defined to include the movement of persons from one setting (an educational program) to another (another educational program, vocational placement, or rehabilitative agency). However, this chapter focuses on issues specific to the transition of students with learning and behavior disorders from secondary schools and presents strategies for improving their post-school adjustment. We begin with an examination of several recent follow-up studies that have dramatized the need for systematic transition programs for handicapped youths, then we present models for transition services. This discussion provides the context for an explication of specific transition strategies.

IMPACT OF FOLLOW-UP STUDIES

Two factors limit the application of follow-up data to the population of young adults who were labeled learning or behaviorally disordered in school. First, because large-scale studies require following many students for extended time periods in many and varied settings, they are impractical. A study by Hasazi and co-workers (1985) of students leaving nine Vermont school districts represents the most comprehensive sample to date, and, as the authors pointed out, it would be inappropriate to generalize findings from such a rural state to more urban locales. Second, follow-up studies have not singled out pupils with learning or behavioral disorders; however, there appears to be little reason to expect that post-school outcomes for this group would be different from those for the special education population as a whole. We will describe the results of three studies of handicapped students who left public school programs.

Hasazi and colleagues (1985) obtained follow-up data on 462 students who, between 1979 and 1983, dropped out of school before reaching the age of 18, left without graduating after the age of 18, or graduated. Their sample came from four urban, four rural, and one metropolitan school district, and included 292 males and 170 females. Procedures included an examination of school records and telephone interviews with parents, guardians, persons familiar with the former student, and/or the student himself.

The current status of the 301 students from whom interview data were obtained is reported in Table 11–1. Sixty percent of the former students who graduated ($n = 271$) were employed, compared with 51% of those who left school ($n = 58$). These figures are well below those for the nation as a whole. Sixty-four percent of those interviewed continued to live with their parents or guardians.

TABLE 11–1

Current work status of former students and job characteristics for those with paid employment: Interviewed sample

Variable	Frequency
What is student doing currently?	
(n = 301)	
Paid employment	166
Homemaker	22
Full-time student (postsecondary)	10
Job training program	1
Mental health center day program	2
Disabled, getting SSI	10
Unable to find job	72
Not employed (reason not specified)	17
For "Paid Employed" only:	
Type of employment (n = 166)	
Nonsubsidized job	164
Sheltered workshop	2
Subsidized job	0
Time status of job (n = 166)	
Full-time	111
21–37 hrs/week	12
Less than 21 hrs/week	30
Variable/unknown	8
Seasonal	5
How did student find job? (n = 166)	
By her/himself	91
Parents/relatives	30
Friend	16
Teacher	9
School counselor	1
Vermont Job Service	3
Vocational Rehabilitation	3
Military	8
Other/unspecified	5

Source: From "Factors Associated with the Employment Status of Handicapped Youth Exiting High School from 1979 to 1983" by S. B. Hasazi, L. R. Gordon, and C. A. Roe, 1985, *Exceptional Children, 61,* pp. 455–469. Reston, VA: Council for Exceptional Children. Copyright 1985 by the Council for Exceptional Children. Reprinted with permission.

Gill (1984) obtained follow-up data, via questionnaires completed by parents or guardians, on 194 former special education students who graduated or left the 10 Pierce County, Washington (Tacoma) schools between 1981 and 1984. Ninety-two (48%) were unemployed at the time of follow-up, compared with a local unemployment rate of 11-12 percent for the entire work force, and 22.7% for youths aged 18 to 24. Twenty-three percent of the sample had not worked during the past three years, and 80% had received no **post-secondary education** experience.

Leone, Fitzmartin, Stetson, and Foster (1986) tracked young persons 2 to 4 years after leaving a residential and day treatment facility. Prior to the follow-up investigation, students were classified as "successful" or "unsuccessful" program leavers based on daily behavior ratings. Sixty-four of the 126 former students were classified as successful, and the remaining 62 were classified as unsuccessful. It was found that successful students had lower rates of absenteeism in school, were more likely to be placed in the day rather than the residential program, and were more likely to be attending school and/ or working when they were followed up. However, the specific status of students at the time of follow-up was not reported.

While these studies sampled all diagnostic categories of handicapped students, none reported the presence of former pupils in correctional or mental health institutions. Based on the analysis of handicapped youths in correctional programs presented in the previous chapter, we would expect to find that *some* of these former students were incarcerated at the time of follow-up. Parents, guardians, and school personnel may have preferred to withold information regarding incarcerated students. As we reported in Chapter Ten, handicapped youths are overrepresented in correctional programs. For example, Morgan (1979) found that more than 42% of children committed to correctional institutions were handicapped, compared with 10.6% in the school-age population as a whole. To our knowledge, no recent study has determined what proportion of clients in mental health or mental retardation institutions were in special education during their public school eligibility, although we would expect this rate to be sizeable. Whereas the proportion of mildly handicapped youths in correctional institutions is much higher than that of persons with moderate to severe handicaps (Keilitz & Miller, 1980; Morgan, 1979; Rutherford, Nelson, & Wolford, 1985), the converse should be the case in mental health/mental retardation institutions.

MODELS FOR TRANSITION SERVICES

A complex array of variables complicates the design and delivery of transition services. Youths requiring these services represent a wide range of functional competence, including the mildly, moderately, and severely/profoundly handicapped. Furthermore, they may exit secondary school programs through graduation, dropping out between the ages of 16 and 18, or leaving without graduating past the age of 18. Regardless of their handicaps or circumstances, all are entitled to special education and related services up to the age of 22. Beyond that chronological limit, they still are eligible for vocational services under Section 504 of the Vocational Rehabilitation Act, which mandates that a handicapping condition may not be used as a basis for excluding any person from a program receiving federal assistance. Financial and programmatic assistance to the handicapped has been strengthened by the Carl D. Perkins Vocational Education Act of 1984 (Cobb & Larkin, 1985).

Another confounding variable is the myriad of human services that may deal with handicapped youth before, during, and after their transition from public school. Edgar, Webb, and Maddox (1987) made several important observations with regard to these agencies. The first is that no apparent plan exists at any level of local, state, or federal government for interagency cooperation. This results in a lack of awareness of other agency programs and services, duplication of services, conflicting philosophies and priorities, and competition over funding and political issues. Section 618 of P.L. 98-199 requires state developmental disabilities and vocational rehabilitation agencies to respond to the lack of adequate transition programs and services, but attempts to initiate interagency communication and collaboration are still in their infancy. The second observation is that agencies differ according to the target population they serve and in entrance and exit criteria. These differences exacerbate problems involving interagency communication and collaboration. Edgar and co-workers observed that agency services frequently are place oriented (e.g., education services are available in schools; counseling services are offered in mental health centers). This means that clients must know where to go for which services, and how to get there.

THE OSERS MODEL

OSERS developed a transitional model leading to employment for handicapped youths (Halpern, 1985). This model includes three bridges to employment: no special services, time-limited services, and ongoing services, which cover the range of transition services handicapped young persons are likely to require. However, as Halpern pointed out, a serious limitation of this model is that it represents only one dimension of post-school adjustment; namely, employment. Halpern's revised transition model is presented in Figure 11–1. It depicts three bridges leading from school to community adjustment: generic services (those available to any youth); time-limited special services; and ongoing special services. Halpern conceptualized community adjustment as including adjustment to a residential environment and to social and interpersonal networks (including daily communications, self-esteem, family support, emotional maturity, and intimate relationships) as well as to employment. Even this model, however, fails to include such services and placement options as parole, corrections, institutional placement, and higher education, all of which may be required by the population of youth with learning or behavior disorders. Our present discussion will emphasize three com-

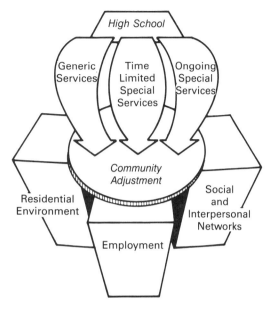

FIGURE 11–1

Revised transition model (Source: From "Transition: A Look at the Foundations "by A. S. Halpern, 1985, *Exceptional Children, 51,* pp. 479–486. Reston, VA: Council for Exceptional Children. Copyright 1985 by the Council for Exceptional Children. Reprinted with permission.)

ponents of adequate transition services, regardless of the student's ultimate placement. These are (a) the regular and special education programming offered the student; (b) a formalized **transition plan**; and (c) specific transition services.

REGULAR AND SPECIAL EDUCATION PROGRAMMING

Most special educators believe that the training students receive in school has an impact on their post-school adjustment. But which of their experiences are most important? What is the most effective blend of curricular programming in terms of successful adult adjustment? Vocational education certainly would appear to be a critical component. Hasazi et al. (1985) found that 60.5% of those former special education students who had received vocational education ($n = 177$) were employed at the time of their follow-up, versus 44.8% of those who had not ($n = 116$). Halpern (1985) reported that a study of secondary special education teachers in Oregon revealed that half of these teachers indicated that vocational education was not available to their pupils. Furthermore, 25% of the special education teachers said that they had no involvement in the vocational education of their pupils. Sixty percent of the administrators indicated that they believed that the coordination of special and regular education services was the responsibility of the special education teacher, but only 30% of the teachers had the same opinion.

Special educators also tend to believe that participation in regular education programs is important in the preparation of handicapped pupils for adult living, especially for the mildly handicapped. Hasazi et al. (1985) found that 54.6% of former students who had been in resource rooms were employed, compared with only 35.3% who had been in self-contained special classes. Halpern (1985) reported that while 80% of the Oregon secondary special education teachers indicated that regular classrooms were an option for their pupils, only 1/3 of parents stated that their children actually were benefiting from this option. Impediments to mainstreaming, according to the special education teachers, included students' lack of entry-level abilities, the resistance of regular classroom teachers to mainstreaming, and the lack of such supportive resources as modified curricula. The findings of Hasazi et al. (1985) indicated that other school experiences related to employment at follow-up included participation in a work experience program, holding a part-time job while in high school, and having a summer job during the high school years.

Predictors of Post-School Adjustment

Thus, existing research, although limited, suggests that a combination of mainstreaming, vocational education, and work experience are important predictors of post-school employment (which is, admittedly, only one aspect of adjustment). However, handicapped students' opportunities for participation in school-related vocational training appear to be limited.

Regular, vocational, and special education programming contribute to the provision of a functional curriculum for handicapped learners; yet these components are not sufficient to guarantee that the curriculum will be functional. Even in special education, secondary curriculum still is heavily influenced by an emphasis on basic or remedial academics (i.e., a developmental curriculum). At the other extreme is a curriculum emphasizing the development of a healthy self-concept and intrapersonal adjustment. We insist that a student has not learned anything useful if he has been taught only to use basic academic skills at an elementary school level or to feel good about himself. Wehman et al. (1985) have argued convincingly for a functional secondary curriculum, which includes preparation for vocational opportunities, assessment of available community employment, the provision of instruction in age-appropriate content and skills, and an emphasis on community functioning, and which begins when the student is young and is extended as he matures.

The Criterion of Ultimate Functioning

Curriculum for the severely handicapped has been significantly influenced by the "criterion of ultimate functioning" (Brown, Nietupski, & Hamre-Nietupski, 1976), that is, the skills the learner will need to function at the maximum level in the least restrictive adult environments, given the opportunity to develop to her fullest potential. This type of curriculum is designed by assessing the skill demands of these environments, arranging them in a hierarchy of successive approximations based on the student's current performance levels, and systematically teaching them in classroom and generalization settings. In general, this "top down" approach to curriculum building has not been followed in programs for the mildly handicapped. However, the development of **social skills training** curricular packages is a step in the right direction (Nelson & Rutherford, in press). For example, Goldstein, Sprafkin, Gershaw, and Klein (1980) have developed a structured learning curriculum for adolescents, which includes six groups of skills: (1) beginning social skills, (2) advanced social skills, (3) dealing with feelings, (4) alternatives to aggression, (5) dealing with stress, and (6) planning skills. These skills are crucial to the successful adjustment of learning and behaviorally disordered youths. So, too, are such community living skills as how to budget an income, pay bills, use public transportation, open and manage banking accounts, converse with strangers, use public facilities, make appropriate use of leisure time, and so forth. In the past, instruction in these skills has been offered primarily in secondary curriculum for mildly retarded individuals. However, even adolescents who are academically talented often display large gaps in such skill areas, and these are overlooked because the students appear otherwise competent. Functional curriculum materials for intellectually average youth are beginning to appear (e.g., Camiel & Michaelsen, 1980).

Functional Versus Developmental Curricula

We believe that a functional curriculum for adolescents with learning or behavior disorders requires early and regular assessment of their academic, vocational, and community living skills and continuous revision of their IEPs based on both new information and their progress. A functional curriculum is one that prepares students for adult living and includes independent living skills, social skills, and vocational skills (Fredericks & Evans, 1987). This entails instruction that has both a classroom and a community base.

The importance of generalization and maintenance programming of functional skills cannot be overemphasized (see Rutherford & Nelson, in press). Such training must include instruction in environments where the skills taught are to be used. Furthermore, a functional curriculum for some students may lead to higher education, and this option should be recognized early enough in the student's school career to permit appropriate educational planning. For a pupil to be denied further educational opportunities because the curriculum has limited the development of her skills to her maximum potential is inexcusable.

Wehman et al. (1985) ranked the components of secondary special education programs in terms of effectiveness. These components are presented in Table 11–2. As you can see, the most effective special education programs are characterized by an integration of regular and special education services and of **classroom-** and **community-based instruction**, as well as by a functional curriculum.

FORMALIZED TRANSITION PLAN

Wehman et al. (1985) advocated individualized transition plans specifying the skills to be acquired by the student and the transition services he will receive prior to and after graduation. Such plans should include annual goals, short-term objectives, and specific skills the student needs to function in the home, community, and workplace (we also would add post-secondary education settings). Wehman and co-workers

TABLE 11–2
Secondary program components ranked from most to least effective

Program Components			
Most effective	Integrated service delivery	Classroom/Community-based instruction	Functional curriculum
↓	Segregated service delivery	Classroom/community-based instruction	Functional curriculum
Least effective	Segregated service delivery	Classroom-based instruction	Developmental curriculum

Source: From "From School to Work: A Vocational Transition Model for Handicapped Students" by P. Wehman, J. Kregel and J. M. Barcus, 1985, *Exceptional Children, 52*(1), pp. 25–37. Reston, VA: Council for Exceptional Children. Copyright 1985 by the Council for Exceptional Children. Reprinted with permission.

recommended that this plan be first developed 4 years before the student's scheduled graduation and modified at least once each year until he has successfully adjusted to his post-school placement. With this mind, we designed Figure 11–2 to facilitate the initial organization of information and the decisions to be made. You probably will want to modify this form to suit your particular needs.

Individualized transition plans are rather uncommon in public special education programs. However, they have been used for some time by vocational rehabilitation counselors. One such plan is presented in Figure 11–3. You will note that the plan contains a description of the client's current level of functioning, long-term goals, and short-term objectives. A significant departure from the format you are used to seeing in IEPs is the narrative style: the plan is written as a direct communication with the client, in recognition of his adult status and the fact that he is directly responsible, with his counselor, for implementation of the plan.

Transition Services

As noted earlier, the transition of handicapped adolescents from secondary schools is a complex process. The multitude of services and agencies needed to guarantee the success of

this process is even more complex. It is possible, although by no means likely, that a single agency, such as a public school, will be able to give students comprehensive educational programs of academic and related services that meet their needs, but once out of school, they enter a confusing array of human service agencies and programs. As we mentioned before, these agencies may have conflicting or overlapping purposes, different eligibility requirements, and a variety of competing political boundary issues. A major problem is that no single public agency has been assigned responsibility for supervision or coordination of transition services (Edgar et al., 1987).

Interagency Communication and Collaboration

A major problem in providing transition services involves interagency communication and collaboration. Cooperative interagency agreements and working relationships have been developed to some extent for the moderately and severely handicapped, because of these persons' need for supervision and structure throughout their lifetimes. However, mildly handicapped youths historically have been left on their own; they or their caretakers usually must seek out the adult services they require.

Student's Name _____

Age _____

Educational history:

Current levels of performance:

Post-secondary placement options

1. Education/training
2. Vocation
3. Living environment

Parental goals   Student's goals

(Evaluate reasonableness of each)

Potential supports and resources for post-school options:

Potential obstacles:

Curricular modifications needed to pursue options:

Progress to be monitored:

Review dates:

Potential transaction plan team members: (names and phone numbers)

FIGURE 11–2
Pretransition planning form

INDIVIDUALIZED WRITTEN REHABILITATION PROGRAM

COMMONWEALTH OF KENTUCKY
DEPARTMENT OF EDUCATION
OFFICE OF VOCATIONAL REHABILITATION

1. Caseload Number (Stamped)
121904

2. Client Number	3. Client Name (Last)	(First)	(Init)
85-1503	Wright	Charles	J.

4. Type of Program	6. Major Disab. Code:	9. Severely Disabled	11. Priority Category:	14.	
1 ☒ Original	**500**	1 ☒ Yes Categ.	**1**	☐ Amend ☐ Ext. Emp. ☐ Review	☐ Closure Inelig. ☐ Dec. Rev.	☐ Periodic Review ☐ Annual Review

	7. Secondary Disab. Code:	2 ☐ Yes Non-Categ.	12. Non-Purchased Services Only:	15. Ext. Emp. Review Outcome Code:	16. Date of Review
2 ☐ Emp. Eval.	**500**		0 ☐ Yes 1 ☒ No		
3 ☐ Post Employ.		3 ☐ No			

5. IWRP Date	8. Eligible Date	10. Vocational Goal Code:	13. Pre-Paid Voc. School	17. Price Contract or Bid Items	(Attach Itemized List)	(BUN)
09/05/85	**09/05/85**	**38**	4 ☐ Yes	☒ No ☐ Yes		

18. Narrative Description:

ELIGIBILITY STATEMENT:

You and I have met on several occasions since you were referred from the treatment team on IT-4. Medical and psychiatric information were obtained from Eastern State Hospital (ESH) and private sources. Your primary disability is Schizophrenia, paranoid, sub-chronic. Other disabilities noted are Adjustment Disorder with depressed mood, Passive Dependent Personality and Malnutrition as noted by the general medical and psychological evaluation.

VOCATIONAL GOAL:

After exploring your interests and aptitudes, we have tentatively agreed upon your vocational goal in the service area as custodian. This is the area you have expressed most interest. An indepth vocational evaluation at Opportunity Workshop of Lexington (OWL) indicates you would do well in this area. This vocational goal is realistic in view of your academic skills, past work history, and physical abilities. Research on the availability of jobs in this location indicates a favorable market for maintenance and custodial workers. This vocational goal is tentatively based upon incoming information from work conditioning at OWL.

INTERMEDIATE GOALS AND OBJECTIVES:

1. Belief in and respect for yourself:

You must realize you are a young man with a full future and life ahead of you. You have come a long way since you were first admitted to the hospital. Keep looking up and strive to be the best person you can. This should be an on-going process. Progress in this area will be measured by self-assessment and counselor contact.

2. Use of public transportation:

You are unfamiliar with the Lexington area and have no transportation. You will need to learn to use the Lex-Tran Bus System to help in getting to OWL, Comprehensive Care Center (CCC) appointments, work, and social activities. Using the bus system will provide you with greater independence and self-esteem. It is hoped that you will be able to use the bus without assistance by September 16, 1985. Progress in this area will be by self-assessment and OWL.

(CONTINUED)

KDE/MIC APPROVED
5010-1168 10/83

Central Office
Use Only
☐

3. Work Adjustment:
You have completed the two-week vocational evaluation at OWL. Now you are ready to enter work adjustment. This adjustment period will last eight (8) weeks with beginning date of 9/5/85 and ending 11/1/85. Progress in this area will be monitored by OWL and counselor contact.

4. Attend Comprehensive Care Center regularly:
You must realize that supportive therapy can enable you to live and work successfully outside of the hospital. You have agreed to attend Comprehensive Care to assist in individual therapy on an on-going basis. Your first Comprehensive Care appointment is scheduled for 9/18/85 and will continue until you and Comprehensive Care feel that it is no longer necessary. Progress in this area will be monitored by Comprehensive Care, self-assessment, and counselor contact.

5. Get involved:
You have expressed that you become depressed when you sit home alone all week-end. Learning to socialize and making new friends will help you in overcoming your depression. We have discussed looking into church activities and Buddy Systems. At the present time, we are both investigating several opportunities. This should be an on-going process. Progress will be monitored by self-assessment and counselor contact.

6. Eat properly to feel good:
One of your diagnoses by the hospital is malnutrition. You must learn to eat well to stay healthy. If you are not healthy, you will not feel like working. An appointment is being made at the Nutrition Clinic at the Lexington Health Department. You must cooperate with your nutritionist and keep scheduled appointments. This should be an on-going process. Progress in this area will be monitored by the Health Department, self-assessment, and your boarding house director.

SERVICES TO BE OR ALREADY PROVIDED BY THE OFFICE OF VOCATIONAL REHABILITATION:
It is being proposed that this agency provide guidance, counseling, help with transportation in the form of bus training and a bus pass, work conditioning, training services, maintenance, and job placement activities. When you are job ready and if all activities go as planned, job placement can be expected to occur by November 30, 1985. Also, you will receive follow-up services for 60 days after job placement occurs.

TERMS AND CONDITIONS FOR THE PROVISION OF VOCATIONAL REHABILITATION SERVICES:
1. Client's responsibilities:
You are responsible for presenting yourself in an alert and responsible manner to OWL staff, Comprehensive Care staff, Vocational Rehabilitation counselor, and the Health Department staff. You are expected to keep all scheduled appointments, participate in training, and strive to achieve all of the agreed intermediate goals.

2. Client's financial responsibilities:
When you begin to earn a paycheck at OWL, you will assume full responsibility for personal needs.

Similar Benefits:
You are to fully utilize the services of Comprehensive Care Center, Eastern State Hospital, and any other agency funds that you might be eligible for before using OVR monies.

PATIENT VIEWS OF VOCATIONAL GOAL:
We are in agreement that these are realistic goals needed to achieve your long-term goal of custodian. You are of the opinion that they are realistic and that with help from this agency and other third parties, you can put it all together.
It is understood that any aid granted by this agency is subject to change with changing needs, economic conditions, and the extent of cooperation on your part. This plan of service is open to amendments following a conference between us.

Cheryll Pearson   9-5-85

Cheryll Pearson, Counselor   Date
Office of Vocational Rehabilitation
627 W. Fourth St.
Lexington, KY 40508

FIGURE 11–3
Individual rehabilitation plan

291

OSERS's designation of transition as a priority area (Will, 1984) has provided incentives for researchers and planners to focus on the needs of learning and behaviorally disordered adolescents for transition services.

Edgar and his colleagues at the University of Washington have addressed the problem of interagency cooperation through an innovative project. They developed and tested a functional transition model for adjudicated youth returning to public schools (Edgar et al., 1987), which focuses on the roles of human services agencies in the transition process. The authors' experience in developing transition strategies has led to a conceptualization of transition services that has important implications for transitions between any agencies. According to Edgar and colleagues, the transition process involves three components: (a) a sending agency, which has the student/client who is being transferred elsewhere; (b) a receiving agency, which obviously gets the client; and (c) the hand-off, which is a process and a set of procedures for moving clients from one agency to another. The hand-off is not a clear responsibility of either the sending or the receiving agency and so is not accomplished systematically. Edgar and coworkers pointed out that transition is not a static process; it involves activities before, during, and after the client is moved. The lack of hand-off procedures can negate effective programming by either the sending or the receiving agency; therefore, the hand-off is the most important component of the transition process. Fortunately, it also is the easiest to change (Edgar et al., 1987).

Issues in Interagency Transition Planning

Edgar et al. (1987) identified six transition issues that have implications for interagency collaboration. These are as follows:

1. *Awareness*. Sending and receiving agencies need to learn about each other's programs and services. Unfortunately, most agencies operate without such information.
2. *Eligibility Criteria*. The sending agency should have a working knowledge of the eligibility criteria of the agencies whose services may help their students or clients. Obviously, a lack of information about other agencies suggests that knowledge of eligibility criteria also is lacking.
3. *Exchange of Information*. The receiving agency needs information before the client arrives. The transfer of student records is a universal problem. Often, records do not arrive in time to be used in placement or planning, and in many cases, the student has left the agency before her school records are obtained.
4. *Program Planning Before Transition*. This should involve both sending and receiving agencies, so that student/clients are adequately prepared for the programs they are about to enter and so their new programs will capitalize on the gains made in the old ones.
5. *Feedback After Transition*. Feedback to the sending agency is essential for program evaluation and modification. Without it, agencies are left to repeat the mistakes of the past, which often is the case.
6. *Written Procedures*. Formal written procedures ensure that important hand-off activities take place. If only one staff person knows the procedures, there will be nothing in place should that person leave, unless procedures are formalized in writing.

Several writers have offered suggestions for improving interagency cooperation. Halpern (1985) recommended that interagency agreements be established between schools and adult service providers. Wehman et al. (1985) called for an exchange of information among such agencies to assure the complete provision of services while simultaneously eliminating wasteful duplication. However, Edgar et al. (1987) have contended that a top-down approach to interagency collaboration is inefficient and often ineffective. Their transition model is based on the procedure of background mapping (Elmore, 1979), which involves isolating the critical points of interaction between agencies (e.g., transfer of student records) and attempting to develop solutions to problems at the grass-roots level, which, if effective, eventually may become adopted at a higher bureaucratic level (e.g., local or state administration offices), and may even become an element of agency policy. Edgar et al. suggested that the bottom-up approach facilitates the commitment of the professionals closest to the actual transition process. They identified three types of transition activities: *Type I* activities are governed by federal or state formal interagency agreements. *Type II* activities, on the other hand, occur at the fundamental level when individuals with decision-making power meet and agree to work together. The personalities of those in power are a critical element, but activities at this level often result in outstanding planning and service delivery. *Type III* activities represent a cookbook approach, in which a set of recipes (strategies) are developed and formalized. The key ingredients of Type III activities are: (a) a perceived need by agencies and a desire to alter current practices, (b) a set of procedures that have proven to be effective, (c) procedures that are easy to implement, and (d) procedures that are detailed. These categories of activities are by no means incompatible; Edgar et al. designed their cookbook strategies through backward mapping (i.e., working with grass-roots agencies). Some of these activities may lead to formal interagency agreements.

Regardless of the manner in which state and local bureaucracies address the problem of interagency collaboration, it is important that school personnel track their graduates and school leavers so that special education programs can be evaluated, refined, and monitored (Edgar, 1985). The following strategies are presented with the assumption that you, as a special education teacher, will be at least partly responsible for their implementation.

STRATEGIES FOR IMPLEMENTING TRANSITION PLANS

Except for the severely handicapped, widespread emphasis on the post-secondary adjustment of the handicapped is so recent that researchers are just beginning to investigate strategies and their relative effectiveness in terms of promoting the successful entry of handicapped students into adult life. We will describe strategies in four areas, which represent the placement options available to handicapped adolescents after high school. These include transition to work, transition to independent community living, transition to post-secondary school, and transition to a correctional or mental health program. Because learning and behaviorally disordered students also may return to public schools from correctional or mental health institutions, we will discuss strategies for facilitating this movement as well. Inasmuch as our common frame of reference is the secondary special education teacher, we first will discuss the teacher's role in the transition process.

Role of the Special Education Teacher

Your first responsibility as a teacher of handicapped adolescents is to initiate transition programming. This obviously is relevant for high school students, but when should transition planning actually begin? Wehman et al. (1985) recommend that transition programming begin when students reach junior high school, at the age of 12. At this level, you should introduce career exploration into the curriculum (Cegelka, 1985). Students should learn about occupational categories, the importance of appropriate social skills in terms of getting and keeping jobs, and work opportunities in their local community. Arrange for employees from your community to speak to your class. Be considerate of their time constraints, and be fairly explicit about your expectations.

In addition, target specific social skills, teach appropriate working habits, and encourage students to explore career interests. Fortunately, career education curriculum objectives and materials have been developed for a wide range of handicapped students (Cegelka, 1985).

Transition Planning at the Junior High School Level

It is by no means too early to introduce students to community-based instruction in junior high school. Wehman et al. (1985) indicated that the major reason for the vocational failure of handicapped persons is their lack of exposure to natural job environments. Community-based instruction does not mean that 12-year-old students have to get jobs in the community; it does mean that they may take field trips, interview relatives about their work, participate in mock job interviews with local employers, and learn about available jobs for adolescents and adults in the area.

Identifying Occupations

As mentioned earlier, each student's values, lifestyle preferences, interests, and abilities will shape his career choices. As information about occupations is presented, students should be encouraged to measure those occupations against their personal set of requirements. They may also need encouragement to modify their expectations, weigh and prioritize wants and expectations, and trade off some negative features for more valued positive features. The selection of a potential career, and to some degree a job, is highly personal, and students should be encouraged to exercise their personal preferences within the boundaries of informed self-awareness and career possibilities. Students may select more than one occupation; this may be particularly wise when the first choice is in a sunset industry or if the opportunity to succeed is highly competitive. Given the variability of the labor market, the youth and the vocational naivete of many of your students, a back-up occupation is, for most students, a good idea.

During the information-gathering stage, students may be able to report the kinds of things that they like to do, the types of volunteer jobs they have liked (and why), and the kinds of chores they do around the house that they find interestings (or odious). Leisure interests also provide information about the student's interests and abilities that can be used to target occupations. It is important to remember that people work for a variety of reasons, including socialization opportunities (or lack of them), money, status, acceptance, and so forth. As you and your students begin to identify these kinds of motivators and needs, you will be better able to target a specific first job to allow the student to discover more about his target occupation.

Junior high school students also should learn about their local community as a living environment; that is, they should learn to use public transportation, to order meals and to eat in public restaurants, to use public recreational facilities, and to understand about local laws and law enforcement. In addition, you should help them begin to think about themselves as adults, living apart from their parents, and maintaining themselves as independent persons. This is why a **functional curriculum** is so important for handicapped adolescents. We are not suggesting that you give up trying to improve basic academic skills. But these skills should be taught for their relevance to your pupils as adults; e.g., reading practice using the newspaper or improving math skills through budgeting an income. Basic academic instruction using traditional materials is still appropriate, but you need to begin to show students how they can use these skills in adult living.

Developing Functional Skills

Wimmer (1981) defined a functional skill as a specific observable and measurable behavior that is essential to carrying out everyday social, personal, and on-the-job tasks. She also described a set of characteristics that are common to functional skills:

1. They are student-centered rather than content-centered.
2. They are built around real life experiences.
3. They are community based.
4. They involve cooperation between students and teachers in the planning of learning experiences.
5. They emphasize process-oriented objectives, such as problem solving.
6. Activities center on small groups or individuals.
7. The teacher functions as a guide to student learning.
8. They often involve teams of teachers from various disciplines.
9. Students acquire skills through active participation. (pp. 613-614)

As these characteristics suggest, a functional skills curriculum is not something that is created haphazardly or piecemeal. Neither is it limited to vocational preparation alone. Such a curriculum represents a significant departure from traditional developmental special educational curricular offerings. Therefore, the decision to implement a functional curriculum should be made by a team of professionals, and should

have the approval of school officials and parents. As we stated earlier, emphasis on a functional curriculum does not mean that instruction in basic academic skills is discarded, only that these skills are taught in such a way that students can see their application to solving real-life problems.

At the senior high school level, a functional curriculum is even more important. However, here the curricular emphasis shifts to more specific vocational training. The primary focus of academic instruction should be on functional skills, and job skills should be systematically taught. Supervised job experience is a useful part of the high school curriculum. Even college-bound students need such preparation, although not at the expense of instruction in skills prerequisite to higher education.

Using School and Community Resources

You may be thinking that these tasks are impossible for one teacher to perform. They are. But secondary schools are rich in terms of staff resources, and you should take advantage of these. Other teachers, guidance counselors, administrators, clerical staff, cafeteria workers, and many other persons have information and skills they can share with your students. Special educators often are guilty of thinking of themselves as working in isolation because no one else wants their pupils or knows how to deal with them. Consequently, they tend to isolate themselves. It is important that you view yourself as part of a professional team and function accordingly. The vignette at the close of this chapter illustrates how one enterprising special education teacher coordinated a strategy to maintain one of her students in the regular secondary school program for six years after he left her special class.

Many resources also exist in the community outside the school, and these too should be tapped. Vocational rehabilitation counselors, law enforcement personnel, public health workers, mental health personnel, employers, and numerous other persons have a vested interest in helping your students become independent, law-abiding citizens. Use these resources to provide instruction, enrichment experiences, generalization training, and follow-up data for your students. But first learn about these resources yourself, then incorporate them into specific instructional strategies rather than enlisting their services without systematic plans.

Thus, in the classroom, your role involves providing a meaningful curriculum based on each student's IEP, updating and revising IEPs consistent with preparing each pupil for adult living, and generalizing relevant academic, social, and vocational skills beyond your classroom. In addition, you should assume a major role in writing students' individual transition plans. As we indicated previously, these plans should include annual goals, short-term objectives, and transition services to be provided. The emphasis on post-school adjustment in such plans dictates that appropriate community personnel (a vocational rehabilitation counselor or a community college or vocational technical school admissions officer), public school staff, and students' parents be involved in writing the transition plan. Team transition plan meetings will provide you with opportunities to learn about other programs and services, as well as to inform agency personnel of the needs and skills of your students.

The classroom teacher also is the most logical person to be responsible for handing off relevant information about his students to the receiving agency. When students are preparing to leave the secondary school, you should see that a current IEP, which includes specific transition plans, is passed on to the appropriate professionals (be sure to obtain parental permission first). The transfer of student records

is perhaps the major bottleneck inhibiting transition procedures (Maddox, Webb, Allen, Faust, Abrams, & Lynch, 1984). Be prepared to do some telephoning and legwork in making contact with agency professionals, and be sure that your principal sees this as part of your job description. Edgar et al. (1987) pointed out that communication within agencies is easier than communication between agencies. To reduce this obstacle, we suggest that you identify reliable contact persons in other agencies, learn about their programs and services, and involve them in developing transition plans.

Monitoring and Follow-up Activities

Responsibility for monitoring and follow-up of former special education students has not been officially assigned to any agency, but educational leaders have indicated this to fall within the province of the school (Edgar, 1985). And, in all likelihood, this task will be assigned to you. Your school district may not have developed systematic follow-up procedures, so you may have to initiate these. Consult reports of the follow-up research we have cited in this chapter (Gill, 1984; Hasazi et al., 1985) for specific strategies. The model for moving adjudicated youth back into community schools from correctional programs (see page 309) also is quite useful.

STRATEGIES FOR TRANSITION PROGRAMMING

We hope that the previous discussion has given appropriate emphasis to the need for pre-transition planning and instruction in skills and content areas that will be functional in each student's adult life. If such is not the case, even the most sophisticated strategies will have little impact at this point. Your first strategy, should your school district not have a curriculum geared to preparing handicapped adolescents for adjustment to the adult world, is to initiate the development of such a plan. One place to start is by examining career education curricula and models that have been developed for secondary special education programs. Examine some of the references cited in this chapter, or contact the Career Education Division of the Council for Exceptional Children, 1420 Association Drive, Reston, Virginia 20202. You should not attempt such planning by yourself; contact your supervisor and appropriate school administrators to enlist their support, cooperation, and assistance. With their permission, you may enlist help from your state department of education and office of rehabilitation services. If you fail to go through proper channels, not only will your chances of developing a transition program be reduced, but also your job will be made that much more difficult (that is, if you are not dismissed for failing to go through proper channels). Indeed, you may want to consider whether to take a position in a secondary school that has little interest in, or specific plans for, a transition program.

School-Based Strategies

The strategies presented below are based on research studies and descriptions of ongoing programs, as well as on our own information and biases. Although we describe these strategies in separate sections, they have in common a set of general procedures, which consist of the following four steps.

Assessment. As we have stressed throughout this text, assessment is a broad-based and ongoing component of effective special education programs. With respect to a transition program, you should assess the academic, social, and vocational skills of your students, as well as their attitudes and interests with regard to their abil-

ities, to school (including further education), and to work. Evans, Hadden, Kraus, Johnson, Fredricks, and Toews (1983) suggested that assessment of students' functional curricular needs should involve a number of steps, including (a) determining the skills students need now and in the future to succeed in a variety of residential and vocational settings, (b) determining possible long-range goals with regard to students' residential and vocational options, (c) assessing students in these skill areas, and (d) incorporating objectives and strategies for developing needed skills into students' IEPs. Your school's guidance counseling staff can help you complete these steps, as can teachers in your vocational education program, community vocational counselors, and other local professionals. Do not forget to include parents in this process; the goals they have for their child will have a significant impact on the transition plan. If large discrepancies exist between their goals and the student's aspirations, interests, or abilities, your first task is to resolve such differences. Referral of the student and his parents for counseling may be necessary at this point. You also should assess the resources and services available in your community in terms of your students' immediate and future needs. One useful strategy is to develop a catalog of jobs available in the local community. This community catalog can be used as a basis for planning career and vocational education content. Your students' parents, who have a vested interest in their children's post-school vocational adjustment, can be recruited to inventory local job sites. The information you obtain can be summarized on the pre-transition planning form presented in Figure 11–2.

Development of a Transition Plan. This step entails setting down specific goals and objectives and putting into operational a set of procedures for their implementation. If you have enlisted the student, her parents, school staff, and other professional in the previous step, this should be a productive experience. However, do not wait until the second semester of the student's senior year to write the plan.

If the plan is to be meaningfully linked to the pupil's post-school life, it should be initiated four years before graduation (Wehman et al., 1985). Then, if the student moves or leaves school, something will be in place with which others can work. We hope that the formulation of a transition plan in the ninth grade will encourage the student to remain in school because she will be a part of the planning process, and because the plan will relate to a functional school curriculum leading to objectives she sees as meaningful to her. Edgar et al. (1987) reported that joint interagency planning of students' educational programs increases the chances that adjudicated youth will remain in school after being released. We have attempted to emphasize the similarity between transition plans and IEPs because we hope it will encourage you to incorporate transition objectives and strategies into IEPs while students are still in school. Transition plans differ from IEPs chiefly in terms of their orientation to post-school adjustment. However, transitions occur whenever students change educational placements (from junior to senior high school, from resource room to regular classroom), and these transitions will proceed more smoothly if the IEP team consists of representatives from the sending and receiving programs, if procedures are developed for handing off relevant information, and if channels of communication between sending and receiving program are used to track students' progress.

It is also important to extend the IEP transition plan beyond high school, so the student and her parents learn to see the school program in the context of ongoing support services. This does not mean that you must plan for the student to enter a specific occupation in the ninth grade; transition objectives should be revised and updated at least annually. As the student approaches graduation, more specific post-school plans can be developed.

Implementation of the Plan. If assessment and planning have gone well, this step also should proceed smoothly. However, if the plan involves a lot of work on your part after school, in the community, or on the telephone, you may find it difficult to be effective. Therefore, job descriptions for secondary special educators should be negotiated with a significant amount of community work in mind. The importance of a comprehensive, community-based secondary special education program cannot be overemphasized. Such programs are becoming more common in large urban school districts, but the lack of resources in rural areas increases the need for individual initiative. Your knowledge of employment and post-secondary educational opportunities in the area may be essential to designing appropriate programs and to convincing school administrators of the need to look beyond the school in providing meaningful experiences. Perhaps you can take advantage of a local industry. For example, Frith, Lindsay, and Reynolds (1981) described a vocational program for handicapped adolescents in northeastern Alabama based on a local horticulture industry. Job sites identified through the process of developing a community catalog can be used in community-based vocational experiences and as job placements after completion of high school.

If students' school programs have been thoughtfully articulated with community resources, the transition from school to the next developmental level will be smoother. However, if the student will be leaving the area— say to a state college, correctional institution, or mental health program—you should not assume that your responsibility has ended. As we have indicated repeatedly, a major shortcoming of special education programming for handicapped adolescents is the failure to transfer records from one agency to another. The existence of a transition plan will encourage parents and professionals within and outside the school to see the transfer of information as important to the transition process, even if the transition occurs unexpectedly. When students leave, you should hand off the IEP and the transition plan to the receiving agency.

Evaluation and Follow-Up. Evaluation of transition plans, like that of IEPs, should be formative; that is, they should be continuously monitored and revised. Formal transition team meetings should occur annually, or more often if important decisions are to be made. After students leave their school program, their status should be monitored until they reach the age of 22.

We concur with Edgar (1985) that responsibility for follow-up rests with the schools and likely will be assigned to you. If a team approach has been used to develop and implement transition objectives, you should find other agencies and professionals more cooperative. A major purpose of follow-up is to evaluate the educational program so it will better prepare other students for future transitions. However, another important purpose is to evaluate and revise the post-school programs of former students. A commitment to transition planning as a multidisciplinary team responsibility will help ensure that both purposes are met.

Specific follow-up procedures and data will depend on local circumstances, but we recommend that each former student's status be reviewed and reported annually. The data should include employment and/or educational status throughout the previous 12 months, marital status, current living situation, and evaluations of adjustment from the student, his parents, and significant others, if available. (Note: Do not violate the student's right to privacy;

obtain his consent or the consent of his caretakers to collect these data.) We also encourage you to obtain information about the perception of students and others concerning the aspects of their school program that were most and least facilitative of their adult adjustment, as these data are important for monitoring and adjusting your educational program.

TRANSITION TO WORK

Programs for achieving the successful transition of handicapped adolescents to the world of work have received more emphasis in the literature because entry into the labor force is a realistic goal for the majority of these pupils. However, we must again emphasize that such a goal is inappropriate if the student's participation in special education is the only reason for selecting it. The labels *learning* or *behavior disorders* do not, and should not, preclude a student's access to higher education, military service, or post-school experiences available to any citizen. If it does, the fault lies with the school system. We urge you not to become a part of a system that sorts students on the basis of prior assumptions about their competence and ultimate adjustment.

Nevertheless, we recognize that many students with learning or behavior disorders will want to seek employment upon completion of high school. A typical transition plan could involve helping one of your students with the task of job finding. Once your students have targeted occupations of interest, they should get firsthand information about jobs within that occupation. It may not be possible for the student's first job to mirror his occupational aspirations, yet that first job should be selected to fit several of the student's needs. It should allow the student to experience the expectations of the work world and the tasks typically assigned to people who work in the target occupation. If possible, it should contribute to a work history that will lead the student to greater opportunity and occupational growth. If it is to be the student's primary source of income after graduation, the job should provide a living wage and acceptable benefits (health insurance, paid vacation, sick leave). Wage and benefit parity are important if students are to rely upon their work rather than family or government subsidy such as Supplemental Security Income (SSI) for their support. If the student is to become a productive member of the work force, working *must* provide more rewards than not working.

Special educators need to help students with in-school transitions as well as transitional activities like job finding. We want to include two primary ways to approach finding entry level jobs. This information should be shared with teachers and passed on to your students. The most traditional is to search through job advertisement listings from newspapers, personnel offices, and the Employment Securities Commission. The second method is to target particular companies that have jobs of interest, identify the person who does the hiring, secure an interview, and present ways that the company will benefit by hiring the applicant. There are also two primary alternatives concerning who should do the job search. Again, the more traditional is for the applicant to search for the position. The alternative is for a teacher or job coach to match the applicant to a specific job. In the latter approach, the applicant will frequently complete all standard employment intake procedures for practice (application form, interview), but hiring has actually been prearranged. It is possible to combine these approaches in four ways: traditional—applicant conducted; traditional—assisted; targeted—applicant conducted; and targeted—assisted. The merits and difficulties of each combination are discussed below.

Traditional—Applicant Conducted. This is the most common method. Students may receive limited assistance in identifying where to search (newspaper advertisement, job posting boards at large organizations, or the Employment Securities Exchange), but the search, application completion, and interview are the student's responsibilities. This method typically takes a great deal of time and effort, especially for young workers who have little experience and few job skills. It can be especially demoralizing if students are frequently rejected. In addition to being young and inexperienced, mildly handicapped youth frequently have difficulty sorting through several job listings, completing applications, and interviewing appropriately. While it can be argued that this method teaches students how to go about finding a job, the lack of directions usually leaves students to draw whatever conclusions they will about the job marketplace. The frequent failures that result from using this technique typically serve to instruct students in their inadequacies rather than their competencies. We would not recommend this method for most mildly handicapped youth.

Traditional—Assisted. This method uses a higher degree of teacher involvement. Searches are broad, yet teacher-directed; frequently they are conducted as a group activity (all students scanning the newspaper). Support systems, such as job-finding clubs are built to ameliorate the difficulties and disappointments of job searching. Proper completion of sample or actual application forms is directly taught; interviewing techniques are practiced and critiqued during class time. Students who secure job interviews report the incidence and content of the interview and are encouraged to take appropriate follow-up measures to secure the position. This method holds much more promise for mildly handicapped students than the traditional—applicant conducted method. It gives students an opportunity to learn job-finding and interviewing skills in a systematic fashion. Compared to the targeted—assisted method, it requires less teacher involvement and produces success for many students.

Targeted—Applicant Conducted. The targeted approach to job finding is a more efficient method of identifying possible jobs because not all options are considered, only those employers who are likely to have specific kinds of jobs. Personal and community contacts are good sources for job leads, and their referral is frequently solicited. These contacts often know whether or not the applicant has a good chance of being hired before referring the applicant to the employer, thus the applicant is spared from time-consuming, frustrating, futile searches. However, the applicant does not receive training in how to search systematically for a job in his field of interest, how to interview, or how to complete applications. Many mildly handicapped adolescents find jobs using this system. They solicit information from friends and family members to determine who might hire them, gauging their success far in advance of the job interview. The prime disadvantage of this method is that it depends solely upon the student's contacts and his knowledge of the labor market. If peers alone are solicited as information sources, the student may not be referred to a job source that would be more beneficial to him.

Targeted—Assisted. This strategy uses two methods of systematic job searching that provide substantial assistance to job finding: targeting specific jobs and systematic training in job-getting skills (application and interview). The assistance can range from teacher direction to teacher involvement in the interview, training, and follow-up activities of the student. Teachers assist students in systematically targeting jobs according to the students' occupational interests and abilities. Companies, and the person with hiring authority, are identified, interviews are solicited, and the applicant's potential benefits to the company are presented or sold to the person with hiring authority. The teacher may solicit cooperation from the person authorized to hire workers or develop job

sites prior to the student's arrival. Frequently these contact persons are not part of the company's personnel department; rather they are directly involved in supervising or producing the company's goods or services. When the teacher develops jobs, he may have a particular student in mind for the job or may know that several students would be candidates for the position.

Successful job development hinges upon presenting the business advantages of hiring the student. Job developers must remember that business and industry survive because of their ability to compete in the marketplace and their ability to produce a specific product. When beginning job development, it is wise to do your homework on the company. Find out as much as you can about the business, its particular difficulties and strengths. Try to present your student as a solution to the problems faced by the company. For example, fast-food businesses are among the fastest growing segment of the economy. The food services industry historically has been faced with high turnover and abrupt resignations among entry-level employees. If your student-applicant is highly dependable, his poor reading and math skills may not be a problem to some food service employers.

When examining the factors that promote success in a particular business or industry, you may find a tolerance of some behaviors that are considered problematic in school settings. We can cite example of students whose conduct and demeanor promoted difficulties in school but were secondary or unimportant (or even an asset) on the job. For example, one high school student's continual cursing was a disaster in school, but went unnoticed on his job at a loading dock; another young woman's intermittent arguments with nonexistent voices did not hinder her ability to perform nighttime building maintenance tasks; yet another adolescent's talkative, off-task, hail-fellow-well-met demeanor was a serious detriment to academic achievement, while serving her well as an airport information and tourism worker. All of these students had problems that made acquiring employment more difficult than usual, but each of them shared work characteristics: All three were always at work when scheduled to be there, each one was productive throughout the work shift, and none of them interfered with other workers' productivity.

Another incentive for employers to hire handicapped workers is government-sponsored tax credits. Businesses are given tax incentives for taking the risk of hiring handicapped workers. Reducing the company's tax debt is undoubtedly a strong reinforcer, yet the job developer's case is strengthened if the company will realize additional benefits such as increased productivity, reduced turnover, or a dependable work force.

Most employers expect to provide on-the-job training to new employees. Your students may present special problems to the employer's typical training format. For example, the format may involve a series of written manuals that the student could not master alone, or the student may have to learn tasks from a peer worker who is not an especially good teacher. Sometimes teachers of mildly handicapped adolescents will need to become part of the employer's training team. You may observe the student and the training that is going on, giving the student feedback at a later time. The most powerful teaching technique is that of the supported jobs model. In this model, the trainer learns the job by working the position, teaches the student to perform to employer specifications by working side-by-side with the student, and gradually fades his presence as the worker's competence increases. Despite the power of this model, it is expensive in terms of time and resources. On the whole, it has been used with severely handicapped adolescents and adults and has produced capable workers. For further information about the supported jobs model and other types of supported work programs,

you may want to review the Mank, Rhodes, and Bellamy (1986) chapter in *Pathways to Employment for Adults with Developmental Disabilities*. The chapter outlines key ingredients for successful implementation of the supported jobs, enclave, mobile crew, and benchwork models of supported employment.

Work-Study Programs

Combining functional academic instruction with supervised and graduated work experience, work-study programs emerged in the 1960s as a major curriculum for mildly retarded adolescents (Cegelka, 1985). This model also has been used with other handicapped students, although the results have not been entirely successful (Ahlstrom & Havighurst, 1971). Webster (1981) described one such program serving 90 behaviorally disordered and socially maladjusted students. The four-year curriculum included exploration of career options and preparatory vocational training in school shop areas along with direct instruction in academic, social, and work-related skills during the first year. In the second year and the first semester of the third year, the emphasis shifted to training in a shop specialty area at the Alternative Vocational School (a special school serving this group of students). Students at this level received three hours of daily instruction in functional academic skills, as well as training in one of the shop specialty areas. Students exhibiting appropriate behavior in school also could participate in a paid after-school work experience program for eight hours per week. During the second semester of their third year, students who obtained appropriate levels of proficiency in academic, social, and vocational training programs were placed in a paid private industry job for up to three days a week, for which they earned credits toward graduation. In their senior year, students demonstrating criterion levels of performance in the curriculum were placed in paid internships for up to 4 1/2 days a week. They spent 1/2 day a week in school to review the week's events, discuss problems, and/or to remedy specific academic deficits. Webster (1981) reported that of 53 students participating in the program in 1979-1980, 32 had held paid jobs for five months at follow-up.

A similar program was described by Levinson (1984). The components of this program included systematic behavioral incentives for progress through a levels system that simulated job advancement, academic instruction, vocational training, work adjustment training in a small local business, and personal counseling by the school psychologist.

Educational programming for more severely handicapped youths must involve a precise and systematic analysis of the characteristics of prospective jobs and work environments. Instruction must then be provided in flexible job competencies (skills applicable to more than one job). Students are taught these skills through an individualized, task-analyzed sequence, in simulated workshop settings. The curriculum also emphasizes career awareness (Bellamy, Wilson, Adler, & Clarke, 1980).

These program descriptions give some idea of the options in the **pre-vocational curriculum** for students who may be directed toward sheltered or independent community employment. However, they do not impart specific strategies for moving students into such employment. We suggest that you attempt to establish a vocational curriculum in your school, if one is not currently operating, by working with local school and state department officials. A comprehensive work-study program requires staff to set up, monitor, and evaluate community work-experience sites, the articulation of community work experiences with academic and pre-vocational curricula, and a continuous flow of data from work site to classroom regarding each pupil's performance. All of this demands a major commitment to such a program by the

school district, as well as linkages to community human services agencies involved in vocational training and adjustment. It also requires that the special education teacher have a block of free time each day to visit work sites and meet with employees, work supervisors, vocational teachers, agency personnel, students, and parents. If such support is not available or planned for the secondary special education program, you may want to consider seriously the advisability of accepting a teaching position. Given what is known about teaching handicapped adolescents, we consider it unacceptable to contain them in watered-down academic programs until they leave school, then assume that another agency will be responsible for their vocational training and guidance. It is also unacceptable to teach in work-study programs without incorporating students' community work experience into the academic curriculum. Therefore, you should obtain information regarding pupils' work performance from their supervisors on a regular basis and use this feedback to adjust their educational programs. Figure 11–4 is offered to facilitate the summary of data regarding students' community work placements. This information should be used in conjunction with an appropriate vocational special education curriculum; that is, one that includes clusters of job-related information and skills that have direct application to students' daily lives and work placements.

TRANSITION TO COMMUNITY LIVING

Brolin's (1978) life-centered approach to career education is based on 22 competencies and 102 subcompetencies organized in three curricular areas: (1) daily living skills, (2) personal-social skills, and (3) occupational guidance and preparation skills. You can thus see that transition to work also involves transition to living as a

Student _____

Grade _____

Work Placement _____

Date Started _____ Date Ended _____

Hours per week _____ Reason for Termination _____

Immediate Supervisor _____ Paid/Unpaid _____

Phone _____

Method of Obtaining Placement
_____ Placed by program staff
_____ Job found by relative
_____ Job found by student
_____ Other (specify) _____
Objectives of Placement:

Evaluation Procedures:

Evaluation Data (attach copies of raw data)

Date   Satisfactory Performance   Needs Improvement
                           (list competencies)   (list competencies)

_____   _____   _____
_____   _____   _____
_____   _____   _____
_____   _____   _____

FIGURE 11–4
Student work experience data summary

private citizen. The strategies for achieving this transition are similar to those for accomplishing successful transitions to the world of work: Assess the student with regard to the daily living and personal-social skills he will need to succeed in his adult living environment; develop a plan for teaching and generalizing these skills; monitor the student's performance of these skills across settings and time; and identify and use resources to accomplish his actual transition. As Hasazi et al. (1985) note, many handicapped youths remain with their parents after second-

ary school. Nevertheless, they should learn independent living skills, as these will be useful both to them and their caretakers immediately, and even more useful when these young adults leave their childhood homes.

A number of curriculum guides for promoting independent living skills exist for students of all ability levels (e.g., Brolin, 1978; Westaway & Apolloni, 1978). These provide a task-analyzed sequence of skills in such areas as health and nutrition, personal grooming, making purchases, using public facilities, managing money, housekeeping, getting around in the community, preparing meals, choosing and making friends, and abiding by the law. Fredericks and Evans (1987) have compiled an extensive list of functional curriculum resource materials. A list of the functional community skills included in the Teaching Research Publications curriculum is provided in Figure 11–5. These materials are available from Teaching Research Publications, Monmouth, OR 97361. Functional community living skills should be an important part of your curriculum, and specific objectives and strategies should be developed in students' IEP team meetings. Incidentally, we highly recommend that high school students participate in their IEP meetings in order to obtain their input and to increase their understanding of the IEP and their cooperation with your procedures.

Transition to Post-Secondary School

Many educators consider high school to be the terminal point of handicapped pupils' education. However, such thinking should not be allowed to limit the access of adolescents exhibiting learning and behavior disorders from post-secondary educational experiences. It also is incorrect to consider only college or university education in thinking about post-high school educational options. Educational alternatives include vocational training centers, vocational/technical schools, business schools and colleges, community colleges, as well as state and private universities.

Your first transition strategy with regard to post-high school training is to assist the student and her caretakers in selecting from these alternatives, if, in fact, further education is an option for the student. You should consider the student's academic abilities, her related skills (e.g., study habits), the goals she and her parents have for her life after high school, her probable living situation after secondary school,

---

Independent Living Skills

Telephone skills
Newspaper skills
Transportation skills
  Using public transportation
  Car ownership and management
Money skills
  Budgeting
  Bill paying
  Banking
Shopping skills
  Food
  Clothing
  Other
Menu planning
Cooking skills
Home and yard maintenance
Survival reading
Use of the calculator
Measurement skills
Leisure time skills

Social Skills

Human awareness
Self-esteem
Personal rights
Relationships
Feelings
Solving problems
Sexual knowledge
Communication
Compliments
Assertiveness
Listening skills
Speaking skills

FIGURE 11–5

Functional community skills (Source: From "Functional Curriculum" by H. Fredericks and V. Evans, 1987. In *Special Education in the Criminal Justice System* edited by C. M. Nelson, R. B. Rutherford, Jr., and B. I. Wolford, Columbus, OH: Merrill Publishing Company. Reprinted by permission.)

and the resources that will be needed for her to succeed in her educational and living settings. We suggest that initial discussions with the student and her caretakers occur early in the student's school career, preferably no later than the seventh or eighth grade, so that you can implement appropriate curricular planning. You may need to help the student and her parents select and evaluate their goals so that neither maintain unrealistic expectations. You may find that the parents need counseling about their child's learning handicaps and the restrictions these place on her further education. Information regarding such discussions can be summarized on the pre-transition planning form (see Figure 11–2) for future reference.

Preparing Students for Post-Secondary Programs

If a student is academically capable of college preparatory courses but lacks the appropriate social and study behaviors to be mainstreamed in such courses, you should make these primary objectives on the student's IEP. This does not necessarily mean that the pupil cannot be mainstreamed until such problems have been remedied, but it does suggest that you should attempt to build such skills systematically in both special and regular education classes. You should find curricula aimed at developing school survival skills useful in this regard (e.g., Zigmond, Kerr, Schaeffer, Brown, & Farra, 1986). Both student and parents should be aware that appropriate social and classroom behaviors are prerequisite to participation in mainstream classes. Furthermore, you should assess the expectations of teachers of these classes and, if necessary, teach students desired behaviors prior to placing them. We have known mainstream placements to fail because students had not completed assignments before class, failed to bring materials, did not get to class on time,

could not remember their assigned seats, or failed to respond when called upon.

Selecting Post-Secondary Programs

Assuming that you have implemented a suitable curriculum for admission into a post-secondary educational placement, your next task is to help the student and his parents select an appropriate school or training program. Your school's guidance office should maintain current lists of post-secondary schools and training programs. In addition, your guidance counselor can administer individualized tests of aptitude in interests and can provide counseling to students and parents regarding appropriate post-school opportunities. Directories of colleges having programs for students with learning disabilities also are now available (e.g., Liscio, 1985). You can obtain additional information from the Association for Children and Adults with Learning Disabilities, 4156 Library Rd., Pittsburgh, Pennsylvania 15234. The student should write to several programs for admission information, then make campus visits with his parents to view the program and meet with admissions officers. Frequently, these programs send recruiters to high school campuses, so you can prepare students for these visits. (This, by the way, is an opportune way to practice interview skills.)

The selection of a post-secondary educational program is an individual matter, but here, too, some general strategies may be applied. We will describe some for selecting college programs, although it should be understood that the same tactics are equally applicable to other kinds of decisions. Cowen (1985) provided guidelines for learning disabled students to use in selecting a college program. These are in the form of an outline of questions the pupil can use to assess himself and the institution he is considering. Questions are grouped into the following categories: (a) know your strengths, (b) know your weaknesses, (c) know about the institution, and (d) know about the services. The questions under these categories would be useful for students when interviewing with admissions officers or when making campus visits. Cowen also listed sources for locating higher education programs for students with learning disabilities.

Strichart and Mangrum (1985) suggested several criteria that you and students' parents can employ in choosing from available programs. These include the availability of diagnostic testing services, of advisors who know about learning problems and can help the student select appropriate courses and instructors, of remedial programs to help the student cope with his learning disabilities and to reduce his academic deficits, and of a counseling program to develop interpersonal relationships and to help the student learn to accept his own limitations. Bireley and Manley (1980) described the services available for learning disabled students at Wright State University. These included special admission procedures in lieu of ACT or SAT examinations; an academic advisory plan suggesting a balance among courses in terms of level of difficulty; a tutorial program consisting of graduate student tutors, proctors to read exams, and tape recordings of textbooks; and weekly advising/counseling sessions during the freshman year.

As with transition to work and to independent living, programming for pupils' movement into post-secondary educational programs should begin well ahead of time. Earlier, we stressed the importance of getting the student into an appropriate college preparatory curriculum by junior high school. Dexter (1982) described specific study skills that should be developed prior to college and then generalized to college settings. These include organizing study times and places, setting priorities for meeting assignments, arranging a suitable en-

vironment for studying, reading assignments twice and devising a system for underscoring reading material. Not only can these skills be taught in secondary school, but they are also immediately useful in both mainstream and special education classes.

When the students interview on a college campus, they should make admissions staff aware of their learning problems, if you have not done so beforehand. During their campus visit, pupils also should locate special student services. Learning disabled students are eligible to have their texts put on audio tapes through Recording for the Blind, Inc. (Dexter, 1982). Once they are enrolled on campus, students can use these services, especially if arrangements have been made in advance. Other strategies for supporting exceptional learners in higher education include having them tape record class lectures (Dexter, 1982) and using special education or psychology graduate students to help the disabled student develop and implement an IEP for college (Gajar, Murphy, & Hunt, 1982).

Although transition services for handicapped learners in higher education are multiplying, relatively few special education services are available to assist adolescents who are pursuing college training programs (National Association of State Directors of Special Education, 1985). Thus, much of the orchestration of services may be up to you, which again indicates the need to work with your local supervisor in designing a job description that takes into account the time you spend in such activities.

Transition to Institutional Placement

As we pointed out in the previous chapter, handicapped youth are overrepresented in correctional programs. Furthermore, in spite of your best efforts, some students will become incarcerated, while others will require placement in restrictive mental health settings. Your knowledge of the juvenile justice system in your locale will help you to reduce the chances that handicapped students will be incarcerated for long periods of time, but if institutional placement is necessary for any reason, you can take some steps to improve the educational program they receive.

An important prerequisite to facilitating transitions to more restrictive placements outside the school system is that you know what is happening in your students' lives that can result in such placements. Obviously, you can observe behaviors in school: the student who is violent or psychotic and sometimes out of control is a likely candidate for institutionalization. But often it is behavior in the home or the community that occasions institutional placement. Therefore, we urge that you maintain a working relationship with your students' parents in order to have access to such information. Lines of communication with community agencies and key professionals also will help you stay informed about your pupils' out-of-school activities. You can respond to some situations with adjustments in students' IEPs (adding instruction in skill alternatives to aggression to your social skills curriculum; see Goldstein et al., 1980). In addition, knowledge about students can lead to long-term planning with parents and other professionals, which may include the decision that institutional placement is a necessary consideration for some. If such is the case, the IEP or transition team should decide among alternative placements. Your specific responsibility should be to obtain information regarding educational programming in the institutions being considered, to arrange for handing off the IEP, and to work out details involving the student's educational program. You also may need to prepare the student for transfer: discuss the reason for it, the experiences offered, and the objectives. (Note: Work this out with the transition team first!)

In other instances, such as when a student is apprehended and adjudicated by the juvenile justice system, you will have little or no advance warning of the impending transition. If you have a working relationship with the local juvenile authorities and they know the student is handicapped, you may be contacted prior to a disposition hearing. If these authorities are not aware that the student is handicapped, you may still be able to intervene before the disposition hearing, if you learn from the parents the reason their child is not in school. In case you do not find this out until the student has been adjudicated, you can still inform the juvenile authorities, and, with appropriate permission, arrange for the transfer of his school records. The model described by Edgar et al. (1987) for achieving the transition of adjudicated youth back to community schools from correctional programs contains several useful strategies for transitions in the other direction as well. This model will be described in the next section.

Transition from Institutions

If you teach in a correctional or mental health institution, returning students to community living will be one of your primary concerns. These programs impose the additional transition problem of moving students from a highly restrictive placement with little or no opportunity for contact with the social or educational mainstream. Mental health institutions tend to offer normalized experiences and training for independent living via progressive movement through systematic level systems; however, these usually are open only to adults who will not be returning to public schools. The transition of school-age youths back to community educational programs generally is coordinated by a case worker, who negotiates the student's placement and transfer of her IEP to local school personnel. As a special education teacher, you may be on the giving or the receiving end of the hand-off process, depending upon your employment and the direction the student is going, but in either case, we hope you can provide input.

The majority of students leaving correctional institutions do not return to public school. Those who do may not be able to obtain appropriate credit for their correctional education experience because these programs are not compatible or because no procedures exist for transferring credits (Leone, Price, & Vitolo, 1986). Furthermore, many correctional education programs, whether regular or special, do not offer a curriculum that provides offenders with functional skills that will facilitate their adjustment to community living (Rutherford et al., 1985). If you teach in such a program, perhaps you can initiate the necessary curricular reform to achieve more appropriate programming. As we pointed out in Chapter Ten, many incarcerated youth, handicapped or not, lack important community survival skills. Our earlier suggestions concerning functional curricula may be useful in terms of redesigning traditional educational programs.

A Juvenile Corrections Transition Model

Edgar and his colleagues (Edgar et al., 1987; Maddox et al., 1984) have designed and evaluated a set of strategies for moving incarcerated adolescents back into community schools. We will present their approach in some detail, because we think the strategies generalize quite well to providing transition services for youths returning from other types of institutional programs. Moreover, as indicated in the previous section, several of these strategies address the movement of students from community to institutional educational programs. This transition model was developed by the University of Washington Networking and Evaluation Team (NET) to provide continuity of educational ser-

vices to youth entering and leaving correctional institutions in Washington's Division of Juvenile Rehabilitation (DJR). The NET staff worked with one of the state's juvenile correctional institutions and the Tacoma Public Schools. They designed more than 40 strategies in four areas: (a) awareness of other agency activities and goals; (b) the transfer of records when entering the institutions and leaving for a local public school; (c) preplacement planning for the transition; and (d) maintaining placement in the school and ongoing communication between agencies regarding youths' progress. Each strategy includes information regarding when the strategy should be initiated, who is responsible, and what materials are required. Personnel directly involved in these strategies included public school and correctional education administrators, juvenile parole counselors, social workers, the public school court liaison, DJR and correctional institution staff, and parents of the adjudicated youth (Maddox et al., 1984). This comprehensive and functional model is summarized in Figure 11–6.

Maddox et al. (1984) reported that their model improved the transition both of educational records and of students between educational programs. In addition, it improved interagency cooperation and provided correctional education staffers with important feedback regarding their curriculum. We think efforts to develop systematic transition models for the agencies serving your students will be well worth the time. Such a model can be used for following up former students as well as for facilitating their transition.

SUMMARY

Specific concern regarding the transition of handicapped adolescents from public educational programs is a recent development. Therefore, few of the strategies we have presented in this chapter are as well developed or evaluated

A. *AWARENESS*
  A.1 Interagency Administrators Meeting
    A.1.1 Develop and disseminate list of roles and responsibilities of schools, regional Division of Juvenile Rehabilitation (DJR), and institutions.
  A.2 Inservice Education
    A.2.1 Conduct an inservice for selected staff from DJR, school district (SD), and correctional institution.
    A.2.2 Conduct inservice for institution staff.
    A.2.3 Conduct inservice for SD principals, counselors, and staff regarding the Juvenile Justice Rehabilitation System and/or the institution education programs.
  A.3 Institution and School District Visits
    A.3.1 Visits to institutions made by SD building teams or other SD representatives.
    A.3.2 Visits made by institution administrators and staff to SD placement options.
B. *TRANSFER OF RECORDS*
  B.1 Establish and implement procedures for students' school records to be sent to institution.
    B.1.1 Educational information is collected and requested prior to juvenile entering institution.
    B.1.2 If records have not arrived within 10 days after student's arrival or have not been requested, institution takes responsibility to obtain records.
  B.2 Establish and implement procedures for transfer of students' records from institution to receiving school.
    B.2.1 Educational information is collected at institution and sent to Juvenile Parole Counselor (JPC).
    B.2.2 In cases of community residential placement (CRP), or short notice placements, the institution expedites record collection using shortened timelines.
    B.2.3 A student withdrawal card is developed and used to gather academic information prior to release.
  B.3 Establish and implement procedures for transfer of students' records from one institution to another.
    B.3.1 When a student is moved from one institution to another, receiving institution takes responsibility to request school records.
    B.3.2 When a juvenile is transferred from a CRP or state group home (GH) back to an institution, GH staff initiates the request for school records.
    B.3.3 Educational information is collected prior to a juvenile being paroled from a CRP or state GH.
C. *PREPLACEMENT PLANNING AND DECISION OF EDUCATIONAL PLACEMENT*
  C.1 Develop a system to screen and assess youth for special education placement
    C.1.1 Identify students needing special education program at institution.
    C.1.2 Use learning center for conducting assessment, making placement decisions, and preparing student for new placement.

FIGURE 11–6

Outline of the juvenile corrections interagency transition model (Source: From "Issues in Transition: Transfer of Youth from Correctional Facilities to Public Schools" by E. Edgar, S. Webb, and M. Maddox (1987). In *Special Education in the Criminal Justice System* edited by C. M. Nelson, R. B. Rutherford, Jr., and B. I. Wolford, Columbus, OH: Merrill Publishing Company. Reprinted by permission.)

C.2 Develop systematic placement procedures.
  C.2.1 Define criteria for learning center (LC) placement.
  C.2.2 Identify potential in-district placement options and adaptations.
  C.2.3 Develop criteria and systematic procedures for credit acceptance.
  C.2.4 Prepare student for moving from LC to other SD program.
C.3 Use all educational information collected to make school placement decision prior to time of release from institution.
  C.3.1 Prepare school progress report at institution school for use by JPC and SD in school placement planning.
  C.3.2 JPC meets with student, institutional school, and residential staff prior to student's release and discusses educational goals after release.
C.4 Plan for placement prior to release.
  C.4.1 Review all placement options within the SD and match to student's needs.
  C.4.2 Education plan is written for each student, from which placement plan is developed.
  C.4.3 Receiving school has staffing prior to student arrival to schedule and pre-register student.
  C.4.4 Hold school registration meeting with student and SD before school program entry.
  C.4.5 Preplacement Planning Team formed.
D. *MAINTAINING PLACEMENT AND COMMUNICATION*
  D.1 Cultivate parent or guardian involvement.
    D.1.1 Develop communication between regional DJR staff and parents.
    D.1.2 Develop communication between parents and receiving school.
  D.2 Design school advocacy program for adjudicated youth.
    D.2.1 All adjudicated youth in each SD school building assigned to one counselor.
    D.2.2 Form an advocacy network by assigning entering paroled youth to SD staff advocate.
    D.2.3 Schedule students into classes with supportive teachers.
  D.3 Monitor attendance and behavior
    D.3.1 Student's school progress and attendance are monitored at scheduled intervals.
    D.3.2 School attendance monitor provides feedback to JPC regarding student attendance.
  D.4 Develop direct communication line between school and JPC for resource sharing and problem solving.
    D.4.1 Develop communication system for contact between JPC and schools.
  D.5 Develop post-placement communication system regarding student's educational placement.
    D.5.1 Provide feedback to institution school about student's educational placement at end of parole.

as the model designed by Edgar and his colleagues (Edgar et al., 1987; Maddox et al., 1984). As Edgar (1985) emphasized, research is badly needed regarding the post-school adjustment of handicapped youth. We need to find out what happens to them after they leave school and to use this information to improve their experiences while in school. We are confident that future research will support the assertion of Wehman et al. (1985) that the characteristics of an appropriate special education program should include: (a) a functional curriculum, (b) schooling with nonhandicapped peers, (c) a formal transitional plan that is being implemented, and (d) varied work (or educational) opportunities for the student after graduation.

We offer the case study to illustrate that transition programming is important throughout the school years of students with learning and behavior disorders. It also will illustrate the dedication that accompanies such a complex task.

RECOMMENDED READINGS

Edgar, E., Webb, S., & Maddox, M. (1987). Issues in transition: Transfer of youth from correctional facilities to public schools. In C.M. Nelson, R.B. Rutherford, Jr., & B.I. Wolford (Eds.), *Special education in the criminal justice system*. Columbus, OH: Merrill Publishing Company.

Goldstein, A.P., Sprafkin, R.P., Gershaw, N.J., & Klein, P. (1980). *Skill-streaming the adolescent*. Champaign, IL: Research Press.

Hasazi, S.B., Gordon, L.R., & Roe, C.A. (1985). Factors associated with the employment of handicapped youth exiting high school from 1979-1983. *Exceptional Children, 51*, 455-469.

Rutherford, R.B., Jr., & Nelson, C.M. (in press). Applied behavior analysis in education: Generalization and maintenance. In J.C. Witt, S.N. Elliott, & F.M. Gresham (Eds.), *Handbook of behavior therapy in education*. New York: Plenum.

CASE STUDY

Getting Robert Through School

Robert came to my intermediate level class angry, street-wise, and tough—but that was all he knew. In school his behavior (knife-wielding, fighting, verbal abuse, and defiance of authority) had earned him only negative consequences and a Behavior Disorder label. Three years of structured behavior management in a self-contained special education classroom with mainstream participation contingent upon systematic level-system criteria accomplished some encouraging behavioral changes, but I was concerned about long-term maintenance and generalization to a junior high school environment. Although behind academically, Robert had above-average intellectual potential and superior athletic ability. He was a particularly talented running back for his intramural football team.

Robert insisted that he begin junior high school in a new district as a "regular" student (without a special education label), and the special education committee agreed to let him. I quickly discovered that the system was not able to provide adequate support for monitoring and aiding special-needs students making transitions between schools or programs. So I decided to see what kind of coalition I could put together myself.

I met individually with the junior high principal, the counselors, and the coaches to alert them and to introduce Robert prior to opening day. I gathered information about academic scheduling, student regulations, disciplinary procedures, and football practice. After school began, I took Robert to breakfast at 6:00 A.M. one morning each week, then accompanied him to school in order to make the rounds of his teachers before my school opened at 8:00. I casually but systematically checked with each teacher, counselor, coach, and the principal for reports on Robert's progress and familiarized myself with their personalities and expectations. This consistent communication enabled me to provide Robert with ongoing feedback and to assist both him and his caretakers in solving problems as they developed rather than after they had accumulated. Over the years, I helped the assistant principal, the football coach, and Robert's parents develop contingency plans for reducing inappropriate behavior, outlined and modeled specific social skills (greeting, conversing with, or apologizing to adults; seeking teacher assistance with assignments; displaying the "proper" atti-

---

This case study was written by Laura Lee McCullough, Fayette County (Kentucky) Schools.

tude; resisting peer pressure), and taught Robert how to take notes and study for tests. Last but not least, I attended numerous football games and ate a lot of pizzas.

High school was easier. Robert's behavior had stabilized, but he needed a tutor, as his slow reading speed and written language deficits triggered a slump in his academic performance and motivation. Tutoring helped, but Robert's coursework remained a struggle. Although I had moved out of town, I continued to call or visit his counselor, tutor, mother, and coach to check on SAT test dates, grades, athletic scholarships, vocational counseling and assessment, and Robert's general progress. Suddenly, Robert was graduating, with a summer job and plans to attend the University of Wisconsin in the offing!

As I watched Robert triumphantly wave his diploma above his head, I thought about the administrator who said Robert would never make

it and about the length and complexity of my role. Then I found myself wondering about other students like Robert who never find someone to coordinate and interweave the network of support, communication, and supervision that are so critical to successful transition.

As this case study suggests, transition services require the commitment of dedicated and skilled persons to work effectively. Edgar et al. (1987) labeled this person a "driver." In the absence of formally assigned responsibility for transition services, agency personnel who are willing to tackle the problems of transition are vital to the process. We hope that you will become a driver. However, Edgar et al. also observed that the staff of one agency cannot change the characteristics of the services offered by another agency. Therefore, we urge you to know and work within the limitations of your agency and professional role.

Glossary

Adaptive Behavior behavior that meets standards of personal-occupational independence consistent with one's age and culture.

Addiction compulsive use of a drug, characterized by a behavior pattern that centers on drug use, procurement, and continued use. According to this definition, evidence of physical tolerance and dependence is not necessary for establishing that a person is addicted.

AIDS (Acquired Immune Deficiency Syndrome) breakdown of the immune system resulting in the body's inability to *combat* disease; common among homosexuals, bisexual men, hemophiliacs, and intravenous drug users. Transmission is thought to take place through intimate contact and blood products.

Amphetamine any of a group of synthetic chemicals that stimulate the central nervous system. Slang: speed, uppers, bennies.

Antecedent Behavior Consequence Analysis (ABC Analysis) a technique used to identify systematically functional relationships among behaviors and environmental variables.

Arrhythmias an alteration in normal rhythm of the heartbeat either in time or force.

Assessment the process of gathering data for the purpose of making education decisions.

Barbiturates a class of drugs that has a sedative effect by depressing the central nervous system.

Behavior Disorders behavior characteristics that (a) deviate from educators' standards of normality and (b) impair the functioning of that student and/or others; manifested as environmental conflicts and/or personal disturbances and typically accompanied by learning disorders.

Caffeine a stimulant drug. Chemically, caffeine belongs in a chemical class named xanthines (pronounced "zanthenes") and is a methyl-xanthine compound.

Carcinogen a cancer-producing agent.

Career Awareness an important aspect of vocational education that helps students target occupations or occupational clusters that interest them.

Classroom-Based Instruction instruction that takes place in the classroom setting, the content of which emphasizes attaining skills and objectives that are appropriate for success in a class, academic, or business/work situation.

Cocaine a narcotic with physiological effects very similar to the amphetamines.

Community-Based Instruction instruction in skills that are necessary for success in independent adult living, which are taught outside the classroom in the actual environment in which the skills will be used.

Contingency Contract contract, usually written, stipulating conditions for certain desired behaviors; conditions typically include precise behaviors desired, stated in clear and objective terms, the time period within which they are to be performed, and the consequences contingent upon successful performance.

Curriculum Modification modification of the curriculum to adapt to student needs by identifying instructional variables important to the selection of instructional materials, and selection of appropriate materials for the entire class and for individual prescription.

Dependence compulsive drug use to ward off physical and/or emotional discomfort. The person depends on the drug to prevent withdrawal or abstinence-related distress. Physical and psychological dependence are distinguished on the basis of overt and predictable withdrawal symptoms.

315

Dependent Group Contingencies a strategy in which the performance of certain group members determines the consequence received by the entire group.

Depo Provera an injectable synthetic hormonal contraceptive, acting on the lining of the uterus, effective for 90 days.

Depressants depressant drugs belonging to the classes of barbiturates (phenobarbital, hexobarbital), benzodiazepine and propanedial minor tranquilizers (Librium, Valium, meprobamate), and antihistaminic sedatives. Barbiturates are commonly prescribed for sleep facilitation and for control of seizures.

Detention a behavioral correction intervention in which students must come 30 to 90 minutes before or after school to complete assignments.

2,5-Dimethoxy 4-methylamphetamine (DOM or STP) an hallucinogenic substance chemically related to amphetamine and mescaline.

Disruptive Behavior behavior that does or is likely to interrupt the class and/or makes it difficult for teachers or peers to continue the task at hand or ongoing classroom activity.

Dimethyl Triptamine (DMT) a frequently encountered hallucinogen belonging to a single chemical class known as indole-amine alkaloids; it is similar in chemical structure to a chemical in the brain (5-hydroxytriptamine), which is involved in the processing of sensory information.

Differential Reinforcement of Low Rates of Behavior (DRL) a procedure in which reinforcement is delivered when the number of responses in a specified period of time is less than or equal to a prescribed limit. This enables the maintenance of a behavior at a predetermined rate lower than that which was occurring at its baseline or naturally occurring frequency.

Drug any chemical that is consumed and is present in abnormal concentration in the body. This includes substances like insulin or other hormones found naturally within the body, which can dramatically influence emotion and behavior if their concentrations are not kept within normal limits.

Drug Abuse the voluntary intake of a chemical in spite of adverse physical and social consequences.

Duration Recording recording the amount of time between the initiation of a response and its con-clusion. Total duration recording is recording cumulative time between the initiation of a response and its final conclusion. For example, one may record cumulative time out-of-seat across several instances. Duration per occurrence is recording each behavioral event and its duration.

Ectopic Pregnancy an abnormal pregnancy in which a fertilized ovum implants outside the uterine cavity.

Educational Assessment a structured method of enquiring into educational settings in order to determine the most appropriate placement and instruction for students.

Environmentally Mediated Strategies techniques for behavior management in the classroom, which rely on changing the environment including: curriculum modifications, scheduling, the physical plan of the classroom, and the placement of work.

Exhibitionism in psychoanalysis, the expression of the infantile sexual aim, or impulse, to display the genitalia; in a loose sense, childish efforts to attract favorable attention by self-display.

Expulsion a behavioral correction strategy in which a student is sent out of school for an indefinite period of time.

Feedback a process by which the teacher corrects or praises a student's behaviors or tasks in a descriptive manner in order to produce a more desired behavior.

Frequency the number of times a behavior occurs during an observation period.

Functional Curriculum a frequently updated educational guide that adequately tests the learner's skill level to prepare students for adult living, including independent living skills, social skills, vocational and educational skills.

Functional Skills those tasks and activities most often required in routinely visited settings.

Generalization expansion of a student's capability of performance beyond those conditions set for initial acquisition. Stimulus generalization refers to performance under conditions (i.e., cues, materials, trainers, and environments) other than those present during acquisition. Maintenance refers to continued performance of learned behavior after contingencies have been withdrawn. Response generalization refers to changes in behaviors similar to those directly treated.

Generalization Training the transference of skills from the student's present environment to a new environment, usually accompanying the movement to a less restrictive classroom.

Group Goalsetting an intervention that consists of two major components: first, the teacher establishes a social behavioral goal for each student; and second, each student receives feedback on his progress towards that goal during highly structured group discussions.

Hallucinogens a chemically heterogeneous group of drugs with the common property of altering sensory experiences and mood.

Hashish a purified resin of the marijuana plant.

Heroin (Diacetylmorphine) a narcotic opiate.

Home Suspension sending a student out of school for a designated time period.

Homework Completion Checklist an objective measure designed to aid students in monitoring various aspects of a peer's assignment.

Homosexuality limitation of erotic interests to members of the same sex.

Individualized Education Program (IEP) written educational plan developed for each student eligible for special education.

Independent Group Contingency a contingency related to the behavior of groups with consequences for behaviors directed toward individual group members.

Inhalants and Volatile Solvents chemicals that easily mix with air and can be inhaled, including hydrocarbons (benzene, carbon tetrachloride), freons (trichlorofluoromethane), ketones (acetone), esters (ethylacetate), alcohols (methyl alcohol), glycols (ethylene glycol), and gasoline. Common sources of these chemicals are aerosols, fingernail polish, household cements, lacquer thinner, lighter fluid, cleaning fluid, and model cement.

Informal Reading Inventory (IRI) an informal assessment device that measures both word recognition and comprehension skills; yields instructional, independent, and frustration reading levels.

In-School Suspension an environmentally mediated behavioral intervention in which students are removed from the classroom, placed in a highly structured environment within the school, and required to pursue their studies.

Interdependent Group Contingency a contingency whose consequences are applied to the group, contingent upon each member reaching a specified criterion level of performance.

Intervention becoming involved with students in an official capacity in order to improve their performance, socially, emotionally, or academically.

Intrauterine Device (IUD) a birth control device placed within the uterus, usually in the form of a small coil.

Juvenile Law jurisdiction for juvenile based on age and behavior, usually concerned with three major areas: criminal behavior, status offenses, and neglect dependency cases.

Learning Disorder a condition that impedes or inhibits the child's acquisition and restructuring of knowledge, hindering adequate intellectual development.

Least Restrictive Environment the environment imposing the fewest restrictions on a pupil's normal academic or social functioning.

Levels System a method of differentiating hierarchically any aspect of an individual's performance (e.g., a token economy or for assessment purposes).

Librium chlordiazepoxide, a minor tranquilizer.

Lidocaine a synthetic anesthetic producing a freezing sensation in the nose when inhaled and often used to dilute cocaine.

LSD (Lysergic Acid Diethylamide) the prototypical hallucinogen.

Mainstreaming the integration of exceptional children with normal peers.

Maintenance the ability to perform a response over time, even after systematic applied behavior procedures have been withdrawn.

Menarche the occurrence of the first menstrual flow.

Mental Retardation subaverage general functioning with impairment of adaptive behavior, manifested during developmental period—classified by etiology and severity; classifications by intellectual functioning are mild, moderate, severe, and profound.

Mescaline (Peyote) a frequently encountered hallucinogen. Mescaline and STP are related to amphetamines and resemble another important brain chemical, norepinephrine. Mescaline is found in the peyote cactus, which grows in the American southwest.

Methylamphetamine Hydrochloride an addictive stimulant affecting the central nervous system, often used orally or intravenously by drug abusers.

Minimum Competency Testing trend among many states to ensure that student promotions and graduations are based on mastery of certain basic skills.

Modeling an instructional procedure by which demonstrations of a desired behavior are presented in order to prompt an imitative response.

Narcolepsy a paroxysmal sleep-like attack.

Narcotics practical and effective drugs for treating specific types of pain; powerful analgesics that reduce pain without seriously altering the ability of the patient to function normally in other ways.

Nicotine a drug found in many forms of commercially grown tobacco. Chemically, nicotine is classified as an alkaloid and is physically highly toxic, causing nausea, salivation, abdominal pain, vomiting, diarrhea, cold sweat, headache, dizziness, confusion, convulsions, and respiratory failure at high doses. Nicotine is a common active ingredient in several insecticides.

On-Task describes the student who is paying attention to and participating in a class activity or is working on a class assignment or project.

Off-Task describes the student who is not paying attention to or participating in a class activity or is not working on a class assignment or project.

Peer-Mediated Intervention an intervention requiring a member of the individual's peer group, rather than an adult, to take the primary role as the behavior-change agent.

Peer-Mediated Task Analysis a behavioral and academic improvement strategy in which the students help each other break major academic tasks into smaller, more manageable ones.

Peer-Monitoring a type of intervention in which a classmate checks on the behavior of another student, or in which monitoring takes place between students reciprocally.

Peer Tutoring formal instruction of one child by another.

Pelvic Inflammatory Disease inflammation in the pelvic cavity, especially the female reproductive organs.

Phencyclidine (PCP) a hallucinogen. LSD and PCP are by far the most frequently abused hallucino-gens (except for cannabis). PCP is more likely to promote aggressive behavior with concurrent increased physical vigor and lack of response to pain.

Phenylpropanolamine (PPA) the active ingredient in many over-the-counter weight-loss pills. It is a stimulant also prescribed for its decongestant properties in respiratory infections (colds and flu) and ear infections, and is very similar to amphetamine in chemical structure.

Pinpointing the specification of behaviors or skills to be modified or taught.

Post Secondary Education the continuing education of handicapped students after secondary school until the age of 21 as stated by P.L. 94-142.

Pre-Referral Intervention a process in which the student's problem is diagnosed briefly with interventions tried and results reviewed before a formal referral for eligibility for special education.

Pre-Vocational Curriculum a curriculum designed for the more severely handicapped, involving precise and systematic analysis of the characteristics of prospective jobs and work environments, enabling instruction for flexible job competencies.

Procaine a drug less toxic than cocaine but similar in effect, often used as a substitute for cocaine.

Psilocybin a frequently encountered hallucinogen. LSD, psilocybin, and DMT belong to a single chemical class known as indole-amine alkaloids and are similar in structure to a chemical in the brain (5-hydroxytriptamine), which is involved in the processing of sensory information. Psilocybin is found in a mushroom common in Mexico.

Pubarche the beginning of puberty; the appearance of pubic hair.

Puberty the stage in an individual's sexual development in which reproduction is first possible.

Pubescence the beginning of sexual maturity.

Public Law 94-142 the Education for All Handicapped Children Act of 1975, mandates free, appropriate, public education for all handicapped students.

Public Law 98-199 the public law for handicapped students empowering P.L. 94-142, which, among other provisions, allots funds for secondary education and transitional services.

Public Posting publicly listing the names of persons who have (or have not) engaged in a target behavior.

Rehabilitation Plan a plan designed for a student in which a schedule of objectives is created, which is appropriately paced for the student and followed through the academic year.

Reinforcement providing reinforcing consequences or removing or withholding aversive consequences contingent upon the occurrence of a desired pupil behavior. Reinforcement results in an increase or maintenance of the rate of that behavior.

Role Playing a therapeutic procedure to introduce new behaviors to enhance social relationships. Here the adult attempts to re-create certain situations for the student, in an effort to help that student practice needed skills.

Salami Technique the process of dividing a large (and overwhelming) responsibility into smaller, more manageable steps.

School Survival Skills those academic skills enabling the student to meet the demands of regular curriculum, of regular educators, and of large group instruction. School survival skills include class attendance and punctuality, class preparedness, time management, assessing teacher demands, remaining on task, handling transitions, getting others' help.

Scopolamine one of a class of drugs known as anticholinergics (because they inhibit the activity of the brain chemical acetylcholine, which is considered important for mood and sensory regulation).

Self-Assessment the systematic examination of a student's own behavior and the evaluation of whether or not she performed a targeted behavior or group of behaviors.

Self-Instruction a procedure through which students practice "coping statements" to themselves.

Self-Mediated Strategies strategies for behavior improvement in which the students control their own planned intervention.

Self-Monitoring a student's observing, counting, and recording of his own behaviors.

Self-Recording a procedure whereby students record their own performance.

Self-Reinforcement a procedure whereby students reinforce their own behavior.

Shaping the gradual reinforcement of behaviors leading to a desired, more difficult behavior.

Social Skills the capacity to develop and choose from a variety of actions when faced with an interpersonal situation.

Social Skills Training an educational curriculum designed to help students learn basic skills for interacting with others (i.e., skills for dealing with feelings, skill alternatives to aggression, skills for dealing with stress) and with the environment (how to budget an income, pay bills, use public transportation, etc.).

Special Education specially designed instruction to meet the unique needs of handicapped students.

Stimulants drugs that have a stimulating effect on the central nervous system. The two drugs of this category that are familiar to most people are amphetamines and cocaine. There are other drugs that fall into this category, including nicotine (cigarettes and other forms of tobacco), phenylpropanolamine, methylphenidate, pemoline, and phencyclidine (PCP).

Task Analysis the process of breaking down a complex behavior into its component parts.

Teacher-Mediated Strategies techniques for behavior management in the classroom that rely on the teacher's adapting to the needs of the students, including teaching study skills, adjusting teacher pace and style, motivating student performance, and assigning homework.

Thelarche the beginning of breast development occurring at puberty.

Time-Out a procedure for the reduction of inappropriate behavior whereby the student is denied access, for a fixed period of time, to the opportunity to receive reinforcement.

Tolerance physical adaptation to the effects of a drug so that more of the drug is necessary to produce the same effect with repeated use.

Token Economy; Token Reinforcement; Token System a system of behavior modification in which tangible or token reinforcers such as points, plastic chips, metal washers, poker chips, or play money are given as rewards and later exchanged for back-up reinforcers that have value in themselves (e.g., food, trinkets, play time, books); a miniature economic system used to foster desirable behavior.

Toxic Shock Syndrome the sudden onset of fever, muscle ache, diarrhea, vomiting, and a peeling rash caused by staphylococcal endotoxin, especially from vaginal infection often associated with the use of tampons.

Transition Plan   a program designed to help students better cope with the move from one setting (educational, vocational, rehabilitative) to another, usually including annual goals, short- and long-term plans, etc.

Transition Services   services and agencies designed to aid students in the move from one setting to another. Services include helping individuals make work and social contacts, helping them to become established, and following-up the individuals in their progress in the new environment.

Trans-sexualism   the conscious desire for an anatomical change of sex.

Transvestism   the adaption of clothing and mannerisms of the opposite sex.

Valium (Diazepam)   a controlled drug intended for relief of mild to moderate anxiety and nervous tension without significant sedation. Thought to reduce activity in parts of the limbic system of the brain.

Vocational Education   a program designed to help students to better understand the work world, pinpoint specific careers, and develop the skills necessary to enter a desired vocation.

Volatility   the ability to mix readily with air in high concentrations.

Work-Study Program   a program designed through vocational education in which students divide their time between school and work, earning experience and credit in preparation for graduation.

References

Chapter One

Gearhart, B. R. (1980). *Special education for the 80's*. St. Louis: C. V. Mosby.

Kerr, M. M., & Zigmond, N. (1986). What do high school teachers want?—A study of expectations and standards. *Education and Treatment of Children, 9,* 239–249.

Chapter Two

Balow, T. H., Farr, R., Hogan, T. P., & Prescott, G. A. (1978). *Metropolitan Achievement Tests* (5th ed.). San Antonio, TX: The Psychological Corporation.

Beatty, L. S., Madden, R., & Gardner, E. F. (1978). *Stanford Diagnostic Mathematics Test*. Orlando, FL: Harcourt Brace Jovanovich.

Brigance, A. H. (1980). *Brigance Diagnostic Inventory of Essential Skills*. N. Billerica, MA: Curriculum Associates.

Buros, O. K. (1978). *Mental measurements yearbooks*. Highland Park, NJ: Gryphon.

Buswell, G. T., & John, L. (1926). *Diagnostic studies in arithmetic*. Chicago: University of Chicago Press.

Children's Defense Fund Report. (June, 1985). Do competency tests really measure up?

Cone, J. D., & Hawkins, R. (1977). *Behavioral assessment: New directions in clinical psychology*. New York: Brunner/Mazel.

Connolly, A., Nachtman, W., & Pritchett, E. M. (1976). *Key Math Diagnostic Arithmetic Test*. Circle Pines, MN: American Guidance Service.

Deno, S., & Mirkin, P. (1978). *Data-based program modification*. Reston, VA: Council for Exceptional Children.

Deutsch-Smith, D., & Lovitt, T. C. (1982). *Computational arithmetic program*. Austin, TX: Pro-Ed.

Dunn, L. M., & Markwardt, F. C. (1970). *Peabody Individual Achievement Test*. Circle Pines, MN: American Guidance Service.

Durast, W., Bixler, H. H., Wrightstone, J. W., Prescott, G. A., & Balow, I. W. (1971). *Metropolitan Achievement Test Survey Tests*. New York: Harcourt, Brace & World.

Durrell, D. D. (1955). *Durrell Analysis of Reading Difficulty*. New York: Harcourt Brace Jovanovich.

Gates, A. I., & McKillop, A. S. (1975). *Gates-McKillop Reading Diagnostic Tests*. New York: Teachers College Press.

Gilmore, J. V., & Gilmore, E. C. (1968). *Gilmore Oral Reading Test*. New York: Harcourt Brace Jovanovich.

Gray, W. S., & Robinson, H. M. (1985). *Gray Oral Reading Test*. Indianapolis: Bobbs-Merrill.

Greene, H., & Petty, W. (1967). *Developing language skills in the elementary school*. Boston: Allyn & Bacon.

Hammill, D. D., & Bartel, N. R. (1986). *Teaching students with learning and behavior problems* (4th ed.). Boston: Allyn & Bacon.

Hammill, D. D., Brown, L., Larsen, S. C., & Wiederholt, J. L. (1980). *Test of Adolescent Language*. Austin, TX: Pro-Ed.

Hammill, D. D., & Larsen, S. (1978). *The Test of Written Language*. Austin, TX: Pro-Ed.

Hawkins, R. P. (1979). The function of assessment: Implications for selection and development of devices for assessing repertoires in clinical, educational, and other settings. *Journal of Applied Behavior Analysis, 12,* 501–516.

Hops, H., & Greenwood, C. R. (1981). Social skills deficits. In E. J. Mash & L. G. Terdal (Eds.), *Behavioral assessment of childhood disorders*. New York: Guilford Press.

Jastak, J. F., & Jastak, S. (1978). *Wide Range Achievement Test*. Wilmington, DE: Jastak Associates.

Kaluger, G., & Kolson, C. J. (1978). *Reading and learning disabilities* (2nd ed.). Columbus, OH: Charles E. Merrill.

Karlsen, B., Madden, R., & Gardner, E. F. (1983). *Stanford Diagnostic Reading Test*. San Antonio, TX: The Psychological Corporation.

Kaufman, A. S., & Kaufman, N. L. (1983). *Kaufman Assessment Battery for Children*. Circle Pines, MN: American Guidance Service.

Keith, T. Z. (1985). Questioning the K-ABC: What does it measure? *School Psychology Review, 14*, 9–20.

Kerr, M. M., & Nelson, C. M. (1983). *Strategies for managing behavior problems in the classroom*. Columbus, OH: Charles E. Merrill.

Madden, R., Gardner, E. R., Rudman, H. C., Karlsen, B., & Merwin, J. C. (1973). *Stanford Achievement Test*. Orlando, FL: Harcourt Brace Jovanovich.

Mager, R. F. (1975). *Preparing instructional objectives* (2nd ed.). Belmont, CA: Fearon Publishers.

Maryland Learning Disabilities Project (1983). *Learning disabilities: A diagnostic handbook*. Baltimore: State Department of Education.

McClung, M. S., & Pullin, D. (1978). Competency testing and handicapped students. *Clearinghouse Review*, 922–927.

Morgan, D. P. (1981). *A primer on individualized education programs for exceptional children* (2nd ed.). Reston, VA: The Council for Exceptional Children.

Myklebust, H. R. (1965). *Picture Story Language Test* (PSLT). New York: Grune & Stratton.

Otto, W., and McMenemy, R. (1980). *Corrective and remedial teaching*. Boston: Houghton Mifflin.

Salvia, J., & Ysseldyke, J. E. (1981). *Assessment in special and remedial education* (2nd ed.). Boston: Houghton Mifflin.

Semel, E. M., & Wiig, E. H. (1980). *Clinical evaluations of language functions*. Columbus, OH: Charles E. Merrill.

Silvaroli, J. N. (1982). *Classroom reading inventory* (4th ed.). Dubuque, IA: William C. Brown.

Smith, D. D., & Lovitt, T. C. (1982). *Computational Arithmetic Program*. Austin, TX: Pro-Ed.

Spache, G. D. (1972). *Diagnostic Reading Scales* (rev. ed.). Monterey, CA: California Testing Bureau/McGraw-Hill.

Sucher, F., & Allred, R. (1973). *Screening students for placement in reading*. Provo, UT: Brigham Young Press.

Tiegs, E. W., & Clark, W. W. (1970). *California Achievement Test*. Monterey, CA: California Testing Bureau/McGraw-Hill.

Wallace, G., & McLoughlin, J. (1979). *Learning disabilities: Concepts and characteristics* (2nd ed.). Columbus, OH: Charles E. Merrill.

Wechsler, D. (1974). *Wechsler Intelligence Scale for Children-Revised*. New York: The Psychological Corporation, Harcourt Brace Jovanovich.

Woodcock, R. (1973). *Woodcock Reading Mastery Tests*. Circle Pines, MN: American Guidance Service.

Woodcock, R. W., & Johnson, M. B. (1978). *Woodcock-Johnson Psychoeducational Battery*. Boston, MA: Teaching Resources Corporation.

Woods, M. L., & Moe, A. (1985). *Analytical reading inventory* (3rd ed.). Columbus, OH: Charles E. Merrill.

Zaner-Bloser (1979). *Zaner-Bloser evaluation scales*. Columbus, OH. Available from Zaner-Bloser, 612 N. Park St., Columbus, OH 43215.

Zigmond, N., Vallecorsa, A., & Silverman, R. (1983). *Assessment for instructional planning in special education*. Englewood Cliffs, NJ: Prentice-Hall.

Chapter Three

Achenbach, T. M., & Edelbrock, C. S. (1980). *Teacher's Form of the Child Behavior Checklist*. Burlington, VT: Thomas Achenbach, Department of Psychiatry, University of Vermont.

Achenbach, T. M., & Edelbrock, C. S. (1983). *Youth self-report*. Burlington, VT: Thomas Achenbach, Department of Psychiatry, University of Vermont.

Alberto, P., & Troutman, A. (1982). *Applied behavior analysis for teachers: Influencing student performance*. Columbus, OH: Charles E. Merrill.

Bell-Dolan, D. J., Foster, S. L., & Sikora, D. M. (1985). *The effect of peer nominations on children's behavior and loneliness in school*. Paper presented at the 19th Annual Meeting of the Association for the Advancement of Behavior Therapy, Houston.

Cone, J. D., & Hawkins, R. (1977). *Behavioral assessment: New directions in clinical psychology*. New York: Brunner/Mazel.

Cooper, J. O. (1981). *Measuring behavior*. Columbus, OH: Charles E. Merrill.

Deno, S. & Mirkin, P. (1978). *Data-based program modification*. Reston, VA: Council for Exceptional Children.

Doll, E. (1985). *Vineland Social Maturity Scale*. Circle Pines, MN: American Guidance Service.

Estes, T. H., Estes, J. J., Richards, H. C., & Roettinger, D. (1980). *Estes School Attitude Scale*. Austin, TX: Pro-Ed.

Gast, D. L., & Gast, K. B. (1981). Educational program evaluation: An overview of data-based instruction for classroom teachers. In *Toward a research base for the least restrictive environment: A collection of papers* (pp. 1–30). Lexington, KY: College of Education Deans Grant Project.

Gelfand, D. M., & Hartmann, D. P. (1975). *Child behavior analysis and therapy*. New York: Pergamon.

Grossman, H. J. (Ed.). (1977). *Manual on terminology and classification in mental retardation: 1973 revision*. Baltimore, MD: Garamonde/Pridemark.

Hall, R. V. (1973). *Managing behavior-behavior modification: The measurement of behavior* (Part 1). Lawrence, KS: H & H Enterprises.

Hayvren, N., & Hymel, S. (1984). Ethical issues in sociometric measures on interaction behavior. *Developmental Psychology, 20*, 844–849.

Hops, H., & Greenwood, C. R. (1981). *Social skills deficits*. In E. J. Mash & L. G. Terdal (Eds.), *Behavioral assessment of childhood disorders*. New York: The Guilford Press.

Kuder, G. F. (1976). *Kuder General Interest Survey. Manual: AAMD Adaptive Behavior Scale, school edition*. Monterey, CA: CTB/McGraw-Hill.

Lambert, D., Windmiller, M., Thoringer, D., & Cole, L. (1981). *Administration and instructional planning manual: AAMD Adaptive Behavior Scale, school edition*. Monterey, CA: CTB/McGraw-Hill.

Roff, M., Sells, B., & Golden, M. (1972). *Social adjustment and personality development in children*. Minneapolis: University of Minnesota Press.

Ullmann, C. A. (1952). *Identification of maladjusted school children*. Public Health Monograph No. 7. Washington, DC: Federal Security Agency.

Walls, R., Werner, T., & Bacon, A. (1977). Behavior checklists. In J. Cone and R. Hawkins (Eds.), *Behavioral assessment: New directions in clinical psychology*. New York: Brunner/Mazel.

Zigmond, N., Kerr, M. M., Schaeffer, A. L., Brown, G. M., & Farra, H. E. (1986). *School Survival Skills Curriculum* (limited published circulation). Available from Department of Special Education, 5M30 Forbes Quadrangle, 230 Bouquet Street, University of Pittsburgh, Pittsburgh, PA 15260.

Chapter Four

Alberto, P. A., & Troutman, A. C. (1982). *Applied behavior analysis for teachers: Influencing student performance*. Columbus, OH: Charles E. Merrill.

Baer, D. M., Wolf, M. M., & Risley, T. R. (1968). Some current dimensions of applied behavior analysis. *Journal of Applied Behavior Analysis, 1*, 91–97.

Bennett, R. E. (1982). Applications of microcomputer technology to special education. *Exceptional Children, 49*, 106–113.

Bliss, E. C. (1984). *Doing it now*. New York: Bantam.

Bliss, E. C. (1983). *Getting things done*. New York: Scribner's.

Brown, G., Kerr, M. M., Zigmond, N., & Harris, A. (1984). What's important for success in high school? Successful and unsuccessful students discuss school survival skills. *The High School Journal, 68*, 10–17.

Brown, N. P. (1982). CAMEO: Computer-assisted management of educational objectives. *Exceptional Children, 49*, 151–153.

Chaffin, J. D., Maxwell, B., & Thompson, B. (1982). ARC-ED curriculum: The application of video game formats to educational software. *Exceptional Children, 49*, 173–178.

Foulds, R. A. (1982). Applications of microcomputers in the education of the physically disabled child. *Exceptional Children, 49*, 155–162.

Frederiksen, J., Warren, B., Gillote, H., & Weaver, P. (1982, May/June). The name of the game is literacy. *Classroom Computer News*, 23–27.

Freedman, B. J., Donahoe, C. P., Rosenthal, L., Schlundt, D. D., & McFall, R. M. (1978). A social behavioral analysis of skill deficits in delinquent and nondelinquent adolescent boys. *Journal of Consulting and Clinical Psychology, 45*, 1448–1462.

Hasselbring, T., & Crossland, C. (1981). Using microcomputers for diagnosing spelling problems in learning-handicapped children. *Educational Technology*, *21*, 37–39.

Hofmeister, A. M. (1982). Microcomputers in perspective. *Exceptional Children*, *49*, 115–121.

Hofmeister, A., & Thorkildsen, R. (1981). Videodisc technology and the preparation of special education teachers. *Teacher Education and Special Education*, *4*, 34–39.

James, W. (1980). *Computer applications for the handicapped*. New York: Institute of Electrical and Electronic Engineers.

Kazdin, A. E. (1975). *Behavior modification in applied settings*. Homewood, IL: Dorsey Press.

Kerr, M. M., & Zigmond, N. (1984). *The school survival skills project: 1983-84 annual report*. (Unpublished grant report.)

Kerr, M. M., & Zigmond, N. (1986). What do high school teachers want?—A study of expectation and standards. *Education and Treatment of Children*, *9*, 239–249.

Kerr, M. M., Zigmond, N., Schaeffer, A. L., & Brown, G. (1986). An observational follow-up study of successful and unsuccessful high school students. *High School Journal, 71*, 20–32.

Malone, T. W. (1981, December). What makes computer games fun? *Byte*, 258–277.

Ragghianti, S., & Miller, R. (1982). The microcomputer and special education management. *Exceptional Children*, *49*, 131–135.

Salend, S. J. (1983). Guidelines for explaining target behaviors to students. *Elementary School Guidance and Counseling*, *18*, 88-93.

Salend, S. J., & Ehrlich, E. (1983). Involving students in behavior modification programs. *Mental Retardation*, *21*, 95–100.

Salend, F. J., & Meddaugh, D. (1985). Using peer mediated extinction procedure to decrease obscene language. *The Pointer, 30*, 8–11.

Salend, F. J., & Santora, D. (1985). Employing access to the computer as a reinforcer for secondary students. *Behavioral Disorders, 11*, 30–34.

Thorkildsen, R., Bickel, W., & Williams, J. (1979). A microcomputer/videodisc CAI system for the moderately mentally retarded. *Journal of Special Education Technology*, *2*, 45–51.

Walker, H. M., & Rankin, R. (1983). Assessing the behavioral expectations and demands of less restrictive settings. *School Psychology Review*, *12*, 274–284.

Walker, H. M., & Rankin, R. (1980). *The SBS inventory of teacher social behavior standards and expectations*. Eugene: University of Oregon.

Wilson, D. (1981). Managing the administrative morass of special needs. *Classroom Computer News*, *1*, 8–9.

Zigmond, N., Kerr, M. M., Schaeffer, A. L., Brown, G. M., & Farra, H. E. (1986). *School Survival Skills Curriculum* (limited published circulation). Available from Department of Special Education, 5M30 Forbes Quadrangle, 230 Bouquet Street, University of Pittsburgh, Pittsburgh, PA 15260.

Chapter Five

Alford, F. (1980). *Inservice on self-management for teachers*. Nashville, TN: George Peabody College for Teachers.

Bliss, E. C. (1984). *Doing it now*! New York: Bantam.

Cohen, R., Polsgrove, L., & Reith, H. (1980). An analysis of the effects of goal-setting, self-management and token reinforcement on oral reading performance of children with learning and behavior disorders. *Monograph in Behavioral Disorders*, 142–149.

Deshler, D. D., Alley, G. R., Warner, M. M., & Schumaker, J. B. (1981). Instructional practices for promoting skill acquisition and generalization in severely learning disabled adolescents. *Learning Disabilities Quarterly*, *4*, 415–421.

Drabman, R. S., Spitalnik, R., & O'Leary, K. D. (1973). Teaching self-control to disruptive children. *Journal of Abnormal Child Psychology*, *82*, 10–16.

Fink, W. T., & Carnine, D. W. (1975). Control of arithmetic errors using informational feedback. *Journal of Applied Behavior Analysis*, *8*, 461.

Gable, R. A., & Kerr, M. M. (1980). Behaviorally disordered adolescents as academic change agents. In R. B. Rutherford and A. G. Prieto (Eds.), *Severe behavior disorders of children and youth: CCBD monograph* (Vol. 4, pp. 117–124). Reston, VA: Council for Children with Behavioral Disorders.

Gallant, J., Sargeant, M., & Van Houten, R. (1980). Teacher-determined and self-determined access to science activities as a reinforcer for task completion in other curriculum areas. *Education and Treatment of Children*, *3*, 101–111.

Greer, D. R., & Polirstok, S. R. (1982). Collateral gains and short term maintenance in reading and on-task responses by inner-city adolescents as a function of their use of social reinforcement while tutoring. *Journal of Applied Behavioral Analysis 15*, 123–139.

Jenkins, J., Mayhall, W., Peschka, C., & Jenkins, C. (1974). Comparing small group and tutorial instruction in resource rooms. *Exceptional Children, 40*, 223–232.

Kastelen, L., Nickel, M., & McLaughlin, T. F. (1984). A performance feedback system: Generalization of effects across tasks and time with eighth-grade English students. *Education and Treatment of Children, 1*, 141–155.

Kazdin, A. E., & Bootzin, R. R. (1972). The token economy: An evaluative review. *Journal of Applied Behavior Analysis, 5*, 343–372.

Kelley, M. L., & Stokes, T. F. (1982). Contingency contracting with disadvantaged youths: Improving classroom performance. *Journal of Applied Behavior Analysis, 15*, 447–454.

Kerr, M. M., & Nelson, C. M. (1983). *Strategies for managing behavior problems in the classroom.* Columbus, OH: Charles E. Merrill.

Kneedler, R. D., & Hallahan, D. P. (1981, November). Self-monitoring of on-task behavior with learning-disabled children: Current studies and directions. *Exceptional Education Quarterly*, 73–82.

Maher, C. A. (1984). Handicapped adolescents as cross-age tutors: Program description and evaluation. *Exceptional Children, 51*, 56–63.

Morrisey, P. A. (1981). *A guide for teachers: How to set up a peer tutoring system in your classroom.* Series No. 4. Bloomington, IN: Center for Innovation in Teaching the Handicapped, Indiana University.

O'Hagan, M. (1985). *How to get the most out of your textbooks.* New York: Association of American Publishers.

Premack, D. A. (1959). Toward empirical behavioral laws: 1. Positive reinforcement. *Psychological Review, 6*, 219–233.

Reith, H. J., Polsgrove, L., Semmel, M., & Cohen, R. (1980, Summer). An experimental analysis of the effects of increased instructional time on the academic achievement of a "behaviorally disordered" high school pupil. *Monograph in Behavior Disorders*, 134–141.

Rosenshine, B. (1977). Review of teaching variables and student achievement. In G. D. Botch & K. S.

Fenton (Eds.), *The appraisal of teaching: Concepts and process* (pp. 144–150). Menlo Park, CA: Addison-Wesley.

Rousseau, J. K., Poulson, C. L., & Salzberg, C. L. (1984). Naturalistic procedures for homework participation by inner-city middle school students. *Education and Treatment of Children, 7*, 1–15.

Rueda, R., Rutherford, R. B., & Howell, K. W. (1980). Review of self-control research with behaviorally disordered and mentally retarded children. In R. B. Rutherford and A. G. Prieto (Eds.), *Severe behavior disorders of children and youth: CCBD monograph* (Vol. 3, pp. 188–197). Reston, VA: Council for Children with Behavioral Disorders.

Ruffin, C., Lambert, D., & Kerr, M. M. (1985). Volunteers: An extraordinary resource. *The Pointer, 29*, 30–38.

Sabatos, M. A. (1986). *The effects of self-monitoring on the on-task behavior of learning handicapped students in mainstream classrooms.* Doctoral dissertation draft, University of Pittsburgh.

Safer, D. J., Saski, J., Swicegood, P., & Carter, J. (1983). Note taking formats for learning disabled adolescents. *Learning Disability Quarterly, 6*, 265–272.

Seligman, M. E. P. (1975). *Helplessness: On depression, development, and death.* San Francisco, CA: W. H. Freeman.

Shepherd, J. F. (1983). *College study skills.* Boston, MA: Houghton Mifflin Company.

Sindeler, P. (1982). The effects of cross-aged tutoring on the comprehension skills of remedial reading students. *Journal of Special Education, 16*, 199–206.

Smith, B. M., Schumaker, J. B., Schaeffer, J., & Sherman, J. A. (1982). Increasing participation and improving the quality of discussions in seventh-grade social studies classes. *Journal of Applied Behavior Analysis, 15*, 97–110.

Sonntag, C. M., & McLaughlin, T. F. (1984). The effects of training students in paragraph writing. *Education and Treatment of Children, 7*, 49–59.

Stokes, T. F., & Baer, D. M. (1977). An implicit technology of generalization. *Journal of Applied Behavior Analysis, 10*, 349–367.

Stowitschek, J. J., Gable, R. A., & Hendrickson, J. M. (1980). *Instructional materials for exceptional children: Selection, management, and adoption.* Germantown, MD: Aspen Publications.

Strain, P. S., & Kerr, M. M. (1981). *Mainstreaming of children in schools.* New York: Academic Press.

Sulzer-Azaroff, B., & Mayer, G. R. (1977). *Applying behavior-analysis procedures with children and youth.* New York: Holt, Rinehart & Winston.

Van Houten, R. (1979). The performance feedback system: Generalization of effects across time. *Child Behavior Therapy, 1,* 219–236.

Van Houten, R., & LaiFatt, D. (1981). The effects of public posting on high school biology test performance. *Education and Treatment of Children, 4,* 217–226.

Van Houten, R., & Van Houten, J. (1977). The performance feedback system in the special education classroom: An analysis of public posting and peer comments. *Behavior Therapy, 8,* 366–376.

Workman, E. A. (1982). *Teaching behavioral self-control to students.* Austin, TX: Pro-Ed.

Chapter Six

Beuhler, R. E., Patterson, G. R., & Furness, R. M. (1966). The reinforcement of behavior in institutional settings. *Behavior Research and Therapy, 4,* 157–167.

Bolstad, O. D., & Johnson, S. M. (1972). Self-regulation in the modification of disruptive classroom behavior. *Journal of Applied Behavior Analysis, 5,* 443–454.

Broden, M., Hall, R. B., Dunlap, A., & Clark, R. (1970). Effects of teacher attention and a token reinforcement system in a junior high special education class. *Exceptional Children, 36,* 341–349.

Broden, M., Hall, R. V., & Mitts, B. (1971). The effect of self-recording on the classroom behavior of two eighth-grade students. *Journal of Applied Behavior Analysis, 4,* 191–200.

Chambers, J. H., Sanok, R. L., & Striefel, S. (1980). Using contingent decreased freedom-of-movement to eliminate classroom running away: A case study. *Education and Treatment of Children, 3,* 123–132.

Dietz, S. M., & Repp, A. C. (1973). Decreasing classroom misbehavior through the use of DRL schedules of reinforcement. *Journal of Applied Behavior Analysis, 6,* 457–464.

Epstein, M. H., Repp, A. C., & Cullinan, D. (1978). Decreasing obscene language of behaviorally dis-

ordered children through the use of a DRL schedule. *Psychology in the Schools, 15,* 419–423.

Garibaldi, A. (1982). In-school suspension. In D. Safer (Ed.) *School programs for disruptive adolescents.* Baltimore: University Park Press.

Gilliland, H. (1974). *A practical guide to remedial reading.* Columbus, OH: Charles E. Merrill.

Glynn, E. L. (1970). Classroom applications of self-determined reinforcement. *Journal of Applied Behavior Analysis, 3,* 123–132.

Hayes, L. A. (1976). The use of group contingencies for behavioral control: A review. *Psychological Bulletin, 83,* 628–648.

Homme, L. (1970). *How to use contingency contracting in the classroom.* Champaign, IL: Research Press.

Kazdin, A. E. (1980). *Behavior modification in applied settings.* Homewood, IL: Dorsey Press.

Kerr, M. M., & Nelson, C. M. (1983). *Strategies for managing behavior problems in the classroom.* Columbus, OH: Charles E. Merrill.

Litow, L., & Pomroy, D. K. (1975). A brief review of classroom group-oriented contingencies. *Journal of Applied Behavior Analysis, 8,* 341–347.

Madsen, C. H., Jr., Becker, W. C., & Thomas, D. R. (1968). Rules, praise, and ignoring: Elements of elementary classroom control. *Journal of Applied Behavior Analysis, 1,* 139–150.

McLaughlin, T. F. (1976). Self-control in the classroom. *Review of Educational Research, 46,* 631–663.

McLaughlin, T. F., Krappman, V. F., and Welsh, J. M. (1985). The effects of self-recording for on-task behavior of behaviorally disordered special education students. *Remedial and Special Education, 6*(4), 42–45.

McLaughlin, T. F., & Malaby, J. E. (1972). Intrinsic reinforcers in a classroom token economy. *Journal of Applied Behavior Analysis, 5,* 263–270.

Muller, A. J., Hasazi, S. E., Pierce, M. M., & Hasazi, J. E. (1975). Modification of disruptive behavior in a large group of elementary school students. In E. Ramp & G. Semb (Eds.), *Behavior analysis: Areas of research and application.* Englewood Cliffs, NJ: Prentice-Hall.

O'Leary, K. D., Becker, W. C., Evans, M. B., & Sudargas, R. A. (1969). A token reinforcement program in a public school: A replication and systematic analysis. *Journal of Applied Behavior Analysis, 2,* 3–13.

O'Leary, K. D., Kaufman, K. F., Kass, R. E., & Drabman, R. S. (1970). The effects of loud and soft reprimands on the behavior of disruptive students. *Exceptional Children, 37,* 145–155.

Rueda, R., Rutherford, R. B., & Howell, K. W. (1980). Review of self-control research with behaviorally disordered and mentally retarded children. In R. B. Rutherford and A. G. Prieto (Eds.), Severe behavior disorders of children and youth: CCBD Monograph (Vol. 3, pp. 188–197). Reston, VA: Council for Children with Behavioral Disorders.

Safer, D. J. (1982). *School programs for disruptive adolescents.* Baltimore: University Park Press.

Solomon, R. W., & Wahler, R. G. (1973). Peer reinforcement control of classroom problems behavior. *Journal of Applied Behavior Analysis, 6,* 49–56.

Strain, P. S., & Ezzell, D. (1978). The sequence and distributional behavioral disordered adolescents' disruptive/inappropriate behaviors. *Behavior Modification, 2,* 403–425.

Trice, A. D., & Parker, F. C. (1983). Decreasing adolescent swearing in an instructional setting. *Education and Treatment of Children, 6,* 29–35.

Van Houten, R., Nau, P. A., MacKenzie-Keating, S. E., Sameoto, D., & Colavecchia, B. (1982). An analysis of some variables influencing the effectiveness of reprimands. *Journal of Applied Behavior Analysis, 15,* 65–83.

Walker, H. H. (1979). *The acting-out child: Coping with classroom disruptions.* Boston, MA: Allyn & Bacon.

Walker, H. M., & Buckley, N. K. (1974). *Token reinforcement techniques: Classroom applications for the hard-to-teach child.* Eugene, OR: E-B Press.

Weiskopf, P. E. (1980). Burnout among teachers of exceptional children. *Exceptional Children, 47,* 18–23.

Wood, F. H., & Lakin, K. C. (Eds.). (1978). *Punishment and aversive stimulation in special education: Legal, theoretical and practical issues in their use with emotionally disturbed children and youth.* Advanced Institute for Trainers of Teachers for Seriously Emotionally Disturbed Children and Youth, Department of Psychoeducational Studies, University of Minnesota. (Grant from the Division of Personnel Preparation, Bureau of Education for the Handicapped, United States Office of Education, Department of Health, Education and Welfare.)

Worell, J., & Nelson, C. M. (1974). *Managing instructional problems.* New York: McGraw-Hill.

Zwald, L., & Gresham, F. (1982). Behavioral consultation in a secondary class: Using DRL to decrease negative verbal interactions. *The School Psychology Review, 11 (4),* 428–432.

Chapter Seven

American Psychiatric Association. (1980). *Diagnostic and statistical manual of mental disorders* (3rd ed.). Washington, DC: Author.

Belsen, W. A. (Ed.). (1975). *Juvenile theft: The causal factor.* London: Harper & Row.

Black, D., & Reiss, A. (1970). Police control of juveniles. *American Sociological Review, 35,* 63–77.

Christian, S. (1985, March 18). New York plans drive to curb dropout rate. *The New York Times,* p. 14.

Cohn, Y. (1963). Criteria for the probation officer's recommendation to the juvenile court. *Court and Delinquents, 9,* 262–275.

Dowrick, P. W., & Gilligan, C. A. (1985). Social skills and children: An annotated bibliography. *The Behavior Therapist, 8*(10), 211–213.

Eisenberg, L. (1980) Adolescent suicide: On taking arms against a sea of troubles. *Paedeatrics, 66,* 315–320.

Farrington, D. P. (1978). The family backgrounds of aggressive youths. In L. Hersov, M. Berger, & D. Shaffer (Eds.), *Aggression and antisocial behaviour in childhood and adolescence* (pp. 73–93). Oxford: Pergamon.

Farrington, D. P. (1980). Truancy, delinquency, the home, and the school. In L. Hersov & I. Berg (Eds.), *Out of school: Modern perspectives in school refusal and truancy* (pp. 49–64). New York: Wiley.

Fulton, R. W. (1975). Job retention of the mentally retarded. *Mental Retardation, 13,* 26–27.

Gabrielson, L. W., Gabrielson, I. W., Klerman, L. W., Currie, J. A., Tyler, N. C., & Jekel, S. F. (1970). Suicide attempts in a population pregnant as teenagers. *American Journal of Public Health, 60,* 2289–2301.

Goldfried, M. R., & D'Zurilla, T. J. (1969). A behavioral-analytic model for assessing competence. In C. D. Spielberger (Ed.), *Current topics in clinical and community psychology* (Vol. 1). New York: Academic Press.

Goldman, N. (1963). *The differential selection of juvenile offenders for court appearance.* New York: National Council on Crime and Delinquency.

Goldstein, H. (1972). Construction of a social learning curriculum. In E. L. Meyen, G. A. Vergason, & R. H. Whelan (Eds.), *Strategies for teaching exceptional children.* Denver, CO: Love Publishing.

Goldstein, A. P., Sprafkin, R. P., Gershaw, N. J., & Klein, P. (1980). *Skillstreaming the adolescent.* Champaign, IL: Research Press.

Goldstein, A. P., Sprafkin, R. P., Gershaw, N. J., & Klein, P. (1983). Structured learning: A psychoeducational approach for teaching social competencies. *Behavioral Disorders, 3,* 161–170.

Gross, S. Z. (1976). The prehearing juvenile report: Probation officer's conception. *Journal of Research in Crime and Delinquency, 4,* 212–217.

Hazel, J. S., Schumaker, J. B., Sherman, J. A., & Sheldon-Wildgen, J. (1981). The development and evaluation of a group of skill-training program for court-adjudicated youths. In D. Upper & S. M. Ross (Eds.), *Behavior group therapy.* Champaign, IL: Research Press.

Hersov, L. (1960). Refusal to go to school. *Journal of Childhood Psychology and Psychiatry, 1,* 137–145.

Hersov, L. (1985). School refusal. In M. Rutter & L. Hersov (Eds.), *Child and adolescent psychiatry: Modern approaches* (pp. 382–399). Oxford, England: Blackwell Scientific Publications.

Holinger, P. C. (1979). Violent deaths among the young: Recent trends in suicide, homicide, and accidents. *American Journal of Psychiatry, 136,* 1144–1147.

Howlin, P. (1985). Special education treatment. In M. Rutter & L. Hersov (Eds.), *Child and adolescent psychiatry: Modern approaches* (pp. 851–870). Oxford, England: Blackwell Scientific Publications.

Kelly, W. J., Salzberg, S. M., Levy, S. M., Warrenfeltz, R. B., Adams, T. W., Crouse, T. R., and Beegle, G. P. (1983). The effects of role-playing and self-monitoring on the generalizational vocational skills by behaviorally disordered adolescents. *Behavioral Disorders, 9,* 27–35.

Kerr, M. M., & Nelson, C. M. (1983). *Strategies for managing behavior problems in the classroom.* Columbus, OH: Charles E. Merrill.

Mackey, D. & Ruta, S. Personal communication, October 11, 1983.

Mathews, R. M., Whang, P. L., & Fawcett, S. B. (1982). Behavioral assessment of occupational skills of learning disabled adolescents. *Journal of Learning Disabilities, 15,* 38–41

Neel, R. (1984, March) Teaching social routines to behaviorally disordered youth. In J. Grosenick, S. Huntze, E. McGinnis, & C. Smith (Eds.), *Social/affective interventions in behavioral disorders.* Des Moines IA: Iowa Monograph Series, State of Iowa, Department of Public Instruction.

Piliavin, I., & Briar, S. (1964). Police encounters with juveniles. *American Journal of Sociology, 70,* 206–214.

Robins, L. N., & Ratcliff, K. S. (1980). Childhood conduct disorder and late arrest. In L. N. Robins, P. J. Clayton, J. K. Wing (Eds.), *The social consequences of psychiatric illness.* New York: Brunner/Mazel.

Robins, L. N., Ratcliff, K. S., & West, P. A. (1979). School achievement in two generations. In S. J. Shamsie (Ed.), *New directions in children's mental health.* New York: Spectrum.

Russell, G. F. M. (1985). Anorexia and bulimia. In M. Rutter & L. Hersov (Eds.), *Child and adolescent psychiatry: Modern approaches* (pp. 625–637). Oxford, England: Blackwell Scientific Publications.

Russell, G. F. M. (1979). Bulimia nervosa: An ominous variant of anorexia nervosa. *Psychologica Medica, 9,* 429–448.

Rutter, M., & Hersov, L. (Eds.). (1985). *Child and adolescent psychiatry: Modern approaches.* Boston: Blackwell Scientific Publications.

Schloss, P. J., Kane, M. S., & Miller, S. (1981). Truancy intervention with behaviorally disordered adolescents. *Behavioral Disorders, 6,* 175–179.

Schmitt, B. D. (1971). School phobia—the great imitator: A pediatrician's viewpoint. *Pediatrics, 48,* 433–441.

Schumaker, J. B., & Ellis, E. S. (1982). Social skills training of LD adolescents: A generalization study. *Learning Disabilities Quarterly, 5,* 409–414.

Schumaker, J. B., Hazel, J. S., Sherman, J. A., & Sheldon, J. (1982). Social skill performance of learning disabled, nonlearning disabled, and delinquent adolescents. *Learning Disability Quarterly, 5,* 388–397.

Shaffer, D., & Fisher, P. (1981) The epidemiology of suicide in children and young adolescents. *Journal of the American Academy of Child Psychiatry, 20,* 545–565.

Shaffer, D., & Caton, C. (1984). *Runaway and homeless youth in New York City.* Unpublished manuscript.

Sheldon, J., Sherman, J. A., Schumaker, J. B., & Hazel, J. S. (1984). Developing a social skills curriculum for mildly handicapped adolescents and young adults: Some problems and approaches. In S. Braaten, R. Rutherford, Jr., and C. Kardash (Eds.). *Programming for adolescents with behavioral disorders.* Reston, VA: Council for Exceptional Children.

Sperling, D. (1985, January 29). 'At-risk' students are losing out. *USA Today,* Sec. D.

Strayhorn, J. M., Jr. (1982). *Foundations of clinical psychiatry.* Chicago: Year Book Medical Publishers.

Tennent, T. G. (1971). School non-attendance and delinquency. *Educational Research, 13,* 185–190.

Chapter Eight

Craft, M., & Craft, A. (1978). *Sex and the mentally handicapped.* London: Routledge and Kegan Paul Ltd.

Gordon, S. (1974). Sexual rights for the people . . . Who happened to be handicapped. 6th in a series: "Notes from the Center. " (Available from Center on Human Policy, Syracuse University, Syracuse, New York).

Guttmacher Institute. (1981). *Teenage pregnancy: The problem that hasn't gone away.* New York: Author.

Kempton, W. (1975). *A teacher's guide to sex education for persons with learning disabilities.* North Scituate, MA: Duxbury Press.

Chapter Nine

Abelson, H., & Fishburne, P. (1976). *Nonmedical use of psychoactive substances, a nationwide survey*

among youth and adults. Princeton, NJ: Response Analysis Corp.

Abelson, H., Fishburne, P., & Cisin, I. (1977). *National survey on drug abuse: Vol. 1, main findings.* Rockville, MD: National Institute on Drug Abuse.

Akil, H. (1977). Opiates: Biological mechanisms. In J. Barches, P. Berger, R. Ciaranello, & G. Elliott (Eds.), *Psychopharmacology* (p. 297). New York: Oxford University Press.

Aronson, E., Felman, R., & Devin-Sheehan, L. (1976). Research on children tutoring children: A critical review. *Review of Educational Research, 46,* 318–341.

Barnes, G. (1979). Solvent abuse: A review. *International Journal of the Addictions, 14,* 1–26.

Barry, H., III. (1974). Classification of drugs according to their discernible effects in rats. *Federal Proceedings, 33,* 1814–1824.

Becker, E. (1972). *Licit and illicit drugs.* Boston: Little-Brown.

Bennett, S. (1979). *Something more than survival.* Lafayette, CA: Center for Human Development.

Berg, D. (1970). Illicit use of dangerous drugs in the United States. Washington, DC: Drug Sciences Division Office of Science and Drug Abuse Prevention, Bureau of Narcotics and Dangerous Drugs, U. S. Department of Justice.

Berger, P., & Tinklenberg, J. (1977). Treatment of abusers of alcohol and other addictive drugs. In J. Barches, et al. (Eds.), *Psychopharmacology.* New York: Oxford University Press.

Beschner, G., & Friedman, A. (Eds.) (1979). *Youth drug abuse.* Lexington, MA: D. C. Heath.

Biase, D. (1984). A drug abuse prevention program developed within a therapeutic community. *Journal of Psychoactive Drugs, 16,* 63–68.

Blount, W., & Dembo, R. (1984). Personal drug use and attitudes toward prevention among youth living in a high risk environment. *Journal of Drug Education, 14,* 207–225.

Blount, W., & Dembo, R. (1984). The effects of perceived neighborhood setting on self-reported tobacco, alcohol, and marijuana use among inner city minority junior high school youths. *International Journal of the Addictions, 19,* 175–198.

Braucht, G., & Berry, K. (1971, April). A survey of drug using behavior in Jefferson County District

Number 1. Social Science Systems, Inc., for Jefferson County, Colorado, Public Schools.

Brecher, E., & the Editors of Consumer Reports (1975, April). Marijuana: The legal question. *Consumer Reports*, 265–266.

Brill, N. O., & Christie, R. L. (1974). Marijuana use and psychosocial adaptation. *Archives of General Psychiatry, 31*, 713–719.

Caracci, G., Migone, P., & Dornbush, R. (1983). Phencyclidine in an East Harlem psychiatric population. *Journal of the National Medical Association, 75*, 869–874.

Carlson, J. (1979, September). Operation snowball. *Seventeen*, p. 18.

Chambers, C., & Moldestad, M. (1970). The evaluation of concurrent opiate and sedative addictions. In J. C. Ball & C. D. Chambers (Eds.), *The epidemiology of opiate addiction in the United States.* Springfield, IL: Charles C Thomas.

Chassin, L. (1984). Adolescent substance use and abuse. *Advances in Child Behavior Analysis and Therapy, 3*, 99–152.

Clements, J., & Simpson, R. (1978). Environmental and behavioral aspects of glue sniffing in a population of emotionally disturbed adolescents. *International Journal of the Addictions, 13*, 129–134.

Cohen, S. (1979). Inhalants and solvents. In G. Beschner & A. Friedman (Eds.) *Youth drug abuse.* Lexington, MA: D. C. Heath.

Collaboretta, E., Fossbender, A., & Bratter, T. (1983). The role of the teacher with substance abusing adolescents in secondary schools. *Psychology in the Schools, 20*, 450-455.

Conrad, D. (1980). *The differential impact of experimental programs on secondary school students.* Unpublished doctoral dissertation, University of Minnesota.

Crawshaw, J., & Mullen, P. (1984). A study of benzhexol abuse. *British Journal of Psychiatry, 145*, 300–303.

Crippen, D. (1983). Substance use–abuse and cognitive learning: Suggested approaches to viable drug education programs. *Journal of Instructional Psychology, 10*, 74–82.

Curtis, B., & Simpson, D. (1976). Demographic characteristics of groups classified by patterns of multiple drug abuse: A 1959 to 1971 sample. *International Journal of the Addictions, 11*, 161–173.

Dembo, R. (1983). Preferred resources for help with a drug problem among youths living in different inner city neighborhood settings. *Advances in Alcohol and Substance Abuse, 2*, 57–75.

Duncan, D. (1978). Family stress and the initiation of adolescent drug abuse: A retrospective study. *Corrective and Social Psychiatry and Journal of Behavior Technology, 24*, 111–114.

Elinson, J. (1975). *A study of teenage drug behavior.* Paper presented at the Second Technical Review on Inhalant Abuse, Rockville, MD.

Ensminger, E., Brown, C., Hendricks, K., & Sheppard, G. (1983). Social control as an explanation of sex differences in substance use among adolescents. *NIDA Research Monograph, 49*, 296–304.

Evans, R., Roselle, M., Mittelmark, M., Hansen, W., Bane, A., & Davis, J. (1976). Deterring the onset of smoking in children: Knowledge of immediate psychological effects and coping with peer pressure, media pressure, and parent modeling. *Journal of Applied Psychology, 8*, 126–135.

Freedman, A., & Kaplan, H. (1965). *Comprehensive textbook of psychiatry, Volume II* (2nd ed.). Baltimore: Williams and Wilkins.

Friedman, A., & Beschner, G. (1985). *Treatment services for adolescent substance abusers* (NIDA monograph No. ADM 85-1342). Rockville, MD: National Institute on Drug Abuse.

Gartner, A., Kohler, M., & Riessman, F. (1970). *Children teach children: Learning by teaching.* New York: Harper and Row.

Gibbs, J., & Allen, A. (1979). *Tribes: A process for peer involvement.* Oakland, CA: Center Source Publications.

Gold, M., & Mattick, H. (1974). *Experiment in the streets. The Chicago youth development project.* Ann Arbor, MI: Institute for Social Research, University of Michigan.

Greenwood, J., & Crider, R. (1978). *Estimated number of heroin addicts: 1977. Forecasting branch reports.* Rockville, MD: National Institute on Drug Abuse.

Harris, L., & Associates, Inc. (1981). Public awareness of the National Institute on Alcohol and Alcoholism advertising campaign and public attitudes toward drinking and alcohol abuse. In F. P. Rice (Ed.), *The adolescent.* Boston: Allyn & Bacon.

Heath, R. G. (1976). *Cannabis sativa* derivatives: Effects on brain function in monkeys. In G. G. Nahos

(Ed.), *Marijuana: Chemistry, biochemistry, and cellular effects*. New York: Springer-Verlag.

Holsaple, R., & White, M. (1984). A model school-based comprehensive alcohol/drug abuse prevention program. *Journal of the Florida Medical Association, 71*, 233–234.

IMS America, Limited. (1975). *Drug abuse early warning network, phase III report*. Washington, DC: National Institute on Drug Abuse.

Jaffe, J. (1970). Drug addiction and drug abuse. In L. Goodman & A. Gilman (Eds.), *The pharmacological basis of therapeutics, Volume 4*. New York: Macmillan.

Jalalai, B., Jalalai, M., Crochetti, G., & Turner, F. (1981). Adolescents and drug use. Toward a more comprehensive approach. *American Journal of Orthopsychiatry, 51*, 120–130.

Jasso, N., & Wolkon, G. (1978). Drug use, attitudes and behaviors of youth in an urban free clinic. *International Journal of the Addictions, 13*, 317–326.

Jessor, R., & Jessor, S. L. (1980). Adolescent development and the onset of drinking. In R. E. Muus (Ed.), *Adolescent behavior and society* (3rd ed.). New York: Random House.

Johnston, L., O'Malley, P., & Bauchman, J. (1985). Use of licit and illicit drugs by America's high school students, 1975–1984. *NIDA Monograph, 14*, 85–1394.

Jordan, C., & Valle, S. (1978). Teenage health consultants. *Synergist, 8*, 43–47.

Kandel, D. (1974). Inter- and intragenerational influences on adolescent marijuana use. *Journal of Social Issues, 30*, 107–135.

Kandel, D., Kessler, R., & Margulies, R. (1978). Antecedents of adolescent initiation into stages of drug use: A developmental analysis. In D. B. Kandel (Ed.), *Longitudinal research on drug use: Empirical findings and methodological issues*. Washington, DC: Hemisphere Publications.

Khavari, K., Mabry, E., & Humes, M. (1977). Personality correlates of hallucinogen use. *Journal of Abnormal Psychology, 86*, 172–178.

Kosman, M., & Unna, K. (1968). Effects of the administration of the amphetamines and other stimulants on behavior. *Clinical Pharmacology and Therapy, 9*, 240–254.

Kupperstein, L., & Susman, R. (1968). Bibliography on the inhalation of glue fumes and other toxic vapors. *International Journal of the Addictions,*

3, 177–197.

Lal, H., Miksic, S., & Drawbaugh, R. (1978). Influences of environmental stimuli associated with narcotic administration on narcotic actions and dependence. In M. W. Adler, L. Manara, & R. Samanin (Eds.), *Factors affecting the action of narcotics*. New York: Raven Press.

Lawton, J., & Malmquist, C. (1961). Gasoline addiction in children. *Psychiatric Quarterly, 35*, 555–561.

Leavitt, F. (1974). Effects of drugs. In F. Leavitt (Ed.), *Drugs and behavior*. Philadelphia, PA: W. B. Saunders Company.

Levitt, E., & Edwards, J. (1970). A multivariate study of correlative factors in youthful cigarette smoking. *Developmental Psychology, 3*, 5–11.

Lingeman, R. (1974). *Drugs from a-z*. New York: McGraw-Hill.

Maddox, G. (1970). *The domesticated drug: Drinking among collegians*. New Haven, CT: College and University Press.

Malvin, J., Moskowitz, J., Schaeffer, G., & Schaps, E. (1984). Teacher training in affective education for the primary prevention of adolescent drug abuse. *American Journal of Drug and Alcohol Abuse, 10*, 223–235.

Marijuana and Youth (1982). Clinical observations on motivation and learning. Rockville, MD: U. S. Department of Health and Human Services, National Institute on Drug Abuse.

Mayer, J., & Filstead, W. (1979). The adolescent alcohol involvement scale. *Journal of Studies on Alcohol, 40*, 291–300.

McCoy, G., McBride, D., Ruse, B., Page, J., & Clayton, R. (1979). Youth opiate use. In G. Beschner, & A. Friedman (Eds.), *Youth drug abuse*. Lexington, MA: D. C. Heath.

McIntosh, W., Fitch, S., Staggs, F., Nyberg, K., & Wilson, J. (1979). Age and drug use by rural and urban adolescents. *Journal of Drug Education, 9*, 129–143.

McMillan, D., Dewey, W., & Harris, L. (1971). Characteristics of tetrahydrocannabinol tolerance. In Marijuana: Chemistry, pharmacology, and patterns of social usage. *Annals of the New York Academy of Sciences, 191*, 3–14.

Miksic, S., Smith, N., & Lal, H. (1976a). Conditioning of discriminable stimuli produced by morphine. *Psychopharmacology Communications, 2*, 357–367.

Miksic, S., Smith, N., & Lal, H. (1976b). Reduction of morphine withdrawal aggression by conditional social stimuli. *Psychopharmacology, 48*, 114–117.

Milman, D. (1982). Psychological effects of cannabis in adolescence. In *Marijuana and youth* (Publication ADM 82–1186). Washington, DC: Department of Health and Human Services.

Mizner, G. L., Barter, J. T., & Merne, P. H. (1970). Patterns of drug use among college students. *American Journal of Psychiatry, 127*, 15–24.

Myrick, R., & Erney, T. (1975). *Youth helping youth: A handbook for training peer facilitators*. Minneapolis, MN: Educational Media Corporation.

Myrick, R., & Erney, T. (1979). *Youth helping youth: A handbook for training peer facilitators*. Minneapolis, MN: Educational Media Corporation.

National Institute on Drug Abuse. (1975). *Alcohol and health*. Washington, DC: U. S. Government Printing Office.

National Institute on Drug Abuse. (1975). *National youth drug survey*. USPHS monograph. Washington, DC: U. S. Government Printing Office.

National Institute on Drug Abuse. (1980). *Saying no: Drug abuse ideas for the classroom* (Publication ADM 80-916). Washington, DC: U. S. Government Printing Office.

National Institute on Drug Abuse. (1982). *Marijuana and youth* (Publication ADM 82-1186). Washington, DC: Department of Health and Human Services.

National Institute on Drug Abuse. (1983). *Adolescent peer pressure* (Publication ADM 83-1152). Washington, DC: U. S. Government Printing Office.

Nemy, E. (1974, August 19). Youth's alcohol abuse called alarming here. *New York Times, 30*.

New York Office of Drug Abuse Services (1977). *Administrative Evaluation of SPARK*. Albany, NY: New York Office of Drug Abuse Services.

Norvenius, G., Widerlov, E., & Lounerholm, G. (1979). Phenylpropanolamine and mental disturbances. *Lancet, 22/29*, 1367–1368.

O'Donnell, J., Voss, H., Clayton, R., Slatin, G., & Room, R. (1976). Young men and drugs: A nationwide survey. Rockville, MD: National Institute on Drug Abuse.

O'Donnell, J., Voss, H., Clayton, R., Slatin, G., & Room, R. (1979). Young men and drugs: A nationwide survey. In G. Beschner & A. Friedman, (Eds.), *Youth drug abuse*. Lexington, MA: D. C. Heath.

Ombudsman: A classroom community. (1980). Charlotte, NC: Charlotte Drug Education Center.

Overton, D. (1966). State dependent learning produced by depressant and atropine-like drugs. *Psychopharmacology, 10*, 6–31.

Pandina, R., & Schuele, J. (1983). Psychological correlates of alcohol and drug use of adolescent students and adolescents in treatment. *Journal of Studies on Alcohol, 44*, 950–973.

Parker, M., Tarlow, M., & Milne-Anderson, J. (1984). Glue sniffing and cerebral infarction. *Archives of Diseases of Childhood, 59*, 675–677.

Pascarelli, E. F. (1973). Methaqualone: The quiet epidemic. In R. P. Shafer et al., *Drug use in America*. (Second report of the National Commission on Marijuana and Drug Abuse). Washington, DC: U. S. Government Printing Office.

Patrick, R., Snyder, T., & Barchas, J. (1975). Regulation of dopamine synthesis in rat brain striated synaptosomes. *Molecular Pharmacology, 11*, 621–631.

Perry, C., McAlister, A., & Farquhar, J. (1978). Peer leadership to help adolescents resist pressures to smoke: A one-year followup. Unpublished paper referenced in *Adolescent Peer Pressure*, Palo Alto, CA: Stanford University.

Peterson, R., & Stillman, R. (1978). *Phencyclidine (PCP) abuse: An appraisal. NIDA Research Monograph 21*. Washington, DC: U. S. Government Printing Office.

Press, E., & Done, A. (1967). Solvent sniffing: Physiologic effects and community control measures for intoxication from the intentional inhalation of organic solvents. *Pediatrics, 39*, 611–622.

Rachal, J., Williams, J., Brehm, M., Cavenaugh, B., Moore, R., & Eikelman, W. (1975). A national study of adolescent drinking behavior attitudes and correlates. (NIAAA Report PB 246-002). Springfield, VA: U. S. National Technical Information Service.

Reagan, N. (1984). The drug abuse epidemic. *Journal of the Florida Medical Association, 71*, 219–220.

Resnick, H. S., & Gibbs, J. (1983). Types of peer program approaches. In S. W. Gardner (Project Officer), *Adolescent peer pressure* (Publication No. 83-1152). Washington, DC: U. S. Government Printing Office.

Ritchie, J. (1980). The xanthines. In L. Goodman & A. Gilman (Eds.), *The pharmacological basis of therapeutics*. New York: Macmillan.

Rosenthal, A. (1970). Readers, experts examine drug problem. *Today's Health, 48,* 50–61.

Samuels, M., & Samuels, D. (1975). *The complete handbook of peer counseling.* Miami, FL: Fiesta Publishing Corporation.

Santos de Barona, M., & Simpson, D. (1984). Inhalant users in drug abuse prevention programs. *American Journal of Drug and Alcohol Abuse, 10,* 503–518.

Schaeffer, G., Schuckit, M., & Morrissey, E. (1976). Correlation between two measures of self-esteem and drug use in a college sample. *Psychological Reports, 39,* 915–919.

Schaps, E., & Slimmon, L. (1976). *Balancing head and heart: Sensible ideas for the prevention of drug and alcohol abuse, Book 2.* Lafayette, CA: Prevention Materials Institute.

Schnoll, S. (1979). Pharmacological aspects of youth drug abuse. In G. Beschner & A. Friedman (Eds.), *Youth drug abuse.* Lexington, MA: D. C. Heath.

Schwartz, S. (1984). A study of drug discipline policies in secondary schools. *Adolescence, 19,* 323–333.

Severson, H. (1984). Adolescent social drug use school prevention program. *School Psychology Review, 13,* 150–161.

Sexter, J., Sullivan, A., Wepner, S., & Denmark, R. (1984). Substance abuse: Assessment of the outcomes of activities and activity clusters in school-based prevention. *International Journal of the Addictions, 19,* 79–92.

Smith, G. (1980). Relations between personality and smoking behavior in preadult subjects. In R. E. Muus (Ed.), *Adolescent behavior and society* (3rd ed.). New York: Random House.

Solleder, M. (1974). New notes. *Journal of School Health, 44,* 44.

Sourindhrin, I., & Baird, J. (1984). Management of solvent misuse: A Glasgow community approach. *British Journal of Addiction, 79,* 227–232.

Soveif, M. (1967). Hashish consumption in Egypt, with special reference to psychosocial aspects. *Bulletin of Narcotic Drugs, 19,* 1–12.

Soveif, M. F. (1976). Differential association between chronic cannabis use and brain function deficits. *Annals of the New York Academy of Sciences, 282,* 323–343.

Steffenhagen, R., Polich, J., & Lash, S. (1978). Alienation, delinquency, and patterns of drug use. In G. Beschner & A. Friedman (Eds.), *Youth drug abuse.* Lexington, MA: D. C. Heath.

Stephenson, J., Moberg, P., Daniels, B., & Robertson, J. (1984). Treating the intoxicated adolescent, a need for comprehensive services. *Journal of the American Medical Association, 252,* 884–888.

Stern, M., Northman, J., & Van-Slyck, M. (1984). Father absence and adolescent "problem behaviors": Alcohol consumption, drug use and sexual activity. *Adolescence, 19,* 302–312.

Sundlee, C., & Stapp, W. (1979). *The YAT manual.* San Rafael, CA: Social Action Research Center.

Thorne, C., & DeBlassie, R. (1985). Adolescent substance abuse. *Adolescence, 20,* 336–347.

Time Magazine. (1981, June). Cocaine. Vol. 118, pp. 56–63.

Time Magazine. (1986, September 15). America's crusade. Vol. 128, pp. 58–60.

Tinklenberg, J., Berger, P. (1977). Treatment of abusers of nonaddictive drugs. In J. Barchas, P. Berger, R. Ciaranello, & G. Elliott (Eds.), *Psychopharmacology,* New York: Oxford University Press.

Verhoeven, A. (1980). Development of the Youth Expression Theatre. Planned Parenthood League of Massachusetts, Cambridge, MA. In NIDA (1983). *Adolescent peer pressure.* (Publication ADM 83-1152). Washington, DC: U. S. Government Printing Office.

Victor, N. (1974). Treatment of alcohol intoxication and the withdrawal syndrome: A critical analysis of the use of drug and other forms of therapy. In P. G. Bourne (Ed.), *A treatment manual for acute drug abuse emergencies* (Publication ADM 75-230). Washington, DC: U. S. Government Printing Office.

Vorrath, H., & Brendtro, L. (1974). *Positive peer culture.* Chicago: Aldine Publishing Company.

Wallgren, H., & Barry, H., III (1970). *Actions of alcohol: Volume 1, Biochemical, physiological, and psychological aspects.* Amsterdam: Elsevier Press.

Watson, S. (1977). Hallucinogens and other psychotomimetics: Biological mechanisms. In J. D. Barchas, P. A. Berger, R. D. Ciaranello, & G. Elliott (Eds.), *Psychopharmacology.* New York: Oxford University Press.

Weisman, T. (1972). *Drug abuse and drug counseling.* Cleveland, OH: Case Western University Press.

Wright, L. (1985). High school polydrug users and abusers. *Adolescence, 20,* 854–861.

Chapter Ten

Abeson, A., Bolick, N., & Hass, J. (1975). *A primer on due process: Education decisions for handicapped children*. Reston, VA: Council for Exceptional Children.

Aiken, T. W., Stumphauzer, J. S., & Veloz, E. V. (1977). Behavioral analysis of non-delinquent brothers in a high juvenile crime community. *Behavioral Disorders, 2*, 212–222.

Abt Associates (1980). American prisons and jails. Washington, DC: National Institute of Justice.

Black, T. E., & Smith, C. P. (1981). A preliminary national assessment of the number and the characteristics of juveniles processed in the juvenile justice system. *Report of the National Juvenile Justice Assessment Center*. Washington, DC: Office of Juvenile Justice and Delinquency Prevention.

Bower, E. M. (1983). Defining emotional disturbance: Public policy and research. *Psychology in the Schools, 19*, 55–60.

Burger, W. E. (1981, December). *More warehouses or factories with fences?* Paper presented at the meeting of the American Bar Association, University of Nebraska.

Cantwell, M. (1983). The offender. In *Report to the nation on crime and justice: The data* (pp. 29–40). Washington, DC: U. S. Department of Justice, Bureau of Justice Statistics.

Coffey, O. D. (1983). Meeting the needs of youth from a corrections viewpoint. In S. Braaten, R. B. Rutherford, Jr., & C. A. Kardash (Eds.), *Programming for adolescents with behavioral disorders* (pp. 79-84). Reston, VA: Council for Children with Behavioral Disorders.

Comptroller General of the U. S. (1981, September 30). *Disparities still exist in who gets special education*. Report to the Chairman, Subcommittee on Select Education, Committee on Education and Labor, House of Representatives of the U. S. Gaithersburg, MD: General Accounting Office.

Edgar, E., Webb, S., & Maddox, M. (1987). Issues in transition: Transfer of youth from correctional facilities to public schools. In C. M. Nelson, R. B. Rutherford, Jr., & B. I. Wolford (Eds.). *Special education in the criminal justice system*. Columbus, OH: Merrill Publishing Company.

Gerry, M. H. (1985). *Monitoring the special education programs of correctional institutions*. Washington, DC: U. S. Department of Education.

Goldstein, A. P. (1987). Teaching prosocial skills to antisocial adolescents. In C. M. Nelson, R. B. Rutherford Jr., & B. I. Wolford (Eds.). *Special education in the criminal justice system*. Columbus, OH: Merrill Publishing Company.

Grosenick, J. K., & Huntze, S. L. (1980). *National needs analysis in behavior disorders: Adolescent behavior disorders*. Columbia, MO: Department of Special Education, University of Missouri.

Huntze, S. L. (1985). A position paper of the Council for Children with Behavioral Disorders. *Behavioral Disorders, 10*, 167–174.

Keilitz, I., & Dunivant, N. (1987). The learning disabled offender. In C. M. Nelson, R. B. Rutherford, Jr., & B. I. Wolford, (Eds.). *Special education in the criminal justice system*. Columbus, OH: Merrill Publishing Company.

Keilitz, I., & Miller, S. L. (1980). Handicapped adolescents and young adults in the juvenile justice system. *Exceptional Education Quarterly, 2*, 117–126.

Kerr, M. M., & Nelson, C. M. (1983). *Strategies for managing behavior problems in the classroom*. Columbus, OH: Charles E. Merrill.

Morgan, D. J. (1979). Prevalence and types of handicapping conditions found in correctional institutions: A national survey. *The Journal of Special Education, 13*, 283–295.

Murray, C. A. (1976). *The link between learning disabilities and juvenile delinquency: Current theory and knowledge*. Washington, DC: National Criminal Justice Reference Service.

Neel, R. S., & Rutherford, R. B., Jr. (1981). Exclusion of the socially maladjusted/delinquent from services under PL 94-142. In F. H. Wood (Ed.) *Perspectives for a new decade: Education's responsibility for seriously disturbed and behaviorally disordered children and youth* (pp. 79–89). Reston, VA: Council for Exceptional Children.

Nelson, C. M. (1985). Behavioral disorders. In W. H. Berdine & A. E. Blackhurst (Eds.), *An introduction to special education* (2nd ed., pp. 427–464). Boston: Little, Brown.

Nelson, C. M. (1987). Handicapped offenders in the criminal justice system. In. C. M. Nelson, R. B.

Rutherford, Jr., & B. I. Wolford (Eds.), *Special education in the criminal justice system*. Columbus, OH: Merrill Publishing Company.

Phillips, E. L., Phillips, E. A., Fixsen, D. L., & Wolf, M. M. (1971). Achievement Place: Modification of the behaviors of pre-delinquent boys within a token economy. *Journal of Applied Behavior Analysis, 4,* 45–59.

Rutherford, R. B., Jr., Nelson, C. M., & Wolford, B. I. (1985). Special education in the most restrictive environment: Correctional/special education. *Journal of Special Education, 19,* 59–71.

Ryan, T. A. (1983). Prevention and control of juvenile delinquency. *The Journal for Vocational Special Needs Education, 5,* 5–12.

Santamour, M. B., & West, B. (1979). *Retardation and criminal justice: A training manual for criminal justice personnel*. Washington, DC: President's Committee on Mental Retardation.

Schilit, J. (1983). Learning and behavior problems of adolescent offenders. In B. J. D'Alonzo (Ed.), *Educating adolescents with learning and behavior problems* (pp. 67–90). Rockville, MD: Aspen.

Snarr, R. W., & Wolford, B. I. (1985). *Introduction to corrections*. Dubuque, IA: William C. Brown.

Stumphauzer, J. S., Aiken, T. W., & Veloz, E. V. (1977). East side story: Behavioral analysis of a high juvenile crime community. *Behavioral Disorders, 2,* 76–84.

Wolford, B. I. (1983). Correctional education and special education—An emerging partnership: Or "Born to lose." in R. B. Rutherford, Jr. (Ed.), *Severe behavior disorders of children and youth* (pp. 13–19). Tempe, AZ: Arizona State University, Teacher Educators for Children with Behavioral Disorders, and Council for Children with Behavioral Disorders.

Wolford, B. I. (1985). Educational interventions in the juvenile justice system. In S. Braaten, W. Evans, & R. B. Rutherford, Jr. (Eds.), *Programming for adolescents with behavioral disorders* (Vol. 2, pp. 74–86). Reston, VA: Council for Children with Behavioral Disorders.

Zawitz, M. W., Mina, T. R., Kuykendall, C. M., Greenfield, L. A., & White, J. L. (1983). The response to crime. In *Report to the nation on crime and justice: The data* (pp. 41–85). Washington, DC: U. S. Department of Justice, Bureau of Justice Statistics.

Zigmond, N., Kerr, M. M., Schaeffer, A. L., Brown, G. M., & Farra, H. E. (1986). *School Survival Skills Curriculum* (limited published circulation). Available from Department of Special Education, 5M30 Forbes Quadrangle, 230 Bouquet Street, University of Pittsburgh, Pittsburgh, PA 15260.

Chapter Eleven

Ahlstrom, W. M., & Havighurst, R. J. (1971). *400 Losers*. San Francisco: Jossey-Bass.

Bellamy, G. T., Wilson, D. J., Adler, E., & Clarke, J. Y. (1980). A strategy for programming vocational skills for severely handicapped youth. *Exceptional Education Quarterly, 1,* 117–126.

Bireley, M., & Manley, E. (1980). The learning disabled student in a college environment: A report of Wright State University program. *Journal of Learning Disabilities, 13,* 13–15.

Brolin, D. E. (1978). *Life centered career education: A competency based approach*. Reston, VA: Council for Exceptional Children.

Brown, L., Nietupski, J., & Hamre-Nietupski, S. (1976). The criterion of ultimate functioning. In A. Thomas (Ed.), *Hey don't forget about me!* (pp. 2–15). Reston, VA: Council for Exceptional Children.

Camiel, R., & Michaelsen, H. (1980). *First time out: Skills for living away from home*. Sacramenta, CA: Jalamar.

Cegelka, P. E. (1985). Career and vocational education. In W. H. Berdine & A. E. Blackhurst (Eds.), *An introduction to special education* (2nd ed., pp. 573–614). Boston: Little-Brown.

Cobb, R. B., & Larkin, D. (1985). Assessment and placement of handicapped pupils into secondary vocational education programs. *Focus on Exceptional Children, 17,* 1–14.

Cowen, S. (1985). College choice for learning disabled students: Know your "SWIS." *Academic Therapy, 21,* 77—82.

Dexter, B. L. (1982). Helping learning disabled students prepare for college. *Journal for Learning Disabilities, 15,* 344–346.

Edgar, E. (1985). How do special education students fare after they leave school? A response to Hasazi and Roe. *Exceptional Children, 51,* 470–473.

Edgar, E., Webb, S., & Maddox, M. (1987). Issues in transition: Transfer of youth from correctional facilities to public schools. In C. M. Nelson, R. B. Rutherford, Jr., & B. I. Wolford (Eds.), *Special education in the criminal justice system*. Columbus, OH: Merrill Publishing Company.

Elmore, R. (1979). Backward mapping: Implementing research and policy decisions. *Political Science Quarterly, 94*, 601–616.

Evans, V., Hadden, C., Kraus, D., Johnson, J., Fredericks, H., & Toews, J. (1983). *The Teaching Research curriculum for mildly and moderately handicapped adolescents and adults: Taxonomy and assessment*. Monmouth, OR: Teaching Research.

Fredericks, H., & Evans, V. (1987). Functional curriculum. In C. M. Nelson, R. B. Rutherford, Jr., & B. I. Wolford (Eds.), *Special education in the criminal justice system*. Columbus, OH: Merrill Publishing Company.

Frith, G. H., Lindsay, J. D., & Reynolds, F. (1981). Horticulture for secondary level handicapped adolescents: The Cherokee County model. *Teaching Exceptional Children, 4*, 58–61.

Gajar, A. H., Murphy, J. P., & Hunt, F. M. (1982). A university program for learning disabled students. *Reading Improvement, 4*, 282–288.

Gill, D. H. (1984). An employment related follow-up of former special education students in Pierce County, Washington. Tacoma, WA: Vocational Special Education Cooperative. (Education Document Reproduction Service No. EC 170 889)

Goldstein, A. P., Sprafkin, R. P., Gershaw, N. J., & Klein, P. (1980). *Skill-streaming the adolescent*. Champaign, IL: Research Press.

Halpern, A. S. (1985). Transition: A look at the foundations. *Exceptional Children, 51*, 479–486.

Hasazi, S. B., Gordon, L. R., & Roe, C. A. (1985). Factors associated with the employment of handicapped youth exiting high school from 1979-1983. *Exceptional Children, 51*, 455–469.

Keilitz, I., & Miller, S. L. (1980). Handicapped adolescents and young adults in the justice system. *Exceptional Education Quarterly, 1*, 117–126.

Leone, P., Fitzmartin, R., Stetson, F., & Foster, J. (1986). A retrospective follow-up of behaviorally disordered adolescents: Identifying predictors of treatment outcome. *Behavioral Disorders, 11*, 87–97.

Leone, P. E., Price, T., & Vitolo, R. K. (1986). Appropriate education for all incarcerated youth: Meeting the spirit of P.L. 94-142 in youth detention facilities. *Remedial and Special Education, 7*(4), 9–14.

Levinson, E. M. (1984). A vocationally oriented secondary program for the emotionally disturbed. *Vocational Guidance Quarterly, 33*, 76–81.

Liscio, M. A. (Ed.). (1985). *A guide to colleges for learning disabled students*. Orlando, FL: Academic Press.

Maddox, M., Webb, S. L., Allen, L., Faust, F., Abrams, D., & Lynch, A. T. (1984). Transitioning adjudicated youth back to community schools. *Journal of Correctional Education, 29*, 124–128.

Mank, D. M., Rhodes, L. E., & Bellamy, G. T. (1986). Four supported employment alternatives. In W. E. Kiernan & J. A. Stark (Eds.), *Pathways to employment for adults with developmental disabilities* (pp. 139–153). Baltimore: Paul H. Brookes Publishing Company.

Mithaug, D., & Horiuchi, C. (1983). *Colorado statewide follow-up survey of special education students*. Denver: Colorado State Department of Education.

Morgan, D. J. (1979). Prevalence and types of handicapping conditions found in juvenile correctional institutions: A national survey. *The Journal of Special Education, 13*, 283–295.

National Association of State Directors of Special Education (1985, October). *Liaison Bulletin, 11* (10).

Nelson, C. M., & Rutherford, R. B., Jr. (in press). Behavioral interventions with behaviorally disordered students. In M. C. Wang, H. J. Walberg, & M. C. Reynolds (Eds.) *The handbook of special education: Research and Practice* (Vol. 2). Oxford, England: Pergamon.

Rutherford, R. B., Jr., & Nelson, C. M. (in press). Applied behavior analysis in education: Generalization and maintenance. In J. C. Witt, S. N. Elliott, & F. M. Gresham (Eds.) *Handbook of behavior therapy in education*. New York: Plenum.

Rutherford, R. B., Jr., Nelson, C. M., & Wolford, B. I. (1985). Special education in the most restrictive environment: Correctional/special education. *Journal of Special Education, 19*, 59–71.

Strichart, S. S., & Mangrum, C. T. (1985). Selecting a college for learning disabled students. *Academic Therapy, 20*, 475–479.

Webster, R. E. (1981). Vocational technical training for emotionally disturbed adolescents. *Teaching Exceptional Children*, *4*, 75–79.

Wehman, P., Kregel, J., & Barcus, J. M. (1985). From school to work: A vocational transition model for handicapped students. *Exceptional Children*, *52*, 25–37.

Westaway, A., & Apolloni, T. (Eds.). (1978). *Becoming independent: A living skills system*. Bellevue, MD: Edmark Associates.

Will, M. (1984). Bridges from school to working life. In S. Alberg, (Ed.) *Division on Career Development News, 8,* 5–6.

Wimmer, D. (1981). Functional learning curricula in the secondary schools. *Exceptional Children*, *47*, 610–616.

Zigmond, N., Kerr, M. M., Schaeffer, A. L. Brown, G. M., & Farra, H. E. (1986). *School Survival Skills Curriculum* (limited published circulation). Available from Department of Special Education, 5M30 Forbes Quadrangle, 230 Bouquet Street, University of Pittsburgh, Pittsburgh, PA 15260.

Name Index

Subject Index

Mary Margaret Kerr received her undergraduate and master's degrees from Duke University and her Ed.D. from The American University, where she worked with Dr. Nick Long. Before going to her present position as Associate Professor of Child Psychiatry and Special Education at the University of Pittsburgh, Dr. Kerr coordinated graduate teacher training in the Special Education Department of George Peabody College. Dr. Kerr has remained close to classrooms throughout her career and may be seen these days teaching in the "Commonwealth Classrooms" alternative program she helped establish for the Pittsburgh Public Schools. A firm believer that university professors should stay in touch with real-world problems, Dr. Kerr teaches school survival skills to middle school students in Pittsburgh and consults in classrooms across the United States. Among Dr. Kerr's many publications is a textbook written especially for classroom teachers, *Strategies for managing behavior problems in the classroom* with Mike Nelson, published by Merrill Publishing Company.

C. Michael Nelson began his special education career as a teacher of adolescents with learning and behavior disorders. After earning a master's degree in school psychology, he worked as a child psychologist at the University of Kansas Medical Center, while simultaneously pursuing a doctorate in special education with an emphasis on behavioral disorders. He received his Ed.D. in 1969 and took a position with the special education faculty at the University of Kentucky. With Robert Rutherford and Bruce Wolford, he co-authored the Correctional/Special Education Training Project and served as the coordinator of in-service curriculum development. He currently is a professor of special education at the University of Kentucky and is a past president of the Council for Children with Behavioral Disorders.

Deborah Lambert received her undergraduate degree from the University of the South and her master's degree in Special Education from George Peabody College of Vanderbilt University. At George Peabody College, she worked with Dr. Mary Margaret Kerr and focused on working with mildly handicapped children and youth. Ms. Lambert now works at the University of Pittsburgh as an education liaison of Project STAR (Services for Teenagers at Risk). She has worked closely with regular and special educators as a consultant in the Pittsburgh City Schools, addressing behavior management issues. Ms. Lambert has co-authored an instructor's guide to accompany *Strategies for managing behavior problems in the classroom,* published by Merrill Publishing Company.